THE SYRIAN CONFLICT IN THE NEWS

Political Communication and Media Practices in the Middle East and North Africa

The popular uprisings that rocked several Arab countries at the beginning of 2011, and the more recent ones in Algeria, Sudan, Lebanon, and Iraq, arose, among other things, in the context of changing media practices and political communication in the region. Beyond visible actions by political elites and institutions, several of these movements were characterized by grassroots communication on social media, and many included creative practises by a diverse range of actors.

Books in this series critically engage with the complex and fluid relationship between politics, communication, and culture in the Middle East and North Africa, taking into account the specificities of social and political local contexts, diverse political and media systems, media institutions, media and political actors and populations as well as differentiations along religious, sectarian, ethnic, gendered and racial lines.

Series Editors
Dina Matar, SOAS, University of London
Zahera Harb, City, University of London

Advisory Board
Omar Al-Ghazzi (LSE); Mohamed Zayani (Georgetown University); Gholam Khiabany (Goldsmiths, University of London); Marwan Kraidy (Northwestern University in Qatar); Adel Iskander (Simon Fraser University); Joe Khalil (Northwestern University in Qatar); Tarik Sabry (University of Westminster); Naomi Sakr (University of Westminster); Annabelle Sreberny (SOAS, University of London)

International Advisory Board
Loubna Skalli Hanna (University of California, Washington); Donatella della Ratta (John Cabot University); Reem Abou-El-Fadl (SOAS, University of London); Laudan Nooshin (City, University of London); Kevin Smets (VUB University, Brussels); Sophie Chamas (SOAS, University of London); Miriyam Aouragh (University of Westminster); Dounia Mahlouly (SOAS, University of London); Sadia Jamil (Khalifa University of Science and Technology)

Published and Forthcoming Titles
Revolutionary Art and Politics in Egypt: Liminal Spaces and Cultural Production After 2011, Rounwah Adly Riyadh Bseiso
The Political Economy of Egyptian Media: Business and Military Elite Power and Communication after 2011, Maher Hamoud
Digital Political Cultures in the Middle East since the Arab Uprisings: Online Activism in Egypt, Tunisia and Lebanon, Dounia Mahlouly

THE SYRIAN CONFLICT IN THE NEWS

Coverage of the War and the Crisis of US Journalism

Gabriel Huland

I.B. TAURIS
LONDON • NEW YORK • OXFORD • NEW DELHI • SYDNEY

I.B. TAURIS
Bloomsbury Publishing Plc, 50 Bedford Square, London, WC1B 3DP, UK
Bloomsbury Publishing Inc, 1359 Broadway, 12th Floor, New York, NY 10018, USA
Bloomsbury Publishing Ireland, 29 Earlsfort Terrace, Dublin 2, D02 AY28, Ireland

BLOOMSBURY, I.B. TAURIS and the I.B. Tauris logo are
trademarks of Bloomsbury Publishing Plc

First published in Great Britain 2024
This paperback edition published in 2025

Copyright © Gabriel Huland, 2024

Gabriel Huland has asserted his rights under the Copyright,
Designs and Patents Act, 1988, to be identified as Author of this work.

Series design by Catherine Wood & Adriana Brioso
Cover image: Barzeh, Syria, 2018. (© LOUAI BESHARA/AFP/Getty Images)

All rights reserved. No part of this publication may be: i) reproduced or transmitted in any form, electronic or mechanical, including photocopying, recording or by means of any information storage or retrieval system without prior permission in writing from the publishers; or ii) used or reproduced in any way for the training, development or operation of artificial intelligence (AI) technologies, including generative AI technologies. The rights holders expressly reserve this publication from the text and data mining exception as per Article 4(3) of the Digital Single Market Directive (EU) 2019/790.

Bloomsbury Publishing Inc does not have any control over, or responsibility for, any third-party websites referred to or in this book. All internet addresses given in this book were correct at the time of going to press. The author and publisher regret any inconvenience caused if addresses have changed or sites have ceased to exist, but can accept no responsibility for any such changes.

A catalogue record for this book is available from the British Library.

Library of Congress Cataloging-in-Publication Data
Names: Huland, Gabriel, author.
Title: The Syrian conflict in the news : Coverage of the War and
the Crisis of US Journalism / Gabriel Huland.
Description: London ; New York : I.B Tauris, 2024. | Series: Political
communication and media practices in the Middle East and North Africa |
Includes bibliographical references and index.
Identifiers: LCCN 2023029307 (print) | LCCN 2023029308 (ebook) |
ISBN 9780755650118 (hardback) | ISBN 9780755650149 (paperback) |
ISBN 9780755650125 (pdf) | ISBN 9780755650132 (epub) | ISBN 9780755650101
Subjects: LCSH: New York times. | Washington post (Washington, D.C. : 1974) |
Wall Street journal. | Journalism–Political aspects–United States. |
Journalism–Objectivity–United States. | Syria–History–Civil War,
2011—Press coverage. | United States–Foreign relations–21st century–Press coverage. |
Syria–Foreign relations–21st century–Press coverage.
Classification: LCC DS98.6 .H85 2024 (print) |
LCC DS98.6 (ebook) | DDC 956.9104/23–dc23/eng/20230630
LC record available at https://lccn.loc.gov/2023029307
LC ebook record available at https://lccn.loc.gov/2023029308

ISBN: HB: 978-0-7556-5011-8
PB: 978-0-7556-5014-9
ePDF: 978-0-7556-5012-5
eBook: 978-0-7556-5013-2

Series: Political Communication and Media Practices in the Middle East and North Africa

Typeset by Integra Software Services Pvt. Ltd.

For product safety related questions contact productsafety@bloomsbury.com.

To find out more about our authors and books visit www.bloomsbury.com
and sign up for our newsletters.

CONTENTS

Figures	vii
Tables	viii
Foreword	ix
A Note on the Referencing Style	x
INTRODUCTION	1
Why Framing Matters	3
Can News Reports Be Objective?	6
Changing Times for US Newspapers	10
The Plan of the Book	12

Chapter 1
MEDIA, FOREIGN POLICY, AND INTERNATIONAL CONFLICTS   15
    The Public Dimension of Foreign Policy   16
    International Conflicts in US Media   17
    The End of the Cold War and the CNN Effect Hypothesis   21
    Reporting the Syrian Revolution   24
    The Cascading Activation Model   28
    The Coverage of the Iraq War: A Return to Cold War Journalism?   29

Chapter 2
THE BEGINNING OF THE SYRIAN UPRISING (PERIOD I)   35
    The *NYT* Supports Obama's Noninterventionist Approach   39
    The *WP* Urges Obama to Support the Protests   44
    The *WSJ* Criticizes US Engagement with the Syrian Regime   49

Chapter 3
THE EASTERN GHOUTA CHEMICAL ATTACK (PERIOD II)   55
    The *NYT* Highlights the Debates inside the Obama Administration   60
    The *WP* Calls for a Strong Response against Assad   64
    The *WSJ* Urges the US to Attack Syria   69

Chapter 4
THE EXPANSION OF ISIS IN IRAQ AND SYRIA (PERIOD III)   77
    The *NYT* Supports Military Intervention against ISIS   84
    The *WP* Opposes Arming Local Groups to Fight ISIS   89
    The *WSJ* Blames Obama for the Instability in the Middle East   94

Chapter 5
THE BEGINNING OF THE RUSSIAN INTERVENTION IN SYRIA
(PERIOD IV) 101
    The *NYT* Highlights the Contradictions of Obama's Policies 106
    The *WP* Claims That Obama's Policies Failed 111
    The *WSJ* Fears Russian Expansionism 117

Chapter 6
THE FALL OF EASTERN ALEPPO (PERIOD V) 123
    The *NYT* Relays a Neutral Frame of Obama's Syria Policy 130
    The *WP* Criticizes Obama's and Trump's Views on Syria 134
    The *WSJ* Focuses on the Incoming Trump Administration 138

Chapter 7
THE US-UK-FRENCH AIRSTRIKES AGAINST SYRIA (PERIOD VI) 145
    The *NYT* Opposes the Airstrikes 150
    The *WP* Considers the Airstrikes Insufficient 155
    The *WSJ* Adopts an Advisory Tone toward Trump 160

CONCLUSION 167
    The Coverage of the Syrian Conflict and the Crisis of US Journalism

Appendix: The Science of News Frames 178
Notes 189
Bibliography 209
Index 237

FIGURES

2.1	Most recurrent topics in period I	39
2.2	Sources in *NYT* articles in period I	41
2.3	Sources in *WP* articles in period I	45
2.4	Sources in *WSJ* articles in period I	50
3.1	Area of fighting and territorial control in Syria's civil war (August 2013)	56
3.2	Topics per newspaper in period II	59
3.3	Sources in *NYT* articles in period II	60
3.4	Sources in *WP* articles in period II	67
3.5	Sources in *WSJ* articles in period II	74
4.1	Number of articles in period III	83
4.2	Genres in period III	83
4.3	Sources in *NYT* articles in period III	87
4.4	Sources in *WP* articles in period III	91
4.5	Sources in *WSJ* articles in period III	97
5.1	Sources in *NYT* articles in period IV	110
5.2	Sources in *WP* articles in period IV	112
5.3	Sources in *WSJ* articles in period IV	120
6.1	Topics in period V	129
6.2	Sources in *NYT* articles in period V	132
6.3	Sources in *WP* articles in period V	137
6.4	Sources in *WSJ* articles in period V	139
7.1	Sources in *NYT* articles in period VI	155
7.2	Sources in *WP* articles in period VI	157
7.3	Sources in *WSJ* articles in period VI	162
8.1	Sources in *NYT*, *WP*, and *WSJ* in periods I to VI	175

TABLES

4.1	Timeline: the expansion of ISIS in Iraq and Syria	82
5.1	Number of articles per newspaper and genre in period IV	105
6.1	Number of articles per newspaper and genre in period V	129
7.1	Number of articles per newspaper and genre in period VI	149
8.1	Summary of frames per newspaper and period	171
A.1	Number of articles per newspaper and period	185
A.2	Number of articles per newspaper and genre	185
A.3	Most recurrent topics and subtopics	186
A.4	Most recurrent codes and subcodes	187

FOREWORD

Gilbert Achcar

The Syrian uprising and especially its mutation into a protracted armed conflict provoked heated political debates, which were only in part a reflection of the conflict itself. As every war in which the United States is involved in some way, the debate also raged within US foreign policy establishment circles. For, whereas simplistic minds believe that there is a homogeneous imperialist attitude embodied in Washington, the truth is that there is hardly any foreign policy issue on which there is unanimity among the US establishment or "ruling class." The range of positions within the establishment reflects several spectra, each of which is privileged by different approaches in their analyses of the debates: socioeconomic interests, ideological orientations, partisan political affiliations, etc.

Gabriel Huland's study focuses on the three most prestigious dailies of the US establishment: The *Washington Post*, the *New York Times*, and the *Wall Street Journal*. By examining their different approaches to the Syrian events and the shifts in those approaches in tune with political shifts in Washington, Huland provides the reader with a set of valuable insights into several issues: US foreign policy in general; US policy toward the Syrian conflict; the three newspapers' positioning; the state of US journalism; and, last but not least, the Syrian events themselves.

This book stands at the junction of media studies and political science, a vast field indeed given how central the media are in modern politics. In addressing the current flaws of journalism in the United States, Huland sheds a special light on a key aspect of what has nowadays become an undisputed truth: the deep crisis of US democracy. This is reflected in the fact that the establishment's most prestigious media outlets have become almost exclusively dedicated to reflecting the power elite's views and interests, and increasingly estranged from the *vox populi* that they originally purported to convey at home, as well as from the comprehensive reporting of evidence—all relevant evidence, including the voices of local populations—that they claimed to offer in performing their duty of informing the US public so as to enable it to develop a truly informed opinion.

A NOTE ON THE REFERENCING STYLE

This book relies extensively on newspapers and periodical publications, such as magazines and online media outlets. For that reason, all footnotes with references to articles from newspapers and periodical publications include the author, the work's title, the publication's name, and the date of publication or most recent update. I decided to use this style to make things clearer for the reader. The URLs of the online versions of all articles cited in this book are included in the bibliography. Note that the titles of some of the articles quoted here might have changed. Although the title might be different, the content and URL are the same (unless expressly indicated to the contrary). When an unsigned piece is quoted, it appears in footnotes and the bibliography with the publication's name standing in place of the author. Thus, an unsigned article published in the *Wall Street Journal* appears in footnotes and the bibliography with "Wall Street Journal" standing in place of the author. The same format was adopted with articles that carry the byline "anonymous." Editorials appear with "Editorial Board" standing in place of the author. I applied the principles of headline-style capitalization to all the works cited in this book, even when the title is not capitalized in the original. For books, book chapters, and journal articles, I have followed a standard form of footnote referencing throughout this book, which consists of the author, the work's title, and, when applicable, the page number. Full references to the books, book chapters, and journal articles cited herein can be found in the bibliography.

INTRODUCTION

The first protests in Syria during March 2011 were met with a dash of incredulity in Western circles. Although popular demonstrations had been occurring in different Middle East and North Africa (MENA) countries since December 2010, when Mohammed Bouazizi set himself on fire in the Tunisian city of Sidi Bouzid, few observers believed that Syrians would follow suit and rise against the dictatorship that had ruled their country since 1970. On March 9, 2011, for instance, an article published in the prestigious think tank Carnegie Endowment for International Peace claimed that a revolution in Syria was unlikely due to "the greater level of contact between the regime and society" and because the Syrian government would refrain from using "excessive violence" against its citizens.[1] Other analysts argued that an uprising was unforeseeable because "people in Syria [were] a lot more afraid of the government and the security forces than they were in Egypt."[2] When the videos of the protests in the southern city of Daraa began to surface on YouTube and Facebook, governments, think tanks, and media organizations were caught by surprise and had to improvise a response to the events unfolding in the country.

Before March 2011, Syria occupied a minor place in the social imaginary of ordinary Americans and Western Europeans. Most people in this part of the world were indifferent to Syria, viewing it as a distant Middle Eastern country and associating it with the vague notions of Islam, authoritarianism, and economic backwardness. Because the coverage of the MENA region in the Western media has been historically dominated by issues such as oil, Islamic fundamentalism, and war, other regional countries received more attention than Syria in international media reports. Syria remained "outside of the headlines" until the emergence of a powerful movement of nonviolent protests resituated it in the geopolitical arena. Since then, the Syrian conflict has attracted overwhelming media attention; some commentators dubbed it "the most documented conflict in history."[3] As the uprising eventually morphed into an armed struggle from mid-2011, the country became the battlefield of a dispute involving local groups, regional countries, and other international powers.

The coverage of the Syrian uprising and civil war has been deeply affected by the divisions that have surrounded this terrible conflict. As international relations scholar Christopher Phillips argues, "a 'war of narratives' [had] been underway from the beginning [of the Syrian conflict], with both sides seeking to manipulate the media and international bodies to present their view."[4] Throughout the conflict, multiple sides, not only two, have struggled to set the prevailing narrative, and journalists covering the events from within Syria have found themselves operating in a highly complex and dangerous situation. On one hand, the emergence of protests prompted the news media to tell the stories of ordinary Syrians fighting for democracy and social justice. On the other, these extraordinary human-interest stories were eclipsed from the outset by the geopolitics of the Syrian conflict. It is not an exaggeration to assert that the coverage of the Syrian uprising and civil war in the mainstream media has been dominated by the strategic interests of the countries with a stake in the conflict.

This book analyzes the coverage of the Syrian conflict in the *New York Times* (NYT), the *Washington Post* (WP), and the *Wall Street Journal* (WSJ) from March 2011 to April 2018. I argue that the three newspapers focused on the elite narratives about the conflict, while taking active stances on the debates about US foreign policy on Syria. The *NYT*, the *WP*, and the *WSJ* consistently aligned with specific segments of the US political establishment, generally adopting a partisan position of support for or opposition to the US government's foreign policies toward the Syrian uprising and civil war. Whereas the *NYT* adopted a pro-Obama tone, the *WP* and the *WSJ* framed President Obama's policy negatively. With respect to the Trump administration, the alignments changed, with the *NYT* and the *WP* criticizing the former US president and the *WSJ* adopting an advisory tone regarding his Syria approach. The three newspapers covered the debates occurring within the US political establishment above all others. By and large, these alignments are a result of the sourcing practices of the journalists writing for the three newspapers and the political views of the columnists who authored the op-ed pieces published during the conflict.

The idea that mainstream news organizations are overly reactive to power dynamics and indexed to elite narratives is by no means new. For instance, Edward Said argued almost forty years ago that the coverage of Islam and non-Western societies in the US media focused almost exclusively on Islamic fundamentalism and terrorism and that media narratives about these topics amounted above all to "assertions of power" rather than objective journalism or "interpretation in the genuine sense."[5] The Palestinian-American scholar further claimed that "anything falling outside the consensus definition of what is important is considered irrelevant to US interests and to the media's definition of a good story."[6] Despite deep transformations in journalism during the intervening decades, these ideas remain strikingly relevant today.

The three newspapers analyzed in this book highlighted certain aspects of US foreign policy on Syria to the exclusion of other facets of the conflict considered less important. The selection and amplification of what is deemed newsworthy constitutes the essence of news framing. One of the first academics to apply the idea of framing to the analysis of news texts was Todd Gitlin, the American sociologist who coined one of the most cited definitions of frame, which runs as follows: "Frames are principles of selection, emphasis, and presentation composed of little tacit theories about what exists, what happens, and what matters."[7]

In *The Whole World Is Watching*, a study about how mainstream media covered the anti-Vietnam War protests and other social movements in the United States in the 1960s, Gitlin untangled the mechanisms, such as selection, emphasis, exclusion, and trivialization, which journalists and media organizations employ in order to shape different versions of events and disseminate those best fitting their interests. Gitlin underscored the idea that "media frames are persistent patterns of cognition, interpretation, and presentation, of selection, emphasis, and exclusion, by which symbol-handlers routinely organize discourse."[8]

Media scholar Robert Entman agreed with this idea, adding that "to frame is to select some aspects of a perceived reality and make them more salient in a communicating text, in such a way as to promote a particular problem definition, causal interpretation, moral evaluation, and/or treatment recommendation."[9] Frames are always present in media texts, emerging as a result of the interactions between media organizations, journalists, sources, and news receivers. Framing involves agency and decision-making, which makes it a political act concerning different players that interact in pursuit of specific objectives. This interaction, like any other act of socialization, can be harmonious or conflictive, collaborative or competitive.

Why Framing Matters

The siege of eastern Aleppo amounted to one of the most dramatic events of the Syrian conflict. Before recapturing it in December 2016, the regime of Syrian President Bashar al-Assad besieged eastern Aleppo for more than six months, preventing food and other essentials from entering the area. Although the siege's full repercussions are difficult to measure, it caused a major humanitarian crisis, leaving thousands of dead, injured, and displaced people. A *Guardian* report spoke of tens of thousands of civilians trapped "without food, water, or medicine under a hail of artillery and airstrikes."[10] In December 2016, Turkey and Russia brokered a deal between the Syrian government and opposition forces whereby civilians and rebel fighters would be evacuated from eastern Aleppo and taken to other rebel-held areas across the country.

The city of Aleppo became divided in July 2012, when opposition groups forced the regime to retreat and seized control of its eastern sector. Four years later, in July 2016, after fierce fighting between the regime and the opposition, the Syrian army and its allies cut the last supply route controlled by the opposition, initiating what would be a six-month-long blockade on the area. The siege of eastern Aleppo attracted a considerable amount of media attention, both from local and international news organizations. Different narratives dominated international news programs in December 2016, when the conditions for civilians became nearly unbearable, and the rebel groups in control of the area showed evident signs of exhaustion.

Besides situating the siege of eastern Aleppo as part of the Syrian civil war, the *NYT* framed it as a humanitarian crisis. On December 16, 2016, the newspaper published an article about the evacuation agreement with the following opening paragraph: "For months, the bodies have been piling up in eastern Aleppo as the buildings have come down, pulverized by Syrian and Russian jets, burying residents who could not flee in avalanches of bricks and mortar."[11] *NYT* Middle East correspondent Ben Hubbard, the author of the piece, argued that Bashar al-Assad's recapture of eastern Aleppo represented the failure of international diplomacy to avoid a humanitarian crisis. For Hubbard, the fact that the Syrian president would get away with the bombing and shelling of schools and hospitals "[proved] the effectiveness of violence and [highlighted] the reluctance of many countries … to get involved."[12] To demonstrate his point, the *NYT* journalist quoted US politicians, such as then-President Barack Obama and President-to-be Donald Trump, as well as experts from prestigious research centers, such as the Tahrir Institute for Middle East Policy in Washington.[13]

Hubbard also discussed the Aleppo crisis against the backdrop of US foreign policy; he highlighted the main features of President Obama's Syria policy and analyzed the possible consequences of the Syrian regime's recapture of the city. The article aligns with the *NYT* editorial line in that it spares President Obama from criticism and depicts the Syrian regime in negative terms. Hubbard's piece relays two important frames: one humanitarian crisis frame and one anti-Assad frame.

On that same day (December 16), the state-controlled *RT* (formerly *Russia Today*) ran a story about the evacuation of Aleppo from an entirely different perspective. Quoting several officials of the Russian military, the article's author asserted that the "liberation" of eastern Aleppo had been completed and that the Syrian government was tackling "separate pockets of militant resistance."[14] *RT* referred to Syrian oppositionists as "gangs," "terrorists," and "radical militants," an expression that is frequently used to describe Salafist and other hardline Islamic movements.[15] The article provides little context about the Syrian civil war or the international reactions to the siege of eastern Aleppo.

RT and the *NYT* conveyed divergent narratives about the same event. Whereas the US newspaper expressed the views of the US political elite and international organizations such as the United Nations, the Russian news channel framed the event from the perspective of the Russian military. It is worth noting that the *NYT*, as a privately owned corporation, independent from the US government, offers a degree of autonomy to its journalists that is not enjoyed by *RT* journalists.

The US-based organization Freedom House concluded, in a 2017 report about the state of the media, that the levels of press freedom in Russia are quite meager. According to the report,

> Vladimir Putin's regime in Russia has been a trailblazer in globalizing state propaganda. It continues to leverage pro-Kremlin reporting around the world … Rebroadcasts of state-controlled Russian television programming, alongside the made-to-export content of the state-owned outlets *RT* and *Sputnik*, fuel distortion campaigns in much of the former Soviet space, warping perceptions

of current and historical events and funneling trust away from domestic authorities[16]

Although this extract emphasizes the influence of Russian propaganda in the former Soviet space, it also applies to Syria, a country that has been in the Russian (and Soviet) sphere of influence for several decades.

Since February 2022, when the Russian invasion of Ukraine began, media freedom in the country has deteriorated rapidly. Roskomnadzor (RKN), the Russian Federal Service for Supervision of Communications, Information Technology and Mass Media, threatened several independent newspapers and news websites, forcing them to interrupt their activities in Russia or shut down completely. This was the case of Novaya Gazetta, one of the last major independent newspapers in Russia, which suspended its operations in March 2022 after receiving two warnings from RKN. The arrest of *WSJ* journalist Evan Gershkovich, detained in March 2023 on charges of espionage, attests to the country's dire situation for media freedom. Journalists can only work in Russia if they reproduce government narratives acritically.

Media scholar Muhammad Idrees Ahmad subscribes to the idea that *RT* functions as a vehicle of propaganda of the Russian government. In his view, the Russian media outlet plays this role, in part, by taking advantage of the shortcomings of Western media:

From Iraq, Israel-Palestine, to the so-called "war on terror," the international media's failings are myriad. This has allowed *RT* to market itself as an "alternative" to this compromised "fourth estate," even though the alternative that it is offering is nothing more than an echo of the Kremlin's adversarial worldview. In some places, this may be a useful counterbalance, but where this coverage aligns with the Kremlin's practical objectives—as in the Ukraine, or Syria—the disinformation becomes lethal.[17]

The *NYT*, by contrast, is driven by a business model and by the principles and tradition of American journalism (I will discuss these topics later in this introduction).

The two articles mentioned above mirror the "war of narratives" that has encircled the Syrian conflict from its beginning in 2011. The siege of Aleppo generated several different news frames. For example, the local newspaper *Enab Baladi*, established by anti-Assad activists in Darayya, Syria, in 2011, shared a unique frame of the evacuation of eastern Aleppo.[18] It focused not only on the fate of the civilian population still trapped inside the area but also on the fact that the Syrian regime did not observe the terms of the evacuation deal. Contrarily to most international media, *Enab Baladi*'s reporters had access to first-hand sources, who witnessed the evacuation of Aleppo *in situ*, and were able to contact residents as they waited to board the busses that would take them to safety. If framing is inevitable, and all news texts are to some extent biased, what is then the place of objectivity in journalism? This is the question I address in the next section.

Can News Reports Be Objective?

This debate is contentious among communication scholars. Objectivity is most importantly an ideology that became predominant in journalistic circles in the late nineteenth and early twentieth century. It came to life as a reaction to the previous era, which was characterized by a highly sensationalist and partisan press that did not see a contradiction in crossing ethical lines in order to increase sales.

The idea of objectivity arose in a period when the journalistic industry was rapidly growing and needed common standards of self-regulation. Journalism historian Michael Schudson explained,

> This newly articulated doctrine was related to the sheer growth in newsgathering. Rules of objectivity enabled editors to keep lowly reporters in check, although they had less control over foreign correspondents. The ideology of objectivity was a kind of industrial discipline. At the same time, objectivity seemed a natural and progressive ideology for an aspiring occupational group at a moment when science was God, efficiency was cherished, and increasingly prominent elites judged partisanship a vestige of the tribal nineteenth century.[19]

Journalists benefitted from the ideology of objectivity as it enabled them to create an identity as a professional group. Crafting rules of ethics and good practices empowered journalists in the face of newspaper owners and politicians.

Objectivity became an all-pervasive ideology in journalism which continues today, as the slogans of different newspapers demonstrate. Authors Bill Kovach and Tom Rosenstiel, for instance, claimed that objectivity in journalism relates to a method for "testing information": "The call for objectivity was an appeal for journalists to develop a consistent method of testing information—a transparent approach to evidence—precisely so that personal and cultural biases would not undermine the accuracy of their work."[20] However, if objectivity became such a sophisticated ideology, grounded on a set of routines and norms on how to treat information, can we say that media texts can be objective and impartial?

The answer to this question is an emphatic no. Newspapers are not objective in the sense of being neutral and perfectly balanced, which is not the same as saying that all media organizations deliberately spread disinformation in order to manipulate their readers. However, my analysis of the coverage of the Syrian conflict in the *NYT*, the *WP*, and the *WSJ* suggests that mainstream newspapers consistently align with specific segments of the political establishment. The claim that mainstream newspapers align with, or reverberate, elite narratives takes us to the question of the relationship between media organizations and political systems.

Edward Herman and Noam Chomsky conceived perhaps the sharpest and most refined critique of the mass media as tools of the elites to shape public opinion. In *Manufacturing Consent*, the two scholars analyzed the "filters" through which governments and private groups inflict their ideas on the public. Herman and Chomsky wrote, "A propaganda model focuses on this inequality of wealth and power and its multilevel effects on mass media interests and choices. It traces the routes by which money and power are able to filter out the news fit to print, marginalize dissent, and allow the government and dominant private interests to get their messages across to the public."[21]

Although Herman and Chomsky did not use the concept of frames, the notion that the media filters the information in its possession alludes to the process of framing. The propaganda model identifies five primary filters:

> (1) the size, concentrated ownership, owner wealth, and profit orientation of the dominant mass media firms; (2) advertising as the primary income source of the mass media; (3) the reliance of the media on information provided by government, business, and "experts" funded and approved by these primary sources and agents of power; (4) "flak" as a means of disciplining the media; and (5) "anticommunism" as a national religion and control mechanism.[22]

It is important to note that two of the filters mentioned above lost validity or underwent significant changes. The role of advertising as an income source of the mass media, for example, has changed significantly in the last fifteen years. Especially the newspaper industry has suffered greatly from declining ad revenues as platforms such as Facebook and YouTube became the recipients of most advertising investments. As I discuss later in this introduction, the three newspapers analyzed in this book rely greatly on online subscriptions to function.

Also, the fifth filter (the anticommunist ideology) has become outdated, as *Manufacturing Consent* was first published in 1988 when the Cold War was still ongoing and constituted a defining paradigm in international relations and political science. The literature on framing, however, accepts the idea that larger frames, or metaframes, influence the mass media's interpretation of issues and events. Metaframes are usually conceived by governments, trickling down to other spheres of society—media organizations included—as strategic narratives that underlie public policies. One of the contemporary strategic narratives is the war on terror discourse, which gained prominence in the aftermath of the September 11 attacks. Especially when covering Middle Eastern affairs, the media widely employ the war on terror narrative as a frame of reference to make events understandable to their audiences. As we will see in the following chapters, this narrative affected the coverage of the Syrian conflict in the US press in numerous ways.

The war on terror narrative is part of a wider set of theoretical and discursive tools employed in the West to describe (and "explain") the Middle East. These narratives, produced mostly in Western universities, government agencies, think tanks and other institutions, became known in academic circles as "Orientalism." Despite not having created the concept, Edward Said was arguably the intellectual who developed it more comprehensively. In his 1978 homonymous book, he claimed that "Orientalism is more particularly valuable as a sign of European-Atlantic power over the Orient than it is as a veridic discourse about the Orient."[23]

Said argued that the Orientalist discourse is an exterior representation of the "Orient", in the sense that it is produced outside of the region by Westerners, and the mass media have become an indispensable vehicle for its proliferation to larger audiences. The Palestinian-American scholar emphasized the connections between knowledge production (primarily about the "Orient") and economic power: "Orientalism, therefore, is not an airy European fantasy about the Orient, but a created body of theory and practice in which, for many generations, there has been a considerable material investment."[24] The three newspapers analyzed in this book reproduced ideas that can be classified as Orientalist when covering the Syrian conflict.

Returning to the discussion on Herman and Chomsky's propaganda model, it is noteworthy that, despite being a useful tool for unveiling the cartography of media power, the model conceives the public as merely a receptor of biased information (or ideology), deprived of agency in the framing process. Herman and Chomsky wrote, "The public is not sovereign over the media—the owners and managers, seeking ads, decide what is to be offered, and the public must choose among these. People watch and read in good part on the basis of what is readily available and intensively promoted."[25] Underestimating the capacity of citizens to interpret and decode media narratives amounts to an evident shortcoming of the propaganda model. Herman and Chomsky overlooked the fact that texts are polysemic and generate different meanings that will vary according to the receivers' background and experiences. The cultural theorist and political activist Stuart Hall referred to this process as "decoding."[26] Furthermore, the unilateral flow of information from the mass media to the public, which predominated in the pre-Internet period, underwent enormous changes in the digital age.

Another theory that examines news framing in the light of political power is the cascading activation model, developed by Entman. Entman and Nikki Usher explained how it functions:

> In the United States the [framing] hierarchy ran from the administration at the apex (president, White House, and cabinet agencies), to nonadministration elites (Congress members and staffers, ex-officials, experts, lobbyists), to institutionalized mainstream media (journalists and news organizations reaching mass audiences and bound to norms of objectivity), to news texts (networks of framing words and images), and, at the bottom, members of the public, whose sentiments were imperfectly communicated to elites and media by such indicators as surveys.[27]

Despite absorbing some aspects of the propaganda model, such as the idea that governments spread frames to the media, the cascading activation model does not pay much attention to the organic relation between the media and the elites. Entman has previously argued that the White House spreads frames to the rest of society through soft power, which stems principally from legitimacy rather than political, military, or economic leverage: "The metaphor of the cascade was chosen in part to emphasize that the ability to promote the spread of frames is stratified;

some actors have more power than others to push ideas along to the news and then to the public."[28]

The cascading activation model helps us to understand how frames rise to a prominent role, but it focuses mainly on the discursive level of power relations. Governments have a privileged position when it comes to projecting frames, but seeing it merely as "the ability to promote the spread of frames" is reductionist. The relationship between political institutions, the mass media, and the elite is more complicated than depicted by Entman's model. Framing cannot be reduced to a top-down, one-sided process in which governments disseminate their views to the rest of society. Entman underestimated the role of struggle and resistance in the process of framing. Framing is above all a political struggle, and as such, it is permeated by conflicting sociopolitical interests.

Media scholar Des Freedman indicated his agreement with this view when he argued that

> we need an approach to the media that focuses on its internal contradictions—tensions that are most clearly expressed in moments of crisis—that not only explains the failures of mainstream media in representing "ordinary" lives and holding power to account but also encourages us to mobilize with others in seeking to open up critical spaces, to press for more accountability and to inspire a democratic and genuinely diverse media.[29]

Media scholars ought to take this idea into account when analyzing news frames. As we will see in the following chapters, the *NYT*, the *WP*, and the *WSJ* shared different views of the Syrian conflict, although they are unquestionably elite newspapers. These different frames reflect not only the internal contradictions within each of these newspapers but also within the US political establishment.

My argument in this book is that mainstream newspapers align with elite narratives when covering political affairs. Nevertheless, my analysis also shows that, occasionally, media organizations are compelled by the circumstances to share alternative frames. These frames are usually relayed by activists, advocates, and intellectuals who do not belong to the mainstream. Alternative narratives constitute a small minority of the frames of the Syrian conflict in the news reports analyzed in this book, but their significance should not be underestimated. They highlight that "nonofficial" actors are sources of information just as legitimate and reliable as government officials and university experts. Syrians acting on the ground are possibly more capable of explaining the conflict than officials and analysts sitting in their offices situated thousands of kilometers away from Syria. Without them, our perception of this multifaceted conflict would be slanted and inaccurate.

In order to understand why mainstream newspapers are increasingly reliant on elite discourses, it is necessary to examine the recent transformations that affected the three newspapers analyzed in this book. This brief overview will help us to identify the reasons behind some of the editorial decisions taken by the three outlets when covering the Syrian conflict.

Changing Times for US Newspapers

The *NYT*, the *WP*, and the *WSJ* belong to the top five US newspapers in terms of circulation, subscribers, and revenues, and are, therefore, considered mainstream. They have been leading newspapers in the United States for several decades and have been able to adapt and reimagine themselves in times of crisis. In the last fifteen years, due to the exponential fall of print circulation and advertising revenues, the three newspapers transitioned to a web-based format, significantly changing their business model. As part of that process, they developed paywalls and began to rely much more on digital subscriptions and online advertising. It can be said that the three newspapers succeeded in adapting to this new reality. In fact, they constitute the top three US newspapers in terms of number of digital subscribers, and the figures seem to be on the rise.[30]

Not all newspapers have had the same luck: many have fallen by the wayside, having either disappeared or undergone major restructuring. According to media scholar Viktor Pickard, of the top one hundred newspapers in the United States, twenty-two filed for bankruptcy between 2005 and 2015.[31] The crisis affecting the US press is deep and it is changing the modus operandi of newspapers on various levels. Above all, this crisis relates to the tension between commercial and public good journalism. In Pickard's words, "These two sides of US journalism within a commercial system—the one, a vital public service; the other, a commodity bought and sold on the market to make profit—have been in conflict since the 1800s."[32]

The history of US journalism is inseparable from the development of American capitalism and its worldwide expansion in the second half of the nineteenth century. For instance, Schudson explained that "after the [American] Civil War, newspapers rapidly expanded as large profitable, industrialized business."[33] The transition from a system characterized by partisan journalism to a commercial business model resulted in the weakening of the symbiosis between political parties and newspapers.

This highly commercial business model, based on mass circulation and advertising revenues, reduced US newspapers' dependence on political parties, allowing them to adjust more or less to power structures regardless of their political affinities. Communication scholars Daniel Hallin and Paolo Mancini pointed to the importance of analyzing political and economic systems when studying the news media: "One cannot understand the news media without understanding the nature of the state, the system of political parties, the pattern of relations between economic and political interests, and the development of civil society."[34] Both scholars further argued that the US media system "is characterized by a relative dominance of market mechanisms and of commercial media."[35]

For that reason, establishing ideological associations between newspapers and political parties in the United States is less than straightforward. Victor Navasky shares this view, suggesting that "mainstream institutions like the *NYT*, the television networks, the news weeklies are no less ideological [than media outlets that are openly left – or right-wing]. They have the ideology of the center and it is part of the ideology of the center to deny that it has an ideology."[36]

However, it is possible to make assumptions about the political orientations of media organizations based on criteria of ownership and political alliances, although shifts occur at times depending on the political context. As large private corporations, the three newspapers analyzed in this book have established idiosyncratic liaisons with the US political and economic elites. For example, the *NYT* stands closer to the political center of the Democratic Party than to any other political group in the United States and it considers itself liberal. In fact, the last Republican candidate endorsed by the newspaper was Dwight Eisenhower in 1956; since then, the *NYT* has only supported Democratic candidates. Notwithstanding the affinity with the Democratic Party, the *NYT* has held critical attitudes toward Democratic presidents.

Although the New York Times Company is still controlled by the Sulzberger family, who bought the *NYT* in 1896, several other private investors, such as Mexican billionaire and media mogul Carlos Slim, have stakes in the company. As a result of lower advertising revenue, the *NYT* underwent a broad restructuring. The company acquired other newspapers in the United States and reduced the number of employees in the newsroom. The *NYT* was one of the first newspapers to launch a paywall, which it did in 2011, and since then it has steadily attracted new subscribers. It reported more than 6 million paid digital subscribers in July 2020.[37] The *NYT* is probably the most influential newspaper in the world. Despite the recent cuts, it retains various international offices around the world, which enables it to obtain firsthand information in different countries.

The *WP* is probably the main competitor of the *NYT* in the United States. Since 2013, it has belonged to Jeff Bezos, the owner of Amazon, who bought it from the Graham family for $250 million. Bezos introduced major changes in the newspaper's technological and social media approaches, which improved the overall performance of the *WP*. The newspaper competes neck and neck with the *NYT* in number of daily unique visits. In July 2020, it reported 3 million paid digital subscribers, which makes it the second newspaper in subscriptions in the United States, behind the *NYT* and ahead of the *WSJ*.

However, the *WP*'s political orientation did not alter substantially following its acquisition by Bezos. The *WP* considers itself the "newspaper of official Washington"[38] and it stands closer to a right-wing, conservative agenda, despite it having opposed the Trump administration on multiple issues, including its Syria policy. According to the Pew Research Center, the US public perceives the *WP* as being more liberal than conservative, although slightly less liberal than the *NYT*.[39] Nevertheless, it has supported Republican candidates on several occasions. The newspaper has numerous international offices, including Beirut, Cairo, and Istanbul, and has actually expanded its international coverage.[40]

The *WSJ* also went through a major change in ownership, when Rupert Murdoch acquired it from the Bancroft family for $5 billion. The deal confirms that the US newspaper industry is becoming less oriented as "family businesses" and more integrated with media conglomerates. The *WSJ* is probably the most conservative of the three newspapers analyzed in this book. Murdoch's News Corp also owns *Fox News* and the British *Times*, among several other media outlets. Since 2007, when the transaction was closed, the *WSJ* has become more conservative and more focused on geopolitics and finance, as well as less attentive to the US corporate world.[41]

In June 2014, in light of the expansion of the Islamic State, the newspaper's editorial board explicitly called for a second invasion of Iraq, echoing the opinion of the neoconservatives inside the Republican Party.[42] The attitude of the *WSJ* toward President Trump was ambiguous; it softened its discourse on the Trump administration on several occasions.[43] The friendship between Trump and Murdoch is well known. In 2017, the newspaper cut some of its international bureaus, which suggests that the *WSJ* is pursuing a more US-focused report strategy, relying more on news agencies for its international coverage.[44] As of June 2020, it reported nearly 3 million digital-only subscribers.

The Plan of the Book

This book is divided into seven chapters. In this introduction, I discussed the concept of news framing and how it relates to power and political systems. Chapter 1 summarizes the other main theoretical topic of this book: the relationship between media and foreign policy. During the analysis of the sample examined in this book, I realized that the coverage of the conflict in the three analyzed newspapers was dominated by the debates about which foreign policies the United States should pursue in Syria. Identifying how these debates shaped the frames relayed by the *NYT*, the *WP*, and the *WSJ* became another focus of this book. Answering this question furthers our understanding of the connections between the political establishment and elite newspapers.

Chapter 1 addresses the existing theories about this relationship and introduces new elements that emerged in the context of the coverage of the Syrian conflict in US media. Sean Aday argued that the scholarship about "the shaping and reporting on the foreign policy of the United States" has been growing steadily in the last decades, especially after the September 11 terrorist attacks.[45] According to Aday,

> The amount of scholarly attention to this area has increased markedly in the last twenty-five years, and—undoubtedly owing to the United States waging two wars (and a "global war on terror") in the aftermath of the 9/11 terrorist attacks—the area has seen an even greater quantity and quality of theoretical, empirical, and qualitative contributions over the last ten years.[46]

These contributions have covered the various dimensions of the portrayal of US foreign policy in the news media, and this book draws on their valuable tradition.

Chapters 2–7 examine the coverage of six events, which I call periods, of the Syrian uprising and civil war. The six events are the beginning of the Syrian uprising in March 2011, the Eastern Ghouta chemical attack in August 2013, the expansion of ISIS in Iraq and Syria in July 2014, the beginning of the Russian intervention in Syria in September/October 2015, the fall of eastern Aleppo in December 2016, and finally, the US-UK-French joint attacks against Syria in April 2018. The structure of each empirical chapter consists of a description of the event followed by the analysis of the coverage in the *NYT*, the *WP*, and the *WSJ*, respectively. For time and resource constraints, visual elements, such as photos and info graphs, were not taken into account. The positions of the articles on their respective websites, though constituting a frame device, were also left unconsidered due to the method of their collection. The total dataset amounts to 414 articles. The total number of articles of the *NYT*, the *WP*, and the *WSJ* are 112, 141, and 161, respectively (see Appendix for a more detailed discussion of the methodology and the sample analyzed in the book).

The six events had considerable geopolitical implications and, for that reason, attracted substantial media attention. The fact that the coverage of the Syrian uprising and civil war alternated between periods of saturation and silence constituted an additional challenge in the selection of the events. Since my primary interest lay in comparing the news frames of the three newspapers, I selected events which put Syria in the spotlight, and when the number of media reports was higher. The conclusion summarizes this book's most relevant findings and makes a few related remarks about the state of contemporary journalism and the relationship between media, foreign policy, and international conflicts.

Chapter 1

MEDIA, FOREIGN POLICY, AND INTERNATIONAL CONFLICTS

On April 14, 2018, a tweet from former US President Donald Trump that confidently declared, "perfectly executed," and "mission accomplished!" made headlines across the world. On the previous day, the United States, the UK, and France had carried out a series of airstrikes against facilities in Syria associated with the country's chemical weapons program. The airstrikes were a response to the Syrian regime's use of toxic gases in the Damascene suburb of Douma on April 7. Donald Trump's tweet spurred a debate about US foreign policy in Syria. In a news analysis published on April 14, for instance, *NYT* White House correspondent Peter Baker asked defiantly what the "mission" in Syria was and condemned the US president for lacking a coherent strategy to end the "bloodshed" in the war-torn country.[1]

President Trump took the opportunity to attack what he called "fake news media" for creating a controversy around his tweet. In the days leading up to the airstrikes, the US president used Twitter on numerous occasions to convey his mood and comment on his policy options. He referred to Syrian President Bashar al-Assad as an "animal" and blamed Russia and Iran for supporting the Syrian regime. A few days after the airstrikes, he stated, also on Twitter, that the United States was "locked and loaded" to deal with the Assad regime.[2] President Trump's decision to order the attacks in the first place was said to have been taken after he saw images on television and social media of the victims of the Douma chemical attack.

Trump's relationship with the media has been the object of an intense debate. Analysts have argued that television and social media have had a profound impact on the former US president's behavior. Like other contemporary far-right politicians, such as former Brazilian President Jair Bolsonaro, social media is Trump's favorite means of communication. Other observers have argued that Trump's and Obama's disparate media consumption habits partially explain their different political approaches. While Barack Obama is known for his indifference to television and social media—which does not mean that he did not consume and use them while he was in office—Donald Trump is a compulsive news consumer, spending several hours daily watching television.

During an event in 2019, former President Obama told the audience that he would advise any president not to watch television or read social media. He mentioned that in his case, a team of assistants filtered the news for him so he could focus on more relevant issues.[3] Ben Rhodes, one of President Obama's top foreign policy advisers, confirmed this information, stating that "each morning, an appointed White House 'media monitor' would send a list of news stories to a large group of staff, anything having to do with Obama or, to a smaller list, national security."[4]

Despite Obama's and Trump's different styles of engaging with the media, it is indisputable that media reports influence politicians in different ways. This chapter analyzes the relationship between news media and foreign policy with a particular emphasis on the Syrian conflict. Since this book examines the media discourses of three mainstream US newspapers, I focus on the debates in the United States. The scholarship on this subject constitutes one of the most prolific subdisciplines of political communication.

The debate about the relationship between media and foreign policy dates back to the first decades of the twentieth century, when US foreign policy became the object of public discussions and the mass media emerged as relevant social actors. Although foreign policy cannot be reduced to war and military intervention, these issues have received far more attention than others, and they will be the primary focus of this chapter.

The Public Dimension of Foreign Policy

The emergence of the United States as a global power at the turn of the twentieth century brought its foreign policy into the spotlight, sparking a national debate that transcended the limits of the political establishment. The conversation involved different segments of the public, such as journalists, intellectuals, newspaper owners, and other members of the elite. Foreign policy scholar Walter Russell Mead argued that the importance of foreign policy throughout US history is comparable to that of domestic politics. Mead reminded us that most US presidents since George Washington faced major international conflicts and had to oversee US troops abroad.[5] The news media, both generalist and specialist publications, have always played a vital role in the US foreign policy debate.

For W. Lance Bennett, "[t]he challenge of understanding the public dimension of foreign policy is to identify the underlying linkages among reporters, publics, and political elites that enable us to talk about different cases within the same analytical framework."[6] The scholarship on the topic has produced several analytical frameworks (to use Bennett's phrase), which have been employed in attempts to unpack the complex connections between media and foreign policy and the mutual influence they exert on one another. The propaganda model, the CNN effect hypothesis, the indexing theory, and the cascading activation model are relevant examples of such frameworks. To understand these connections, it is necessary to examine the political context, the predominant foreign policy discourses, and the relationship between media organizations, journalists, and the foreign policy establishment.

There is a broad consensus among scholars and other analysts that the mass media tend to reproduce the strategic narratives propagated by political elites. Media and international affairs scholar Sean Aday, for instance, claimed that foreign policy coverage in the United States is ethnocentric, elite-driven, and uncritical. Aday held that "in the foreign policy domain the press is far less likely to adequately fulfill its Fourth Estate function than it is in the domestic policy arena."[7]

As we will see in the following chapters, this book confirms this hypothesis, indicating that mainstream media focus almost exclusively on elite debates about foreign policy. I also argue that the current US media environment has become more polarized and indexed to the political views of elite circles. In fact, media polarization has become an essential feature of the public sphere of different societies across the globe. Although this increased polarization creates the appearance of diversity, I believe that the opposite is true: we are currently seeing less variety of opinions and critical views in the so-called quality press. In part, the sourcing practices of most mainstream media organizations explain this lack of diversity. Victor Pickard highlighted that an "over-reliance" on official sources constitutes a significant weakness of the US news media. In his opinion, this arrangement, in which mainstream party politics becomes the overarching element of news reports, creates "a media environment through which misleading information is easily amplified."[8] Media narratives that neglect unconventional voices restrain the public debate, becoming an obstacle to the optimal functioning of a democratic system.

Media scholar Dina Matar argued that "sourcing practices derive from a symbiotic and consensual process in which both parties—journalists and their sources—have much to gain in making news."[9] This is no different in foreign policy reporting. Most of the sources quoted in the articles analyzed in this book are either members of one of the two major US political parties or experts from a few think tanks and elite universities. Moreover, the fact that "most democratic governments have more power to keep secrets in foreign policy than they do in domestic affairs," as Mead argued,[10] constitutes a major deterrent for the achievement of a vigorous public debate. In the name of preserving national and security interests, governments insulate their discussions about foreign policy from public scrutiny.

By becoming more indexed to elite views, media organizations reduce their power to facilitate what Jürgen Habermas called the "deliberative legitimation process." The German philosopher argued that only an independent media system could properly mediate the public debate that is a basic requirement of a functioning democracy.[11] The following sections examine the coverage of international conflicts in US media, showing how this coverage intrinsically relates to the theoretical discussions about the relationship between media and foreign policy.

International Conflicts in US Media

In August 1920, Walter Lippmann and Charles Merz authored one of the pioneering studies in media content analysis, which examined the *NYT* coverage of the Russian Revolution. The two journalists analyzed more than one thousand *NYT* issues over three years, from March 1917 to March 1920. When the *New Republic* published the essay, the *NYT* was already a newspaper of prestige and international reputation, reaching a daily audience of several thousand. Two years before, in 1918, it had won its first Pulitzer Prize for its coverage of the First World War.

Lippmann and Merz found that the coverage of the Russian Revolution in the *NYT* was biased in favor of the interests of the US elite and the old Russian nobility. They wrote, "From the point of view of professional journalism, the reporting of the Russian Revolution [in the *NYT*] is nothing short of a disaster. On the essential questions, the net effect was almost always misleading, and misleading news is worse than none at all."[12] The two media analysts criticized the *NYT* for portraying opinions as facts and relying essentially on sources that supported one side of the conflict. It is noteworthy that Lippmann and Merz spoke of "professional journalism" in their analysis of the *NYT* coverage of the Russian Revolution. As previously seen, the idea that journalists should write news in a nonpartisan and professional manner was relatively new at the time, although it was gaining terrain among US journalists, editors, and newspaper owners.

In 2004, a study conducted by scholars Howard Friel and Richard Falk concluded that the *NYT* misreported the claims of the Bush administration about the existence of weapons of mass destruction (WMD) in Iraq. Friel and Falk wrote, "[T]he [*NYT*] aided and abetted the administration's deception efforts by reporting without challenge the claims about Iraqi WMD, and by not challenging on international law grounds the illegal unilateralism of the president."[13] In the run-up to the Iraq invasion, the two scholars further suggested, the *NYT* aligned with the Bush administration's narratives on issues such as the claim that the Saddam Hussein regime had links with terrorist groups. Although separated by more than seventy years, these two studies draw similar conclusions about the coverage of foreign affairs in one of the leading US newspapers.

Slanted coverage of the Iraq invasion is not an exclusive feature of the *NYT*. Todd Gitlin wrote in 2003 that the editorial pages of the *WP* gave more space to pro-war voices than to those opposing the invasion of Iraq. Gitlin argued that the *WP* editorials "read like direct transcriptions from the West Wing," instead of nurturing a broader debate about the consequences of toppling Iraqi President Saddam Hussein.[14] These examples suggest that US mass media reverberate elite narratives uncritically. To answer the question of whether this is always the case, it is necessary to examine the coverage of international conflicts in US media in conjunction with the theoretical models that have been employed to explain the complex relationship between media and foreign policy.

The propaganda model, which was introduced in the previous chapter, is possibly the most well-known analytical framework (even outside academic circles) as to how US media portray international affairs. In the previously cited *Manufacturing Consent*, Herman and Chomsky analyzed media reports about US involvement in different international events, such as the Indochina wars and elections in El Salvador and Nicaragua. As we have seen, Herman and Chomsky concluded that mainstream US media function as a platform for elites to spread their narratives and foster public consent for their policies: "It is our view that, among other functions, the media serve, and propagandize on behalf of, the powerful societal interests that control and finance them. The representatives of these interests have important agendas and principles that they want to advance, and they are well positioned to shape and constrain media policy."[15]

For Herman and Chomsky, mass-media firms had become an oligopoly, owned by a handful of businesspeople and increasingly dependent on advertising from the public and private sectors. One of the consequences of the entanglement between governments, large corporations, and media organizations has been that journalists mainly turn to government officials when looking for sources to inform their stories. The two scholars further argued, "The mass media are drawn into a symbiotic relationship with powerful sources of information by economic necessity and reciprocity of interest. The media need a steady, reliable flow of the raw material of news."[16]

Bennett's indexing hypothesis reinforces this aspect of the propaganda model. Drawing on research about the *NYT* coverage of US funding of paramilitary groups in Nicaragua,[17] the indexing hypothesis states that "news is 'indexed' implicitly to the range and dynamics of governmental debate but has little relation to expressed public opinion."[18] Bennett found that sources in news stories about US involvement in the Nicaraguan civil war were overwhelmingly government officials, which created a distorted, unilateral representation of events unfolding in the Central American country. In a more recent article, Bennett claimed the mass media has become a homogenous institution driven by elite narratives: "This indexing process gives the media-as-institution its remarkable homogeneity in terms of what stories matter, what sources are used to frame those stories, and what narrative lines emerge as stories develop."[19] In the same article, which was published in 2017, Bennett also argued that the Internet did not change this aspect of the press-government relationship in a tangible way. Whereas the indexing hypothesis focuses primarily on sourcing practices, the propaganda model provides a broader view of the relationship between governments and the media sector by looking at the media industry's political economy and the influence of the private sector in setting the agenda of the press.

Another contribution of the propaganda model is in identifying the role of ideologies in the news-making process. As noted in the previous chapter, Herman and Chomsky saw anticommunism as a vital force in the shaping of mainstream media reports during the Cold War:

> The anticommunist control mechanism reaches through the system to exercise a profound influence on the mass media. In normal times as well as in periods of Red scares, issues tend to be framed in terms of a dichotomized world of communist and anticommunist powers, with gains and losses allocated to contesting sides, and rooting for "our side" considered an entirely legitimate news practice.[20]

The influence of anticommunism on US media was also analyzed by Daniel Hallin, who concluded that, during the Vietnam War, the *NYT* editorial line "never broke with the assumption that the cause of the war was communist aggression" and that US defeat would have negative consequences for the "free world."[21] Hallin's analysis of the coverage of the Vietnam War in US media, especially in television, constitutes a groundbreaking work in media studies. Although he did not subscribe to the propaganda model in its entirety—his study was published before the publication of *Manufacturing Consent*—his analysis of the relationship between mass media and the US government confirmed some of the ideas proposed by Herman and Chomsky.

Despite acknowledging that ideology plays an important role in how journalists report international conflicts, Hallin does not see the mass media as a monolith that reverberates elite narratives uncritically. The author of *Uncensored War* paid greater attention than Herman and Chomsky to the discrepancies between the media and the political establishment, arguing that occasionally, media reports challenge government narratives. For Hallin, the coverage of the Vietnam War shifted throughout the conflict, from a more "patriotic" perspective at its early stages to a more critical stance as the war unfolded.[22] This shift was caused by the divisions in the political establishment and the growing opposition to the war among soldiers and the US public in general.

The impact of television on news production and consumption accelerated these trends, as Vietnam was the first "televised" war in history. The relative freedom that reporters enjoyed during the conflict partly explains the negative frames of the war relayed by numerous television networks and other media vehicles. In Hallin's words,

> Surely it made a difference, for instance, that many journalists were shocked both by the brutality of the war and by the gap between what they were told by top officials and what they saw and heard in the field, and were free to report all this. But it is also clear that the administration's problems with the "fourth branch of government" resulted in large part from political divisions at home, including those within the administration itself, which had dynamics of their own.[23]

Herman and Chomsky, by contrast, see the media as less autonomous organizations, more vulnerable to political and economic pressures. Despite acknowledging that media narratives might vary when the "powerful are in disagreement," reflecting a "diversity of tactical judgments on how to attain generally shared aims,"[24] the two scholars neglect the agency of journalists in the construction of news stories and of the public in the reception of news frames. Hallin seems more sensitive to these issues, which amount to two key subdisciplines of media studies and have been studied in detail by the scholarship.

As previously argued, the propaganda model is unmistakably shaped by Cold War politics, when a solid foreign policy consensus around anticommunism prevailed among US policymakers, scholars, and media practitioners. Despite constituting a relevant contribution to the field, it fails to integrate important aspects of the news-making process into the analysis of how the media interact with political systems.

In an interview conducted in 2009, Herman and Chomsky reaffirmed the fundamental aspects of the propaganda model, stating that their model "[could] do very well even without a firm elite consensus."[25] The two scholars cited the coverage of the Vietnam and the Iraq wars as examples of how the mass media were deferential to government narratives: "In both cases [Vietnam and Iraq] the media failed to give serious space to news and opinion reflecting the position of the majority. In neither case would the media ever refer to the US government's action as 'aggression.'"[26] Herman and Chomsky continued to downplay the fact that media narratives occasionally divert from official discourses. They argued that the US media not only supported the Iraq War but also "failed to give serious space to news and opinion reflecting the position of the majority." They also claimed that the experts quoted in the mainstream media "differed only on tactics." This opinion, as we will see, is far from being unanimous among scholars.

The End of the Cold War and the CNN Effect Hypothesis

The end of the Cold War changed US foreign policy in various ways. Following the collapse of the Soviet Union, a new triumphalism emerged among US politicians and foreign policy circles, who came to see the United States as the sole superpower. Several analysts adhered to new foreign policy discourses, such as the end of history, according to which states would gradually evolve toward market economy and liberal democracy, and the clash of civilizations, which advocates that cultural and civilizational conflicts would replace ideological struggles. For obvious reasons, anticommunism lost its place as a grand narrative of US foreign policy. The administrations of George H. W. Bush and Bill Clinton, for example, justified foreign interventions, such as in northern Iraq (1991), Somalia (1992–3), and Bosnia (1992–5), on humanitarian grounds, as a way of saving native populations from genocide and other crimes against humanity.

The shift to a foreign policy discourse focused on the defense of human rights took place in the aftermath of the US withdrawal from Vietnam, during Jimmy Carter's presidency (1977–81). The US defeat in Vietnam was arguably the event that most importantly contributed to the change. President Carter argued that the United States should abandon the Cold War paradigm and adopt a foreign policy based on values such as human rights, democracy, and self-determination. Although the new narrative advocated the end of US intervention in foreign countries, the approach was short-lived. With the ascension of Ronald Reagan to the presidency in 1981, US interference in the affairs of third countries stepped up markedly, as the examples of Nicaragua, Afghanistan, Iran, and Iraq attest. It was not until the defeat of the Soviet Union in 1992 and the subsequent end of the Cold War that the idea of humanitarian interventions became hegemonic within US foreign policy circles.

International relations scholars Jon Western and Joshua Goldstein explained how the idea came into existence:

> Modern humanitarian intervention was first conceived in the years following the end of the Cold War. The triumph of liberal democracy over communism made Western leaders optimistic that they could solve the world's problems as never before. Military force that had long been held in check by superpower rivalry could now be unleashed to protect poor countries from aggression, repression, and hunger.[27]

Among these "new" problems, which would pervade peripheral countries in particular, ethnic and national conflicts occupied a central place. This was the case in northern Iraq (Iraqi Kurdistan), Somalia, Rwanda, Bosnia, Serbia, and Kosovo, which constituted some of the most severe conflicts of the 1990s.

In addition to these geopolitical transformations, the media landscape underwent drastic changes during the 1990s due to the spread of satellite television that broadcast live worldwide to millions of households. These political and technological changes created a fertile ground for the emergence of new analytical frameworks to interpret the relationship between media and foreign policy. The CNN effect hypothesis emerged in this context, as scholars Eytan Gilboa et al. argued: "Since the 'CNN effect' was first coined in 1991 in the wake of the US intervention during the Kurdish crisis in Northern Iraq, the term has grasped a range of the novelties brought about by live 24-hour news reporting from conflict scenes, and its catchiness quickly made it a popular concept both in scholarly and policy circles."[28]

According to the proponents of the CNN effect hypothesis, international media, especially cable television networks, had acquired the capacity to influence governmental responses to international crises significantly. Piers Robinson, a former academic and one of the proponents of this hypothesis, argued in a 2002 book that "the emotive and graphic coverage of the Kurds in 1991 clearly pressured politicians to 'do something.' This pressure would not have existed if news media reports had been framed in a less emotive and more distancing manner."[29]

Robinson was referring to Saddam Hussein's violent response to the Kurdish uprising in northern Iraq in March/April 1991 in the aftermath of the Gulf War, which included the use of gunship helicopters and artillery barrages. Following the Iraqi regime's repression of the insurrection, the United States, the UK, and France launched Operation Provide Comfort to enforce a no-fly zone over northern Iraq. Proponents of the CNN effect hypothesis rejected the assumption that the media report international events in an objective and neutral fashion. Robinson, for example, argued that the media and governments mutually influence one another, especially in the context of elite dissent and policy uncertainty. His policy–media interaction model, which stems from the CNN effect hypothesis, tried to elaborate on this notion. In Robinson's words, "The policy–media interaction model is designed to help identify instances when media coverage comes to play a significant role in persuading policymakers to pursue a particular policy. As such the model is designed to capture instances where media reports helped drive or push policymakers down a particular path."[30]

Robinson is a member of the Organization for Propaganda Studies and also of the Working Group on Syria, Propaganda, and Media. His research transcends the topic of media influence on policymakers, focusing more broadly on conflict, war, and propaganda. He has been involved in various debates and controversies in recent years, and some academics have criticized him for promoting conspiracy theories and for "whitewashing" some of the crimes committed by the Assad regime in Syria.[31] Robinson has authored or endorsed studies disputing that the Syrian government carried out chemical attacks against civilians in rebel-controlled areas.[32] In a 2018 essay, for example, he wrote, "The issue of alleged chemical weapon attacks in Syria remains disputed at an international level and is now subject to emerging evidence that opposition groups have been staging attacks, so-called false flags, in order to implicate the Syrian government."[33] Robinson also seems to support theories according to which al-Qaeda militants did not execute the September 11 attacks.[34]

Despite the controversies surrounding one of the proponents of the CNN effect hypothesis, the model—or some variations of it—became popular among mainstream politicians and foreign policy scholars. George Kennan, one of the most prestigious US foreign policy scholars of the Cold War era, endorsed the idea in a 1993 opinion piece: "The reason for this acceptance [by the US Congress and public of the Somalia intervention] lies primarily with the exposure of the Somalia situation by the American media, above all, television."[35] Kennan further argued that the media had grown capable of influencing foreign policy decision-makers, especially when it involved foreign military operations: "If American policy from here on out, particularly policy involving the uses of our armed forces abroad, is to be controlled by popular emotional impulses, and particularly ones provoked by the commercial television industry, then there is no place—not only for myself, but for what have traditionally been regarded as the responsible deliberative organs of our government."[36]

Livingstone agreed with this idea when he suggested that media organizations act as "accelerants" of the foreign policy decision-making process. Rather than shaping policy, real-life television compels the foreign policy establishment to respond faster to international crises. Livingstone wrote, "Understood as an accelerant to the policy process, global, real-time media have also had an effect on the operation of the foreign policy bureaucracy, particularly intelligence agencies and desk officers in the State Department."[37] However, this is not the only effect of real-time news reports on policy. Livingstone also maintained that on some occasions, especially during wars and humanitarian crises, the media can function as an "impediment" to specific policy options because they have the power to generate emotional responses, such as aversion or sympathy, on the public.

The discussion about the CNN effect hypothesis continued throughout the 1990s, and it is still part of the conversation to this day, although current research has discredited most of its claims. Aday, for example, argued that "since the [CNN effect] hypothesis was crafted, most studies have found little evidence of direct effects on the public in line with it."[38] Other scholars agree with this view. Peter Jakobsen, for instance, did not establish a causal relationship between media coverage and the decision of governments to embark on so-called humanitarian interventions:

> The CNN effect did not cause the three interventions commonly regarded as the prime examples of media-driven humanitarian interventions: the intervention in northern Iraq to save the Kurds in April 1991, the intervention in Somalia in December 1992 to create a secure environment for the distribution of humanitarian relief, and the intervention in Rwanda in June 1994 which set up a security zone for refugees.[39]

Jakobsen maintained that other political factors caused these three interventions and that media coverage was one among them.

In a 2018 article titled "Syria & the CNN Effect," *BBC* Senior Correspondent Lyse Doucet argued that even when media coverage plays a role in the foreign policy choices of presidents, it does not constitute the primary factor. Doucet analyzed how presidents Obama and Trump reacted to media reports on the Syrian conflict. She concluded that although President Trump was influenced by images of the Syrian war when authorizing the 2018 airstrikes against the Assad regime, these attacks were one-off and did not change US policy substantially. Doucet agrees with Aday and Jakobsen that media influence exists, but that it is not the determinant factor causing a government to act in a certain way: "Extensive studies have highlighted how powerful images can only make a real difference in the choices of decision-makers if an avenue already exists for them to act."[40]

Nevertheless, advocates of the CNN effect hypothesis made a useful contribution to the conversation about the relationship between media and foreign policy. In a hyper-mediatized era, understanding the influence of the news media on the public and on members of the political establishment is crucial. The case of Syria is particularly relevant to assess the efficacy of the CNN effect hypothesis to untangle the relationship between media and foreign policy because the Syrian civil war has been one of the most covered conflicts in recent history. Before resuming the analysis of the analytical frameworks about media and foreign policy, it is helpful to examine the coverage of the Syrian conflict in more detail.

Reporting the Syrian Revolution

Since the Syrian uprising erupted in March 2011, images of the protests and the regime's violent response have spread to every corner of the world through social media and countless websites. Syrian activists circumvented the restrictions imposed by the government on the use of the Internet to broadcast their protests on Facebook, YouTube, and other social media. Syria has for a long time been one of the most closed and isolated countries of the region, as the Assad regime banned virtually all types of public spaces in which citizens could freely express themselves. In the words of Syrian scholar Samer Abboud, "[p]rior to the uprising, Syria did not have an autonomous civil society. There was very limited space for the expression of political dissent. From the 1960s onwards the only associations that were formed and licensed by the state were charitable organizations that were almost all religious."[41]

The situation was similar regarding the digital sphere, Syrians often having to deal with regime-imposed restrictions on the use of the Internet. For that reason, as media scholar Donatella Della Ratta attested, online activism was scarce: "Online activism was close to nonexistent, and even at a regional level, prior to 2011, very few Syrians had ever attended community gatherings revolving around the use of technology for social and political change."[42] During the first months of the uprising, in an attempt to persuade the protesters to leave the streets, the Assad regime introduced a few political reforms, including limited liberalizations of the use of digital spaces. However, as the demonstrations continued, the government reinforced the restrictive laws that banned social media and other websites.

In 2012, the Committee to Protect Journalists—an independent, nonprofit organization—ranked Syria the third most censored country globally. The committee's editors wrote,

> In its campaign to silence media coverage, the government disabled mobile phones, landlines, electricity, and the Internet. Authorities have routinely extracted passwords of social media sites from journalists through beatings and torture. The pro-government online group the Syrian Electronic Army has frequently hacked websites to post pro-regime material, and the government has been implicated in malware attacks targeted at those reporting on the crisis.[43]

Bashar al-Assad, who had been the head of the Syrian Computer Society before becoming president, knew perfectly well the potential of social media activism.

This scenario created immense obstacles affecting the Western media's ability to cover the conflict from the ground. When the protests began, only a few outlets had journalists based in Damascus, and those who happened to be in Syria were unable to move freely and speak with protesters. The emergence of an extraordinary movement of citizen journalists partially filled the void created by the absence of international media outlets. Citizen journalists played a crucial role in documenting the uprising and communicating to the world a counternarrative to that relayed by the state-controlled media. Hundreds of newspapers, media centers, and Facebook pages surfaced in the first months of the uprising, shaking the media landscape of the country in an unprecedented way.

Antoun Issa, a journalist at the Middle East Institute,[44] claimed in 2016 that "Syria's media culture [was] undergoing significant transformation from a top-down, state-run industry, to a diverse arena populated by competing viewpoints and driven by communities."[45] This community-led journalism, which is still active inside and outside the country to this day, constitutes one of the most enduring legacies of the Syrian uprising.

Kholoud Helmi, one of the founders of the Syrian newspaper *Enab Baladi*, stated in an interview that she decided to become a journalist exactly because international media could not work freely in Syria and the state-owned media reproduced the regime narrative about the protests.[46] Helmi further claimed that women played a unique role in the emergence of this new Syrian media: "Of the twenty-five co-founders of [*Enab Baladi*], around 75 percent were women. It was our choice to be part of the newspaper as we had been present for every single moment since the revolution's beginning. We were taking to the streets and organizing demonstrations. We were not just witnessing but participating in everything that was happening."[47]

Syrian media scholar Omar al-Ghazzi shares a similar view. In a study about how affective proximity and emotion influenced the work of Syrian media practitioners during the uprising, al-Ghazzi argued that, in Syria, the boundaries between activism and journalism were often difficult to identify. Al-Ghazzi interviewed several professionals who worked as or with Syrian media practitioners in the period 2015–16. The Syrian scholar wrote, "When asked about their media engagement, and in recalling their experiences in 2011, several interviewees spoke of feeling they were 'forced to report' because if they do not tell the world what was happening, no one else would."[48] Al-Ghazzi further argued that journalists in Syria "faced a tension between reporting what was happening, and lending support to what one wanted to happen."[49] For him, as the Syrian uprising evolved into a civil war, and Islamist, foreign-backed armed groups proliferated, it became more difficult for media practitioners in Syria to deal with this dilemma.

Overreliance on this newly formed local media engendered great challenges for the coverage of the Syrian conflict by international media organizations. For Doucet, the shortcomings of having to rely on information produced by untrained media practitioners were enormous:

> Syria's war is arguably the first "social media war." Security risks and visa restrictions often kept many of the world's leading media, including most mainstream Western broadcasters, off the front lines. That led to a reliance on streams of information on social media provided mainly by activists. There was often valuable material, but it was hard to verify and, at times, turned out to be wrong or misleading.[50]

Syria became more accessible once the civil war was underway and once the Assad regime began to withdraw from specific areas. In rebel-controlled territory, foreign journalists were welcomed and could move freely, at least during the first years of the uprising. Moderate Syrian rebels were interested in showing to the world what was happening in the territory controlled by anti-Assad groups. Different media outlets sent teams to these liberated areas so they could report the conflict from multiple perspectives. Journalists, humanitarian workers, and activists who sympathized with the Syrian uprising crossed into Syria from

Lebanon and Turkey with the help of the Free Syrian Army (FSA) and other local groups.

However, this period of relative freedom was short-lived. At the beginning of 2014, as ISIS became a strong player and set about targeting foreign journalists and humanitarian workers, the situation on the ground rapidly deteriorated. The strengthening of ISIS and other jihadist groups resulted in the withdrawal of most international media from rebel-controlled areas. As the conflict progressed, several media groups established partnerships with local Syrian outlets, providing training and funding to enable them to produce reports in accordance with professional journalistic standards.

Della Ratta analyzed the singularity of the collaboration between citizen journalists and international media outlets, highlighting that it was particularly important in Syria:

> After the outbreak of the 2011 uprisings and the increasing need to process a formidable amount of information almost in real-time, and, sometimes, from places—particularly Syria—where no other sources were available, volunteer-based digital activism sought to adopt a more professional approach. This was a consequence both of the need for material survival in countries where the unrest had caused inflation, financial instability, and unemployment, and of the demand of international news outlets for more accurate and verified data.[51]

Several of the local media outlets that established partnerships with international groups are still active in Syria, functioning as an essential source of alternative news reports.

The combination of challenging conditions for international journalists and a prolific movement of citizen journalists, who became experts in using the Internet to spread information and counternarratives, made the coverage of the Syrian conflict an exceptional activity. The coverage of the Syrian uprising and civil war constitutes a one-off opportunity to test and reassess the CNN effect hypothesis. As noted earlier, the unprecedented number of reports, videos, and images produced in Syria reached virtually every corner of the world, affecting governments in different ways. Some scholars have coined new expressions, such as the "YouTube effect," to describe this new reality. Nevertheless, the graphic images of this terrible humanitarian catastrophe did not persuade international powers to act decisively to end the conflict. Geopolitical factors prevailed, creating an impasse that prevented the United Nations and the so-called international community from finding a solution to the civil war.

The geopolitical quagmire around the Syrian civil war confirms that dissent among elites, both on the international and domestic levels, amounts to a defining feature of the current world order. The cascading activation model, proposed by Entman, offers a range of theoretical tools to analyze the relationship between media and foreign policy in the context of growing elite dissent.

The Cascading Activation Model

The end of the Cold War eroded the foreign policy consensus over containing Soviet expansionism, which had been in place in the United States since the late 1940s, giving rise to new US foreign policy priorities. In the words of British historian Perry Anderson,

> During the Cold War, it had been the great tradition of American statecraft, combining a heavy investment in military force with a strong commitment to international institutions—power and partnership held in a balance that commanded a bipartisan consensus. Now, amid increasing polarization in Congress and public opinion, broad agreement on American foreign policy had faded, and the compact on which it was based had broken apart.[52]

The increasing polarization to which Anderson referred has become an intrinsic feature of the current political landscape. At the same time, the mass media have become more indexed to political elites, which means that they are more likely to echo the ongoing debates within these groups. The propaganda model and the CNN effect hypothesis fail to capture the complexities of this new political reality, as they overemphasize either the absolute power of governments to shape media discourses or the media's capacity to significantly influence foreign policies. Entman's cascading activation model, which has also been addressed previously in the introduction, constitutes an alternative view to both the propaganda model and the CNN effect hypothesis. In Entman's words, "the [cascading activation] model highlights what the hegemony model neglects: that the collapse of the Cold War consensus has meant differences among elites are no longer the exception but the rule."[53] By hegemony model, Entman referred to different traditions, including the propaganda model, according to which governments have a decisive influence on media narratives.

Entman does not ignore the power of government officials over newspaper owners and journalists, but he argued that media framing transforms (not only reproduces) official narratives in different ways. In his view, the notion that the media merely reproduce elite views is an oversimplification. Each news outlet refines government (and other elite) narratives by adding new layers of meaning that relate to factors such as editorial lines, levels of disagreement between elites, and indicators of public opinion. The fundamental feature of the cascading activation model is the notion that the framing process begins at the government level, trickling down to other elite groups, the press, and finally, the public.

The cascading activation model integrates the notion of frame into the analysis of the press-government relationship. It highlights that different media apply a variety of frames in the coverage of similar events, issues, and actors. If frames, as Entman argued, contain aspects such as problem definitions, causal analyses, remedy proposals, and moral judgments, they may not be understood simply as narratives or discourses. I argue in this book that the *NYT*, the *WP*, and the *WSJ* framed the Syrian conflict differently and that these differences relate primarily to how the three newspapers positioned themselves with respect to the foreign policies pursued by the US government.

The cascading activation model also considers how news frames trigger different mental associations within a particular public. For example, one of the challenges of reporting the Syrian conflict was dealing with the cultural abyss that separates the United States and Syria. The fact that the general interest in Syria among American readers is low adds a layer of complexity to explaining the conflict. This observation helps us to understand why journalists employ general categories, such as sectarianism, religious extremism, humanitarian crisis, uprising, or civil war, to explain issues that otherwise would be inaccessible to a significant part of the public.

As discussed in the introduction to this book, the cascading activation model does not consider in detail issues such as media ownership concentration and the relationship between journalists and the political establishment. Without integrating these two issues in the analysis of the press-government relationship, it is impossible to fully unpack how power dynamics operate in the production of news frames. Entman reduces power to the political capability of governments to spread frames to media groups, leaving political-economic aspects out of his analytical framework. In the context of growing ownership concentration and digital sphere predominance, this narrow notion of power hinders the capability of the cascading activation model to provide an accurate picture of the relationship between media and foreign policy. Regarding this particular aspect, the propaganda model offers a broader range of theoretical tools.

Despite this weakness, Entman's model represents a novel contribution to the debate, more in line with the new realities of post-Cold War politics. However, the September 11 attacks against the World Trade Center and the subsequent military interventions in Afghanistan and Iraq posed new challenges to the discussion about the relationship between media and foreign policy. These dramatic events resulted in the revival of narratives and policies that some believed to be buried forever, such as the notion that the United States was facing an existential threat, this time from Islamic extremism. The analysis of how the US media reacted in the face of these challenges, especially the invasion of Iraq, is the focus of the next section.

The Coverage of the Iraq War: A Return to Cold War Journalism?

No event in recent history influenced US foreign policy as profoundly as the September 11 attacks against the World Trade Center. The 2001 terrorist attacks that destroyed the Twin Towers gave rise to a new US National Security Strategy (NSS) that came to be known as the war on terror or the global war on terrorism. By establishing that terrorist groups operated in different countries through unconventional ways, the 2002 NSS deterritorialized the notion of war. The NSS represented a significant shift in US foreign policy, as it endorsed preemptive wars against regimes or organizations perceived as threats to US national security.

Historians Stephen Ambrose and Douglas Brinkley argued that al-Qaeda operated within a similar model as NGOs, "recruiting members across borders and using technology to coordinate training, planning, and action."[54]

In the aftermath of the attacks, the Bush administration identified the terrorist group al-Qaeda as the main enemy to be defeated. It also singled out Afghanistan's Taliban regime for harboring al-Qaeda militants and the Iraqi regime of Saddam Hussein for having weapons of mass destruction and links with different terrorist networks. President George W. Bush claimed that the United States could not wait for threats to materialize and that, therefore, preemptive attacks should become an integral part of US foreign policy. However, as political scientist Ian Lustick argued, the war on terror doctrine was not only about defeating terrorism; it was predominantly about projecting US power:

> The notion of a war against al-Qaeda-type terrorists arose as an immediate reaction to 9/11. It then rapidly developed into an abstract and far-reaching war on terror. The supremacist faction within the Bush administration advanced that slogan to launch a neoimperial war in Iraq; a war that had nothing to do with terrorism but everything to do with extravagant ideological and political ambitions.[55]

The Bush administration embarked on an effort to involve the US public, multilateral organizations, and its international allies on the war on terror. Immediately after the attacks, the US government was able to build strong alliances around the legitimacy of fighting terrorism and how it represented an existential threat to so-called Western values. President Bush amassed high approval rates, with more than 90 percent of the US population supporting the fight against terrorism.

The narrative of the Bush administration resembled Cold War discourses in numerous ways. In the introduction of the 2002 NSS, for example, the then-US president stated,

> The great struggles of the twentieth century between liberty and totalitarianism ended with a decisive victory for the forces of freedom—and a single sustainable model for national success: freedom, democracy, and free enterprise. In the twenty-first century, only nations that share a commitment to protecting basic human rights and guaranteeing political and economic freedom will be able to unleash the potential of their people and assure their future prosperity.[56]

Despite President Bush's rhetoric about supporting democracy and freedom, the United States provided arms and security assistance to several dictatorships and so-called poorly performing countries during his administrations. Some of the regimes to which US military and police assistance increased exponentially after 9/11 included Pakistan, Afghanistan, Yemen, Tajikistan, and Djibouti.[57] These partnerships were justified with narratives such as the war on drugs, the fight against terrorism, and the need to help these countries transition to democracy.

For Lebanese scholar Gilbert Achcar, the narratives of the US government in the aftermath of the September 11 attacks "[called] on the imagery of the Second World War for the third time since the end of the Cold War, after having resuscitated Hitler successively in the shape of Saddam Hussein and then of Slobodan Milošević."[58] The invoking of the "metaphysical notion of evil" to refer to Islamic terrorism, Achcar argued, was a conscious attempt to associate the fight against terrorism with the one against communism.

Media scholars Pipa Norris, Montague Kern, and Marion Just claimed that "the replacement of the older Cold War frame with the new war on terrorism frame offered a way for American politicians and journalists to construct a narrative to make sense of a range of diverse stories about international security, civil war, and global conflict."[59] To a certain extent, this notion epitomizes what news frames are all about: relaying problem definitions, causal relations, and perceived solutions to mass audiences in a palatable way. The mass media absorbed this new war on terror frame uncritically, at least in the period immediately after the September 11 attacks, when support for President Bush's policy was widespread.

According to media scholar Robert McChesney, US media did not promote a balanced public debate about how to respond to the attacks: "What is most striking in the US news coverage following the September 11 attacks is how that very debate over whether to go to war, or how best to respond, did not even exist. It was presumed, almost from the moment the South Tower of the World Trade Center collapsed, that the United States was at war, world war."[60]

Several media scholars agree with McChesney's views. For example, Entman, analyzing the media coverage of the Iraq War, argued that most TV networks in the United States supported the Bush administration's narrative about the urgency to overthrow Saddam Hussein: "Although comprehensive studies of war news were not available at press time, informal observation and impressions gleaned from obtainable data suggest that television supported the administration line in most respects, from the studio to the battlefield—at least until Bush's declaration in a May 1 speech given on an aircraft carrier that 'major combat operations' [in Iraq] were over."[61] Things were no different regarding print media, Entman continued, stating (also about the Iraq invasion) that "[the *WP*] ran nine pro-war (and no antiwar) unsigned editorials between December 1, 2002, and February 21, 2003, along with 39 pro-war and just 12 antiwar op-ed columns."[62] Research around this issue is unequivocal in concluding that the US media failed to provide a counternarrative to the war on terror frame.

For Schudson, this tendentious coverage of the Iraq War is partly explained by the fact that in moments of tragedy, when a country is mourning a large number of deaths and there is widespread fear among the population, journalists tend to assimilate these feelings, "abandoning" the effort to report from a neutral stance.[63] Schudson further argued that this lack of objectivity also occurs in moments of public danger and threat to national security. The September 11 attacks combined these three features: tragedy, public danger, and perceived threat to national security.

John Richardson, a media scholar who undertook extensive research about the coverage of the build-up to the Iraq invasion in British newspapers, found that even newspapers deemed left-leaning and progressive reproduced the frames spread by the US and UK governments. According to Richardson,

> A search of the *Guardian* website, for instance, shows that there were only thirteen articles that contained the phrase "weapons of mass destruction" in 1998, all in November and December, the first dated November 14, a month before the US "Desert Fox" cruise missile attacks on Iraq.[64] This number rose to seventy-five articles in 1999, 204 in 2001, 2007 in 2003 and then dropped off to only 251 in 2005 (to the time of writing).[65]

As we know, the Bush administration's central justification for the 2003 Iraq invasion was the claim that Saddam Hussein had an arsenal of weapons of mass destruction that needed to be eliminated. It is interesting to note how the coverage of this topic (the existence of such weapons in Iraq) increased exponentially as the invasion became imminent.

Richardson's work paid significant attention to the ways in which journalists are exposed to official narratives in times of war. His work corroborates the idea that governments exert a strong influence in setting the mass media's agenda. In the case of the Iraq War, the US government employed several strategies, such as embedding vetted journalists in the US army, to shape media discourses.

The fact that the media behaved deferentially to government narratives in the aftermath of the September 11 attacks, reproducing the war on terror strategy, does not mean that the relationship between governments and news organizations had returned to a context similar to the Cold War period. Despite the similarities between anticommunism and the war on terror narrative, the mass media's uncritical acceptance of government frames about the Afghanistan and Iraq Wars did not last long.

For instance, President Bush's *carte blanche* to act in Iraq expired after a few months. According to Entman, the first critical reports on the invasion of Iraq surfaced in US media once the Bush administration started to face its first setbacks:

> Pressure from media and foreign (and internal) dissent imposed real diplomatic and economic costs on the United States and political costs on the administration. The latter became especially acute when Saddam Hussein's fall was followed not by peace but by mounting American casualties and financial costs. Although the media celebrated the deaths of Saddam's two villainous sons in late July 2003, questions about Bush's main justifications for going to war (and Saudi complicity in 9/11) kept percolating, and by then Bush's approval ratings were down significantly in various polls from their April peak.[66]

These dynamics represent a crucial distinction between Cold War and post-Cold War politics. Not only did the US political establishment present fissures early on during the invasion of Iraq, but also at the international level, US allies manifested their disagreement with the way the Bush administration conducted the Iraq invasion. Popular dissent also played a role in opening the way to critical reports about the Iraq invasion. As media scholar Des Freedman argued, "[t]he media are open to challenge particularly when the frames they propose do not seem to match the experiences or aspirations of their audiences. This is all the more likely at times of social struggle and political instability when existing narratives are under stress and when audiences themselves are actively seeking out new perspectives that better fit with changing circumstances."[67]

In the face of increasing dissent around the Iraq War, the cascading activation model, with its focus on how frames cascade from governments to the rest of the system, provides an adequate picture of the relationship between media and foreign policy. Despite adopting a narrow depiction of power, it integrates the notion that dissent among elites has become an integral part of mainstream politics. As the following chapters demonstrate, elite dissent marked the coverage of the Syrian conflict in US mainstream newspapers in different ways. Although the three newspapers analyzed in this book often covered the same topics (mostly related to US foreign policy), the frames that each one of them relayed are shaped by the different views within the US political and foreign policy establishments.

Chapter 2

THE BEGINNING OF THE
SYRIAN UPRISING (PERIOD I)

The first demonstrations in Syria against the regime of Bashar al-Assad erupted in March 2011. Inspired by the revolts that were shaking other countries of the region, such as Tunisia, Libya, Yemen, Bahrain, and Egypt, Syrians took to the streets peacefully to demand reforms in the country's political system. Al-Assad's presidency started in 2000 after the death of his father, Hafez al-Assad, a Syrian Air Force commander who became president after leading a coup d'état in 1970. According to most accounts, the Syrian revolution started on March 15 in Daraa, as thousands of protestors demanded the release of fifteen children who had been arrested for painting anti-Assad slogans on a wall. In a clear demonstration of the regime's brutality, local security forces not only arrested these children but tortured them, burning their bodies and pulling their fingernails. When they were released two weeks after the arrests, a wave of indignation washed over Daraa and then other parts of the country.

Events in Syria cannot be understood in isolation from the uprisings that started in 2010/11 in different countries of the MENA region or the Arab Spring. Compared to the Tunisian and the Egyptian revolutions, the initial protests in Syria were followed by high levels of popular organization. As Samer Abboud argued, "[w]ithin several weeks, the Syrian protests evolved into a movement that became more organized and which possessed a national momentum, but did not enjoy central coordination."[1] Although building national centralization amounted to a permanent challenge for Syrian revolutionaries throughout the conflict, the *Tansiqiat* (or Local Coordinating Committees) emerged almost instantaneously during the uprising's early stages, playing a determinant role in organizing and shaping the struggle against the Assad regime.

By and large, the mass media identified some of the common aspects underpinning the Arab revolts, although most Western media reduced them at first to democratic upheavals with the foremost objective of bringing about more political freedom. Such a reductionist interpretation fell short of explaining these highly complex events, as Gilbert Achcar explained: "Given the diversity of the region's political regimes, logic suggests we search for underlying socioeconomic factors which may have laid the common ground for the regional shock wave. Despotism by itself, moreover, can hardly be sufficient cause for the outbreak and subsequent success of a democratic revolution."[2] The three newspapers analyzed in this book emphasized the political dimensions of the Syrian uprising at the expense of the socioeconomic factors mentioned by Achcar, such as growing unemployment and economic precarity among young Syrians.

In the case of Syria, for instance, the years that preceded the uprising were marked by the implementation of various neoliberal reforms such as the liberalization of trade, the approval of the 2008 Competition and Anti-Monopoly Law, the licensing of private banks, and the deregulation of the real-estate sector.[3] Although the pace of the neoliberal transformation was slower than in other countries of the region, such as Egypt, Tunisia, and Morocco, the dismantling of the welfare state in Syria deeply affected the livelihoods of the majority of the population. According to Dahi and Munif, "[t]he neoliberal practices of Makhlouf [Bashar al-Assad's cousin] and others like him have devastated Syrian citizens' standard of living in the past ten years. The concentration of wealth, since the time of the United Arab Republic, has never been as uneven where 5% of the population owns 50% of the wealth."[4] Unemployment and poverty rates also multiplied during al-Assad's presidency.

The first demonstrations in Syria caught the Obama administration by surprise, which was busy responding to the crises in Egypt, Tunisia, and Libya. As previously noted, several analysts ruled out an uprising in Syria, arguing, among other things, that the Assad regime was different from other Middle Eastern regimes in that it was stronger and more repressive. Michael Bröning, a German political scientist, expressed this view in an article for *Foreign Affairs*: "Despite various parallels, a closer look at Syria reveals that the Assad regime—led for the past decade by Bashar al-Assad—is unlikely to fall. Paradoxically, Syria's grave economic situation and its Alawi minority rule, which has been safeguarded by repressive mechanisms, will prevent oppositional forces from gaining critical mass in the near future."[5]

The Assad regime has indeed not fallen, although it is disputable that the Syrian opposition did not "gain critical mass," as Bröning anticipated. The protesters formed thousands of councils and other networks that not only organized the demonstrations but also took up administrative roles in some areas. The reasons for al-Assad's permanence in power must be found elsewhere. The intervention of al-Assad's external allies in support of the Syrian regime, on the one hand, and the unwillingness of Western powers to arm and equip the Syrian democratic opposition more decisively, on the other, are more significant factors that explain the outcome of the Syrian conflict.

In March 2011, the White House, the US State Department, and several members of the US Congress shared the view that an uprising was unlikely to occur in Syria. In fact, several officials of the Obama administration, such as then-Secretary of State Hillary Clinton, saw the Syrian leader as a reformer. On March 27, 2011, Clinton made the following remarks: "There is a different leader in Syria now. Many of the members of Congress of both parties who have gone to Syria in recent months have said they believe he is a reformer."[6] The Syrian president also discarded the possibility of an uprising occurring in his country. In an interview for the *WSJ* in January 2011, President al-Assad assured that Syria was a stable country whose people would not go to the streets as in Tunisia and Egypt.[7] Thus, almost everyone was caught by surprise by the first protests in Syria. When the first demonstrations began, the US establishment found itself improvising a response in the heat of events.

Two of President Obama's priorities in the Middle East at the time consisted in withdrawing US forces from Iraq and reaching out to Iran. In 2011 and 2012, lower-level US and Iranian officials held secret backchannel bilateral meetings to discuss Iran's nuclear program.[8] As of 2013, more robust negotiations between the two countries were taking place, culminating two years later in the signing of the Joint Comprehensive Plan of Action by Iran, the members of the UN Security Council, Germany, and the European Union. Related to the strategy of negotiating with Iran was a policy of engaging with the Assad regime, a sort of *détente* after the Bush years of distance and hostility. The US ambassador in the country at the time, Robert Ford—but also John Kerry, the future secretary of state who was then chairman of the Senate Foreign Relations Committee—strived to normalize relations with Syria.

For its part, Syria also sought to build better political ties with Western countries and Israel. The 2009 Association Agreement with the European Union and some attempts of peace talks with Israel mediated by the United States and Turkey demonstrate this. In fact, the United States conducted and moderated secret negotiations between Israel and Syria between 2009 and 2011. According to Frederic C. Hof, who served as special adviser for transition in Syria under President Obama, Bashar al-Assad was willing to reach a peace agreement with Israel that would consist primarily of Syria's reorientation away from Iran, Hezbollah, and Hamas in exchange for the recovery of the territory lost to Israel during the 1967 Six-Day War.

In Hof's words,

> Bashar had explicitly acknowledged that peace with Israel would have two essential elements: Syria's strategic reorientation away from Iran, Hezbollah and Hamas; and Syria's full recovery of all land lost to Israel in June 1967. Netanyahu acknowledged the territorial price Israel would have to pay and had authorized his team to work with me to define exactly the line of June 4, 1967. Both sides protected the confidentiality of the effort, and both sides gave every indication of seriousness.[9]

The Syrian president told Hof during a private conversation in 2011 that Iran and Hezbollah would accept such a deal.[10]

The Assad regime broke ties with Hamas in 2012 after some leaders of the Palestinian group voiced support for the anti-government protests occurring in Syria. In 2011, when the protests began, Hamas had links with the Muslim Brotherhood, whose Syrian branch actively participated in the uprising. In 2022, the Syrian regime restored ties with Hamas after the Palestinian group made conciliatory statements toward the Syrian government and announced it had broken ties with the Muslim Brotherhood. Iran brokered the negotiations.

Although the relationship between the United States and Syria had been marked during the Bush years by disagreements and tensions, especially over the US-led occupation of Iraq, President Obama was willing to establish a new relationship with the Assad regime. The *NYT* reported on this issue. Mark Landler, who in March 2011 was the newspaper's White House correspondent, wrote, "Last June, the State Department organized a delegation from Microsoft, Dell, and Cisco Systems to visit Mr. Assad with the message that he could attract more investment if he stopped censoring Facebook and Twitter. While the administration renewed economic sanctions against Syria, it approved export licenses for some civilian aircraft parts."[11]

As the Syrian security forces responded to the 2011 demonstrations with extreme violence, arresting and killing protesters in large numbers, the United States saw itself obliged to distance itself from Bashar al-Assad. The US government demanded that the Syrian dictator stop the violence and listened to the protestors who had taken to the streets. Despite this, several US officials continued to believe that the Syrian president could be persuaded to take the path of gradual political and economic opening, an assessment that proved to be erroneous. To add more fuel to this already explosive situation, the first demonstrations of the Syrian uprising began as NATO forces were about to initiate their intervention in Libya, which began on March 19 and required a great deal of attention from the US foreign policy establishment. The Syrian uprising urged the Obama administration to reassess its approach to the Assad regime in a context of significant regional instability and economic uncertainty.

Period I covers the weeks from March 15 to March 30, 2011. A period of roughly two weeks enabled the collection of a more extensive and representative dataset, as the Syrian uprising was still in an embryonic stage and the number of articles in a period of one week was limited. Like the political establishment, the media was also caught by surprise by the events in Syria. As previously mentioned, few newspapers had correspondents in Damascus due to the various restrictions that the Syrian regime imposed on foreign journalists.

The dataset of period I consists of fifty-five articles: fifteen from the *NYT*, twenty-four from the *WP*, and sixteen from the *WSJ*. Of these fifty-five articles, thirty-seven are news articles, fourteen are opinion pieces, three are editorials, and one is a news analysis. Twenty-eight authors sign the articles analyzed in period I, both news and op-ed pieces. Twenty-one of the authors are men, and seven are women. The protests in Syria, the Syrian government repression, US foreign policy, and the Libya intervention are the most common topics or subtopics found in the articles (see Figure 2.1).

In news articles, the frames of the Syrian protests are similar in the three newspapers, focusing on describing the protests and the regime's violent response. The newspapers also reported on the situation in Libya and how the US political establishment reacted to it. In period I, the coverage of the Libya intervention intertwined with the reports on the protests in Syria, and for this reason the discussion about this issue is included in this chapter. The most recurrent types of sources in the three newspapers in period I are US politicians, pro-Assad Syrian sources, other politicians (largely European and UN officials), NGO members, anti-Assad activists, and experts from universities and think tanks. Joshua Landis,

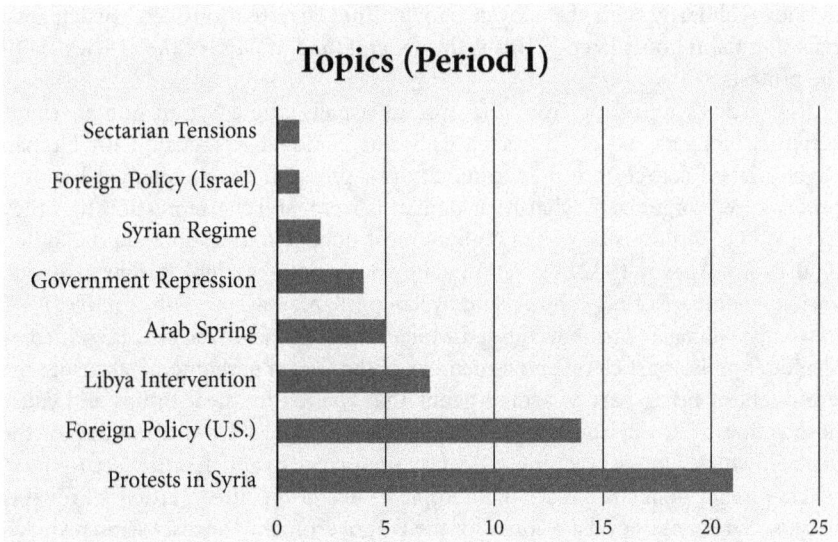

Figure 2.1 Most recurrent topics in period I.

head of the Center for Middle East Studies at the University of Oklahoma and an expert on Syria, was the most-quoted expert in period I. The three newspapers cited him during these two weeks.

If the frames about the protests are similar, the same does not apply to the discussion about US foreign policy, in which the three newspapers articulated distinct views. These differences, however, do not relate to the causes of the protests, which were generally presented as part of a pro-democracy movement but rather to how the United States should respond to them. Whereas *NYT* authors usually aligned with the Obama administration, their colleagues writing for the *WP* and *WSJ* presented views that most of the time opposed it. In the following sections, a more detailed analysis of how these similarities and differences played out is presented.

The NYT *Supports Obama's Noninterventionist Approach*

The *NYT* published fifteen articles in period I, of which ten are news, four are opinion pieces, and one is a news analysis. The most common topics addressed are the protests in Syria, the Syrian government repression, the Arab Spring, US foreign policy, and the Libya intervention. Seven pieces report on the first protests and how the Syrian regime responded to them. The overall tone is favorable to the demonstrations and against the Syrian regime. The protests are framed in most cases as part of a pro-democracy movement. On March 16, one news article states, "The government has repeatedly been ferocious in quelling protests. Security forces chased and beat young people who gathered for a vigil on February 23 to show solidarity with the Libyan people. They arrested fourteen participants, releasing them hours later."[12] This is the general tone in most of the articles about the protests.

The articles reporting from the ground usually quote Syrian human rights activists, bloggers, and NGOs such as Syria's National Association for Human Rights. These sources are predominantly pro-protests. They explained how the protests were organized, what their demands were, and the repression that they were facing. On the side of the regime, most quoted sources include the Syrian Arab News Agency (SANA), Syrian state television, President Bashar al-Assad, various members of his cabinet, and Syrian parliamentarians. For example, *NYT* journalist Michael Slackman quoted Mohammed Habash, who was identified as a "moderate Islamist cleric and a member of the Syrian parliament," accusing the protesters of being part of armed gangs that wanted to "steal things and cause destruction."[13] Pro-Syrian regime sources usually appear toward the end of the articles, which suggests that the *NYT* gave preference to anti-Assad voices.

US foreign policy is a topic or subtopic in five of the fifteen articles. Probably because Syria was not yet a priority for the US government, the discussion revolved primarily around the situation in Libya. The first article discussing Syria as a matter of foreign policy came out on March 26, 2011.[14] The implementation of a no-fly zone over Libya, authorized by UN Security Council Resolution 1973 in March 2011, is the topic of four articles—three news articles and one opinion piece. The three news articles portray the intervention as a necessary enterprise, a frame that is built basically by allowing President Obama and various US officials to express their views without contrasting them with different opinions. In this way, the frames of the Libya intervention relayed by *NYT* authors are similar to those of the US government. There is hardly any source opposed to the Libya intervention, President Obama being by far the most-quoted politician. Then-Secretary of State Hilary Clinton and then-Defense Secretary Robert Gates also appear on the pages of the *NYT* supporting the enforcement of a no-fly zone over Libya.

The Libya intervention is deemed necessary on the grounds of Gaddafi's brutality toward the uprising that broke out in early 2011 and challenged the decades-long Libyan regime. Although the operation is framed as a humanitarian intervention, some journalists suggested that the United States should not deploy ground troops. Mark Landler and Thom Shanker, for example, quoted Secretary Gates stating that "the unrest in Libya did not pose an immediate threat to the United States."[15] The two journalists also quoted Hillary Clinton saying that Libya would not set a precedent for how the United States would behave in other countries of the region.

Helene Cooper, in turn, quoted President Obama comparing Libya and Iraq to argue that the United States should play a limited role in the North African country: "'To be blunt, we went down that road in Iraq,' Mr. Obama said, adding that 'regime change [in Iraq] took eight years, thousands of American and Iraqi lives, and nearly a trillion dollars. That is not something we can afford to repeat in Libya.'"[16] As these two articles suggest, the fact that *NYT* journalists framed the Libya intervention as necessary did not mean that they were promoting a more

2. The Beginning of the Syrian Uprising   41

aggressive US policy in the Middle East. The *NYT* showed almost unrestrained support for the Obama administration's approach in Libya and Syria, although these two approaches differed in several aspects.

Most sources that comment on foreign policy in *NYT* articles are government officials, which gives the reports a pro-Obama tone (see Figure 2.2). Only on one occasion are Republicans quoted criticizing the Obama administration. Helene Cooper, the journalist who quoted them, did not disclose the identity of these politicians. Cooper wrote, "Some Republicans continued to criticize Mr. Obama for moving too slowly, while another strain of conservative thought argued that the intervention [in Libya] was overreach, a military action without a compelling national interest."[17] This passage is the only occasion on which the Libya intervention was questioned. In all other articles, the sources are either direct members of the administration or supporters of the US president. Especially in news articles, sourcing practices played a distinct role in how the *NYT* built its frames in period I.

Landler signs another piece, this time a news analysis, about US foreign policy. The article discusses how the unrest in Syria and Jordan would force the United States to readapt its Middle East strategy. Before the protests in Syria, the *NYT* journalist argued, Obama sought to engage with the Syrian regime hoping to pull it away from Iran: "For two years, the United States has tried to coax Damascus into negotiating a peace deal with Israel and to moving away from Iran."[18] Landler also discussed the possible consequences of "deepening chaos" in Syria to the

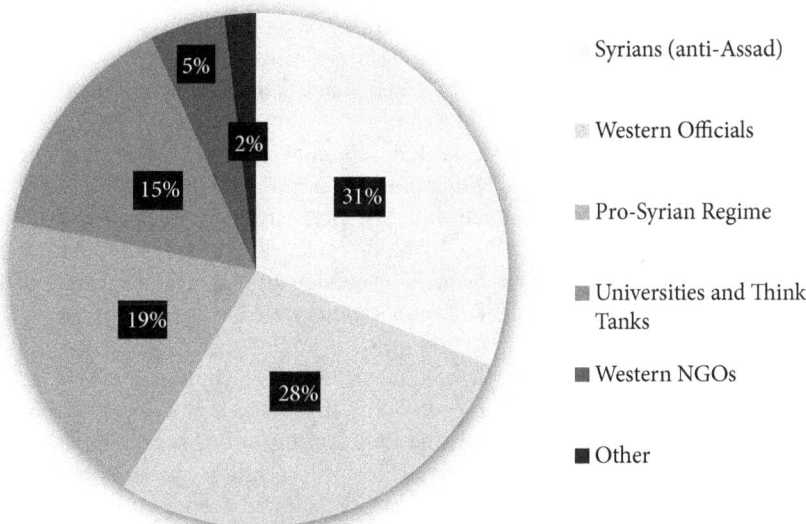

Figure 2.2 Sources in *NYT* articles in period I.

peace process in the Middle East and to Israel's security: "Deepening chaos in Syria, in particular, could dash any remaining hopes for a Middle East peace agreement, several analysts said. It could also alter the American rivalry with Iran for influence in the region and pose challenges to the United States' greatest ally in the region, Israel."

Landler went on to claim that part of the Obama administration was skeptical of a Libyan-style intervention in Syria, as they lacked sufficient information about the Syrian opposition. He portrayed Syrian rebels in sectarian terms, mentioning the possibility of a new Sunni-led regime in Damascus: "Some analysts predicted the administration would be cautious in pressing Mr. Assad, not because of any allegiance to him but out of a fear of what could follow him—a Sunni-led government potentially more radical and Islamist than his Alawite minority regime."[19] The *NYT* journalist did not specify who these analysts were or provide any evidence of why the opposition could be "more radical and Islamist" than the Assad regime. Apparently, he reduced the Syrian protests to a Sunni-Alawite dispute, which amounts to a highly inaccurate depiction (a misrepresentation) of what was happening in Syria in March 2011.

The *NYT* opinion pieces published in period I are also in line with most of the US foreign policy in Libya and Syria. Of the four opinion pieces, three are signed by Thomas Friedman, the prominent *NYT* foreign affairs columnist, and the fourth by British historian Simon Sebag Montefiore. Friedman's pieces are almost exclusively about US foreign policy. Montefiore's piece, on the other hand, discusses the Arab Spring in a broader sense, comparing it with other revolutions throughout history. In two of his articles, Friedman seconded the Iraqi occupation, identifying it as "the most important liberal experiment in modern Arab history."[20] He claimed that once dictators are toppled in Middle Eastern countries—he called it the "removal of the authoritarian lid"—sectarian tensions will eventually arise in what he described as multisectarian Arab states. Using the Iraq War as an example, the *NYT* columnist argued that the United States had a significant role to play in bringing democracy to the Middle East.[21]

While reading Friedman's texts, it is difficult to overlook the influence of Francis Fukuyama's *The End of History and the Last Man*, especially the part where the American sociologist claimed that American-style liberal democracy is the most evolved political system.[22] In "Looking for Luck in Libya," Friedman stated, "When an entire region that has been living outside the biggest global trends of free politics and free markets for half a century suddenly, from the bottom up, decides to join history … you're going to end up with some very strange-looking policy animals."[23] The *NYT* columnist situated Libya outside of "the biggest global trends" (and also of history), since it had been out of free markets and liberal democracy for the last five decades. However, the idea that Libya had been completely out of free markets for this interval is debatable. As Libya expert Ronald Bruce St. John argued, Gaddafi adopted several political and economic reforms in the second half of the 1980s that moderately liberalized Libya's economy, especially its hydrocarbon sector.[24] As a matter of fact, different scholars have claimed that neoliberalism and authoritarianism have reinforced each other in several Middle East countries.[25]

The similarities between the ideas of Friedman and Fukuyama are striking. In 1992, Fukuyama argued that

> all countries undergoing economic modernization must increasingly resemble one another: they must unify nationally on the basis of a centralized state, urbanize, replace traditional forms of social organization like tribe, sect, and family with economically rational ones based on function and efficiency, and provide for the universal education of their citizens. Such societies have become increasingly linked with one another through global markets and the spread of a universal consumer culture. Moreover, the logic of modern natural science would seem to dictate a universal evolution in the direction of capitalism.[26]

The civilizatory potential of free markets and liberal democracy has been a recurrent argument in Orientalist discourses conveyed by Western analysts claiming the status of authorities on Middle Eastern societies. Friedman's ideas about the MENA uprisings fit within Edward Said's definition of Orientalism. In the introduction of his famous book, Said stated, "I myself believe that Orientalism is more particularly valuable as a sign of European-Atlantic power over the Orient than it is as a veridic discourse about the Orient (which is what, in its academic or scholarly form, it claims to be)."[27] The Palestinian-American scholar also argued that the idea of an alleged Western superiority pervaded the media: "These contemporary Orientalist attitudes flood the press and the popular minds. Arabs, for example, are thought of as camel-riding, terroristic, hook-nosed, venal lechers whose undeserved wealth is an affront to real civilization."[28]

Friedman's views are also aligned with the main narratives of the Obama administration. In "Hoping for Arab Mandelas," for example, he went on to argue that the Arab Spring had no clear leaders, an argument which was extensively used by US officials to justify their noninterventionist approach in the beginning of the Syrian uprising: "This is what the new leaders of these Arab rebellions will have to do—surprise themselves and each other with a sustained will for unity, mutual respect, and democracy. The more Arab Mandelas who emerge, the more they will be able to manage their own transitions, without army generals or outsiders. Will they emerge? Let's watch and hope."[29] The discussion about leadership in the Syrian uprising is complex. Indeed, there was no unquestionable leader in Syria with the same stature as Ayatollah Khomeini in Iran in 1979 or Gamal Abdel Nasser in Egypt in 1952. Nevertheless, the first stage of the revolution saw the emergence of thousands of local leaders who played a prominent organizational role in the local councils and other civil society organizations.

In brief, the *NYT* portrayed the first demonstrations in Syria as peaceful and antidictatorial, thereby building an unambiguously anti-Assad frame. Nevertheless, *NYT* journalists reverberated the noninterventionist policy that marked the Obama administration's approach in the first period of the Syrian protests. The Libya intervention, in turn, was seen as a necessary humanitarian enterprise, although *NYT* authors argued that the United States should avoid sending ground troops to Libya, as the country did not represent a threat to US national security. To a great extent, the *NYT* built this pro-Obama frame by using sources that expressed similar views to those of the US administration.

The *WP* Urges Obama to Support the Protests

The *WP* published twenty-four articles in March 2011, ten more than the *NYT*. Fourteen of them are news, seven are opinion pieces, and three, editorials. The most common topics in the *WP* are similar to those in the *NYT*. They are the protests in Syria, the Syrian government repression, US foreign policy, the Libya intervention, and the Arab Spring. The higher number of op-ed articles in comparison to the *NYT* (ten and four, respectively) shows that the *WP* was interested not only in describing the situation in Libya and Syria but also in analyzing it. The op-ed pieces are mostly critical of the Obama administration, although a few of them convey a more neutral tone. Only one piece is openly pro-Obama, an interview with then-Secretary of Defense Robert Gates.

As with the *NYT*, the "protests in Syria" is the most recurrent topic in the *WP* coverage in period I. In twelve articles, the protests feature as a topic or subtopic. The Syrian government repression, which appears in eleven articles, is the second most popular topic. Nine articles discuss US foreign policy as their central theme. Unlike the *NYT*, the *WP* presented frames that are critical of the Obama administration, which may also explain the high number of opinion pieces in the *WP* in period I. Additionally, the *WP* published one article discussing Israel's foreign policy, another discussing the sectarian tensions in Syria, and a third article about the MENA regional context.[30] These topics do not receive the same attention in the *NYT* coverage.

The *WP* also framed the protests as part of a pro-democracy movement that was sweeping the region. An article published on March 16 stated, "Syrian forces fired into the air Monday to disperse a pro-democracy demonstration in the southern flash point of Daraa, where reformers want to end the Assad family's 40-year rule."[31] Compared to the *NYT*, the *WP* used a broader spectrum of sources, quoting more Syrians, more non-American politicians, and more NGOs. The number of pro-Assad sources in the two newspapers, however, is similar. In news articles, both newspapers preferred to quote US officials aligned with the Obama administration, rather than the opposition (see Figure 2.3). *WP* op-ed pieces, by contrast, are signed by experts and politicians expressing a critical view of Obama's policy.

Most *WP* op-ed articles advocate a more active US Middle East strategy. Syria is depicted as an ally of Iran and the Lebanese militia Hezbollah and, therefore, as a regime that should be confronted. For example, the neoconservative politician Elliot Abrams, who served in several Republican administrations and consistently writes for the *WP*, called for the implementation of sanctions against Syria, expressing

Sources in *WP* Articles in Period I

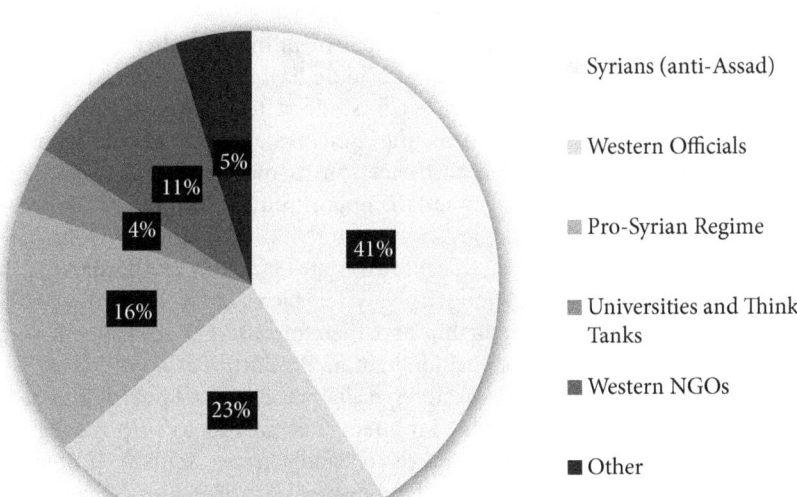

Figure 2.3 Sources in *WP* articles in period I.

the view that the International Criminal Court, the UN Security Council, and the UN Human Rights Council should prosecute the Syrian president. Abrams wrote, "We should prosecute Syria in every available multilateral forum, including the UN Security Council and the Human Rights Council. Others should refer Assad to the International Criminal Court. With blood flowing, there should be no delays; this is the moment to call for special sessions and action to prevent more killing."[32]

In an editorial published on March 24, the newspaper called for the imposition of sanctions against members and allies of the Assad regime. The *WP* editorial board wrote, "[The Obama administration] should also look for ways to tighten US sanctions on Damascus, including freezes on the assets of those involved in the repression as well as private companies linked to the regime."[33] In another editorial, this one published on March 29, the idea that Bashar al-Assad could be a reformer was openly challenged.[34] The *WP* editorial board argued that the Syrian president's ethnic group, the Alawites, represented only 6 percent of the Syrian population and this would prevent him from reforming the political system for fear of losing power. The editorial also demands that the Obama administration supported the protesters:

> Most likely the dictator [Bashar al-Assad], like Mr. Mubarak before him, is seeking to deflect the demands for change with a mixture of violence and false promises. If that proves to be the case, the Obama administration, Mr. Kerry and others who have reached out to Mr. Assad should be ready to respond—by siding decisively with those in Syria seeking genuine change.[35]

Zalmay Khalilzad, a diplomat who served as ambassador to the United Nations under President George W. Bush and was appointed special representative for Afghanistan reconciliation at the State Department in September 2018, criticized President Obama for not having a clear Middle East strategy: "President Obama has reportedly settled on a country-specific strategy for the Middle East uprisings. Instead of crafting a regional plan, the United States will deal with protests for democracy and freedom in each state on its own terms. This approach is inadequate to both the challenges and the opportunities arising from the political turbulence."[36] Khalilzad further argued that in the Middle East, the United States should differentiate between "transitional states, friendly authoritarians, and enemy dictatorships," and define its policy for each country accordingly. Syria amounted to an enemy dictatorship and therefore the US government should devise a plan to support the opposition fighting President Bashar al-Assad.

David Ignatius, a prominent *WP* foreign affairs columnist, favored this selective approach as well. In his opinion, President Obama should help the Egyptian revolution succeed but, in a reference to Saudi Arabia and the United Arab Emirates, should not shy away from defending pro-US monarchies: "Obama should not be shy about defending America's friends, even when they are conservative monarchies and have lots of oil. The United Arab Emirates may not be a perfect place, but it is a lot freer and more progressive than Iran, say, or Russia or China. Saudi Arabia has its problems, but it is not an Iran-style menace, either."[37] The use of the word "menace" by the *WP* columnist is revealing of the meaning behind this sentence. An attentive reader would naturally ask, "Menace to whom? To regional stability under US hegemony?" Ignatius did not clarify what he meant by "Iran-style menace."

In another article, this one less critical of the US president, Ignatius described President Obama's foreign policy as a blend of realism and humanitarian interventionism. While in Libya the principles of humanitarian interventionism had prevailed, in other countries of the region, such as Bahrain, Yemen, and Syria, realist principles seemed to be guiding the US president. In Ignatius' words,

> Obama appears to be evolving a hybrid strategy, blending "realist" and "humanitarian interventionist" themes. Several weeks ago the administration seemed almost to be allying with Shiite protesters in Bahrain against the minority Sunni monarchy. But Obama has recognized that America has an abiding interest in the stability of neighboring Saudi Arabia, which sees Bahrain as its 51st state and will not tolerate the overthrow of its ruling family.[38]

Additionally, the *WP* columnist argued that the Arab uprisings amounted to the "core riddle" to be solved by Obama's presidency: "If Obama can connect his Af/Pak policy with the democratic wave that transformed Tunisia and Egypt, he will solve the core riddle of his presidency." With Af/Pak policy, Ignatius referred to the set of policies unveiled by the Obama administration in March 2009 to neutralize Islamist groups, such as al-Qaida and the Taliban, in Afghanistan and Pakistan. The US government intended to weaken these groups by increasing regional integration, financing development projects, and arming both countries' militaries.

Jim Hoagland, a distinguished *WP* journalist winner of two Pulitzer Prizes, stated in an op-ed piece that President Obama was recalibrating US power in the new world order. His tone was neutral rather than critical of the US president, as he recognized that Obama combined diplomacy and force in his foreign policy. Without being specific, Hoagland asserted that such a strategy, of balancing diplomacy and the use of force, could produce ambiguities in some situations: "I confess to some ambivalence about what could be characterized as Obama's intervention-lite approach. But over the past month he has adeptly balanced diplomacy and the use of force to protect Libyan civilians from wholesale slaughter by Muammar Gaddafi, while advancing less tangible goals of reshaping the politics of the Middle East."[39] Among these "less tangible goals," Hoagland included the revitalization of the "concept of humanitarian intervention," the "support to the spreading Arab political uprising," and a "form of burden sharing inside NATO that should be nurtured." Hoagland praised the NATO intervention in Libya for saving civilian lives and encouraging citizens of other Middle East countries to protest against their governments. However, he did not make any reference as to what policy should the Obama administration pursue in Syria.

A *WP* editorial published on March 26 criticizes the UN Human Rights Council for being "dominated by abusers of human rights and [having] devoted most of its energies to demonizing Israel."[40] Although this article does not discuss Syria or Libya directly, it highlights two aspects of the *WP*'s editorial line that deserve attention. On the one hand, it shows that Israel's security has a preponderant position in the newspaper's analysis of the Middle East. On the other, the editorial board criticized what it called "President Obama's ideologues of multilateralism" for expending too much energy to "rehabilitate the deeply flawed human rights council." The criticism of multilateralism indicates that, for *WP* editorialists, the United States should adopt a unilateral and more assertive approach to the Middle East, particularly in Syria. As we will see throughout this book, the *WP* repeatedly argued that the United States should play a more active role in Syria.

In an apparent attempt to influence the debate about US foreign policy, *WP* authors drew attention on several occasions to Obama's supposed lack of strategy in the Middle East. By placing Syria and Libya on the same level of importance, they conveyed a different narrative than that of the Obama administration and the *NYT*. For example, Abrams argued that the United States should lead an international campaign against the Syrian regime:

The Obama administration erred badly by sending an envoy [to Syria]—in a recess appointment—for this move was understood in the region as a reduction of US pressure on Syria despite its increasingly dominant role in Lebanon. We should pull our ambassador, as we did in Libya, and unveil a hard-hitting political and human rights campaign against a bloody regime whose people want it gone.[41]

In fact, different *WP* analysts highlighted the similarities between Libya and Syria—both countries amounted to anti-US dictatorships facing popular uprisings—and demanded that the United States cut diplomatic relations with Syria and impose sanctions on it. If the two countries are in a similar state, it can be inferred that an intervention in Syria should not be ruled out. *NYT* authors, in contrast, seemed more concerned with justifying the Libya intervention and stressing its exceptionality. *WP* op-ed articles never openly advocated an intervention in Syria; most authors demanded instead that the United States adopt a stricter stance against the Assad regime.

This was not the case in the *NYT* coverage. Friedman, writing for the *NYT*, argued that the United States could not repeat in Syria what it had done in Libya. The *NYT* columnist wrote, "For now, we are being cautious. We are not trying nearly as hard to get rid of the Syrian dictator as we are of the Libyan one because the situation in Syria is just not as clear as we would like and because Syria is a real game-changer. Libya implodes. Syria explodes."[42] Without explaining precisely what he meant, Friedman attributed to Syria the quality of being a "game-changer" that would influence events in the whole region ("Syria explodes"). Thus, President Obama was right to be "cautious" in Syria. In the same text, Friedman stated that it was not clear who the Syrian opposition was, implying that active support for anti-Assad groups was not yet the most adequate response.

WP and *NYT* authors framed the Iraq War differently. In the *NYT*, Friedman described the Iraq War as a genuine attempt to oust a dictator and democratize the country. Abrams, in contrast, mentioned the Iraq War in an opinion piece for the *WP* to argue that the United States should not consider the Syrian regime an ally. He condemned Bashar al-Assad for making "Syria the pathway for jihadists from around the world to enter Iraq to fight and kill Americans."[43]

The only pro-Obama opinion piece published by the *WP* is an interview with Secretary Gates, in which he analyzed US foreign policy in the context of the Arab uprisings. He defended President Obama's Libya strategy of not taking a leading role in the intervention and acting as part of an international coalition. Gates believed that the Arab Spring highlighted the ethnic, sectarian, and tribal differences in several countries of the region, and it was not clear "whether more democratic governance [could] hold ... countries together in light of these pressures."[44] Friedman expressed a similar opinion in one of his pieces for the *NYT*. As previously noted, the view that the Arab Spring highlighted the ethnic, sectarian, and tribal differences within Middle Eastern countries is highly contentious, amounting to a serious misrepresentation of the uprisings occurring in the region. In the case of Syria, for instance, the opposite was also the case. At the least in the beginning of the protests, people belonging to different ethnic and religious groups came together to protest against the Syrian regime.

The *WP* published one news article that discusses the Syrian conflict from the perspective of Israeli officials. In this article, Janine Zacharia depicted the Assad regime in contradictory terms, as having kept the Syrian-Israeli border quiet since Israel occupied the Golan Heights[45] in 1967, but also as a supporter of Iran and Hezbollah, two entities broadly regarded as anti-Israel:

Israel has long complained about Syrian President Bashar al-Assad's alliance with Iran, his support for the Shiite militia Hezbollah and his sheltering of leaders from Palestinian militant groups, such as Hamas, in Damascus. But with Assad facing the most serious threat to his rule since he took power nearly eleven years ago, Israelis have been forced to confront the notion that they may well be better off with him than without him.[46]

Although the different Israeli officials quoted by Zacharia were not particularly supportive of President al-Assad, they did not seem to believe that there was a better alternative to the Syrian president available.

In summary, the *WP* framed the first demonstrations in Syria as a legitimate pro-democracy movement that should be supported by the United States mainly through the imposition of sanctions against the Syrian regime. This frame is found both in news pieces and op-ed articles. In editorials and opinion pieces, however, most *WP* analysts assessed President Obama's policy critically, condemning the US president for not having a more resolute Middle East strategy. Khalilzad, for example, urged the United States to help opposition movements in countries governed by "anti-US dictatorships."[47] Some *WP* authors stressed the similarities between Libya and Syria, although they did not advocate an intervention in the latter straightforwardly.

The WSJ *Criticizes US Engagement with the Syrian Regime*

The *WSJ* published sixteen articles about the Syrian conflict in period I: thirteen news articles and three opinion pieces. The number of op-ed articles in the *WSJ* in this period is lower than in the *NYT* and *WP*. The most discussed topics are US foreign policy, the protests in Syria, and the Syrian government repression. In general, *WSJ* authors depicted the demonstrations in Syria positively and urged the United States to support them actively. One opinion piece is signed by Ahed al-Hendi, a former detainee of the Syrian regime and now an activist living in the United States. He is the only Syrian to sign an article in period I in the three newspapers. In a vivid account, al-Hendi described the beginning of the protests in Daraa and how they rapidly spread to the rest of the country.[48]

Two *WSJ* articles address the divisions within the US political establishment, a topic that merits special consideration as the Syrian conflict was the source of much dissent in the United States. The first of the two explains how US officials differed in their assessments of the Syrian regime.[49] For Jay Solomon, a *WSJ* journalist who writes about foreign affairs and US national security, the view that Bashar al-Assad was a reformer was losing ground. Solomon claimed that an increasing number of US officials were beginning to think that the United States should put more pressure on the Syrian president.

The second article about the divisions within the US political establishment reports on the divisions in the Republican Party concerning the Libya intervention. The *WSJ* covered the Republican Party more extensively than the other two newspapers. Naftali Bendavid, the author of this piece, argued that Republicans were divided into two wings: one supportive of foreign interventions and another opposed to them: "The GOP's divisions reflect long-time cross-currents on foreign policy. The party has always had a faction wary of overseas intervention. But it has also had a faction favoring a muscular US presence overseas, personified in recent years by neoconservatives, many of whom served in the administration of George W. Bush."[50] According to Bendavid, the faction that was reluctant to foreign interventions was more popular with the younger generation of the Republican Party.

As for the *WSJ*'s sourcing practices, the number of Republican politicians quoted in news pieces is slightly higher than those belonging to the Democratic Party. This represents a change in the trend observed so far, as both the *NYT* and the *WP* quoted more Democrats than Republicans. Apart from US politicians, *WSJ* journalists quoted Syrian opposition members, NGOs (though less than the other two newspapers), pro-Assad politicians, and experts from universities and think tanks (see Figure 2.4).

On one side, the *WSJ* focused on the protests and how the Syrian government responded to them. On the other, it published various articles on US foreign policy. The *WSJ*'s tone regarding the Obama administration is critical, both in news and opinion pieces. The *WSJ* advocated a more active US role in the region, some journalists noting that the Arab Spring represented an opportunity to weaken countries such as Iran and Syria.

Sources in *WSJ* Articles in Period I

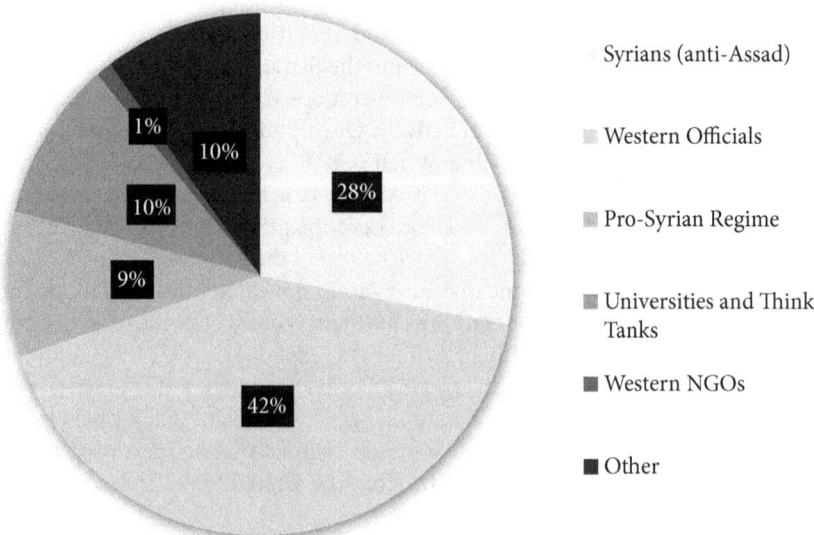

Figure 2.4 Sources in *WSJ* articles in period I.

In period I, the *WSJ* openly criticized one of its "competitors," without specifying which newspaper it was referring to, for supporting more engagement with the Syrian regime before the protests. The article states,

> We mention Brand X because it is one of those liberal voices that for years has been telling us that Assad is the kind of dictator the US should "engage." He is a modern guy, his wife reads Vogue, and democracy and human rights are preoccupations of American neocons, not of Syrians. The Obama Administration bought this line in toto, sending a US ambassador to Damascus after many years without one, dispatching assorted emissaries to court Assad, and beseeching him to break with his Iranian patrons.[51]

In all the dataset analyzed in this book, this fragment is the only occasion on which a newspaper criticizes a competitor.

Two other articles discuss the Obama administration's engagement with the Syrian regime. The *NYT* reported on this aspect of US foreign policy as well, but the *WSJ* highlighted and criticized it. Solomon, for example, quoted US officials saying that President Obama's overtures toward Bashar al-Assad did not generate anything in return and that Syria was at that point closer to Iran than before.[52] In the same piece, John Kerry is portrayed as a "supporter" of the Assad regime. The Syrian president is portrayed not only as an authoritarian leader that was repressing peaceful demonstrations but also as an enthusiast of Hamas and Hezbollah: two organizations classified by the US government as terrorist groups that were involved in confrontations with Israel.

In one opinion piece, the *WSJ* argued that "the US national interest in this season of Arab uprisings is to have anti-American regimes fall while helping pro-American regimes to reform in a more liberal (in the nineteenth-century meaning of that word) direction."[53] In another, the *WSJ* stated that the United States should support the opposition "in as many ways as possible."[54] Except for this rather vague reference to supporting the opposition, no other possible actions, such as sanctioning the Syrian regime or enforcing a no-fly zone, are suggested in *WSJ* articles published during this period. The *WP* was more emphatic than the *WSJ* in suggesting policies.

The idea that the United States should actively seek the fall of anti-US regimes, present in one opinion article, is not echoed (in the same way) in news pieces, which relay a more pragmatic view of what could happen in the event of the fall of Bashar al-Assad. Farnaz Fassihi and Jay Solomon, for example, claimed that "Syria's neighbors, especially Israel, worry about what might happen if the regime fell, removing a force that has held together the country's disparate array of ethnic and sectarian groups."[55] The two journalists reminded *WSJ* readers that "Mr. Assad kept the Golan Heights border quiet." Fassihi and Solomon also quoted an Israeli official, without disclosing their identity, as saying that they would not mourn the demise of Bashar al-Assad, but they did not know who the opposition was.

These somewhat divergent narratives in news and opinion articles illustrate an essential difference between these two journalistic genres. In the first, journalists report from the ground, communicating the views of actors involved in or affected by the conflict. Thus, news articles are more fact-based and less ideological than opinion pieces, which are written from a distance by an authoritative author conveying a clear opinion and usually taking sides on the issue at hand. However, my research of the coverage of the Syrian conflict in the *NYT*, the *WP*, and the *WSJ* suggests that newspapers tend to present similar frames in news and op-ed articles, although dissonant discourses may occasionally coexist.

As previously mentioned, in March 2011, US policy in Syria was characterized by nonintervention. President Obama was unwilling to take action unilaterally in Syria, especially if it involved deploying US ground troops. This position grew stronger as Libya fell into a state of disarray following the fall of Gaddafi in August 2011. The first sanctions against the Syrian regime were imposed in May 2011, and it was not until August 2013 that the first CIA program to train and equip Syrian opposition groups came into existence.

In March 2011, amid the Libya intervention, then-Secretary of State Hillary Clinton ruled out military intervention in Syria. In as many as four articles, the *WSJ* reported that nonintervention was the official US policy in Syria. The US president was quoted by Farnaz Fassihi on one occasion explaining the decision: "President Barack Obama said that while the US would 'monitor the situation' in Syria, he did not think military intervention was appropriate. 'When it comes to military intervention ... the circumstances in which we start getting engaged in military operations have to be very narrowly drawn,' he said on the 'CBS Evening News.'"[56]

On another occasion, Solomon quoted anonymous "US lawmakers" as saying that the United States should be more interested in overthrowing the Syrian regime than the Libyan regime: "Some US lawmakers have argued that Washington has more of a justification—and interest—in seeking Mr. Assad's overthrow than Libyan leader Muammar Gaddafi's. Syria is Iran's closest strategic partner, and Damascus has played a central role in arming militant groups operating in Iraq, Lebanon, and the Palestinian territories."[57] The references to these lawmakers' opinions appear in the beginning of the article, which suggests that Solomon wished to highlight them. The *WSJ* journalist did not go into detail about these armed operations.

In brief, the *WSJ* presented a positive frame of the first demonstrations in Syria and depicted the Syrian government as not deserving any sympathy from the US government. The newspaper also urged that assistance be given to the Syrian opposition, without specifying the manner in which this support should be provided. Various uncertainties associated with the fall of the Assad regime were highlighted, especially in news articles: Firstly, that the fall of the Syrian regime could unleash sectarian forces that might pose a threat to Israel. Secondly, that although Bashar al-Assad supported alleged terrorist groups, it had kept the Golan Heights safe. Like the *WP*, the *WSJ* also depicted the Obama administration in negative terms, raising doubts about the US president's noninterventionist approach and criticizing it for engaging with the Syrian regime before the uprising.

...

Differences and similarities mark the coverage of the first two weeks of the Syrian uprising in the *NYT*, the *WP*, and the *WSJ*. On the one hand, the topics discussed in the three newspapers present striking similarities. Also, the *NYT*, the *WP*, and the *WSJ* relayed analogous frames regarding the first protests and the violent response from the Syrian regime. On the other hand, the articles analyzed in period I expose significant differences among the three newspapers, especially with respect to the nature of US interests in the Middle East and which approach the Obama administration should take toward the Syrian regime.

Most articles in period I report on the protests and how the Syrian government responded to them: the protests in Syria are a topic or subtopic in thirty-one of the fifty-five articles comprising period I; the Syrian government repression is a topic or subtopic in twenty-two articles. The three newspapers portrayed the protests as legitimate and part of a pro-democracy movement. The Assad regime was depicted as an authoritarian regime that used unnecessary violence to suppress a movement calling for political reforms. Although the demonstrations are framed positively, the three newspapers expressed wariness of the Syrian opposition, which is analyzed ambiguously, sometimes as democratic, sometimes in sectarian terms. Some analysts saw President al-Assad as a strong man who held Syria together despite the country's multisectarian nature.

US foreign policy is the third most recurrent theme discussed in the articles, featuring as a topic or subtopic in twenty-one articles. Whereas the *NYT* presented frames that were usually aligned with the Obama administration—supporting his unwillingness to intervene in Syria—the *WP* and the *WSJ* distanced themselves from the US president, calling instead for a more resolute Middle East policy. The sourcing practices of the journalists writing for the three newspapers played a significant role in building these different frames. Whereas *NYT* authors relied mostly on politicians and experts who supported President Obama, most sources that appear in the *WSJ* opposed his policy. *WP* authors, for their part, quoted more Democratic politicians than Republicans, but, in general, they presented a broader and more balanced array of sources. As we have seen, the negative frame of the Obama administration relayed by the *WP* is built mostly in op-ed pieces.

WP authors supported the use of sanctions as a coercive measure against the Syrian regime. However, it was not clear whether they believed that the United States should pursue regime change or pressure Bashar al-Assad to implement democratic reforms. Several *WP* authors implied that US goal should be regime change, whereas others employed a more cautious tone. It is noteworthy that most Syrian protesters called for political and economic reform rather than regime change in the first two weeks of the Syrian uprising. As the protests evolved and the government repression generalized, the protestors adopted the demand for regime change, which materialized in the famous slogan: "The people want the fall of the regime."

WSJ authors did not go as far as demanding sanctions, at least during these two weeks, but one opinion piece states—rather vaguely, however—that the United States should help the opposition "in every possible way." Both *WSJ* and *WP* authors quoted Israeli and US officials expressing concerns as to what could happen if the Syrian president was removed from power. Furthermore, the three newspapers reported on the Obama administration's intention to engage with Syria to pull it away from Iran. *WP* and the *WSJ* authors, however, criticized this engagement as inappropriate and contrary to US national interests.

Chapter 3

THE EASTERN GHOUTA CHEMICAL ATTACK (PERIOD II)

As of August 2013, the Syrian uprising had long become an armed conflict between the Syrian regime and its external backers, and various opposition groups with distinct ideologies. Navi Pillay, the UN High Commissioner for Human Rights from 2008 to 2014, reported in June 2013 that almost 93,000 people had died since the beginning of the protests in March 2011.[1] The Syrian Observatory for Human Rights, an independent human rights organization based in the United Kingdom, recounted a much higher figure: 260,000 deaths. Although peaceful demonstrations still occurred and civil society groups were organized and active, by August 2013 armed factions had gained prominence in the ranks of the Syrian opposition. The Carter Center,[2] a nongovernmental organization that, with other partners, launched the Syria Conflict Mapping Project, estimated that "approximately 3,250 'battalions' and 'companies' [had] been created that often (but not always) [operated] beneath a total of 1,050 'brigades.'"[3]

Islamist groups were growing fast, although it was not easy to determine at that point their precise size and influence. For example, the al-Nusra Front, which had gone public in early 2012, had become one of the major opposition groups fighting the Assad regime. The group had a similar ideology to that of al-Qaeda, defending that Syria should be governed by a particular version of Sharia law. Furthermore, a dispute between Islamic and secular groups was underway within oppositional forces.

For Yassin al-Haj Saleh, a Syrian intellectual and activist who was in Syria in the summer of 2013 and witnessed this dispute, the spread of black flags with the white *shahada*[4] suggested the growth of Islamic fundamentalist groups. Al-Haj Saleh wrote, "In the summer of 2013, it seems that banners with this basic design, in all its variations, have spread across many antiregime armed groups. I have often seen them in 'liberated zones' that I have visited or lived in for a while."[5] Among other reasons, the growth of Islamist brigades was linked to the fact that these groups were receiving financial support from different regional players. As shown in Figure 3.1, almost half of Syria was outside the control of the Syrian government in March 2013.

The Syrian regime conceived the conflict as a full-scale war, treating the opposition as terrorists or foreign fighters, while frequently disregarding the principle of distinction under International Humanitarian Law between combatants and civilians. Syrian citizens that happened to reside in rebel-controlled areas often became targets of collective punishment in the form of indiscriminate

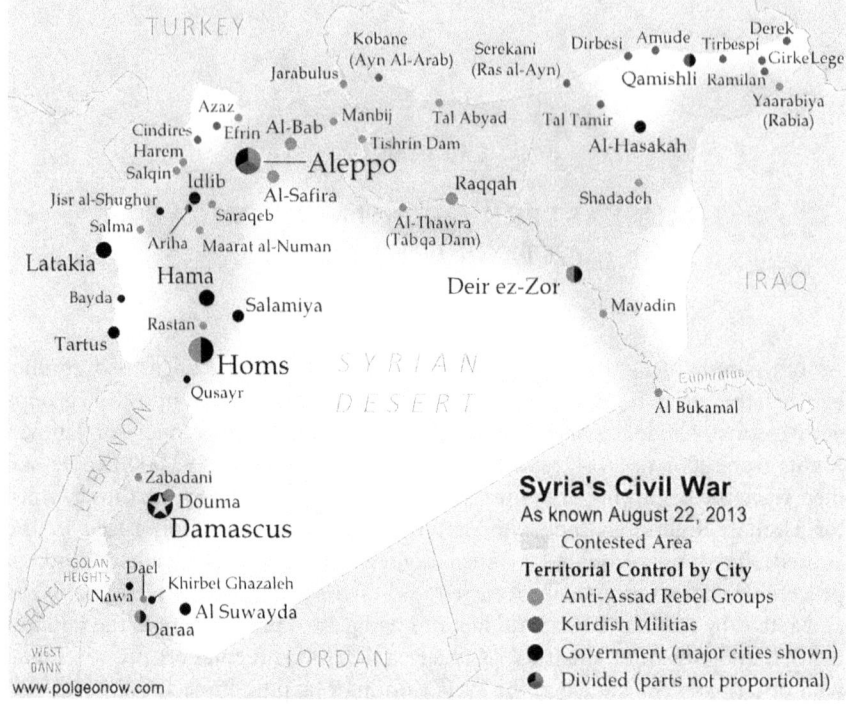

Figure 3.1 Area of fighting and territorial control in Syria's civil war (August 2013). Map by Evan Centanni. Retrieved on January 19, 2023, from https://www.polgeonow.com/2013/08/syria-civil-war-map-august-2013-11.html. Used under Creative Commons Attribution-ShareAlike 3.0 Unported (CC BY-SA 3.0).

attacks perpetrated by the Syrian army and its allies. Hundreds of thousands of detainees were subject to torture, rape, and mass killings in regime prisons. The exact number of detainees is unknown, although civil society groups worked with a six-digit figure of missing persons. According to Amnesty International, "Between 2011 and 2015, every week and often twice a week, groups of up to fifty people were taken out of their prison cells and hanged to death. In five years, as many as thirteen thousand people, most of them civilians believed to be opposed to the government, were hanged in secret at Saydnaya [prison]."[6]

Chemical attacks, the siege of civilian populations, mass executions, and torture amounted to some of the tactics used by the Syrian regime in its war against the armed and unarmed opposition groups. On August 21, 2013, dozens of videos uploaded to YouTube by Syrian activists suggested that the Assad regime had been using Sarin gas—a nerve gas banned by the international community in the 1993 Chemical Weapons Convention—against civilians in the rebel-controlled area of Eastern Ghouta, in the suburbs of Damascus. The images showed piles of dead bodies lying on the streets displaying symptoms of exposure to the highly toxic gas that attacks the nervous system. Experts have considered it the most significant use of chemical weapons in the Middle East since Saddam Hussein's attack on Kurdish villages in northern Iraq in March 1988. The NGO *Médecins Sans Frontières* reported that "they received approximately 3,600 patients displaying neurotoxic symptoms in less than three hours on the morning of Wednesday, August 21, 2013, and four hundred people died in the incident."[7] A UN investigation team found "clear and convincing" evidence of the use of Sarin gas in Eastern Ghouta. The team found traces of Sarin in blood samples collected in Eastern Ghouta and rocket fragments found in the area of the attack.[8]

The outcry was immediate after the attack. Different countries, especially those opposed to President Bashar al-Assad, demanded a strong response in the form of a military strike against the Syrian regime. Politicians, journalists, and analysts referred to a speech delivered by President Obama in August 2012 where he warned the Syrian government that the use of chemical weapons "in large quantities" would be considered a "red line" that could change US policy toward the conflict. In the days that followed the Eastern Ghouta chemical attack, the Obama administration engaged in internal debates about the appropriateness and scope of a potential attack against Syria. US officials consulted possible international partners—mainly France and the UK—about the viability of building a coalition to carry out strikes against facilities belonging to the Syrian regime. Although members of the Obama administration and part of the press considered a military response imminent, as the days passed, the US president grew increasingly skeptical of it.

On August 31, ten days after the attack, President Obama announced that he would seek congressional approval before striking—a decision likely influenced by the fact that, a day earlier, the UK parliament had denied British Prime Minister David Cameron authorization to use military force in Syria. A few days later, Russia stepped in to mediate the crisis. In the face of such a complex scenario and under enormous pressure, the US president decided not to use military force against the Syrian regime. The last-minute turnaround inevitably changed the dynamics of the conflict. As international relations scholar Christopher Phillips explained:

> The "nonstrike" of late summer 2013 was something of a watershed in the Syrian civil war. Until that point, some form of American-led military intervention, modelled on the actions in Libya in 2011, seemed a realistic prospect to many of the key actors and impacted their behavior. Afterwards, while some still clung to the dream of a more limited NATO no-fly zone, most recognized that US-led military action against Assad was unlikely.[9]

Obama's decision to abort the plan to use military force against the Syrian regime reassured al-Assad and his external allies that they could continue to act with impunity against the Syrian opposition and part of Syria's civilian population. It also created a vacuum inside the anti-Assad front, which would be eventually filled by countries such as Turkey, Saudi Arabia, and Qatar. The Syrian opposition, on its part, concluded that the West was not a reliable partner in the fight against the Syrian regime. On September 14, approximately three weeks after the Ghouta attack, Russia and the United States announced an agreement, which foresaw the

Syrian regime's signature of the Chemical Weapons Convention and voluntary surrender of its chemical arsenal under UN supervision.

The debates about the levels of US involvement in the Syrian conflict exposed the divisions within both the US political establishment and the Obama administration. In August 2013, these divisions reached their highest level since the beginning of the uprising, perhaps of the entire conflict. Whereas Hillary Clinton, who had stepped down as secretary of state some months earlier, and then-Secretary of State John Kerry advocated an attack, officials such as General Martin Dempsey, chairman of the joint chiefs of staff, took a more cautious standpoint. The discussions revolved around not only whether or not to attack Syria but also what kind of support the United States should give to rebels fighting the Assad regime.

The Eastern Ghouta chemical attack solidified President Obama's decision to increase US support to rebel groups deemed moderate. The United States had indeed decided to start arming Syrian rebels with light weapons in June 2013, although the program, called Timber Sycamore, was not launched until August of the same year. It has come to public attention that the program was run by the CIA and was partly funded with Saudi money. Until August 2013, an arms embargo on Syria had been in force, affecting above all the Syrian opposition, as Muhammad Idrees Ahmad argued:

> The United States ... has spent many years trying to ensure that no antiaircraft weapon would reach Syrian rebels lest it affect its ally Israel's ability to bomb Syria with impunity. Instead, its support has taken the form of nonlethal aid, such as night-vision goggles and satellite phones. It took many years before it supplied outdated TOW [Tube-launched Optically-tracked Wire-guided] antitank missiles but has refrained from passing on any game-changing technology.[10]

Military aid to the Syrian opposition was insignificant if compared, for example, to the billions of dollars the United States and several EU countries sent to Ukraine in the aftermath of the 2022 Russian invasion. According to some estimates, the CIA program to arm and train Syrian rebels totaled U$1 billion during its four-year existence. Although the program allowed thousands of rebels to enter the battlefield in Syria, it was not enough to allow these groups to make a difference on the ground.

The US press not only covered the debates taking place within the country's political establishment, but it also took sides to a certain extent. This was done by highlighting a particular political position to the detriment of others and also by deciding to publish certain opinion articles that were either aligned with or critical of the Obama administration. In some cases, newspapers blatantly supported a specific policy. In other cases, they merely reacted to government declarations or policies. Four general frames appear in the articles analyzed in period II. First, some pieces report on the attacks, showing evidence of it and analyzing how the situation developed on the ground. Second, several articles cover the reactions coming from the US administration and political establishment. A third frame focuses on the international reactions and how the international community should act. Finally, the newspapers published opinion articles by politicians and political commentators arguing for or against US intervention in Syria.

The *NYT*, the *WP*, and the *WSJ* combined these frames in different ways, depicting general frames that resulted in a clear alignment or disagreement with the Obama administration. Period II starts on August 20, 2013, and ends on August 26, 2013. The compiled articles regarding this one-week time period provide a comprehensive picture of the coverage of the attacks in the three analyzed newspapers. The Eastern Ghouta chemical attack is considered one of the most challenging events to which the US foreign policy establishment had to respond, as it placed direct military intervention in the Syrian conflict on the agenda of countries opposing the Assad regime. As previously seen, the debates around it exposed the divisions within the US political establishment: one side supporting intervention and the other side opposing it. The division between the two groups did not follow clear party lines.

The dataset analyzed in this period consists of eighty-five articles: twenty published in the *NYT*, twenty-five published in the *WP*, and forty published in the *WSJ*. As shown in Figure 3.2, the coverage in the *WSJ* is by far the most extensive. Of the eighty-five articles, sixty-two are news, sixteen are opinion articles, three are editorials, two are news analysis, and two are transcripts of a statement from John Kerry in which he blamed Bashar al-Assad for the attack. In period II, op-ed pieces account for 23 percent of the total number of articles, 9 percent less than in period I but the same percentage as in the whole dataset. Fifty-three authors or co-authors sign the articles of period II. Forty of these authors are men and only thirteen are women. Two general topics dominate the frames in this period: the Eastern Ghouta chemical attack and US foreign policy. As in the previous period, in period II, the general topics covered in the three newspapers are quite similar; however, the framing of US foreign policy differed significantly.

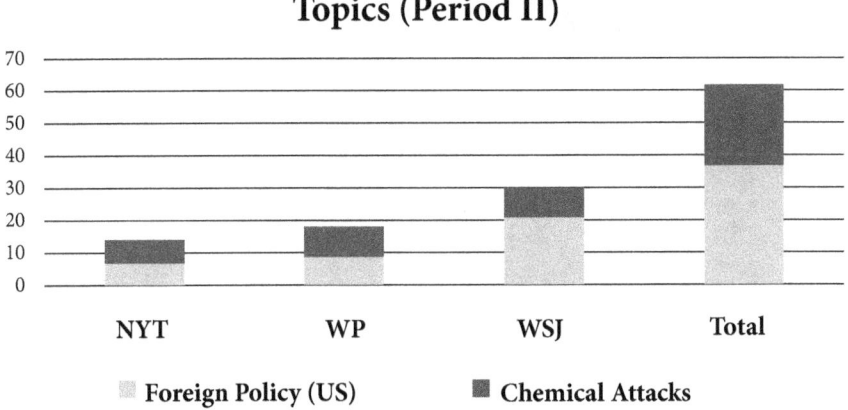

Figure 3.2 Topics per newspaper in period II.

The NYT Highlights the Debates inside the Obama Administration

The *NYT* published twenty articles in period II: seventeen news, one opinion article, one editorial, and a transcript of John Kerry's statement. The two op-ed pieces are aligned with the views of the Obama administration. In the news articles, the journalists focused on three topics: the chemical attack, the UN attempt to conduct on-site investigations, and the reactions of the US foreign policy establishment. The Eastern Ghouta chemical attack is the main topic in seven articles and the subtopic in five articles. US foreign policy features as the main topic in seven articles and as a subtopic in four articles. On the ground, coverage of the conflict relies on testimonies from survivors of the attacks as well as UN personnel (see Figure 3.3). Videos uploaded to YouTube by residents of Eastern Ghouta were also an important source of information. As the days passed, the coverage acquired an analytical tone rather than a purely descriptive one, focusing on the debates in the United States and the reactions from international actors—especially, the United Nations, the European Union, and Russia.

On August 21, the day of the attack, *NYT* journalists Ben Hubbard and Hwaida Saad adopted a cautious tone: "Even with videos, witness accounts, and testimonies by emergency medics, it was impossible to say for certain how many people had been killed and what exactly had killed them. The rebels blamed the

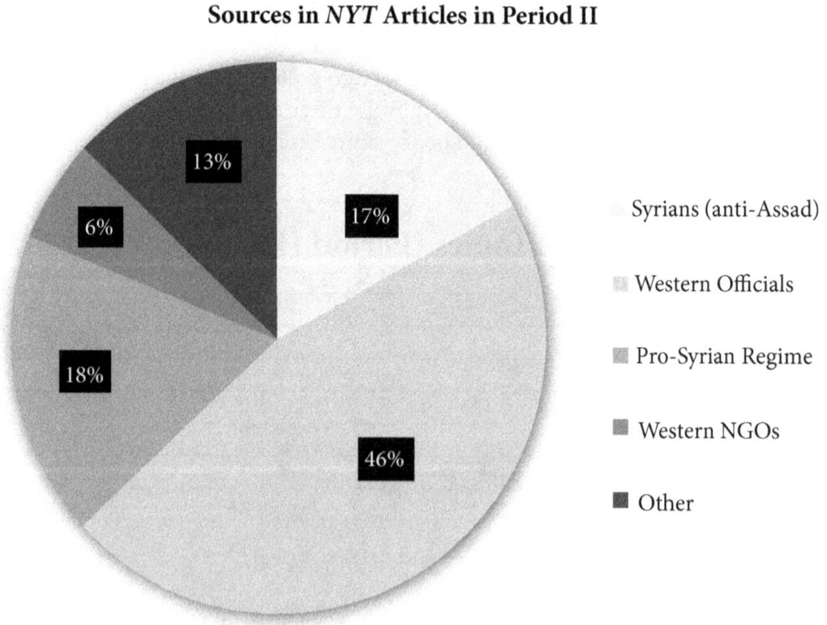

Sources in *NYT* Articles in Period II

- Syrians (anti-Assad): 17%
- Western Officials: 46%
- Pro-Syrian Regime: 18%
- Western NGOs: 6%
- Other: 13%

Figure 3.3 Sources in *NYT* articles in period II.

government, the government denied involvement, and Russia accused the rebels of staging the attack to implicate President Bashar al-Assad's government."[11]

As more evidence emerged and the US government began to blame the Syrian government, *NYT* authors started using a more hostile language against the Assad regime. For instance, an editorial published on August 22 stated, "If the killings … prove to be the work of President Bashar al-Assad's cutthroat regime … the United States and other major powers will almost certainly have to respond much more aggressively." In the same piece, the editorial board declared that it "[had] supported Mr. Obama's cautious approach to Syria, his unwillingness to embroil the United States in another Middle East war, and his push for a negotiated solution."[12]

In period II, as will be shown, the *NYT* disseminated frames—both in news and op-ed pieces—which agree with the previous statement. In the aftermath of the chemical attack, *NYT* authors paid particular attention to President Obama's decision-making process and to the debates taking place inside his administration. By so doing, the newspaper primarily highlighted the views of US government officials, not those of the opposition or other nongovernmental actors, such as advocacy and other political groups. As previously noted, framing can be defined as "selecting and highlighting some facets of events or issues, and making connections among them so as to promote a particular interpretation, evaluation, and/or solution."[13]

At least five articles analyze the internal White House debates. In one of them, Ben Hubbard, Mark Mazzetti, and Mark Landler wrote, "The debate was robust, officials said. Some officials argued forcefully for military action, while others raised potential dangers about American missile strikes, including fears that they would destabilize the region and set off a vast new refugee flow into Turkey, Jordan, and Lebanon."[14] Another news article, published one day after the Eastern Ghouta events, reported that "a sharply divided" Obama administration was weighing a response to the attack.[15]

A strike against Syria was practically imminent until August 26, the date when the US President finally decided to seek congressional approval before engaging militarily in Syria. John Kerry was one of the most outspoken voices favoring an intervention. In a news conference on August 25, he assured, "President Obama believes there must be accountability for those who would use the world's most heinous weapons against the world's most vulnerable people. Nothing today is more serious, and nothing is receiving more serious scrutiny."[16] As Hubbard reported, the US military seemed to be preparing an attack: "Pentagon officials also said that the Navy had increased its presence in the eastern Mediterranean Sea to four destroyers, each carrying long-range Tomahawk cruise missiles similar to those launched in past American attacks on Afghanistan, Iraq, and Libya."[17]

Mark Landler and Michael Gordon argued that the 1999 NATO intervention in Kosovo could provide a legal precedent for a strike in Syria: "Kosovo is an obvious precedent for Mr. Obama because, as in Syria, civilians were killed and Russia had longstanding ties to the government authorities accused of the abuses. In 1999, President Bill Clinton used the endorsement of NATO and the rationale of protecting a vulnerable population to justify seventy-eight days of airstrikes."[18] In March 1999, a US-led NATO operation conducted an air campaign against Serbian military targets without a UN mandate. US officials knew that Russia, as an ally of Yugoslav President Slobodan Milosevic, would veto any resolution authorizing the use of military force against Serbian troops fighting the Kosovo Liberation Army.

The previous extracts demonstrate that the US government did not have a unified view about the exact form an attack against Syria should take. *NYT* journalist Tom Shanker quoted General Dempsey as saying that the Syrian opposition was not "ready" to take power. Shanker wrote, "The nation's top military officer [General Dempsey], just back from the Middle East, has told Congress that the Pentagon could forcefully intervene in Syria to tip the balance in the civil war, but that there were no moderate rebel groups now ready to fill any power vacuum there."[19] According to the *NYT* journalist, one wing of the US military had doubts about an intervention. Moreover, it was not clear what being "ready to fill any power vacuum" meant for Dempsey. Dempsey was quoted further arguing that a military intervention in Syria "[could not] resolve the underlying and historic ethnic, religious, and tribal issues that [were] fuelling this conflict."[20] As we can see, his explanation of the Syrian uprising and civil war is simplistic and Orientalist.

When General Dempsey argued that the Syrian opposition was not ready to take power and that an intervention would not resolve the ethnic, religious, and tribal issues in Syria, he was referring in reality to the fact that the United States did not wield enough influence over the leaders of the anti-Assad movement. As previously discussed, the Syrian opposition was decentralized and divided, and the US general knew very well that a new government in Damascus formed out of such a diffused movement could create more instability in the region and encourage protest movements in neighboring countries to seek regime change.

NYT authors never advocated intervention in Syria, though the newspaper's editorial board held that the United States should "respond much more aggressively" in case the Assad regime was to blame for the use of chemical weapons.[21] In fact, the *NYT* framing of the Eastern Ghouta events reinforced an anti-interventionist stance. By disclosing the divisions inside the administration and portraying the Syrian opposition as sectarian and "not ready," *NYT* authors suggested that an attack on the Assad regime would be unsuitable for the United States as it could have led groups to power that were in conflict with US interests. The *WP* and *WSJ*, by contrast, reported not only on how the Obama administration reacted to the attack but also on how Republican politicians urged the US president to respond more forcefully.

In an opinion article published by the *NYT* on August 23, Edward Luttwak, a senior associate at the conservative Center for Strategic and International Studies, claimed that a "prolonged stalemate is the only outcome that would not be damaging to American interests."[22] Luttwak further stated that President Obama should "resist the temptation to intervene more forcefully in Syria's civil war." According to the senior scholar, the idea of a stalemate being in the best interest for the United States would make sense because all sides in the conflict were hostile to the United States.

Indeed, Luttwak saw the possibility of a rebel victory as extremely dangerous:

> A rebel victory would also be extremely dangerous for the United States and for many of its allies in Europe and the Middle East. That is because extremist groups, some identified with al-Qaeda, have become the most effective fighting force in Syria. If those rebel groups manage to win, they would almost certainly try to form a government hostile to the United States. Moreover, Israel could not expect tranquility on its northern border if the jihadists were to triumph in Syria.[23]

The Syrian opposition is portrayed in negative terms—usually as "Islamists" or excessively religious—in four other articles. Luttwak was in tune with the Obama administration. US policy in Syria under President Obama aimed at prolonging the stalemate between the Syrian regime and oppositionist forces and avoided providing more decisive support to anti-Assad rebels. Among other reasons, the US government justified this approach by arguing that the Syrian opposition was Islamist and incapable of defeating the Syrian government and governing the country.

This noninterventionist stance is predominant in the *NYT* coverage of the Eastern Ghouta chemical attack. There is sufficient evidence to conclude that the newspaper sided with the cautious wing of the Obama administration. Ben Rhodes explained in his book *The World as It Is* how the debates unfolded in the White House once all the doubts about Bashar al-Assad's responsibility were dispelled. According to him, the US president, who was initially inclined to authorize an attack, became increasingly skeptical as the days passed and the possibility of forming an international coalition vanished. Most US officials, Rhodes continued, actually favored a limited strike against Syria (not aimed at regime change). However, important figures belonging to President Obama's closest circle, such as Denis McDonough—Obama's chief of staff at the time—raised doubts about it.[24]

In period II, the *NYT* criticized President Obama's Syria policy only on one occasion: when the editorial board deemed his decision to draw a red line as "unwise."[25] An interesting fact about the *NYT* coverage of the aftermath of the Eastern Ghouta attack is that only one article describes how Republicans assessed the situation. Scott Shane and Ben Hubbard reported that President Obama was facing "criticism from Congressional Republicans and others" for not enforcing the "red line."[26] In this article, the two *NYT* journalists also quoted then-Israeli Prime Minister Benjamin Netanyahu as saying that the chemical attack in Eastern Ghouta demanded a response. As to the reactions in Israel, the two journalists claimed that "some Israelis have argued that international intervention in Syria would distract the world from the crucial effort to prevent a nuclear Iran," which suggests that opinions in Israel were not entirely favorable of military intervention.

This brings us to a final comment on the sourcing practices of *NYT* authors in period II. Seven general categories of sources can be identified: pro-Assad officials, Syrian oppositionists, US officials, international officials, UN officials, humanitarian organizations, and experts. The most quoted sources are US officials, followed by Syrian oppositionists, the United Nations, and other humanitarian groups. *NYT* authors preferred quoting Democrats and members of the Obama administration. Pro-Assad sources are mostly Syrian and Russian officials. Only two experts are quoted in the articles published by the *NYT* in period II: Jeffrey White, a former Middle East analyst with the Defense Intelligence Agency—then fellow at the Washington Institute for Near East Policy[27]—and Ivo Daalder, a former US ambassador to NATO—then president of the Chicago Council on Global Affairs.[28]

In conclusion, the *NYT* coverage of the Eastern Ghouta attack centers on the debates that occurred inside the Obama administration. The most diffused frame champions a cautious response to the attack. No author advocated intervention in Syria, although the tone vis-à-vis the Assad regime was highly critical. This frame is attained by highlighting the US president's decision-making process, on one hand, and by overlooking voices that supported a more energetic response, on the other. Sourcing practices play a critical role in building the idea that an attack against Syria might not have been the best option. The following sections discuss the narratives in the *WP* and the *WSJ*, arguing that they were quite different from the one relayed in the *NYT*.

The WP *Calls for a Strong Response against Assad*

The *WP* published twenty-five articles in period II: sixteen news pieces, five opinion articles, two editorials, one news analysis, and a transcript of John Kerry's statement. The topics addressed in the *WP* are similar to those reported by the *NYT*. The Eastern Ghouta chemical attack, US foreign policy, and the international reactions to the attack amount to the three most popular topics. In the articles reporting on the chemical attack, the sources are mainly opposition activists giving testimonies from the ground. In the articles discussing US foreign policy, the sources are mostly American and international politicians.

The *WP* relied on sources and analysts that called for a strong response against the Syrian regime, such as late Republican Senator John McCain and French officials.[29] In period II, the *WP* published seven opinion pieces—five more than the *NYT*—at least four of which are critical of the Obama administration. Among the commentators who held particularly negative views of President Obama are Michael Gerson, a visiting fellow at the Center for Public Justice[30] who served as a senior speechwriter for President Bush, and Elliot Cohen, who served as counselor in the US Department of State under Condoleezza Rice. As we will see, several *WP* articles in period II urge the Obama administration to strike Syria.

WP authors seemed more interested in highlighting opinions that urged the US government to act in light of the attack rather than covering the internal debates in the White House. This constitutes a significant difference with the *NYT* coverage. On August 22, one day after the Eastern Ghouta events, the *WP* editorial board suggested that the United States should have a more proactive attitude:

The United States should be using its own resources to determine, as quickly as possible, whether the opposition's reports of large-scale use of gas against civilians are accurate. If they are, Mr. Obama should deliver on his vow not to tolerate such crimes—by ordering direct US retaliation against the Syrian military forces responsible and by adopting a plan to protect civilians in southern Syria with a no-fly zone.[31]

Three policies are found in *WP* articles in August 2013: the use of military force against the Syrian regime, the training and equipping of rebel forces, and the enforcement of a no-fly zone. However, *WP* authors overall argued against the deployment of US ground troops to Syria. Jennifer Rubin, an American journalist who writes the *Right Turn* blog for the *WP*, regarded President Obama's cautious behavior as "cringe-worthy." Rubin condemned the US president for not understanding the role of the United States in the liberal world order: "Obama has never fully understood the centrality of the United States to preserving international stability and preventing mass horrors. His entire scheme of 'leading from behind' and deferring to international bodies is designed to refute the idea that the United States must lead, sometimes on its own, in order to prevent great evil."[32] Obama's failure to act, Rubin continued, represented a "stain" on US foreign policy. The journalist is not the first *WP* columnist to condemn President Obama's apparent deference to international bodies. Other authors writing for the newspaper shared this mistrust in multilateral organizations, indicating that the *WP* favors a more assertive foreign policy approach.

On August 27, the *WP* published another editorial, this time arguing that the United States could influence the Syrian conflict by combining "military measures with training, weapons supplies, and diplomacy."[33] The editorial board went on to specify what these military measures should be, arguing that they "could include destroying forces involved in chemical weapons use and elements of the Syrian air force that have been used to target civilians, as well as helping to carve out a safe zone for rebels and the civilian populations they are seeking to protect."

WP journalist Liz Sly, in turn, stated in a news piece that President Obama was left with "few options" since Russia had "repeatedly blocked action against Syria at the UN Security Council."[34] It is not clear what these options were. The *WP* journalist quoted members of the Obama administration accusing the Assad regime of being responsible for the chemical attack, as well as British, French, and Turkish officials as saying that "they would be prepared to back US action outside the parameters of a UN mandate." Eugene Robinson, a senior *WP* columnist, suggested the same, arguing that Obama should use force against the Assad regime: "I believe we are obliged to hit Assad."[35] However, Robinson did not express the same resolve for sending weapons to Syrian rebels, as this "materiel could end up in the hands of Islamist, anti-Western factions that seem a good bet to prevail in a post-Assad Syria." The fear of US weapons falling into the "wrong hands" was a recurrent argument used by US officials for not arming Syrian opposition groups.

The *WP*'s pro-interventionist frame can also be seen in articles that cover the international reactions in the aftermath of the Eastern Ghouta attack. In a news article that discusses the Russian reactions to the attack, Will Englund underlined the country's role in blocking any international response under the framework of the United Nations. Englund further asserted, "Moscow would appear to have little recourse ... in the event of a Western attack" and that "Turkey, Britain, and France indicated ... they would back the Obama administration if it decided to act against Syria."[36] The journalist paints a favorable scenario for a US intervention in Syria.

WP authors depicted the US government as hesitant and divided in the response to the chemical attack. In a news piece published on August 21, journalists Loveday Morris and Karen DeYoung quoted General Dempsey casting doubt on the effectiveness of providing military support to the Syrian opposition. In Dempsey's words, "more robust military assistance, including US air assaults against Assad's air force, could not ensure that US-favored moderates in the fractured opposition would prevail."[37] Dempsey further argued that the only "way forward" for the United States in Syria was providing "more humanitarian aid and support for opposition moderates." In the same article, the Obama administration is portrayed as "divided over the wisdom of the more direct military support that the rebels and some US lawmakers have demanded." Using testimonies from survivors and videos uploaded to YouTube, Morris and DeYoung described the situation in Eastern Ghouta as "terrible" and quoted Syrian opposition leaders as demanding a response. Furthermore, the two journalists quoted Syrian oppositionists complaining that the "light arms and ammunition shipments that [US] administration officials said [had been] recently cleared for delivery [had] not arrived."[38]

Morris and DeYoung's article frames the Eastern Ghouta attack in such a way that the United States appears to be urged to act against the Syrian regime. First, the two journalists described the scenes of the attacks, quoting scholars who verified the authenticity of the videos. Then, they moved on to quote members of the Syrian opposition demanding a response and complaining about the lack of support from the United States. Finally, the two journalists depicted the divisions inside the administration and its "hesitation" to act. By organizing the narrative in this particular way, Morris and DeYoung induce the reader to conclude that acting decisively against the Syrian regime was the best option. After all, as Berinsky and Kinder argued, "frames are never neutral. By defining what the essential issue is and suggesting how to think about it, frames imply what, if anything, should be done."[39]

The *WP* and the *NYT* used different sources. For example, in a news article published on August 27, the vast majority of sources quoted by *WP* journalists DeYoung and Anne Gearan support military intervention in Syria.[40] Among these sources were US politicians—both Republicans and Democrats—YouTube videos, Syrian oppositionists, members of the Obama administration, and members of humanitarian groups. In another article, DeYoung and Colum Lynch quoted McCain as saying that the United States "would lose credibility if it did not respond forcefully to Bashar al-Assad's repeated use of chemical weapons."[41]

Gearan, Morris, and Lynch, in turn, claimed that "two top US lawmakers" (John McCain and Republican Senator Lindsey Graham) called for an immediate US military response.[42]

WP journalists also quoted different French officials—especially, then-Foreign Minister Laurent Fabius—advocating a response to the attacks. In comparison with the *NYT*, the *WP* quoted a higher number of experts who verified the authenticity of the videos uploaded from Eastern Ghouta or discussed the possible responses to the attacks. For instance, Mahmoud Irdaisat, head of the Center for Strategic Studies at Jordan's King Abdullah II Academy for Defense Studies, declared that "the West and Arab states" should have reached an agreement over military action in Syria.[43] As can be seen, the pro-interventionist frame that the *WP* disseminated in period II relies mostly on the strategic selection of sources (see Figure 3.4).

In opinion pieces, criticism of the Obama administration and calls to act in light of the attack is more straightforward than in news articles. Elliot Cohen, for example, asserted that "as weak as the United States now appears in the region and beyond, we would look weaker yet if we chose to act ineffectively. A bout of therapeutic bombing is an even more feckless course of action than a principled refusal to act altogether."[44] Cohen's argument is that the United States should engage in a "serious bombing campaign" against the Syrian regime. He further argued that "not to act would be, at this point and by the administration's own

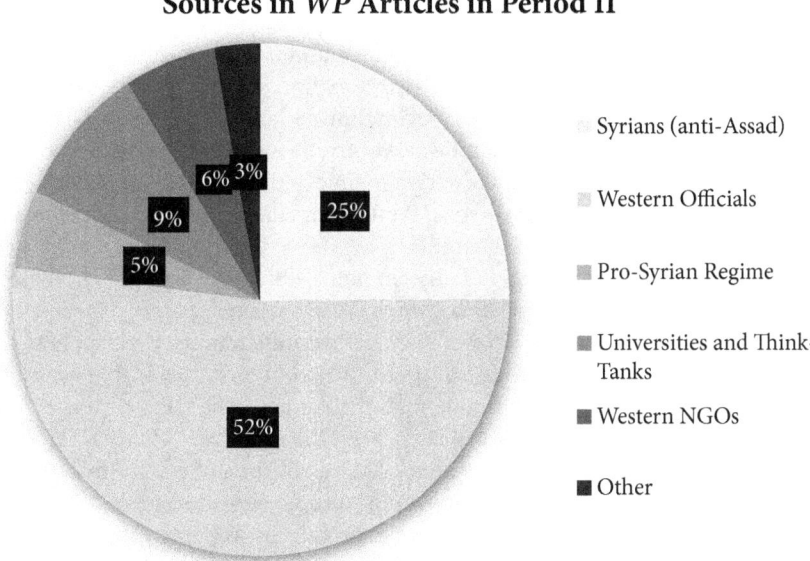

Figure 3.4 Sources in *WP* articles in period II.

standards, intolerable" and that it was "late, perhaps too late, to prevent Syria from becoming the new Afghanistan or Yemen, home to rabidly anti-Western jihadis." His primary concern seemed to be the growth of groups that could later challenge US interests in the region.

Another opinion piece, one by Michael Gerson, condemns the entire Syria policy adopted by the Obama administration. In Gerson's words,

> US policy is making difficult adjustments as well. Since the worst elements in Syria have grown stronger over time, delay has complicated every course. At first, the Obama administration hoped that Bashar al-Assad would fall without being pushed. Then it adopted a policy of wait-and-see as the tide of battle turned in Assad's favor, with help from Russia, Iran, and Hezbollah. Then a policy of arming selected rebels that does not seem to have armed any rebels.[45]

By "worst elements" Gerson meant what he called "the jihadist opposition to Assad."

The Free Syrian Army is depicted in negative terms in *WP* articles on two occasions. The first negative depiction appears in a piece by journalist Taylor Luck where he reported on the recruitment of teenagers by the FSA in Jordan's Zaatari refugee camp. Luck quoted a UN official expressing his concerns about this practice and an FSA commander justifying it. He also quoted a teenage soldier—stating that he fights "in the name of God to take back the country from government forces"—and the father of another one saying that his son "decided to join the FSA not only to save his country, but to save his family."[46]

The second occasion on which the FSA is depicted negatively is the previously mentioned article by Gerson. In it, the *WP* columnist associated it with religious and ethnic divisions. Nevertheless, he drew a line between the FSA and other jihadist groups, blaming the Assad regime for sectarianizing the conflict. As to possible solutions, he argued that the best outcome for the United States would be a negotiated solution between the Syrian regime and the opposition, which could only be attained with a "Kosovo-style, Western air campaign" that would force the Assad regime to the negotiating table.[47]

In brief, the *WP* and the *NYT* disseminated different frames of the Eastern Ghouta chemical attack. Whereas the *NYT* presented narratives which do not question the main aspects of the US administration's Syria policy, and do not support intervention as a response to the attack, the *WP* depicted the administration's policy as hesitant and incoherent. The *WP* coverage, both in news and op-ed articles, urges President Obama to act. Multiple responses were suggested, such as a military attack, the establishment of a no-fly zone, and the training and equipping of opposition groups. However, most *WP* articles in period II depict the Syrian opposition negatively, as if consisting mainly of "jihadist" groups. *WP* authors used sources advocating for a response against the Syrian regime, such as Republican politicians, international officials, and Syrian oppositionists.

The WSJ Urges the US to Attack Syria

The *WSJ* published forty articles between August 20 and August 26, 2013, being the newspaper with the most extensive coverage in period II. Of the forty pieces, twenty-nine are news articles, ten are opinion pieces, and one is a news analysis. The *WSJ* did not publish any editorial articles in period II, but it published the highest number of opinion pieces among the three newspapers. US foreign policy is by far the most recurrent topic covered by the newspaper, being the main subject of twenty-one articles. The second most recurrent topic is the Eastern Ghouta chemical attack, which features as the principal topic in nine articles. Five articles analyze the Syrian civil war, a topic barely discussed by the *NYT* and the *WP* in this period. As in the *WP*, the coverage of the chemical attack in the *WSJ* is highly critical of President Obama.

In opinion pieces especially, *WSJ* contributors advocated a strong response to the chemical attack as well as the overthrow of Syrian President Bashar al-Assad. *WP* authors also called for a strong response to the attack, but they were not as straightforward in arguing that the United States should aim at regime change. This represents an important difference between the two newspapers.

In news articles, however, *WSJ* journalists employed a more pragmatic tone with respect to the future of the Syrian president. By using sources that cast doubts about toppling the Syrian dictator, the journalists counterbalanced the idea spread by *WSJ* opinion columnists that Bashar al-Assad should step down. *WSJ* journalists relied, on one side, on the US officials who were not convinced of a military attack against Syria. On the other, they counted on officials from countries that held a more cautious position regarding the removal of the Syrian president, such as Israel and Saudi Arabia. The foreign policy analysis in the *WSJ* is the most complete of the three newspapers, as it discussed the views of both Democrats and Republicans as well as the perspectives of other countries, such as Israel, Saudi Arabia, Russia, and Iran.

Three opinion articles discuss US foreign policy in broad, almost theoretical terms, focusing not only on Syria but also on the strategic importance of the Middle East for the United States. For example, Walter Russel Mead, who is also a prominent *WSJ* columnist, identified the five problems of what he called President Obama's Middle East "grand strategy."[48] The first problem was the belief that "moderate Islamists"—with reference to groups such as the Egyptian Muslim Brotherhood and the Turkish Justice and Development Party—would run governments wisely. Mead argued that US officials wrongly assumed that these groups would trigger democratic reforms in the Middle East. The second problem was misreading what happened in Egypt as a "transition to democracy." Thirdly, the professor continued, the United States failed to identify the impacts of its Middle East policy on Israel and Saudi Arabia, the two most important US allies in the region. According to Mead, both countries were unsettled by President Obama's proximity to moderate Islamist groups. The fourth problem was underestimating the "vitality and capability" of terrorist cells to resist and spread. Lastly, Mead claimed that President Obama had failed to grasp in good time the costs of a noninterventionist approach in Syria.

The growth of Islamist groups (his precise words were "terrorists" and "jihadists"), on the one hand, and the loss of influence in the Middle East to Russia and Iran amount to the most relevant costs the United States would bear.

At the end of his article, Mead suggested that the United States should deter Iran and implement a "much tougher policy in Syria." In order to defeat terrorism, he continued, the United States would need to build "pragmatic alliances" with other Middle Eastern countries that shared similar objectives:

> In the Arab world, in parts of Africa, in Europe, and in the United States, a constellation of revitalized and inventive [jihadist] movements now seeks to wreak havoc. It is delusional to believe that we can eliminate this problem by eliminating poverty, underdevelopment, dictatorship, or any other 'root causes' of the problem; we cannot eliminate them in a policy-relevant time frame. An ugly fight lies ahead. Instead of minimizing the terror threat in hopes of calming the public, the president must prepare public opinion for a long-term struggle.[49]

Mead's opinions seem to align with the neoconservative ideas that view Islamic fundamentalism as an existential threat to the United States. Also, his failure to mention the democratic forces still operative in Syria in 2013 amounts to a misrepresentation of the conflict.

In the second article that analyzes US foreign policy in a more general sense, journalists Jay Solomon and Julian Barnes claimed that the two most influential paradigms among US foreign policy thinkers—"realism and neoconservatism"—are no longer capable of explaining Middle East politics or of providing guidelines on how to respond to the various crises besetting the region. The two *WSJ* journalists, who write about foreign affairs and national security, argued that "two pillars have guided American foreign policy for a generation: the realist school that sought stability and tackled the world as it came, and the neoconservative trend that was willing to use force to realize American goals and values. Both are now struggling to provide answers for how the United States should respond to the Middle East's continuing upheaval."[50]

Solomon and Barnes quoted several scholars who held critical views of the "backseat approach" of President Obama's foreign policy. They saw US influence in the region as receding, while some Middle Eastern countries—such as Iran and Turkey—moved to "fill the leadership void, often in ways contrary to American interests." The two journalists went on to depict Iran as the main antagonist of the United States in the region, although they did not state clearly what should have been done in Syria to contain Iranian presence.

The third article discussing US foreign policy—titled "Obama's Foreign Failure," written by Pete du Pont, a member of the Republican Party—criticizes the US administration's attempt to "reset" relations with Russia and President Obama's "lead-from-behind" approach in Libya.[51] Du Pont was particularly harsh on the US president, anticipating that his policy mistakes would cause immeasurable damage to the United States:

The great sorrow is that the damage caused by this administration will take years to repair, and America and the world will be less safe, less peaceful, and less secure. The great irony is that a man and his team who are so good at domestic politics, and understanding how the American voters think, can be so bad at foreign policy and understanding how the real world works.

Du Pont did not propose any concrete policy, though his criticism of the "lead-from-behind" approach suggests that a more proactive stance should be adopted. These three articles are truly revealing of the *WSJ*'s foreign policy views and of why it assessed the Obama administration so negatively.

Several articles (both news and opinion) imply that the Obama administration was actually to blame for the Eastern Ghouta chemical attack, for it had refused to act against the Syrian regime earlier in the conflict. For example, an opinion article claims that Bashar al-Assad had "grown more brazen" as a result of President Obama's willingness to stay out of Syria.[52] The author used an ironic tone when referring to how the White House first responded to the chemical attack, stating that "any concerns Assad might have had that the attack would prompt Mr. Obama to act were allayed by Wednesday's [August 21, 2013] White House press conference." In another opinion piece, the *WSJ* argued that President Obama's refusal to form a coalition to attack Syria encouraged Bashar al-Assad to use chemical weapons against civilians, thereby implying that a coalition should be formed.[53]

At least six *WSJ* articles call for an attack against the Syrian regime. Andrew Roberts, a historian at King's College London, compared the Syrian dictator to Hitler, Mussolini, and Saddam Hussein, suggesting that the United States attack and topple him. Roberts wrote, "The White House ties itself into rhetorical knots in order to avoid having to topple [Bashar al-Assad]."[54] The historian further argued that chemical weapons should be seen as a boundary between civilization and barbarism: "There is a long and honorable history of the civilized world treating those dictators who use poison gas as qualitatively different from the normal ruck of tyrants whose careers have so stained the 20th and 21st centuries. President Obama, who talks endlessly of the importance of civilized values, must now uphold this one." This idea, based on the binary opposition between civilized and uncivilized, is one of the most popular Orientalist tropes used by Western analysts when discussing the Middle East.

In another piece, Gary Fields, a *WSJ* journalist and a board member for the Fund for Investigative Journalism,[55] quoted one Republican senator as saying that the United States should attack "in a very surgical and proportional way" without sending ground troops to Syria. Fields quoted former Democratic Congressman Elliot Engel calling for an attack even without UN approval.[56] In contrast to the *NYT*, *WSJ* journalists used several pro-interventionist sources—both politicians and experts—in news articles.

Sam Dagher, Maria Abi-Habib, and Ellen Knickmeyer sign a detailed news piece, published on August 27, reporting on the international reactions to a possible attack against Syria. The authors collected opinions from officials and international organizations of different countries—France, the UK, Saudi Arabia, and the Arab League. Although the article's title ("Arab League Cautious as US Gears for Strike") conveys the idea of restraint, most of the cited officials defended an international response to the Syrian regime's use of gas Sarin in Eastern Ghouta. This response, the authors argued, should be carried out by an international coalition, not as a unilateral act by the United States. The article suggests that an attack against Syria would not face opposition from international and regional actors as long as it was proportional and not part of a long-term intervention.[57]

Bret Stephens, a political commentator with links to the Israeli political right,[58] not only championed that the United States should attack Syria but also that it had to kill Bashar al-Assad and some of his closest allies. Just like Andrew Roberts had done a few days earlier, Stephens compared the Syrian dictator with Saddam Hussein, the Iraqi president toppled in 2003 by a US-led coalition:

> Should President Obama decide to order a military strike against Syria, his main order of business must be to kill Bashar al-Assad. Also, Bashar's brother and principal henchman, Maher. Also, everyone else in the Assad family with a claim on political power. Also, all of the political symbols of the Assad family's power, including all of their official or unofficial residences. The use of chemical weapons against one's own citizens plumbs depths of barbarity matched in recent history only by Saddam Hussein. A civilized world cannot tolerate it.[59]

In this same line, another opinion piece urges the Obama administration to overthrow the Assad government, arguing that a limited attack would not be sufficient and that there would be "no good outcome in Syria until Assad and his regime [were] gone."[60] A third opinion piece enumerates three different ways in which the United States could have responded to the attacks: a "surgical attack," a more extensive attack aimed at ousting Bashar al-Assad, and no attack at all.[61] The piece continues by saying that overthrowing the Syrian regime was the best path for the United States, as it would prevent the continuous growth of "jihadist" groups. The author concluded that supporting "nonjihadist" opposition groups with an air campaign was the best way to remove the Syrian president from power.

As previously mentioned, not all *WSJ* articles relay such a pro-interventionist frame. Three news pieces reflect the debates that were occurring inside the Obama administration as well as the views of officials from countries involved in the conflict, such as Saudi Arabia, Iran, Russia, and Israel. In an article published on August 27, Ellen Knickmeyer and Nour Malas showed how the Arab League and different regional countries reacted to the possibility of a unilateral US strike in Syria.[62] They depicted a highly divided region with, for example, Turkey being supportive of intervention even without a UN resolution, and with the Arab League and other smaller countries (such as Lebanon and Jordan) calling for a response only if authorized by the UN Security Council. Adam Entous, Julian Barnes, and Inti Landauro, in turn, reported that the United States weighed "plans to punish Assad."[63] The three journalists quoted US officials as saying that "their purpose would not be to topple the regime, but to punish Mr. Assad if there is conclusive evidence that the government was behind poison-gas attacks."

Farnaz Fassihi authored a news article in period II discussing a possible strike against the Syrian regime from an Iranian perspective: "An attack on Damascus would likely give Iranian hard-liners, who oppose a nuclear compromise, the upper hand over moderate President Hasan Rouhani, who has made foreign policy and nuclear talks a priority."[64] The *WSJ* journalist claimed, however, that Iran would not have engaged in a direct military confrontation with the United States in the event of a US attack against Syria.

Joshua Mitnick, for his part, reported on the Israeli perspective. Although the title of his article ("Israel Worries Rise over a Syrian Attack") suggests that Syria might use chemical weapons against Israel, his conclusion stressed the unlikeness of such an attack. According to Mitnick, "[t]he prevailing assessment of many Israeli security and regional experts is that the Syrian regime, despite veiled threats of an attack on Israel, is unlikely to attack the Jewish state in order to avoid having to fight on another front and risk losing to the rebels. The experts also do not expect the US intervention to topple Mr. Assad."[65]

Adam Entous wrote a news article describing the role of Saudi Prince Bandar bin Sultan al-Saud—Saudi Arabia's ambassador to the United States from 1983 to 2005 and former director general of the Saudi Intelligence Agency—as a liaison between the Saudi kingdom and US officials during the Syrian conflict.[66] According to Entous, Saudi Arabia was pressuring the United States to carry out a more aggressive Syria policy, which should have materialized in the training and equipping of rebel forces fighting the Syrian government. Relatedly, the Syrian rebels are the main topic of one news article published by the *WSJ* in period II. Solomon quoted different Syrian oppositionists, from a senior official in the Supreme Military Council to activists lobbying in the United States or active on the Turkish-Syrian border. The rebels expressed their frustration with US policy ("We're tired of just words"[67]), urging the US administration to retaliate against the Syrian government by targeting "Damascus's artillery batteries and airfields and the command-and-control centers of the elite Republican Guards."

In conclusion, the *WSJ* coverage of the Eastern Ghouta chemical attack is the most extensive and complete of the three newspapers. In the opinion pieces, the tone is mostly in favor of an attack against the Syrian regime. Whereas some commentators openly called for the overthrow of Bashar al-Assad, others leaned toward a surgical attack aimed at punishing the Syrian dictator or an air campaign to support rebel forces backed by the United States. In the news pieces, the story is slightly different. Several articles deliver a more cautious frame as to the future of the Syrian regime, although several journalists used pro-interventionist sources, especially US politicians and experts.

The *WSJ* used a more balanced selection of sources than the *NYT*, which, as we have seen, relied primarily on US officials and supporters of the Obama administration (see Figure 3.5). Furthermore, the *WSJ* gave importance to the perspective of regional countries, which did not receive the same attention in either the *NYT* or the *WP*.

Sources in *WSJ* Articles in Period II

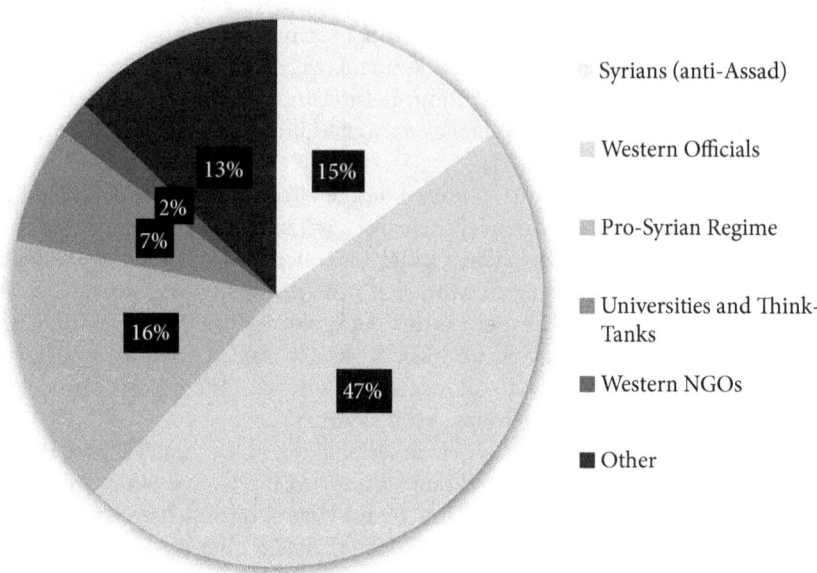

Figure 3.5 Sources in *WSJ* articles in period II.

...

The Eastern Ghouta chemical attack represented a turning point in the Syrian conflict. On the one hand, it showed that the Assad regime was sufficiently confident to go as far as using chemical weapons against civilians, despite several international treaties prohibiting their use in armed conflicts. By using these kinds of weapons in Eastern Ghouta, Bashar al-Assad defiantly crossed the "red line" set by President Obama in August 2012. Thus, the events of August 2013 forced the US government to make the strategic decision of whether it would enforce the "red line" or not. The US president and his team engaged in a complex debate about the viability and the extension of a possible attack. Not only was the Obama administration divided over the issue, but so too was the whole US political elite. President Obama faced a dilemma on whether or not to attack Syria; the consequences of his decision to not do it would "haunt" him until the end of his second term.

The three newspapers not only reflected these debates but to some extent took sides. In op-ed articles, each newspaper carefully selected a variety of contributors who supported or condemned President Obama's Syria policy and called for different actions—from keeping a "wait-and-see" approach to a limited attack and the training of Syrian rebels. Politicians, political analysts, academics, and journalists participated in this energetic discussion. The *NYT* published only two op-ed pieces in period II, thereby adopting a more cautious approach. To substantiate their news pieces, *NYT* journalists relied mostly on sources aligned with President Obama's views. Conversely, the *WP* and the *WSJ* ran a higher number of op-ed pieces, most of which are critical of the Obama administration and favorable to a strong response against the Assad regime. In the case of the *WSJ*, several columnists went as far as calling for the overthrow (and even assassination) of Bashar al-Assad by the United States.

In news articles, the topics addressed in the three newspapers vary only a little, making the strategic selection of sources a crucial factor in the frame-building process. The *NYT* focused on the internal debate in the White House, while the *WP* and the *WSJ* highlighted the discussion within the entire US political establishment and also on an international scale. Thus, the scope of the coverage (a narrower or broader coverage of the debates occurring in the United States and in other countries) determined how each newspaper built and disseminated a particular frame about what to do in the light of the Eastern Ghouta chemical attack. By focusing on Obama's decision-making process, the *NYT* spread an anti-interventionist frame, as *NYT* journalists used very few sources that defended a military strike. The *WP* and the *WSJ* adopted a different approach, relying extensively on sources that favored a more forceful stance against the Syrian regime. However, the *WP* was more propositive, suggesting a number of policies that could be adopted by the US government.

Chapter 4

THE EXPANSION OF ISIS IN IRAQ AND SYRIA (PERIOD III)

In July 2014, after almost three years of a bloody civil war, the Syrian uprising showed signs of exhaustion. Opposition forces were divided and deprived of resources, despite the United States having started to equip and train rebel fighters in August 2013. Most military factions fighting the Syrian regime had become predominantly dependent on regional powers, such as Turkey, Saudi Arabia, and Qatar, and fund-raising networks, which in many cases meant carrying forward their sponsors' agendas. The lack of support for secular, democratic groups led to increasing numbers of opposition activists and fighters becoming disappointed with the United Nations and the so-called international community, especially in light of the fact that the 2013 chemical attack perpetrated by the Assad regime in Eastern Ghouta, went relatively unchallenged. In fact, the Independent International Commission of Inquiry on the Syrian Arab Republic, established in August 2011 by the UN Human Rights Council, found that the Syrian regime used chemical weapons on at least five occasions from August 2013 to July 2014.

This scenario created a breeding ground for Islamic fundamentalist groups, an assessment that the Syrian regime shared, as it had been employing strategies to accentuate tensions among sects and ethnicities since the beginning of the uprising. These strategies included the use of a sectarian narrative to delegitimize the protests (Bashar al-Assad referred to the uprising on some occasions as a Sunni movement against the minorities[1]) and the release from prison of Salafist militants as the protests erupted in 2011. In March 2011, for example, the Syrian government issued a general amnesty as part of a package of reforms aimed at containing the initial protests.

However, as Michael Weiss and Hassan Hassan claim, the amnesty was part of a wider strategy to sectarianize the conflict:

> In the first amnesty, 246 of the 260 people freed were from the infamous Saydnaya prison that houses the violent Islamists. Plenty of protestors and activists were kept in jail, while an untold number of Salafist-jihadists were let out. Of these, many had not long ago been on ratlines to Iraq only to return to Syria and be collared and locked up by the very Mukhabarat [the Syrian secret service] that had sent them to Iraq in the first place.[2]

The formation of the Islamic State of Iraq and Syria in 2013, and its expansion in both countries in 2014, needs to be analyzed against this backdrop.

In August 2011, Abu Bakr al-Baghdadi, the leader of the Islamic State of Iraq (ISI), sent some of his men from Iraq to Syria to explore the possibility of expanding the group's operation into the neighboring country. One of ISI's main goals was the establishment of a caliphate in Iraq. Al-Baghdadi had been active in the fight against US troops in Iraq since 2003, when he founded a radical Islamist group called Jamaat Jaish Ahl al-Sunnah wa-l-Jamaah (the Army of the Sunni People Group). "Jamaat" merged with other groups in 2006 to form the Islamic State of Iraq. By 2010, Baghdadi had risen as one of Iraq's most prominent and radical Islamist leaders. Finally, in April 2013, ISI became the Islamic State of Iraq and Syria.

When ISIS became active in Syria in 2013, it targeted mostly rebel-held areas, especially those controlled by the Free Syrian Army, the Islamic Front (IF)—an organization formed in November 2013 following the unification of several Salafist groups—and the al-Nusra Front, which until July 2016 was al-Qaeda's branch in Syria. The Syrian regime, being spared attacks, received an additional boost in its campaign against the opposition and was able to retake territories it had lost to rebel forces at the beginning of the conflict. Some rebel groups had to fight on two fronts—against ISIS and the Syrian army—which led them to experience heavy losses and combat fatigue. The fact that ISIS prioritized assaulting rebel-held areas did not mean that it never clashed with the Syrian regime. The terrorist group did attack Syrian regime forces, as the three newspapers analyzed in this book have documented, but these confrontations were less frequent than the clashes between ISIS and Syrian oppositionist groups such as the FSA. The Syrian regime, on its part, attacked ISIS positions occasionally in the context of a strategy to regain legitimacy among the West and strengthen the idea that it was the most reliable partner in Syria against the fundamentalist group.

By August 2014, ISIS controlled approximately a third of Syria and 40 percent of Iraq. The sudden rise and expansion of the group prompted the United States to reassess its Syria policy, and on August 7, President Obama authorized airstrikes against the terrorist organization, launching a new large-scale US intervention in the Middle East. Christopher Phillips argued that the US president decided to attack ISIS because it represented a more significant threat to US interests in the region:

> First and foremost, ISIS' advance represented an immediate danger to US regional interests in a way that Assad did not. ISIS was dismembering a state the United States had only just left [Iraq], having invested time and money in rebuilding its institutions that Washington was not willing to write off. It also was advancing on the [Kurdistan Regional Government], a key US regional ally, home to a joint operations center with the US and Iraqi military in Erbil, and one of the Middle East's few stable entities.[3]

In October 2014, the US Department of State launched the Combined Joint Task Force-Operation Inherent Resolve (CJTF-OIR) with the objective of damaging the leadership and infrastructure of ISIS. Previously, US policy in Syria had focused on providing certain FSA units with training, nonlethal equipment, and light weapons. As previously mentioned, the CIA program was limited and did not include the transference of heavy weapons.

International relations scholar Stephen Zunes argued that President Obama's hesitation to support moderate Syrian rebels more decisively stemmed from the fact that the US president was afraid of ISIS overcoming the FSA, gaining the upper hand among anti-Assad forces, and capturing the weapons provided by the United States to these groups. According to Zunes,

> It was an awareness of ISIS's potential dominance of the Syrian rebel movement, which served as an important reason why the Obama administration did not go beyond the relatively limited arming and training of a few small groups affiliated with the Free Syrian Army. Indeed, part of ISIS's military prowess comes from weapons they captured from overrunning FSA positions and from their ranks supplemented by FSA fighters who, in the course of the three-year battle with Assad's regime, became radicalized and switched sides.[4]

The rise of ISIS intensified the debates within US political circles about the Syrian conflict. Two of the most vocal critics of Obama's hitherto Syria policy were Hillary Clinton and John McCain, both long-time advocates that the United States should support anti-Assad rebel groups more effectively. In the summer of 2012, Clinton and then-CIA Director David Petraeus sketched a plan, according to which the United States would "vet and train opposition groups and supply certain parts of the Syrian opposition with weapons."[5] The plan was rejected by the White House with the argument that the weapons could end up in the "wrong hands," which was probably a reference to Iran and Islamic fundamentalist groups such as al-Qaeda. It was only in August 2013 that the first program to arm Syrian rebels was put in place, after EU and US intelligence became convinced that the Syrian regime had on several occasions used chemical weapons against civilians in opposition-held areas.

In August 2014, with ISIS already seen by the United States as a major threat, Clinton adopted an aggressive tone against President Obama's Syria policy, denouncing it for allowing the rise of the Islamic fundamentalist group. In an interview for *The Atlantic*, she argued, "The failure to help build up a credible fighting force of the people who were the originators of the protests against Assad—there were Islamists, there were secularists, there was everything in the middle—the failure to do that left a big vacuum, which the jihadists have now filled."[6] In this interview, in which Clinton announced her intentions to run for president in 2016, she drew a clear line between President Obama's foreign policy strategies and her own. The differences were plain to see: while the US president opposed the view that ISIS represented an existential threat to the United States, Clinton, expressing a more hawkish foreign policy approach, equated its defeat to the fight against communism. Jeffrey Goldberg, the journalist who conducted the interview with the former secretary of state, wrote, "[Hillary Clinton] said that the resilience, and expansion, of Islamist terrorism means that the United States must develop an 'overarching' strategy to confront it, and she equated this struggle to the one the United States waged against Soviet-led communism."[7]

Obama had a different view. According to President Obama's foreign policy adviser Ben Rhodes,

> ISIL was a serious enough threat to warrant launching thousands of airstrikes, but [President Obama] cringed when he heard the threat described as "existential." ISIL had killed four Americans, a tiny fraction of those lost in Iraq and Afghanistan. It was not, as some of our critics roared, analogous to Nazi Germany—the same rhetoric Bush used after 9/11 when the government was authorizing torture.[8]

In practical terms, however, the main difference between President Obama and Clinton was the scope of the programs to arm anti-Assad rebels. Both politicians believed that ISIS was a threat, but the former secretary of state had been calling for the armament of part of the Syrian opposition since at least 2012. As mentioned above, the US president only acceded to the idea of a limited version of such a plan in 2013. For him, the so-called moderate rebels could not have defeated the Assad regime even if provided with American weapons. In a widely quoted 2014 interview with *NYT* columnist Thomas Friedman, the US president stated,

> This idea that we could provide some light arms or even more sophisticated arms to what was essentially an opposition made up of former doctors, farmers, pharmacists, and so forth, and that they were going to be able to battle not only a well-armed state but also a well-armed state backed by Russia, backed by Iran, a battle-hardened Hezbollah, that was never in the cards.[9]

Despite these differences, in 2014, both President Obama and Hillary Clinton pursued a similar strategy regarding how to end the conflict and restabilize Syria, namely that Bashar al-Assad and the Syrian opposition reach a settlement to initiate a political transition during which the Syrian dictator would probably have to step down, while the core of his regime would remain in place. As Gilbert Achcar argued, the Obama administration and other members of the US establishment were obsessed "with securing an 'orderly transition' and avoiding the repetition of the Iraqi debacle by preserving the bulk of the Syrian state apparatus."[10] This had been President Obama's policy since the beginning of the Syrian uprising, even after he demanded Assad to step down in August 2011, remaining the general US government strategy throughout the conflict.

McCain shared Clinton's view on the issue of arming Syrian rebels. As early as February 2012, he argued that the United States should offset the support that Iran and Russia were giving to the Syrian regime by assisting Syrian opposition groups with armaments. The fact that Clinton and McCain had similar views indicates that this debate did not follow clear party lines. The vote in September 2014 in the US House of Representatives, authorizing the Obama administration to arm and train Syrian rebels to fight ISIS, revealed that Republicans and Democrats were internally divided on the issue. While 159 Republicans and 114 Democrats supported the bill, totaling 273 votes in favor of it, 71 Republicans and 85 Democrats voted against it.

Another factor to take into account was that the emergence of ISIS changed how the US public viewed the involvement of the United States in the Syrian conflict. In 2013, after the Eastern Ghouta chemical attack, a YouGov survey showed that 64 percent of the American public opposed military action in Syria, while 20 percent supported it. One year later, with ISIS in the center of the debates, the numbers reversed almost entirely, with support for US intervention growing to 63 percent against 16 percent of respondents who opposed it.[11]

McCain argued that the United States should arm not only Syrian rebels but also other groups (mostly in Iraq) that were fighting ISIS on the ground. In a piece co-authored with Republican Senator Lindsey Graham, he wrote, "Such a plan [of confronting ISIS] would seek to strengthen partners who are already resisting ISIS: The Kurdish Peshmerga, Sunni tribes, moderate forces in Syria, and effective units of Iraq's security forces. Our partners are the boots on the ground, and the United States should provide them directly with arms, intelligence, and other military assistance."[12] The Obama administration ended up implementing programs to support nearly all the groups mentioned, although the Republican senator expected them to be broader in scope.

The *NYT*, the *WP*, and the *WSJ* covered the emergence of ISIS and the debates that followed it with great enthusiasm. They were particularly concerned about how to respond to the apparent security threat that the terrorist group posed to Western countries. Thus, following the emergence of ISIS as a central player in Iraq and Syria, terrorism and the war on terror narrative became recurrent topics in the coverage of the Syrian conflict. Despite the differences that persisted between the three newspapers regarding how to deal with the group, they all seemed to agree that Bashar al-Assad was a lesser threat for US interests in the Middle East. Another key issue in July 2014 was the nature of the Syrian opposition, especially the influence of moderate groups within rebel factions. The three newspapers had been describing parts of the Syrian opposition as "radicals" since the beginning of the conflict, but the emergence of ISIS changed the situation dramatically.

Period III comprises twenty-six days, from July 6 to July 31, 2014, being the longest of the six periods analyzed in this book; the other periods consist of either one or two weeks. The decision to make period III longer allowed for the collection of a more representative sample. After ISIS had captured the Iraqi cities of Tikrit and Mosul in June 2014, most US mainstream media changed focus, prioritizing the activity of the group in detriment of the Syrian civil war. Some of the articles analyzed in period III cover the activity of ISIS in both Iraq and Syria equally;

Table 4.1 Timeline: the expansion of ISIS in Iraq and Syria

	Timeline: The Expansion of ISIS in Iraq and Syria
November 2006	Following the death of Abu Musab al-Zarqawi, al-Qaeda's leading operator in Iraq, his successor Abu Ayyub al-Masri dissolves al-Qaeda in Iraq and pledges allegiance to the Islamic State of Iraq (ISI).
July 2012	The al-Nusra Front, which in 2014 proclaimed its allegiance to al-Qaeda, launches its first public operations in Aleppo.
April 2013	Abu Bakr al-Baghdadi announces the formation of ISIS.
August 2013	ISIS captures Raqqa in Syria.
December 2013/ January 2014	ISIS captures oil fields in Northeastern Syria.
February 2014	Global al-Qaeda formally ends its association with ISIS, issuing a public statement: "ISIS is not a branch of the Qaedat al-Jihad group [al-Qaeda's official name], we have no organizational relationship with it, and the group is not responsible for its actions."[13]
June 2014	ISIS captures Tikrit and Mosul in Iraq while al-Baghdadi announces the creation of a caliphate stretching from Aleppo in Syria to Diyala in Iraq and renames the group the Islamic State.[14]
July/August 2014	ISIS expands in Iraq and Syria, extending its control to a third of Syria and a quarter of Iraq.
October 2014	The US Department of Defense formally establishes Combined Joint Task Force-Operation Inherent Resolve (CJTF-OIR) in order to formalize ongoing military actions against ISIS in Iraq and Syria.[15]

others prioritize the group's activity in Iraq. Nevertheless, they were included in this sample because the development of ISIS in Iraq had a profound impact on the Syrian conflict. Moreover, the foreign policy debates around ISIS affected the discussion about Syria in different ways—for example, regarding what to do with the Assad regime and the Syrian opposition.

The total number of articles analyzed in period III amounts to forty-four, of which twenty-six are news articles, fifteen are opinion pieces, two are editorials, and one is a news analysis (see Figures 4.1 and 4.2). The *NYT* published twelve articles; the *WP* published eleven, and the *WSJ*, twenty-one. Thirty-nine journalists or commentators authored or co-authored articles in period III: thirty-three men and six women. The most recurrent topics in July 2014 are US foreign policy (seventeen articles), ISIS (five articles), and the United Nations (five articles). As for subtopics, the three most popular are the Syrian regime (six articles), the Syrian civil war (three articles), and the Syrian opposition (three articles).

Number of Articles in Period III

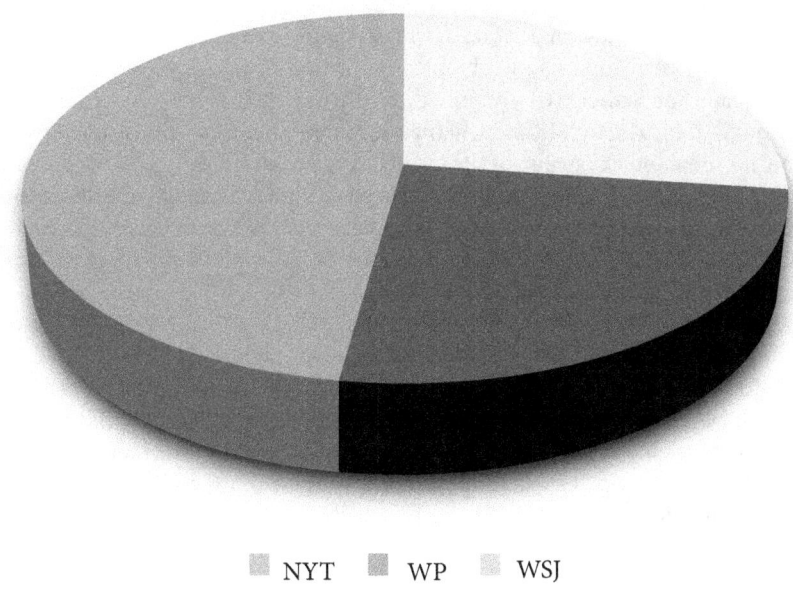

Figure 4.1 Number of articles in period III.

Genres in Period III

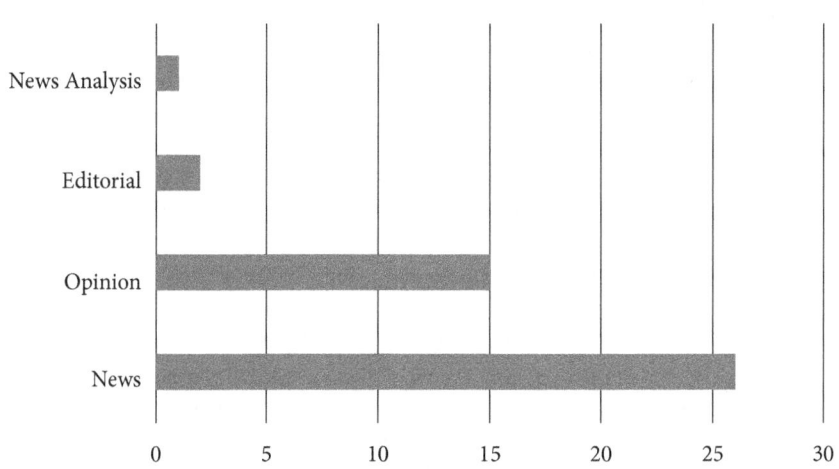

Figure 4.2 Genres in period III.

The NYT Supports Military Intervention against ISIS

The *NYT* published seven news articles, four opinion pieces, and one news analysis about the Syrian conflict in period III, which amount to a sample of twelve articles. The most frequent topics and subtopics are US foreign policy, ISIS, the United Nations, and the Syrian civil war. The foreign policy debates revolve around how to respond to the rise of ISIS and whether or not the Obama administration was to blame for the rapid expansion of the terrorist organization. As in the two previous periods, the *NYT* disseminated an anti-Assad frame, although the discussion around ISIS gained prominence over the depiction of the Syrian regime in negative terms. In period III, the *NYT* published one opinion piece that is particularly critical of the Obama administration but in general the newspaper continued to support the US president's approach to the Syrian conflict. Most *NYT* articles suggest that the United States ought to intervene in Iraq and Syria to defeat ISIS.

Matthieu Aikins, a journalist based in Kabul in 2014, signs the first *NYT* op-ed article worth mentioning. Aikins visited a building in Aleppo (Syria) that had served as headquarters and prison for ISIS until January 2014, when a coalition of oppositional groups expelled the terrorist group from the city. The journalist was accompanied by members of the IF, which had become by then one of the most powerful rebel groups fighting the Syrian regime, outweighing various FSA brigades in fighters, weapons, and resources. The decisive role that IF played in expelling ISIS from Aleppo led some Western officials to believe that the group could be a reliable partner in the fight to contain the Islamic State. Aikins argued that the West should consider this option: "The Islamic Front is entirely Syrian in leadership, and its central goal is overthrowing President Bashar al-Assad—good credentials in the eyes of Western governments hoping to roll back ISIS without strengthening the Syrian regime."[16]

Aikins quoted a former British intelligence official (who remained anonymous) as saying that the FSA was "divided and weak," a statement which implied that Western countries should consider an alliance with other oppositional groups. He was aware of the ideology of the IF's most relevant brigades, as he mentioned that one of its key members, Ahrar al-Sham, had links with al-Qaeda. Ahrar al-Sham emerged in January 2012 as a Salafist group founded by former prisoners of the Syrian regime who had been released in 2011. Its main goals were the overthrow of the Syrian regime and the establishment of a government based on Sharia law. Nevertheless, Aikins's article still frames the group as the best option to serve as a ground force in the fight against ISIS. The former British official was quoted a second time by the journalist, as saying that "the Islamic Front is really the only game in town if you want to attack ISIS in Syria." This article clearly illustrates the new political narrative that would predominate in US foreign policy circles as ISIS emerged as a relevant player in the Syrian conflict. According to this narrative, the fight against the terrorist organization should prevail over the one against the Syrian regime.

Clemens Wergin, in turn, signs an op-ed piece holding President Obama's "deed of omission in Syria" responsible for the emergence of ISIS. In 2014, Wergin was foreign editor of the conservative German newspaper *Die Welt* and a regular contributor for the *NYT* op-ed section. The German journalist described US foreign policy as too "European":

> While Mr. Obama's new style of diplomacy—soft power and nonintervention—was at first seen as a welcome break with the Bush years, five years later a dismal realization has set in. It turns out that soft power cannot replace hard power. On the contrary, soft power is merely a complementary foreign policy tool that can yield results only when it is backed up by real might and the political will to employ it if necessary.[17]

Wergin, an advocate of the 2003 Iraq War, argued that the use of hard power was indispensable for maintaining world stability—he did not specify what he meant by stability. He also claimed that other players, such as Russia, Iran, and the Syrian regime, would fill the void left by the United States in the Middle East.

Wergin's piece is one of the few *NYT* articles that openly criticize the foreign policy pursued by the Obama administration toward the Syrian conflict. The author did not recommend concrete guidelines to deal with "the crisis in Iraq," but his defense of hard power implied that the United States should employ military action against ISIS. Wergin's arguments to oppose President Obama's Syria policy mirrored those of Clinton and McCain, although his article does not advocate that the United States arm and train Syrian rebels, as the two politicians often did. The question that arises is whether Wergin's op-ed represents an outlier in the *NYT* coverage or a change of tone in the newspaper's framing of US foreign policy in Syria. As we will see next, the former seems to be the case.

One day after the publication of Wergin's sharp criticism of the Obama administration, Michael Cohen, a political analyst with links to the Democratic Party, published an op-ed piece titled "Obama's Understated Foreign Policy Gains." Cohen's main argument runs as follows: The Obama administration had achieved significant foreign policy gains in the Middle East and other parts of the world by using "a combination of diplomacy, economic sanctions, and the coercive threat of military force."[18] In Cohen's opinion, these gains would not have been possible had the United States attacked Syria after the 2013 Eastern Ghouta chemical attack. An attack against the Syrian regime back then, Cohen argued, would have imperiled the negotiations of the Iran nuclear deal and the discussions with Russia regarding the Crimea annexation and the armed conflict in Ukraine. The political analyst also listed the chemical weapons agreement with Russia, which led to the destruction of part of Syria's chemical weapons arsenal, as a foreign policy achievement of the Obama administration.

According to Cohen, the Syrian conflict did not exist in isolation and could only be understood in the context of the broader scenario of crises besetting the world in 2014. Therefore, it was imperative to accept the limitations of US power and abandon the "simplistic idea that force is a problem solver" and should constitute the United States' main foreign policy tool. The United States, Cohen continued, "[could] not stop every conflict or change every nefarious regime." It should, instead, adopt "painstaking diplomacy, [seek] multilateral consensus, and [act] with an understanding of its own limitations." Cohen's article amounts to a strong defense of President Obama's foreign policies.

In a book published in 2012, *NYT* journalist and foreign policy commentator David Sanger shared a similar opinion. However, Sanger argued that Obama's "approach to the world" oscillated between "his embrace of working in coalitions to support shared goals, and his willingness to strike unilaterally, and often in secret."[19] He mentioned the Libya intervention as an example of the United States adopting a collaborative attitude and the capture and assassination of Bin Laden as an occasion when the US president acted unilaterally.

On July 6, Jake Flanagin posted a text on *Op-Talk*, a blog hosted by the *NYT*, analyzing the rise of ISIS in Iraq. Although the blog entry is not directly about Syria—the Syrian civil war is mentioned only in passing—its inclusion in this sample stemmed from the fact that the piece reinforces the idea that ISIS should become the United States' priority in the Middle East. Flanagin quoted two Reuters journalists who supported this strategy: "The important objective is the defeat of the Islamic State of Iraq and the Levant (or ISIL), the terrorist group that now controls large swaths of both Syria and Iraq with its extreme brutality, its strong allegiances to an al-Qaeda-like ideology, and its ambitions to do even more damage in the region and beyond."[20]

Apart from framing ISIL as the main concern in the region, the article discusses the future of Iraq, recapping a debate that had been hovering over US foreign policy circles since the beginning of the 2003 Iraq invasion. For some members of the US political elite, Iraq should be divided into three semi-autonomous regions that would form a federation. According to this neocolonial plan, each one of these regions, which would be based on ethnicities or religious sects, would have Sunni, Shiite, and Kurdish majorities. Two of the advocates of the plan were Joe Biden, then-US vice president, and Leslie Gelb, then-president emeritus of the Council on Foreign Relations. Flanagin referred to a 2006 article authored by the two politicians in which they argued, "The Kurdish, Sunni, and Shiite regions would each be responsible for their own domestic laws, administration, and internal security. The central government would control border defense, foreign affairs, and oil revenues. Baghdad would become a federal zone, while densely populated areas of mixed populations would receive both multisectarian and international police protection."[21]

Flanagin mentioned the discussion about the partition of Iraq to argue that the most effective way for the United States to defeat ISIS would be by building alliances with Sunni, Shiite, and Kurdish forces on the ground. Quoting the two Reuters journalists again, Flanagin stated, "In the end, what is needed is a joint campaign plan for defeating the Islamist militants that is developed and supported by the United States, and the region, but led by Iraqi Shiite and Sunni and Kurds."[22] As we can see, the *NYT* journalist seems to believe that the United States should not deploy ground troops to fight ISIS.

In news articles, *NYT* journalists reported on the developments of ISIS on the ground, especially its expansion in Iraq and Syria and how it was rapidly conquering new territory. Hwaida Saad signs a news piece about the capture by ISIS of a Syrian military base in the northern province of Raqqa. During the assault, ISIS militants killed dozens of Syrian government soldiers. According to one of the persons interviewed by Saad, approximately three hundred government soldiers fled the base leaving behind corpses, heavy equipment, weapons, and ammunition. The *NYT* journalist echoed the claims of part of the Syrian opposition that the Assad regime refrained from fighting ISIS in order to allow the group to focus on rebel-controlled territory. Quoting the Syrian Observatory for Human Rights, Saad asserted, "There have long been accusations that Mr. Assad's government— despite its repeated denunciations of its opponents as terrorists—had been secretly collaborating with ISIS and other Islamist organizations to undermine more moderate rebel groups."[23] Besides quoting the Syrian Observatory for Human Rights, Saad spoke to an ISIS combatant who participated in the confrontation (see Figure 4.3).

Three *NYT* articles analyze the attempts by the United Nations to deliver humanitarian aid to civilians in rebel-controlled areas. The articles report on the frictions among the members of the UN Security Council over the issue. Russia and China, two allies of President Bashar al-Assad, pushed for the Syrian regime to have the prerogative to receive and distribute humanitarian aid. The UN Secretary-General Ban Ki-moon and most Security Council members opposed that view, arguing that the Assad regime was preventing humanitarian relief from entering opposition-held areas. In this contentious context, the

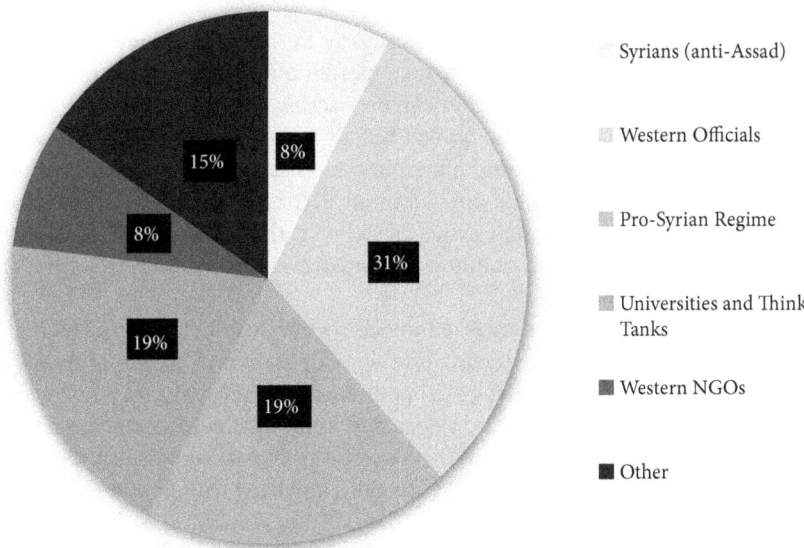

Figure 4.3 Sources in *NYT* articles in period III.

Security Council approved resolution 2165, which allowed UN relief agencies to enter Syria from Turkey, Iraq, and Jordan, and distribute relief supplies in rebel-controlled areas without the Syrian government's supervision. Despite some initial reluctance from China and Russia, the resolution passed unanimously on July 14, 2014.

Somini Sengupta wrote a news article reporting on the tensions that preceded the vote on resolution 2165. The *NYT* journalist quoted Vitaly Churkin, then-Russian ambassador to the United Nations, who complained about the draft text being politicized and leaving "open the possibility of military intervention" in Syria. Sengupta wrote, "Mr. Churkin said last week that he was wary of any language that could suggest justifying military action in Syria. The current draft contains no such explicit suggestion."[24] The approval of resolution 2165 was one of the few occasions on which the UN Security Council acted undivided on the Syrian conflict.

On July 14, the day in which the vote took place, Rick Gladstone published another news piece arguing that the approval of the resolution meant a diplomatic setback for the Syrian regime. The journalist framed the passing of the resolution as a positive measure, mentioning that the previous resolution, which had been approved a few months earlier, in February 2014, had not fulfilled its goals: "The Security Council resolution on Syria passed in February, aimed at allowing the widespread distribution of aid, has been repeatedly subverted or ignored."[25] Gladstone went on to state that Russia and China accepted the resolution on the condition that the United Nations did not respond with military or economic sanctions in case of noncompliance on the part of the Syrian regime. The *NYT* journalist quoted the UN secretary-general and different Western diplomats endorsing resolution 2165.

Sengupta signs the third article that discusses the delivery of humanitarian aid into Syria. This time, the *NYT* journalist reported on the delivery of "food, water purification tablets, and other relief supplies across the Turkish border … into rebel-held areas."[26] Sengupta also quoted Ban Ki-moon, who criticized all warring parties in Syria for "[obstructing] humanitarian assistance to those most in need and [withholding] consent for operations in a completely arbitrary manner."[27] These three articles, which reflect the divisions in the international community regarding the Syrian conflict, reinforce the anti-Assad frame conveyed in the *NYT* coverage in period III.

The last two *NYT* articles analyzed in this section feature the Assad regime as their central topics. The first reports on the inauguration of Bashar al-Assad for his third term as Syrian president. Bashar al-Assad obtained almost 90 percent of the votes in an election considered rigged and unfair by the United States and the European Union. Hwaida Saad and Alan Cowell, the journalists who sign the article, agreed with this view, arguing that the elections had been "closely choreographed" and that Western powers had called it a "sham."[28] In mentioning Bashar al-Assad's speech in the ceremony of inauguration, Saad and Cowell highlighted the parts where he called the opposition "terrorists" and denounced Western countries for sponsoring them.

The second article on the Assad regime focuses on the use of cluster bombs by the Syrian army. Rick Gladstone accused the Syrian regime of using these weapons, which "maim and destroy indiscriminately," on different occasions during the civil war. This article is not only about Syria but about the use of cluster bombs in different conflicts in the world, such as Syria, Ukraine, and South Sudan. It is included in this sample because it focuses mostly on Syria. Gladstone quoted different NGOs and consultancy groups, including Human Rights Watch, the United Nations Mine Action Service, and Armament Research Services, all of them confirming that cluster weapons were being used in these conflicts.

In conclusion, most *NYT* articles in period III relay a pro-Obama sentiment, except for the piece authored by Wergin, which is critical of the US president. In July 2014, the *NYT* coverage of the Syrian conflict is consistent with previous periods in relaying a strong anti-Assad frame. This time, however, an anti-ISIS narrative gained prominence and *NYT* journalists implied that the United States should intervene militarily in Iraq and Syria to defeat the group. In order to accomplish this goal, most journalists argued that Western countries should build alliances with local groups. In period III, *NYT* authors also highlighted the divisions in the UN Security Council regarding the delivery of humanitarian aid in rebel-controlled areas.

The WP *Opposes Arming Local Groups to Fight ISIS*

The *WP* published eleven articles about the Syrian conflict in period III: seven opinion articles, two news pieces, and two editorials. The most recurrent topics are US foreign policy, the Syrian regime, and the Syrian opposition. This highly opinionated coverage is critical of President Obama's policy toward Syria—at least four articles criticize it. Like the *NYT*, most *WP* authors relayed an anti-Assad frame and argued that ISIS should become the US priority in the region. However, the coverage of ISIS is not as extensive in the *WP* as it is in the *NYT* and the *WSJ*. Additionally, *WP* articles depict both the Syrian regime and the Syrian opposition negatively.

Most *WP* columnists saw the Syrian opposition and other regional groups as dominated by Islamist factions, which implied that the United States should confront ISIS on its own, without building alliances with local armies. As previously seen, one *NYT* author (Matthieu Aikins) held that the United States should establish a partnership with the IF against ISIS. The views relayed in *WP* articles in period III resemble those of Wergin, the German journalist who wrote an op-ed article for the *NYT* criticizing President Obama's policy in Syria. Although no *WP* author went as far as blaming the US president's inaction for the emergence of ISIS, most of them demanded a more confrontational attitude against the terrorist organization.

Two *WP* analysts criticized President Obama's strategic views regarding the Middle East. *WP* columnists Marc Thiessen and Dana Milbank sign opinion articles stating that President Obama failed to project US power in a moment of great turbulence in the world. The year 2014 was a convulsive year. Not only did ISIS represent a threat to the stability of the international liberal order but also the civil wars in Syria and Ukraine, the Israeli shelling of Gaza, and the growing tensions in Afghanistan and the South China Sea.

In his article, Thiessen, who served as a speechwriter for President George W. Bush, compared President Obama with Jimmy Carter, a president he thought had left a meager foreign policy legacy:

> [President Obama] is looking like another Carter in the making. Obama has presided over a recent string of disasters that make even Carter look competent. From his failure to enforce his own red line in Syria to the release of five senior Taliban leaders from Guantanamo Bay to the Russian invasion and annexation of Crimea to the implosion of Iraq, the world is on fire—and Obama's foreign policy legacy is in tatters.[29]

Although the *WP* columnist did not state it clearly, he advocated a much more aggressive US foreign policy.

Thiessen's critique encompassed not only the Obama administration's foreign policy but also some of its domestic plans, such as the Affordable Care Act. He used President Obama's health care reform to argue that the then-US President was an advocate of extensive government intervention in public services and other areas of the economy. Also, the *WP* analyst cited a Gallup poll, according to which the majority of the US population had lost faith in the US president.

In another opinion piece, Dana Milbank also criticized Obama's foreign policy in its entirety. The article focuses on refuting a statement from then-White House press secretary Josh Earnest in which he claimed that President Obama "was bringing tranquility to the world."[30] The former press secretary mentioned the disposal of Syria's chemical weapons, John Kerry's mediation of Afghanistan's electoral dispute,[31] and progress in negotiations with China as examples of the Obama administration's role in mitigating international conflicts. To challenge Earnest's statements, the *WP* columnist cited the crises in Syria, Iraq, and Ukraine, among other events, to argue that the world was far from being in a state of tranquility. Milbank claimed that President Obama acted as a "bystander" in light of this turmoil. His article amounts to a sharp critique of President Obama's foreign policy, although it does not address the Syrian conflict specifically.

The *WP* published an editorial that discusses the US president's antiterrorism strategy. The editorial board criticized the idea that the establishment of alliances with "local armies" was the best approach to fight terrorism, especially in countries such as Iraq, where "US-trained forces have allowed much of the country to be overrun by al-Qaeda and Sunni tribal fighters and [appeared] to lack the firepower to prevent the consolidation of a terrorist-ruled state."[32] The *WP* editorial warns about the risk of resources and weapons transferred to these potential partners ending up in the hands of human rights violators or groups that could turn against the United States: "Allowing aid to flow to foreign military units that commit major human rights crimes cannot be in the US interest in any circumstances."

This argument suggests that the United States should attack ISIS directly, without the support of local groups.

However, not all *WP* analysts agreed with this view. Jane Harman, a member of the Wilson Center,[33] wrote an opinion article for the *WP* arguing that the United States lacked a strategic narrative that allowed it to gain the hearts and minds of Middle Eastern peoples. In her view, US policy should not focus exclusively on military intervention: "For every jihadist our airstrikes might kill, left behind are scores of Iraqis and Syrians whose only contact with the United States came by way of a Hellfire missile. Instead, we need a 'track two' surge, a dynamic partnership with Middle Eastern citizens seeking stability, economic growth, and freedom from corruption."[34] Although Harman did not explicitly refer to the Obama administration's Middle Eastern policy, the idea of there being a deficiency in the strategic narrative suggested that she did not agree with the White House's Syria approach. Harman further warned about the United States "losing people to jihad." Her article suggests that military intervention should not be the only focus of US foreign policy and that the United States should look for partners in the region if it wished to reestablish its hegemony. Although she did not discuss ISIS specifically, her views seem to contradict those of Thiessen and Milbank, who maintained instead that the United States ought to attack ISIS.

Fareed Zakaria is a renowned US-based journalist and foreign policy analyst. Besides writing an opinion column for the *WP*, he collaborates with different media outlets, such as *CNN*, *The Atlantic*, and *Foreign Affairs*. Zakaria has

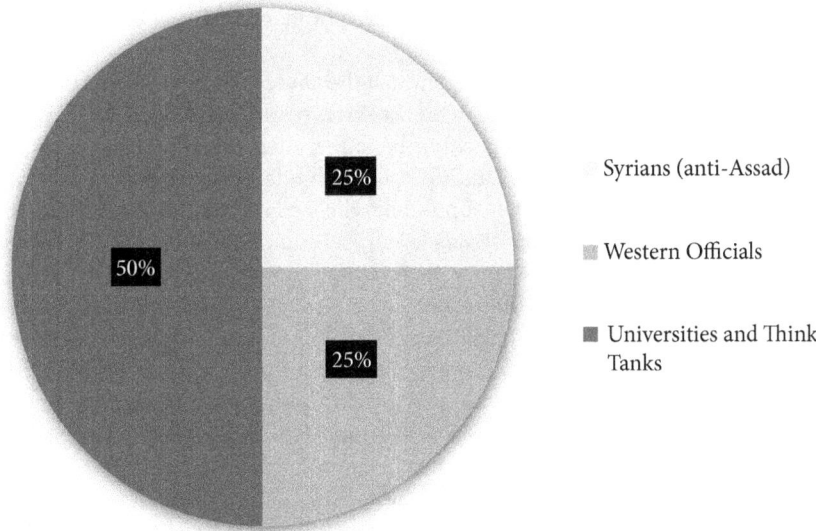

Figure 4.4 Sources in *WP* articles in period III.

authored several books on international relations and US foreign policy. He wrote an opinion piece for the *WP* in July 2014 in which he analyzed the Syrian opposition and opposed the idea that funding rebel groups from the beginning of the uprising would have avoided the emergence of ISIS. Zakaria resisted any plan to fund and train moderate oppositionist groups on the grounds that Islamist factions controlled most of them: "There are about 1,500 separate insurgent groups in Syria, with between 75,000 and 115,000 insurgents. In addition, there are 7,500 foreign fighters from neighboring countries. The strongest groups are all radical Islamist—the Islamic State, Ahrar al-Sham, and Jabhat al-Nusra."[35]

Zakaria went further, claiming that the Syrian opposition had been Islamist for more than three decades, since the Hama uprising in the early 1980s.[36] His article reinforces the argument that the United States should not build alliances with local groups, an idea that prevailed in the *WP* coverage of the Syrian conflict in July 2014. Moreover, by stating that "Syria [had] been unstable from its birth," Zakaria flirted with the Orientalist cliché which characterizes the Middle East as a region immersed in a permanent state of instability due to ethnic and religious conflicts. The *WP* columnist failed to explain the reasons for this alleged instability; he attributed it simply to ethnic and religious divisions: "By the late 1970s, [Syria] was already divided into camps, largely defined by Islamism and sect. Outside powers in the Middle East—Saudi Arabia, Iraq, Iran—have been funding, arming, and training militants on both sides. In 2011, these long-simmering tensions bubbled over."[37] Despite acknowledging that "outside powers" have stoked these divisions, Zakaria conveyed a reductionist view of Syria's history. Since 1970, when Hafez al-Assad became president, Syria has enjoyed periods of relative, despotic stability. Zakaria seems to ignore that aspects such as authoritarianism, colonialism, and Western interventions also played a role in Syria's evolution as a country. Religious and ethnic diversity alone does not constitute a fundamental reason for the failure of a particular state.

Eugene Robinson supported the view that the United States should refrain from arming Syrian rebels. However, unlike Zakaria, he acknowledged the existence of moderate Syrian oppositionists, but he still argued that American arms and resources could end up in the hands of Islamic fundamentalist groups: "Imagine that the Pentagon had given US-supported rebels enough shoulder-fired missiles to seriously threaten the Syrian army's low-flying aircraft, including its helicopters. Imagine that these weapons were captured by the Islamic State. Imagine the grave threat this would pose, not just to allied forces struggling against the Islamic State but potentially to commercial aviation as well."[38] Although Robinson was not as critical of the Obama administration as other *WP* authors, he thought that the US president should have enforced a no-fly zone to prevent the Assad regime from bombing civilians. A no-fly zone was a long-time demand of the Syrian opposition that President Obama always resisted.

In period III, only one *WP* article advocates that the United States should support moderate forces in Syria. Its author, Ray Takeyh, is a member of the Council on Foreign Relations, a prominent, bipartisan US think tank. Takeyh's article focuses on the need to contain Iranian expansionism in the Middle East.

The author argued that the only way to resume the nuclear negotiations with Iran, which in his view were stalled, was through the imposition of more sanctions on the Iranian regime by the United States and the European Union. The imposition of stricter sanctions and the support for moderate opposition groups fighting the Syrian government would, in Takeyh's view, amount to effective policies to offset the Iranian regime: "By aiding reliable rebels in Syria and helping rehabilitate an inclusive order in Iraq, the United States could go a long way toward blunting Iran's surge."[39] Most *WP* authors, however, did not agree with this view, maintaining instead that Islamist groups dominated the Syrian opposition.

WP authors advocated a tough stance on Russia as well, a country that was considered a threat to the stability of the United States and Europe. According to an editorial published on July 30, "[t]he West also should not shrink from the destabilization of Mr. Putin's regime. Once considered a partner, this Kremlin ruler has evolved into a dangerous rogue who threatens the stability and peace of Europe. If he can be undermined through sanctions and the restoration of order in eastern Ukraine, he should be."[40] Whereas the *NYT* echoed President Obama's strategy of rapprochement toward Iran, the *WP* advocated a more aggressive stance on Iran, Russia, and the Syrian regime.

Liz Sly and Ahmed Ramadan wrote a news article overviewing the situation in Syria after the June 3 elections in which Bashar al-Assad won a landslide victory. The journalists quoted experts from two internationally renowned think tanks—the Washington Institute for Near East Policy and the Carnegie Middle East Center[41] (see Figure 4.4). One of the experts was Yezid Sayigh, a distinguished Middle Eastern scholar who has worked for different academic and research institutions. Sayigh claimed that Bashar al-Assad had made substantial gains in the civil war and had reasons to feel confident about the future.[42] Sly and Ramadan quoted the Syrian president as saying in his inauguration ceremony that "Arab, regional, and Western countries, which supported terrorism, will also be paying a high price of their own."[43]

Sly and Ramadan pointed out that the Syrian regime's recent gains in the civil war were attributable primarily to Russia and Iran. The two *WP* journalists also affirmed that the Syrian regime and ISIS rarely clashed on the battlefield—a similar statement can be found in a *NYT* article of the same period. The other expert quoted by Sly and Ramadan, Andrew Tabler, a member of the Washington Institute for Near East Policy, argued that ISIS had become the priority of the White House. It is striking that the Syrian opposition does not appear in the article at all, which suggests that the *WP*'s focus had shifted to ISIS.

In brief, the coverage of the Syrian conflict in July 2014 both in the *NYT* and the *WP* concurs that the United States should consider ISIS the greatest threat to its interests in the region. In addition, the two newspapers relayed anti-Assad frames, although the *WP* also built a negative frame of the Obama administration. Most *WP* authors advocated that the United States should confront ISIS without building alliances with rebels on the ground, which stemmed from the opinion that the Syrian opposition amounted mainly to Islamist groups. *NYT* authors, by contrast, not only relayed a pro-Obama frame but also endorsed the building of alliances with local groups. Lastly, it is noteworthy that the *WP* coverage of the Syrian conflict in period III is more balanced than that of the *NYT*, as it allowed for a greater variety of opinions and a more vibrant debate of ideas.

The WSJ *Blames Obama for the Instability in the Middle East*

The *WSJ* published twenty-one articles in period III, of which seventeen are news pieces and four are op-eds. The *WSJ* coverage of the Syrian conflict in July 2014 is the most extensive among the three newspapers analyzed in this book. The most recurrent topics are US foreign policy, ISIS and the war on terror, the Syrian civil war, and European foreign policy. The *WSJ* relayed both anti-Obama and anti-Assad frames in period III, although the discussion about toppling the Syrian president virtually disappeared. It is worth remembering that in period II, the *WSJ* openly called for the overthrow of Bashar al-Assad. In July 2014, the focus shifted to covering ISIS and discussing the threat of terrorism to world stability.

Various *WSJ* articles in period III examine the role of the United States as a world power. It was almost a consensus among columnists and journalists that US power had receded, and its foreign policy in the Middle East had failed. In an opinion piece published on July 6, for example, Bret Stephens argued that the emergence of ISIS was a consequence of President Obama's reluctance to project US power in the region. For Stephens, the United States could have removed the Syrian president a long time ago:

> The United States could have long ago dispatched Assad with targeted airstrikes. Fearing unforeseen consequences, we did not, and so we got the foreseeable consequence that is Syria and Iraq today. The United States could use Apache gunships to blunt the offensive of ISIS and kill a lot of jihadists. Fearing entanglement we do not, and so we risk acceding to the creation of an Islamic caliphate.[44]

As we can see, Stephens considered the creation of an Islamic caliphate the greatest threat to US interests and blamed the Obama administration for the emergence of ISIS and the turmoil that beset Iraq and Syria.

Another aspect of President Obama's Syria policy discussed in the *WSJ* was the plan announced by the Pentagon in mid-July 2014 to train and equip Syrian rebels to fight ISIS. The Pentagon announced a plan to provide Syrian rebel forces with weapons, intelligence, logistics support, and military advice in July 2014, but the US Congress only approved it in September. Journalists Adam Entous and Julian Barnes sign a news article in which most of the sources criticize the plan for being too limited. Their first paragraph runs as follows: "A Pentagon plan to aid Syrian rebels is emerging as far smaller than advocates hoped, ramping up slowly over an extended period while offering no quick support to moderate fighters, who are losing ground both to the Assad regime and to jihadists."[45]

Entous and Barnes's piece amounts to another excellent example of how the use of sources plays a crucial role in the construction of frames. Throughout the article, the two journalists gave particular emphasis to critics of the plan, such as members of the Syrian opposition and US representatives who opposed it. A few Pentagon officials who supported the plan were quoted by Entous and Barnes, although these voices appear toward the end of the article. In the second paragraph, they went on to state, "Critics inside and outside the administration say the limited steps [that the Obama administration] is taking are too modest to make a difference on the battlefield, reflecting his own and the Pentagon's reluctance to get entrenched in another Middle East conflict." The article suggests that the United States should support moderate Syrian rebels more vigorously. This view, which was shared by politicians like Clinton and McCain, is similar to the one relayed in the *NYT* articles in period III.

In line with the idea that the United States should build alliances on the ground to confront ISIS, Jonathan Foreman, a journalist who covered the Iraq War for the conservative newspaper *New York Post*, published an op-ed in which he advocated that the "West" should support Kurdish independence. Foreman further argued that the United States should build a military base in the Kurdish-Iraqi city of Erbil: "The time has come for America and the West to support Kurdish independence and, simultaneously, to set up US bases in Iraqi Kurdistan that would make it America's military hub in the region."[46] Foreman invited President Obama to break with "past policies and with the State Department's traditional preference for maintaining postcolonial borders." Although this article does not focus on the Syrian conflict, it was included in this sample because it highlights the foreign policy debate about how to confront ISIS. Foreman's article suggests that the *WSJ* sympathized with the idea that the United States should seek regional allies.

The *NYT* also published an opinion piece in period III echoing the idea that the dismemberment of Iraq would be in the interest of the United States. The article, signed by Joe Biden and Leslie Gelb, advocates the partition of Iraq into three countries with Kurdish, Sunni, and Shiite majorities, respectively. These articles illustrate that US foreign policy decision-makers and analysts consider being in a position to discuss the borders of Middle Eastern countries publicly. Interestingly, the authors of both pieces did not even try to hide the fact that keeping US hegemony in the region was their primary concern when suggesting the division of Iraq into different political entities.

Jay Solomon signs a news article arguing that US foreign policy failed to bring stability to the Middle East.[47] The article is mainly about the failed attempt by the United States to organize peace talks between the Israeli government and the Palestinian Authority in 2013/2014. Solomon's piece was published on the second day of the 2014 Gaza War, also known as Operation Protective Edge. Although the *WSJ* journalist did not mention the Israeli attack on Gaza, and that Israeli forces attacked mostly civilian areas, the article implies that the Obama administration is partly to blame for the interruption of the negotiations between Israel and

Palestine and, therefore, for the escalation of the conflict in Gaza. Quoting several US officials, the *WSJ* journalist explained that the United States had shifted its priorities from the Israeli-Palestinian conflict to Syria, Iran, and Ukraine. One of the quoted officials is Aaron Miller, who served as a Mideast peace negotiator in the Clinton and George H. W. Bush administrations. According to him, the United States had lost its credibility as a broker among Middle Eastern state and nonstate actors.

Another news article authored by Solomon, this time in collaboration with Carol Lee, maintains the same line of criticism toward President Obama's foreign policy. The two *WSJ* journalists argued that the world was, in July 2014, living its worst period of turmoil—what they called "security crises"—since the 1970s: "The breadth of global instability now unfolding has not been seen since the late 1970s, US security strategists say, when the Soviet Union invaded Afghanistan, revolutionary Islamists took power in Iran, and Southeast Asia was reeling in the wake of the US exit from Vietnam."[48] The article amounts to a sharp critique of the Obama administration's handling of this "global instability." In the first paragraph, for instance, Solomon and Lee stated that "US global power [seemed] increasingly tenuous."

Since it is a news article (not an op-ed), criticism of President Obama's policy is expressed indirectly, largely by the use of sources expressing concern about US foreign policy. The first two sources cited in the article are John McCain and former Republican Senator Bob Corker, two prominent opponents of the Obama administration. The use of sources in this article is skewed toward critics of the US president. Voices that support the US administration do not appear until halfway through the text and are always countered by voices who criticize President Obama's policy. One expert, for example, compared the US president to a quarterback who did not know how to organize his team.

Solomon and Lee's rationale is that the Obama administration's inaction aggravated the conflicts instead of solving them—a logic that also applies to the Syrian conflict:

> The president's critics in Washington, as well as some diplomats abroad, believe Mr. Obama's policies have fueled today's conflicts. They cite his decision to pull back from wars in Iraq and Afghanistan, his rejection of a more decisive US and allied role in the Syrian civil war, and what they see as his reluctance to provide greater support to American allies in Asia and Europe as they face down the newly aggressive foreign policies of China, Iran, and President Vladimir Putin's Russia.

This article is another example of how sourcing practices affect framing (see Figure 4.5).

WSJ authors also discussed the divisions within the US political establishment regarding the Syrian conflict. Jason Riley, a member of the newspaper's editorial board, wrote an opinion article explaining the differences between Hillary Clinton and President Obama in foreign policy matters. Riley, citing a *WSJ/NBC*

Sources in *WSJ* Articles in Period II

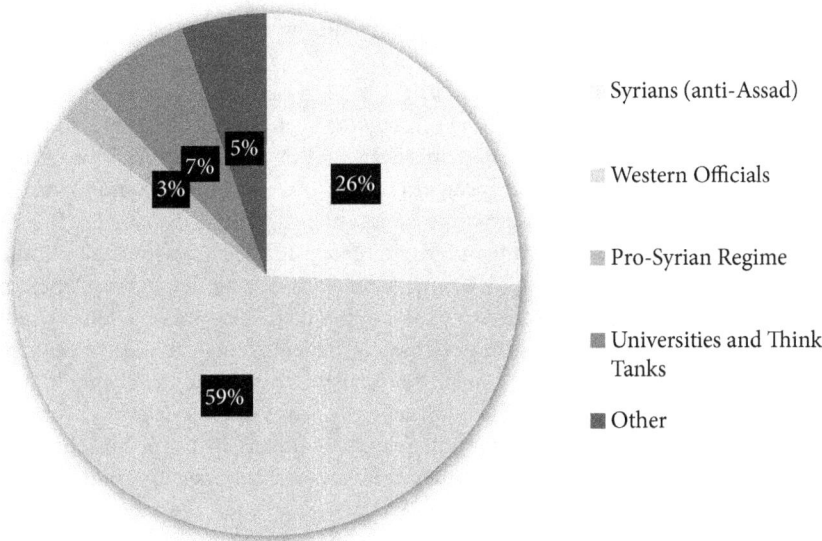

Figure 4.5 Sources in *WSJ* articles in period III.

News poll to corroborate his statement, argued that the US president's falling popularity prompted Clinton to take a position in favor of "a more assertive stance toward global crises."[49] Riley criticized the Republican party as well, stating that "Republicans seem happy to shoot spit balls at the White House over its handling of Iraq, Syria, Russia, Benghazi, Iran and so forth, but they are reluctant to put forth an alternative foreign policy vision." He went further, arguing that some Republicans shared many of President Obama's foreign policy views, even if they did not acknowledge it.

European foreign policy is the topic of two *WSJ* articles in period III. Laurence Norman wrote an article reporting on the European Union's decision to expand the sanctions imposed on Syrian companies and individuals.[50] The article suggests that the European Union should step up the pressure on the Syrian regime as a way to force Bashar al-Assad to resign. In another article about the same topic, Stephen Fidler discussed the imposition of EU sanctions on Russia.[51] Fidler reported on the divisions that surrounded the issue, which, in his view, stemmed from the fact that, in 2014, several European countries had political and economic ties with Russia. According to Fidler, countries such as France, Italy, Germany, and Hungary feared that new sanctions on Russia could backfire and affect the supply of Russian energy to Europe. In turn, other countries saw the sanctions as an essential tool to compel President Vladimir Putin to downgrade Russian interference in countries such as Syria and Ukraine. It is interesting to note the difference regarding how the debate about the imposition of sanctions on Russia unfolded in 2014, in the context of

Russian support to the Syrian regime, and in 2022, in light of the Russian invasion of Ukraine. In 2022, the European Union acted in unison to impose sanctions on Russia as it deemed Ukraine a strategic ally and saw the possibility of a Russian takeover of the country as a security risk.

The second most discussed topic in the *WSJ* in period III is ISIS; at least five articles report on the terrorist group directly or on issues closely related to it. The *WSJ* gave more importance to this topic than the *NYT* and the *WP*. Two of these articles discuss the wave of European citizens who were going to Syria to join the ranks of ISIS. In the first, Andrew Grossman warned about the growing threat of terrorist attacks in the world due to the emergence of ISIS.[52] The journalist argued that the group's "anti-Western ideology" had a considerable impact on American and European young Muslims. On explaining which measures US allies should take to counter the terrorist group, Grossman relied extensively on the opinions of two high-profile US officials—former Attorney General Eric Holder and former FBI Director James Comey. The different measures mentioned by Grossman included the enhancement of surveillance mechanisms in European countries, the implementation of extended border controls, and the sharing of information among intelligence services.

Stacy Meichtry wrote the second piece on the topic, which analyzes how France stepped up efforts to prevent its citizens from joining rebel groups in Syria. Meichtry described the numerous measures that were about to be taken by French authorities to hinder the flow of French citizens to Syria, such as imposing travel bans on "suspected radicals" and blocking jihadist websites. It is worth noting that the *WSJ* journalist depicted the Syrian opposition as dominated by extremist factions. He wrote, "[French] Interior Minister Bernard Cazeneuve ... proposed new obstacles ... to stop French citizens from trying to reach the front lines of the Syrian conflict, where offshoots of al-Qaeda and other Islamist militants have come to dominate the rebel side."[53] The WSJ did not relay a homogeneous frame of the Syrian opposition in period III. Whereas some authors argued that the alliances could be built with some of the groups fighting the Assad regime, others, like Meichtry, advocated that most of these groups were Islamic fundamentalists.

The possibility of terrorist attacks in the United States is the topic of an article written by Siobhan Gorman, a *WSJ* journalist who focuses on terrorism, counterterrorism, and intelligence. The article analyzes a report authored by former members of the National Commission on Terrorist Attacks upon the US, in which they criticized the US government for responding to terrorism inadequately. The commission, also known as 9/11 Commission, was formed in the wake of September 11 and mandated to fulfill two tasks: produce a full account of the facts surrounding the terrorist attacks against the twin towers and provide recommendations to prevent future attacks on American soil. Gorman argued in the article that the United States faced "a growing array of threats, from new terrorist havens to cyberattacks, but the American public [did] not appreciate these dangers and [was] growing complacent."[54] According to the journalist, the authors of the report employed a grim, prophetic tone to describe the situation, claiming that "history may be repeating itself." These three articles suggest that the *WSJ* echoed the view that ISIS should become a priority for the United States.

The two remaining articles, of the five that focused on terrorism and ISIS, report on the history of the Islamic State and its expansion in Iraq and Syria. Maria Abi-Habib signs a news piece that analyzes the group's territorial gains in July 2014. She highlighted that ISIS was in control of a territory that covered over four hundred miles in Syria and Iraq. To illustrate this rapid expansion, Abi-Habib described an ISIS assault on a Syrian military base in Hasakah, a city located in northeastern Syria, which she considered a strategic position: "If the Islamic State militants can seize Hasakah city that will help them to consolidate their control over the major Syrian and Iraqi cities they have occupied on either side of the border. Hasakah sits in the middle of the Islamic State's two centers of power in both Syria and Iraq—Raqqa and Mosul."[55]

Abi-Habib saw the confrontations between ISIS and the Syrian regime as an alteration of the dynamics of the civil war: "A recent surge in fighting between the government and Islamic State is a marked change. The two have rarely faced off on the battlefield, with President Bashar al-Assad's forces generally avoiding the same large-scale offensives it has launched against the Western and Arab-backed Free Syrian Army." The three newspapers analyzed in this book reported on the fact that the Syrian regime and ISIS seldom clashed in the initial stage of the latter's expansion in Syria.

Finally, the fifth *WSJ* article that focuses on ISIS is a long piece on the history and ideology of the terrorist organization, written by veteran war journalist Margaret Coker. The article, which has the suggestive title of "The New Jihad," argues that the Islamic State emerged as the product of the split between two generations of Salafist leaders. Whereas the younger generation, represented by ISIS leader Abu Bakr al-Baghdadi, had developed a more radical view, the older generation of militants remained loyal to Osama bin Laden's ideas. Coker explained,

> Mr. Baghdadi and his followers reject this doctrine of an evolving religious and social consensus. They believe instead that a pure Islamic regime can be more swiftly imposed by force. This basic split has existed for a decade between al-Qaeda and its one-time offshoot in Iraq, which formed after the United States invaded in 2003 and helped establish the first Shiite government in Iraq in centuries.[56]

Coker warned *WSJ* readers that ISIS represented an unprecedented threat to global stability, although she nuanced this opinion by recognizing that the full consequences of its expansion were not yet clear. Like other *WSJ* authors, she seemed particularly concerned about the risk of young European Muslims becoming radicalized through exposure to sectarian ideologies.

In brief, the *WSJ*'s coverage of the Syrian conflict in July 2014 is the most extensive and complete of the three newspapers analyzed herein. It relies more on news pieces than op-eds, and it relays anti-Assad and anti-Obama frames. The critical frame of President Obama is achieved mainly by the use of sources, such as John McCain, that criticized the US president for his passivity in light of the emergence of ISIS. Some commentators even blamed President Obama for the rise of ISIS. Some *WSJ* analysts suggested that the United States should build alliances with local groups, such as the Iraqi Kurds. *WSJ* authors did not pay significant attention to the Syrian opposition, although one article argues that it was dominated by Islamist factions. They focused instead on the security threat that terrorism represented to the United States and the European Union, especially regarding the flow of Western citizens to Syria who could later return and carry out terrorist attacks.

…

The emergence of ISIS in Iraq and Syria ushered in a new phase in the Syrian conflict. Alliances on the ground shifted, as ISIS posed a challenge to both the Syrian regime and rebel groups. On the international level, the rapid expansion of the terrorist group urged the United States and the European Union to adjust their approaches and turn the fight against the group into a priority. The coverage of the Syrian conflict in the *NYT*, the *WP*, and the *WSJ* in July 2014 reflect these changes. This chapter argues that, in period III, the coverage of ISIS gained prominence over other aspects of the conflict; the fewer number of articles about Syria supports this claim. The attention given to ISIS indicates that the narratives around the Global War on Terrorism still wield influence over the editorial boards of the three newspapers analyzed here. As discussed in Chapter 1, there is a quasi-consensus in the literature about the coverage of wars and international conflicts that the US media reproduce governmental narratives about Islamic terrorism almost uncritically.

The three newspapers agreed that the United States should intervene in Syria and Iraq against the Islamic State, although there was no consensus about the specifics of such an intervention. Whereas *NYT* and *WSJ* authors advocated that the United States could build alliances with groups on the ground, such as Syrian rebels and Iraqi Kurds, their colleagues writing for the *WP* were more reluctant about such alliances. In fact, the coverage of the Syrian opposition in the *WP* was negative, with most authors holding that it was formed almost exclusively by Islamist groups. In the *WSJ*, rebel groups did not receive the same attention as in the *NYT* and the *WP*.

In period III, the three newspapers maintained anti-Assad frames, although calls for the overthrow of the Syrian dictator virtually disappeared from their narratives. The coverage in the *WP* is more balanced than in the *NYT* and the *WSJ* in that it presented a wider variety of opinions about US foreign policy. The *NYT* shared a pro-Obama frame, while the other two newspapers were consistent in framing President Obama's foreign policy negatively. This aspect did not change in comparison to periods I and II. The coverage in the *WSJ* is the most complete, as it covered more topics than the *NYT* and the *WP*. A facet of the *WSJ* coverage is the importance given to the threat of terrorism to the United States and Europe.

Chapter 5

THE BEGINNING OF THE RUSSIAN INTERVENTION IN SYRIA (PERIOD IV)

In September 2015, the Assad regime was on a tightrope, facing challenges from multiple opponents. President Bashar al-Assad had not found himself in such a difficult position since 2013, when the Lebanese Hezbollah came to his rescue, assuming a more direct combat role in the civil war. The Syrian regime was accumulating defeats on the battlefield. Jaish al-Fatah (Army of Conquest), an alliance of rebel groups including the al-Nusra Front, Ahrah al-Sham, and several FSA brigades, captured the northwestern city of Idlib in March 2015. Ahrar al-Sham was a Salafist organization that emerged in January 2012, founded by Syrian Islamists who had been released from prison in 2011 following al-Assad's general amnesty. Most of its founders had been active in the anti-US insurgency in Iraq. The group's leadership advocated the establishment of an Islamic State in Syria, which would follow similar principles to those of the Islamic Republic of Iran, with Sharia law as its base, but governed by elected officials. Unlike other Salafist organizations active in the Syrian civil war, such as the al-Nusra Front and ISIS, Ahrar al-Sham claimed to operate only within Syria.

In May 2015, ISIS seized the ancient city of Palmyra in the Syrian desert, after a two-month fight with the Syrian army, and in June, the FSA's Southern Front—a coalition of moderate brigades including some supported by the CIA—took control of an important military base in the southern province of Daraa.

While the Syrian government faced human resource shortages and dissent from its ranks, opposition groups showed greater political and military coordination, which compelled Assad forces to retreat and defend its most important strongholds, such as the center of Damascus and parts of Aleppo. Charles Lister, a scholar at the Middle East Institute, described the situation as if the Syrian regime fought for its survival: "Frustration, disaffection, and even incidences of protest are rising across al-Assad's most ardent areas of support on Syria's coast—some of which are now under direct attack. Hezbollah is stretched thin and even Iranian forces have begun withdrawing to the areas of Syria deemed to be the most important for regime survival."[1] While the belief that the Assad regime was close to collapse was not consensual among observers, nearly everyone agreed that the situation for the Syrian president was extremely complicated.

The Syrian refugee crisis, which had been a relentless humanitarian problem since the beginning of the armed conflict, added more turmoil to the Syrian situation. In

2015, with tens of thousands of refugees reaching European shores from Turkey, the crisis attained a global dimension. Up until the summer of 2015, most Syrian refugees had settled in Turkey, Lebanon, or Jordan, making it a primarily regional problem. Nonetheless, from July 2015, a growing number of refugees and migrants decided to make their way into Europe, triggering what several commentators dubbed the worst refugee crisis on the continent since the Second World War. William Spindler, the spokesperson of the UN Refugee Agency, summarized the extent of the humanitarian disaster, claiming that "911,000 refugees and migrants had arrived on European shores since the year [2015] began and some 3,550 lives had been lost during the journey."[2] The majority of these refugees were Syrians, though many also came from Afghanistan, Iraq, and other countries.

The wave of refugees arriving in Europe, and the significant amount of media coverage they received, changed the way most Western countries assessed the Syrian conflict. *NYT* journalist Somini Sengupta captured the new sentiment of EU elites: "The rush of migrants into Europe, combined with the continent's fear that Islamic State (IS) fighters may cross porous borders to carry out attacks, has stirred new urgency among Western leaders to address the war in Syria and push harder for an end to it."[3]

As discussed in the previous chapter, the emergence of ISIS prompted several world leaders to change their calculations about the Syrian conflict, especially regarding al-Assad's role in a possible political transition. The escalation of the refugee crisis in 2015 reinforced the idea that the Syrian president was the lesser evil: an "undesired guest" that Western leaders ought to tolerate. Despite maintaining an anti-Assad discourse, the United States and the European Union were more concerned about containing ISIS and finding a political solution to the conflict than about pushing for regime change. In this context, they expressed their willingness to collaborate with Russia, the Syrian regime's most important supporter, and even Iran. The Russian military buildup in Syria and the subsequent intervention occurred against this intricate backdrop.

On September 30, 2015, Russian warplanes started a bombing campaign in Syria. The operation consisted of the deployment of Russian aircraft to the Hmeimim Air Base, built in 2015 in the province of Latakia, and the country's Northern Fleet to the Syrian coast. According to the Russian Defense Ministry, the country's aircraft "flew 420 combat missions, ... striking 1,252 targets from September 2015 to March 2017."[4] Christopher Phillips stated that "at least twenty-eight [Russian] planes were dispatched [to Syria], along with up to two thousand personnel, while Russia's Black Sea Fleet was sent to the eastern Mediterranean."[5] Unquestionably, the Russian intervention turned the tide in the Syrian civil war in favor of the Assad regime; for some, it was the determining factor, eliminating any hope of a rebel victory against Assad forces. The aerial bombings of rebel positions were followed by a ground offensive led by the Iranian Revolutionary Guard (IRGC) and Hezbollah militias against opposition forces in Idlib, northern Hama province, Daraa, Latakia, and Homs.[6]

Russian President Vladimir Putin framed the military campaign as part of the fight against ISIS and other terrorist groups, although the operation, at least at the outset, targeted mainly moderate opposition groups and civilians in rebel-held areas. A few days before the operation began, during his speech before the UN General Assembly, the Russian president had called for an international coalition against ISIS. He also defended the Syrian president, saying that he was a reliable partner in the fight against the Islamic State. President Obama, on his part, reaffirmed in his speech before the UN General Assembly his willingness to work with Russia to contain ISIS, although he defended al-Assad's removal from power. President Obama's actual words were, "The United States is prepared to work with any nation, including Russia and Iran, to resolve the [Syrian] conflict. But we must recognize that there cannot be, after so much bloodshed, so much carnage, a return to the pre-war status quo."[7]

The agendas of the United States and Russia in Syria were different, but not incompatible, as some implied. Whereas the United States (and the European Union) prioritized the defeat of ISIS, Russia and its allies were more concerned with shoring up the Syrian regime. Gilbert Achcar argued that President Obama's attitude in the face of the Russian intervention gave Russia *carte blanche* in Syria. The Lebanese professor wrote, "By condoning Russia's reinforcement of the regime, and showing more and more inclination to retreat from previous Western insistence that al-Assad must step down and cede power as an indispensable precondition for a political settlement … Washington and its Western allies [were] only encouraging al-Assad to stick to his post, and Russia and Iran to stick to al-Assad."[8] Achcar went further to argue that both President Obama and President Putin shared the view that the Syrian state should not be allowed to collapse, as had happened in Libya after Muammar Gaddafi's ousting in 2011.[9]

Once Russian involvement in the Syrian civil war became a *fait accompli*, the United States initiated an effort to deconflict Russian forces operating in the Syrian airspace. Immediately after the first Russian bombs fell on Syrian soil, then-US Secretary of State John Kerry met with Russian Foreign Minister Sergei Lavrov to negotiate a de-escalation. The European refugee crisis and the Russian intervention prompted the United States and the European Union to seek arrangements with Russia to find a political solution to the Syrian civil war.

More importantly, the Russian intervention indicated that the United States had lost its position as the single hegemon in the Middle East. After their defeat in Iraq and failed intervention in Libya, the United States and its closest allies faced more resistance from other countries, such as Russia and China, when trying to interfere in the region's political affairs. Despite this resistance, President Obama opted to keep the level of confrontation with Russia to a minimum. In an interview with Jeffrey Goldberg published in *The Atlantic*, the US president explained why he refrained from trying to "shape the Syria situation." President Obama said,

> Any president who was thoughtful … would recognize that after over a decade of war, with obligations that are still to this day requiring great amounts of resources and attention in Afghanistan, with the experience of Iraq, with the strains that it is placed on our military—any thoughtful president would hesitate about making a renewed commitment in the exact same region of the world with some of the exact same dynamics and the same probability of an unsatisfactory outcome.[10]

The US president could not have been more straightforward; he had no intention of responding to the Russian air offensive with military force.

A heated debate within the US political establishment followed President Obama's limited response to the Russian intervention. For instance, John Kerry openly advocated that the United States ought to carry out sporadic attacks against Syrian positions to force Russia, Iran, and Syria to the negotiating table. John McCain, in turn, accused the US president of accepting Russia's role in Syria and Bashar al-Assad's brutal actions against the Syrian people. Hillary Clinton, then a presidential candidate for the Democratic Party, defended the creation of a no-fly zone and humanitarian corridors to protect civilians and anti-Assad moderate rebels.

This debate, which did not follow a "Democrat versus Republican" line, brings us to the broader question of US foreign policy toward Russia. British historian Perry Anderson argued that "the field divides between advocates of containment and apostles of co-option."[11] Although President Obama was seemingly an "apostle of co-option," the number of voices advocating a more combative policy toward Russia has been growing ever since. For example, Robert Blackwill and Philip Gordon argued that the "United States [needed] to confront Russia more forcefully."[12] Blackwill served as deputy national security adviser for strategic planning in the George W. Bush administration. Gordon, in turn, worked as special assistant to the president during the Obama administration. Both former officials wrote in January 2018, "Washington needs to impose real costs on Moscow, while also enhancing defences against future attacks and bolstering its military commitment to European allies most threatened by Moscow's aggressive posture."[13]

Some analysts saw President Obama's approach to Russia above all as a pragmatic foreign policy, one from a president unwilling to take unnecessary risks in countries deemed secondary for US national security. Regardless of whether the US president was a pragmatist or not, the Russian intervention underscored once again the divisions within the US political establishment over the Syrian conflict. Another consequence of Russia's bombing campaign was that it prompted the Obama administration to step up its support of Syrian-Kurdish militias fighting the Islamic State. The previous programs to support and train Syrian rebels—one CIA program to arm moderate groups fighting the Assad regime and one Pentagon program to arm Syrian rebels fighting ISIS—had been ineffective and faced sharp criticism. In October 2015, the Syrian Democratic Forces (SDF), which consisted mainly of Kurdish and Arab militias fighting ISIS, was established, receiving immediate endorsement from the United States.

But why did Putin intervene so resolutely in support of the Assad regime? A combination of reasons explains his decision to authorize the first direct Russian military operation abroad since the Soviet invasion of Afghanistan in 1979. First, Syria was a long-time Russian client, the relationship between the two countries dating back to Cold War times. Russia and Syria had always maintained a robust commercial relation, especially in the arms trade. Between 2007 and 2011, for example, Russia supplied 72 percent of all Syrian arms imports. Second, Syria hosts the only Russian naval base in the Mediterranean, located in the province of Tartus, and President Putin was unwilling to lose it in the event of a rebel victory.

Third, in the Russian president's view, the vacuum left by the United States in Syria presented a unique opportunity for Russia to expand its influence in the Middle East. Putin used the failed NATO-led Libya intervention and the fact that al-Assad requested support from Russia as political justification for his bombing campaign in Syria. In March 2011, Russia had abstained on UN Security Council Resolution 1973, which authorized the use of "all necessary means" to protect civilians from the Libyan regime, later expressing serious reservations about it being used to promote regime change. Russia wanted to ensure that the Syrian president did not face the same fate as his Libyan counterpart Gaddafi, who had been killed by Libyan rebels in October 2011 during the Battle of Sirte.

The fourth reason that explains the Russian intervention relates to the fact that President Putin saw the military operation in Syria as an opportunity to gain legitimacy domestically, lift the national morale, and further isolate his internal opponents. Finally, the Russian president would never have proceeded with the operation in Syria had he not been convinced that the United States would not retaliate. Despite some observers predicting that the intervention could become Russia's "new Afghanistan,"[14] it arguably succeeded in its foremost objective of maintaining al-Assad in power.

Period IV comprises seven days, from September 28 to October 4, 2015. The number of articles amounts to ninety-five, of which twenty-seven appeared in the *NYT*, thirty-three in the *WP*, and thirty-five in the *WSJ* (see Table 5.1). The most common journalistic genres are news articles (sixty-four), followed by opinion pieces (twenty-one), and editorials (five). Sixty-three authors sign pieces in period IV; forty-one men and twenty-two women. The two most important topics and subtopics are US foreign policy and Russian foreign policy.

Other topics and subtopics, such as the civil war and the refugee crisis, appear in the articles analyzed in period IV, but those above constitute the overwhelming majority. The relationship between the United States and Russia dominates the coverage of the Syrian conflict in period IV. This period starts on September 28, rather than on September 30 when the intervention began, because both the

Table 5.1 Number of articles per newspaper and genre in period IV

Period IV	NYT	WP	WSJ	Totals
News	14	22	28	64
Opinion	7	7	7	21
Editorial	2	3	0	5
News Analysis	2	0	0	2
Background	2	0	0	2
Interview	0	1	0	1
Totals	27	33	35	95

US and the Russian presidents delivered their speeches before the UN General Assembly on that day, generating a significant amount of media coverage. The three newspapers covered the friction between the two leaders with great interest. They also focused on the preparations for the intervention and the first days of the Russian attacks in Syria.

The NYT Highlights the Contradictions of Obama's Policies

The *NYT* published twenty-seven articles in period IV, of which fourteen are news articles, seven are opinion pieces, two are editorials, two are background analyses, and two are news analyses. The most relevant topics and subtopics are US foreign policy, Russian foreign policy, and the refugee crisis. In period IV, the newspaper continued to relay a pro-Obama frame, but the Russian intervention and the flaws of the train-and-equip programs spurred *NYT* authors to point out the contradictions in President Obama's Syria policy. For example, the newspaper's editorial board claimed that the US president lacked a strategy in Syria;[15] in another editorial, it was pointed out that his policy to equip and train Syrian rebels had failed.[16]

On one side, the *NYT* depicted Russia, ISIS, and the Assad regime in negative terms; on the other, it framed Kurdish groups positively, describing them as the most reliable partners in the fight against ISIS. The Syrian opposition nearly disappeared from the newspaper's coverage of the Syrian conflict in October 2015, although Syrian rebels are quoted denouncing the Russian bombing campaign. The Russian intervention prompted the *NYT* to discuss the relationship between the United States and Russia in detail. The newspaper also gave considerable coverage to the divisions within the Democratic Party, particularly the debate between President Obama and former secretaries of state John Kerry and Hillary Clinton.

On September 28, presidents Obama and Putin laid out before the UN General Assembly their views of the Syrian conflict and the role of the Syrian President Bashar al-Assad in a possible political settlement. The three newspapers analyzed in this book focused mostly on the disagreements between the two leaders. However, several *NYT* journalists noted that despite the differences, there was sufficient common ground for a compromise regarding the fight against the Islamic State.

An editorial published on September 28 emphasize that the United States and Russia ought to engage in negotiations to avoid the collapse of the Syrian state: "There should be grounds for a political compromise [between the United States and Russia]. As the American invasion of Iraq showed, destroying state institutions leads to chaos. Every effort should thus be made to ensure that institutions in Syria continue to function once Mr. al-Assad is moved out of the government."[17] The *NYT* editorial board endorsed President Obama's policy, although it did not ignore that his attempts to "create a proxy force" on the ground had failed. In another article, Michael Gordon, who was chief military correspondent for the *NYT* at the time, and Gardiner Harris, a journalist who covers international diplomacy, quoted President Obama and Secretary Kerry assuring that the United States was ready to negotiate with Russia and Iran to find a solution to the conflict.[18]

When Russia finally launched a military campaign in Syria, several authors pointed out that the Russian aircraft targeted mainly moderate anti-Assad rebels, not ISIS, contrary to President Putin's avowal. Most of these articles focus on the reactions of US officials, who were critical of Russia, but they also relay the opinion of rebel leaders, who, in turn, criticized the United States for "allowing" Russia to attack them. *NYT* journalist Anne Barnard, who was based in Beirut at the time, quoted one activist from Homs as saying, "Russia is an accomplice in al-Assad's crimes today, with approval from both the United States and the international community to kill us."[19] The activist went on to presage, "If these raids continue this way, Russia will kill a larger number of civilians than Bashar did in four years."

In another article, Barnard and Andrew Kramer pointed out that Pentagon officials had held a deconfliction meeting with Russian officials and that John Kerry had made clear to Foreign Minister Lavrov that Russia should limit its attacks to ISIS strongholds. The two journalists further argued that US policy in Syria was ambiguous: "The Army of Conquest itself embodies the ambivalence of American policy. The United States considers the al-Nusra Front a terrorist organization, but other groups, including some that have received American funding, fight alongside the al-Nusra Front, saying that they have no choice if they want to unseat Mr. al-Assad."[20] In October 2015, the al-Nusra Front, which still claimed to be al-Qaida's branch in Syria, was part of the Army of Conquest (Jaish al-Fatah). Some groups that received US support fought alongside them. Barnard and Kramer seem to agree with the *NYT* editorial board on the assessment that US policy to train and equip Syrian rebels had failed.

In periods I, II, and III, the *NYT* supported President Obama's Syria policy almost uncritically. This overall assessment remains valid in period IV, but during this period, *NYT* authors felt compelled to identify more clearly the contradictions of the US president's plan. The Russian intervention amplified these contradictions in a way that made them difficult to overlook. On one occasion, the editorial board claimed that "despite American-led airstrikes, the administration [had] no real strategy for Syria."[21] It is the first time so far in this book that such strong as well as negative language had been used by the *NYT* editorial board to describe President Obama's policy. As the situation in Syria became more complicated, the *NYT* struggled to propose a coherent policy. The editorial above did not go beyond the general suggestion that the US president work with "America's partners on a unified response to Russia's moves and seek a way to end the war." As we will see in the following sections, both the *WP* and the *WSJ* proposed explicit policies to handle the situation.

Peter Baker, the *NYT* White House correspondent at the time, echoed the idea that the US campaign to contain ISIS had been unsuccessful. Baker quoted some of President Obama's "aides" explaining what the US strategic interests in the conflict were: "As disturbing as the destruction in Syria has been, aides said Mr. Obama's main priority was to safeguard American interests, leaving him willing to take direct action against the Islamic State but not Mr. al-Assad's government."[22]

President Obama's response to the Russian intervention reinforced the notion that his priority had long shifted from confronting al-Assad to containing ISIS. His apparently timid reaction intensified the divisions within the US political establishment, which the *NYT* reported in detail. As a newspaper with links to the Democratic Party, the *NYT* gave special attention to the debates involving President Obama, John Kerry, and Hillary Clinton. Baker continued his article outlining the differences between the US president and Kerry: "The distinction between [President Obama's] approach and Mr. Kerry's has played out in a variety of areas, including Middle East peace talks and nuclear negotiations with Iran. White House officials give Mr. Kerry plenty of latitude to pursue deals they do not view as likely to come to fruition, while keeping a distance."[23] According to Baker, US officials close to the US president saw Kerry as an idealist, as someone who relied extensively on diplomacy. As previously mentioned, President Obama was often depicted as a pragmatist and down-to-earth politician, not willing to engage in negotiations unlikely to succeed.

Baker signs another article, this time about the discrepancies between the US president and Clinton, in which he pointed out that the then-Democratic presidential candidate had opposed President Obama's views on Syria since her tenure as secretary of state. Baker wrote, "As secretary, [Clinton] was there next to Mr. Obama and offered a different prescription then as well, long before she was a candidate. As secretary, she joined with David Petraeus, then the CIA director, and Leon Panetta, then the defense secretary, to push a plan to arm and train moderate Syrian rebels."[24] That Baker reported on these debates in such detail reveals an interest in the divergences inside President Obama's inner circle and in the Democratic Party. This interest is also seen in the *NYT* coverage of the Eastern Ghouta chemical attack, discussed in Chapter 3.

Ross Douthat, a senior *NYT* columnist, analyzed the reasons that led President Putin to give the green light to a military campaign in Syria. Douthat laid out the same argument as President Obama, stating that the Russian president's decision to intervene was a sign of weakness rather than of strength. For the *NYT* columnist, President Putin felt cornered by the Ukrainian crisis and the possibility of al-Assad losing the war. Douthat also saw the Russian intervention as an indication that US influence in the Middle East had reached a new low: "[Putin's] Syrian machinations … have helped prove that America's 'al-Assad must go' line is just empty bluster, and that a regime can cross Washington's red lines and endure."[25]

Even Thomas Friedman, one of President Obama's most ardent advocates, accepted that US policy had shortcomings, although he argued that the US president was not the one to blame for them. Friedman argued that President Obama kept "getting pummeled into" pursuing the wrong policies in Syria, but he did not specify who "pummeled" the US president.[26] In light of the Russian intervention, the *NYT* columnist prescribed a "wait-and-see" policy, as he seemed confident that Syria would become a quagmire for Russia, a scenario from which the United States could benefit. He also stated that there were no moderate Syrian rebels, suggesting (somewhat ironically) that the United States would have to forge them. Friedman joined the majority of commentators arguing that the defeat of ISIS should be the number one priority for the United States.

Using an ironic tone again, Friedman further argued that democracy would only thrive in Syria if the United States helped to nurture it: "If we want something better—multisectarian democracy in Syria soon—we would have to go in and build it ourselves. The notion that it would only take arming more Syrian moderates is insane."[27] This statement attests that Friedman not only essentialized the sectarian component of the Syrian society (it is not clear what he meant by "multisectarian democracy"), he also implied that democracy-building amounts to a legitimate objective of US foreign policy. This view reiterates the Orientalist cliché, according to which Middle Eastern peoples are incapable of building democratic institutions by themselves.

Four *NYT* articles discuss the reasons for and possible outcomes of the Russian intervention. The journalists who sign these articles focused mainly on how the intervention would affect the Middle Eastern geopolitical balance. They all agreed that the Russian president's primary goal was not only to protect the Syrian regime and prolong its existence but also to project Russian power in the region. For example, Barnard and Neil MacFarquhar quoted one Russian expert explaining that President Putin intended to project Russia as a relevant international player, and that establishing a military presence in Syria would help him to achieve this goal.

Barnard and MacFarquhar further argued that it would be difficult for Russia to defeat the anti-Assad rebels and that President Putin's move might prompt a large number of rebels to radicalize and join extremist groups:

> Russia remembers its own disastrous battle with Islamist insurgents—American-backed groups that over time spawned al-Qaeda—in the 1980s in Afghanistan. And fears that the strikes would further radicalize people seemed to be coming true … as one previously independent Islamist brigade declared its allegiance to the al-Nusra Front, saying unity was necessary because America and Russia were allied against Muslims.[28]

The *NYT* journalists did not provide details about the "independent Islamist brigade" that they referred to.

Sengupta signs a news piece reporting on a press conference by Foreign Minister Lavrov in which he explained that Russia intervened in Syria because al-Assad had asked for assistance to fight ISIS and "other terrorist groups." The article constitutes an accurate summary of the Russian government's narrative regarding the intervention in Syria. According to Sengupta, "Moscow's position then—and now—is that any military action on a country's territory should be done with the consent of that country's legitimate government. In the case of Syria, the Russian government considers President Bashar al-Assad to be the sovereign authority."[29]

As the Russian intervention in Syria demonstrated, Lavrov used the expression "other terrorist groups" to refer to any group opposed to the Assad regime.

On a different note, Steven Myers signs a news analysis that unpacks President Putin's ideology. Myers recounted the Russian president's trajectory as an official of the KGB, the Soviet Union's main security agency, who made his way to becoming the most powerful person in the country.[30] The *NYT* journalist argued that President Putin's years as a young official in East Germany during the 1989 Peaceful Revolution played a decisive role in forging his political views, which are strongly influenced by the idea that the United States and Europe share a foreign policy that is based on violating the sovereignty of nations and creating revolutions aimed at bringing political change in specific countries. For the Russian president, Myers continued, the mass demonstrations in Syria in March 2011 had been orchestrated by Western powers interested in destabilizing a hostile government.

As mentioned, the Russian intervention in the Syrian conflict occurred amid the refugee crisis that befell Europe in the summer of 2015 and affected its foreign policy in different ways. Most importantly, the crisis prompted EU leaders to soften their attitude toward the Syrian president. Reaching a political agreement to end the conflict became a priority for the European Union, as Sengupta argued.[31] The *NYT* journalist quoted EU officials—which included members of the German and French foreign offices—expressing their willingness to negotiate with Russia and Turkey (see Figure 5.1 for a more detailed breakdown of the sources used in the *NYT* articles in period IV).

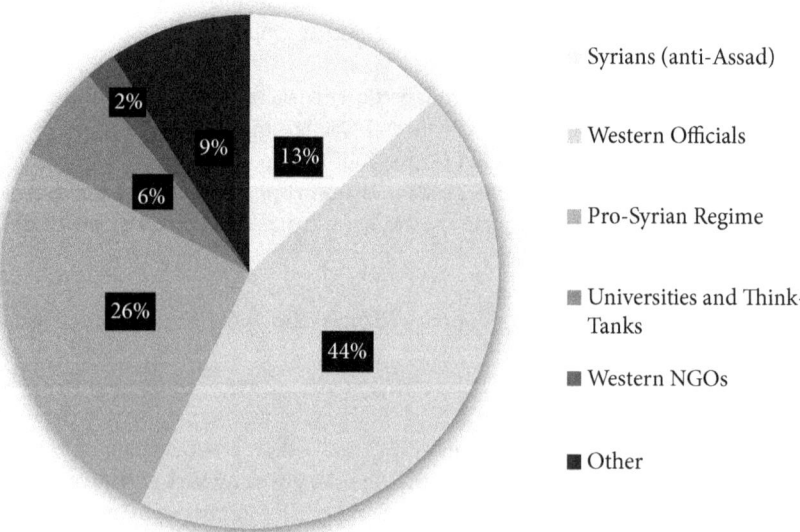

Figure 5.1 Sources in *NYT* articles in period IV.

5. The Beginning of the Russian Intervention   111

The *NYT* published an opinion piece by Sinan Ulgen, at the time a member of the Istanbul-based EDAM think tank, in which he advocated for greater engagement between Europe and Turkey to solve the refugee crisis. Ulgen argued that Turkish President Recep Tayyip Erdoğan wished to negotiate with the European Union, although he would demand something in return: "[The European Union] desperately needs Turkey to improve its border security in order to stem the further outflow of refugees. The only incentive that will ensure Turkey's long-term cooperation is visa-free travel for its own citizens."[32]

In period IV, the *NYT* relayed a positive frame of the Kurdish militias that had been active since the beginning of the conflict and played an important part in the fight against ISIS. Baker and MacFarquhar quoted President Obama saying that the program to arm Syrian rebels had failed and that the United States would move on to work more closely with "Kurdish allies who have enjoyed some success against the Islamic State."[33] On a similar note, Carne Ross, a former British diplomat, signs an opinion piece about the autonomous region of Rojava[34] in eastern Syria. She claimed that the Kurdish militias that controlled the region ran an experiment in direct democracy in which women were treated equally to men, and hierarchies had been abolished.[35] The former diplomat praised this political system as an exception in the Middle East and urged the West to support it unequivocally. The idea of a "Kurdish exceptionalism," as if Kurds (especially the Kurdish communities in Syria and Iraq) were different and superior to other peoples in the region, is popular among Western politicians and scholars. As mentioned, the *NYT* did not pay particular attention to the rest of the Syrian opposition. Only one article briefly discusses Jaish al-Fatah, portraying it as a coalition of moderate and Islamist groups.

In brief, the *NYT* continued to relay a pro-Obama frame in period IV, although during this time, *NYT* authors laid some emphasis on the setbacks of the US president's Syria policy. The newspaper also focused on the divisions within the US political establishment, particularly the debates inside the Democratic Party. The relationship between the United States and Russia occupies a prominent place in the *NYT* coverage of the Syrian conflict in period IV. However, the newspaper refrained from suggesting clear policies regarding how the United States should act in light of the Russian intervention. It did not go beyond affirming that the United States should engage in deconfliction talks with Russia. One columnist suggested a wait-and-see policy as the best approach. As we will see next, the *WP* and the *WSJ* proposed a number of policies.

The WP *Claims That Obama's Policies Failed*

The *WP* published thirty-three articles in period IV. Twenty-two are news articles, seven are opinion pieces, three are editorials, and one is an interview with Federica Mogherini, who was at the time the EU head of foreign affairs and security policy. The most recurrent topics and subtopics discussed in these articles are US foreign policy and Russian foreign policy.

The *WP* relayed a negative frame of President Obama, holding him responsible for the tumultuous situation in Syria and urging the US president to take more decisive action against ISIS, Russia, and the Syrian regime. Most *WP* authors concurred that President Obama's approach was partly to blame for the United States' decreasing influence in the Middle East. Like the *NYT*, the *WP* also analyzed the relationship between the United States and Russia and the divisions inside the Democratic Party. This section focuses on US and Russian foreign policy, although other topics are tackled in the *WP* during period IV.

The *WP* was more critical than the *NYT* of Obama's Syria policy. In news articles, *WP* journalists built this critical frame by relying on sources who assessed US policies negatively (see Figure 5.2). The journalists also relayed this negative frame by covering and highlighting the dissent inside the Obama administration. In op-ed articles, by contrast, criticism was leveled directly by authors who challenged the US administration and suggested alternative plans. The negative frame with which the newspaper portrayed the Obama administration's policy amounted to the most evident difference between the coverage of the Syrian conflict in the *WP* and the *NYT* in period IV. For example, the *WP* editorial board asserted that the US president lacked a strategy to promote democracy and "respect for universal values" in Syria. The editorial board also implied that the lack of support for moderate Syrian rebels paved the way for the conflict's sectarianization: "Mr. Obama failed to lend timely, effective support to Syria's

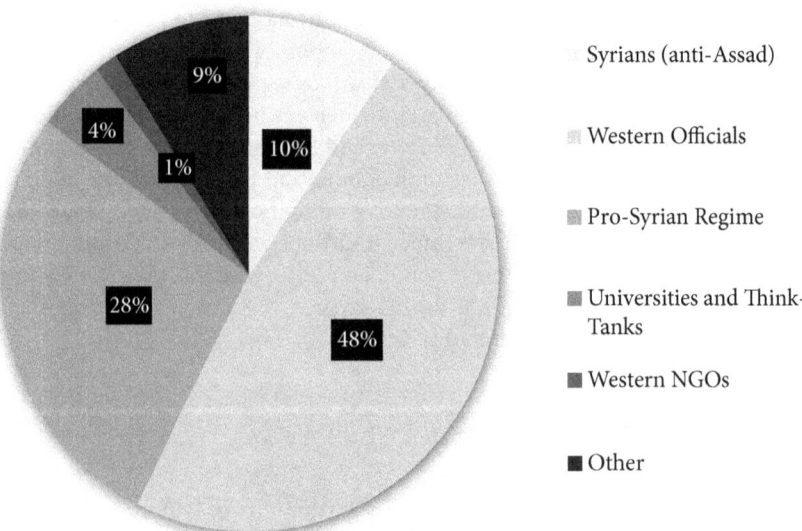

Figure 5.2 Sources in *WP* articles in period IV.

rebellion before extremists took it over. Then he laid down a blurry 'red line' against Mr. Assad's chemical weapons use, threatening to enforce it with airstrikes before backing down in return for a Russian-brokered disarmament deal that kept Mr. Assad in power."[36]

Fareed Zakaria expressed a similar view, claiming that the most evident difference between presidents Obama and Putin was that the Russian leader had an unambiguous Syria policy. The *WP* columnist argued that the United States would have to engage more actively in Syria if it intended to build democratic institutions: "If Obama's goal is a peaceful, stable, multisectarian democracy, then it requires a vast US commitment on the scale of the Iraq war. If not, Washington has to accept reality and make some hard decisions. The two big ones are whether to stop opposing al-Assad and whether to accept that Syria is going to be partitioned."[37] Like the *WP* editorial board, Zakaria held that the Syrian opposition was formed mostly by jihadists, an idea which led him to conclude that it would be best if Bashar al-Assad stayed in power: "If Assad falls and jihadis take Damascus, that would be worse than if Assad stays." Zakaria and the *WP* editorial board seem to agree that democracy building is a legitimate principle of US foreign policy. As shown in the previous section, *NYT* columnist Thomas Friedman shares this view as well.

Not only did *WP* authors reproach President Obama's lack of a coherent Syria strategy, but they also claimed that his policy had failed. *WP* authors made particular reference to the CIA and Pentagon programs to train and equip Syrian rebels. Philip Carter, an Iraq veteran and a researcher at the Center for a New American Security,[38] authored an opinion article in which he identified the alleged inconsistencies of both programs. He claimed that both programs left the United States in a worse position to fight the Islamic State. Therefore, Carter continued, the country should change its approach to security assistance:

> We must think about security assistance the same way we think about long-term alliances, looking for alignments of interests, not convenience. Our assistance should be narrowly tailored to the existing capabilities and needs of the recipients and must be sustainable long after we leave. We should balance military training and equipment with support for civilian institutions that promote the rule of law and stability, to guard against blowback and to help address the root causes of instability.[39]

Carter seemed to favor a more comprehensive, Iraq-like US intervention in Syria.

Karen DeYoung, Juliet Eilperin, and Greg Miller sign a news article almost exclusively about the CIA program launched in June 2013. Their conclusion was unequivocal: "The CIA program has failed to shift the course of the conflict in Syria, and agency-backed fighters have long complained about the US refusal to provide more powerful weapons, air support, or no-fly zones."[40] DeYoung, Eilperin, and Miller also reported on the fact that President Obama was not willing to confront Russia directly in Syria. Although the three *WP* journalists quoted the

US president repeatedly, they also gave plenty of space to politicians who criticized Obama's Syria approach.

Three articles claim that US influence in the Middle East was decreasing. Missy Ryan, a journalist who covers the Pentagon, military issues, and national security, signs a news piece highlighting how Russia posed a challenge to US hegemony in the region. Ryan quoted John McCain as saying that the agreement between Russia, Syria, and Iraq to share intelligence, established in September 2015, amounted to an example of the curtailment of US power.[41] Another *WP* editorial, published a few days after Russia initiated its bombing campaign, follows the same direction, arguing that Syria's turmoil was the result of years of US disengagement in the Middle East.[42] Furthermore, the editorial board advocated that the United States should establish safe zones, destroy Syria's helicopter fleet, and provide aid to Kurdish militias fighting ISIS.

Even more emphatic in his criticism was Charles Krauthammer, a long-time neoconservative political analyst, who stated that the Russian intervention amounted to humiliation of the United States. Krauthammer reminded *WP* readers that Russian airstrikes in Syria started less than forty-eight hours after presidents Obama and Putin had met to discuss the situation in the war-torn country. He further argued that the United States had lost its position as the hegemonic power in the Middle East:

> When Obama became president, the surge in Iraq had succeeded and the United States had emerged as the dominant regional actor, able to project power throughout the region. Last Sunday [September 27, 2015], Iraq announced the establishment of a joint intelligence-gathering center with Iran, Syria, and Russia, symbolizing the new "Shiite-crescent" alliance stretching from Iran across the northern Middle East to the Mediterranean, under the umbrella of Russia, the rising regional hegemon.[43]

It is debatable, to say the least, whether the United States was still the dominant power in the Middle East in 2009, when Barack Obama became US president, as Krauthammer claimed. Other analysts, such as Fareed Zakaria, argued that the "beginning of the end" of US hegemony in the region started much sooner, in 2003, with the invasion of Iraq.[44]

Another distinction between the *NYT* and the *WP* coverage is that the latter did not hesitate to suggest policies to respond to the Russian intervention. As previously mentioned, the *WP* urged the Obama administration to engage more actively in the conflict. For instance, Walter Pincus wrote an article discussing the views of David Petraeus, the retired Army general and former CIA director who had been advocating the establishment of a no-fly zone and a more aggressive stance against Bashar al-Assad since the beginning of the conflict. Petraeus agreed with Clinton in proposing that the United States train and equip moderate rebel groups. In light of the emergence of ISIS, however, the retired general adjusted his position, moving on to argue that the United States should not force the Syrian president to step down, as it was not clear who would succeed him: "We should not rush to oust Assad without an understanding of what will follow him."[45] Notwithstanding his new position, Petraeus maintained that the Obama administration should not hesitate to prevent the Assad regime from using barrel bombs against civilians. For him, President Obama's policy was not a fiasco, but it lacked fortitude; he believed the US president should enforce measures such as the establishment of safe enclaves, which would be supported by US airpower and a local ground force ("a moderate Sunni force" were his actual words).

DeYoung, Eilperin, and Miller, in turn, quoted Clinton as saying that "the United States should create no-fly zones and humanitarian corridors to protect civilians and moderate anti-Assad rebels."[46] Clinton made this remark as part of a public discussion with President Obama in which she clearly distanced herself from the US president. The three *WP* journalists also quoted former US Ambassador to Syria Robert Ford and other "current and former US officials" as claiming that Syrian rebels would become frustrated with the low levels of support provided by the United States.

In an opinion piece, David Ignatius also expressed his disagreement with President Obama's Syria policy. Ignatius accused the United States of being absent and unable "to organize a winning strategy to deal with the Islamic State."[47] Like other *WP* commentators, Ignatius advocated "safe zones in northern and southern Syria to allow humanitarian assistance and greater security." In his view, the US president should negotiate with Russia and simultaneously step up support for Kurdish militias fighting ISIS. The above articles suggest that the *WP* promoted clear-cut policies for the Syrian conflict in both news and opinion pieces.

Nevertheless, not all *WP* articles in period IV condemn President Obama's Syria approach. Eilperin, a journalist covering domestic policy and national affairs, signs at least two pieces portraying US foreign policy positively. In one of them, she maintained that President Obama had reshaped US foreign policy: "This year's General Assembly session of the UN illustrates the extent to which Obama's foreign policy approach has reshaped the global landscape over the past seven years, with historic deals with Iran and Cuba as well as a big climate agreement with China."[48] Despite admitting that President Obama's Syria policy had shortcomings, she argued that they were outweighed by its positive outcomes. In another article, Eilperin claimed that the US president's multilateralist approach was bearing fruit.[49] She referred again to the agreement with Cuba in 2014, which reestablished diplomatic relations between both countries, and the 2015 Iran nuclear deal. To substantiate her views, she quoted a member of the Obama administration and experts from two think tanks: the Brookings Institution and the Council on Foreign Relations.[50] Eilperin's opinions amount to an outlier in the general frame built by the *WP* in period IV.

The second leading topic in the *WP* coverage of period IV is Russian foreign policy. Several *WP* articles discuss aspects such as the Russian intervention, the reasons behind it, and its possible geopolitical consequences. The *WP* and the *NYT* relayed similar frames of Russian foreign policy toward the Syrian conflict. The *WP* coverage of this topic, however, is more extensive than that of the *NYT*.

Several *WP* authors agreed that Russia's primary objective in Syria was not to fight ISIS but to protect Bashar al-Assad and assure his permanence in power.

For example, Anne Applebaum, a historian with expertise in the history of communist and post-communist Europe, argued that the principal reason underlying President Putin's involvement in the Syrian conflict was the safeguarding of Russian domestic stability, not his geopolitical aspirations. In her words, "Putin's entry into Syria, like almost everything else that he does, is part of his own bid to stay in power. During the first ten years he was president, Putin's claim to legitimacy went, in effect, like this: I may not be a democrat, but I give you stability, a rise in economic growth, and pensions paid on time."[51] As we will see in the next section, one *WSJ* author also singled out this aspect as the reason behind the Russian intervention.

Conversely, Adam Taylor, a *WP* journalist who writes about foreign affairs, claimed that the Russian intervention represented a radical shift in the country's foreign policy, as Syria was "outside [Russia's] traditional sphere of influence."[52] By traditional sphere of influence, the *WP* journalist probably meant the republics that formed the former Soviet Union and the countries of the Warsaw Pact. Taylor added that "Moscow usually distanced itself from direct involvement in conflicts in the Middle East and several times pressured states to avoid fighting." David Ignatius also discussed this topic, echoing the more sweeping narrative that the Russian president's decision to intervene was spurred mainly by the Obama administration's lack of strategy in the Middle East.[53] Ignatius pointed out that US officials were not completely averse to Russian involvement in the Middle East, as long as it was in line with US interests.

When discussing the possible consequences of the Russian involvement in Syria, *WP* authors—like several of their *NYT* colleagues—predicted that Russia would face enormous challenges. Some even predicted that Russian airstrikes would not change the course of the war; a view that proved erroneous. For instance, Andrew Roth, a journalist who focused on Russia, stated, "Russia has limited capacity to influence the chaotic situation in the Middle East, officials and analysts say. The Russian public does not support sending large numbers of troops to Syria, according to opinion polls, and Russian authorities are wary of accidentally being drawn into a conflict with US and other Western forces in the region."[54] Roth signs another article, this time in collaboration with Thomas Gibbons-Neff, claiming that "Moscow's contribution [was] unlikely to be decisive in the war."[55]

Pincus, in turn, quoted Petraeus as saying that Russia could run out of funds as a consequence of the sanctions imposed by the United States and the European Union.[56] Pincus also quoted the former CIA director arguing that Russia became involved in Syria to defend its military base in the country. As of this writing, Russia maintains a military presence in Syria and continues to support the Syrian army in its fight against Syrian rebels. In September 2021, for instance, the country brokered a truce between the Syrian regime and opposition forces still active in Daraa. The deal, which was highly advantageous to the Assad regime, allowed government forces to reestablish checkpoints in the city and required that armed rebels surrender their weapons. According to different reports, Russia committed numerous human rights violations and war crimes, such as the mass killing of civilians, during its military operations in Syria.[57]

In short, the *WP* relayed a negative frame of President Obama's policy toward Syria in period IV. After Russia's involvement in Syria escalated in September 2015, numerous *WP* authors urged the US president to play a more active role in the conflict. Some of the policies suggested included the establishment of safe zones and support for Kurdish militias fighting the Islamic State. A few *WP* authors predicted that Russian military power would not alter the course of the war, an idea that proved to be wrong.

The WSJ *Fears Russian Expansionism*

The *WSJ* published thirty-five articles in period IV. Of these, twenty-eight are news pieces, and seven are opinion articles. Like the other two newspapers, US and Russian foreign policies are the most recurrent topics and subtopics. The *WSJ* coverage of the beginning of the Russian intervention in Syria is the broadest of the three newspapers. *WSJ* authors discussed the geopolitical consequences of the intervention in detail, assessing it from the perspective of different countries, such as Russia, Saudi Arabia, and Iran. However, the newspaper left out the standpoint of those most affected by the conflict, the Syrian civil society. The *WSJ* portrayed the US administration's Syria approach negatively, deeming it a failure, criticizing President Obama for not defending US interests in the Middle East, and holding him responsible for the growth of ISIS. The *WSJ* coverage of period IV is similar to that of the *WP*, although *WSJ* columnists were not as blunt as their *WP* colleagues in recommending policies. In matters of policy proposals, *WSJ* columnists urged the United States to establish safe zones and step up sanctions on Russia.

Gerald Seib, one of the *WSJ*'s editors and most prominent foreign policy commentators, signs an opinion piece that analyzes what he described as "Obama's security doctrine." He claimed that US foreign policy had shifted away from the "endless" Middle Eastern wars to issues such as climate change and China's rise. Seib argued that President Obama's approach in Syria, based on avoiding military engagement, had failed to maintain the United States as the hegemonic power in the Middle East. For Seib, the US president fell short of achieving his two primary goals in the conflict, namely getting rid of President Bashar al-Assad and containing ISIS. Without stating it explicitly, the *WSJ* analyst advocated a change toward a more active foreign policy aimed primarily at containing ISIS. Seib wrote, "Mr. Obama's gamble that the US could steer Syria toward a better outcome without having to intervene directly has not worked. Syria has become the insoluble problem, and along the way has tested some of the basic precepts of the Obama security doctrine."[58]

Bret Stephens also wrote an opinion piece that is critical of President Obama's foreign policy, which he called a "strategy of retreat and accommodation." Using an ironic tone, Stephens accused the US president of refusing to exercise power in a tumultuous world: "Having declared our good intentions, why muck it up with the raw and compromising exercise of power? In Mr. Obama's view, it is not the man in the arena who counts. It is the speaker on the stage."[59] The *WSJ* columnist continued, "History will remember Barack Obama as the president who conducted foreign policy less as a principled exercise in the application of American power than as an extended attempt to justify the evasion of it." He ended the piece holding the US president responsible for the chaos in Aleppo (Syria), Donetsk (Ukraine), and Kunduz (Afghanistan).

Echoing similar reasoning, an unauthored opinion piece titled "What US Retreat Looks Like" argues that President Obama's lack of willingness to counter Russian expansionism in the Middle East would make the situation in Syria more chaotic. The author refuted the idea, which was quite widespread within US foreign policy circles, that Syria was prone to become a "quagmire" for Russia:

> The world is watching [the Russian bombing campaign in Syria] …,yet we are now told by the same people who told us to stay out of Syria that Mr. Putin has fallen into his own quagmire. We doubt that is how they see it in Moscow, Tehran, or Damascus. For a limited deployment of two thousand soldiers and some weapons, Mr. Putin is showing Russians their country has global influence again.[60]

The article recommends the establishment of a no-fly zone as the most effective way to protect refugees fleeing the Assad regime and ISIS. Nevertheless, the author seemed convinced that President Obama would not implement such a policy.

Garry Kasparov, the chairman of the Human Rights Foundation,[61] argued that US retreat from the Middle East was the main explanation for the growth of ISIS. Kasparov denounced the United States for abandoning the Sunni population of Iraq and Syria:

> A look at a map of Iraq and Syria shows that the rise of ISIS was a logical response to American abandonment of the region's Sunnis. A group like ISIS cannot thrive without support from locals, in this case Sunnis who see no other way to defend against the Shiite forces of Iran and Syria that are slaughtering them by the hundreds of thousands.[62]

Kasparov exaggerated the role of sectarianism in the Syrian conflict; he made constant references to the disputes between Sunni and Shiite forces. Kasparov is not alone in overestimating the Sunni-Shiite divide in the Middle East and using it as an all-encompassing explanation for contemporary political conflicts. Different Western commentators interpreted the Syrian conflict through these same lenses. Nader Hashemi and Danny Postel call this "sectarian essentialism" a new form of Orientalism. Hashemi and Postel further argued, "Major world leaders, public intellectuals, policy analysts, and media commentators have sought to explain the current instability in the Middle East as a function of ancient blood feuds rooted in putatively primordial hatreds and antagonisms between Sunnis and Shiite. These conflicts, we are told, have been brewing beneath the surface since the dawn of Islam."[63] Also, the article's explanation for the growth of ISIS is overly simplistic. Any serious discussion about the emergence of the Islamic State should refer back to the 2003 invasion of Iraq as a threshold.

Kasparov's (Orientalist) views epitomize the standpoint of the *WSJ* editorial board. He further argued that Obama's "refusal" to oust Bashar al-Assad earlier in the conflict increased insecurity in the region. The US president's hesitant policy, Kasparov continued, encouraged President Putin to expand Russian influence in Syria. Another unsigned opinion piece maintains that the US president was ready to accept the permanence of Bashar al-Assad in power and Russia's growing role in the Middle East. The author wrote, "Mr. Obama is likely to accept Russia's presence in Syria and thus eventually the survival of Mr. al-Assad or some other Tehran-Moscow factotum in Damascus."[64]

Carol Lee, the *WSJ*'s White House correspondent at the time, signs a news article which reports on the divisions produced by the Syrian conflict among US politicians.[65] After quoting President Obama in the first part of the article, Lee gave voice to two Republican politicians, former Senator Bob Corker and Senator Marco Rubio, who expressed their reservations regarding US policy in Syria (see Figure 5.3). Both politicians argued that the United States ought to revise its priorities. Whereas Corker argued that President Obama should focus on defeating the Syrian president, Rubio advocated a stronger stance against Russia. Lee did not elaborate on the details of such policies, although she suggested that the US president's hitherto Syria approach was inadequate.

A few days later, however, an opinion piece signed by two former US officials who had served under Republican presidents outlines a plan of action to offset Russian expansionism. Paula Dobriansky and David Rivkin argued that President Obama should impose stricter sanctions on Russia and avoid any alliance with President Putin, even if such an alliance aimed at containing the Islamic State.[66] Both former officials stated that the Russian president used the war on terror narrative as an excuse to protect the Syrian president. In their view, Bashar al-Assad was a war criminal who did not deserve any sympathy. Dobriansky and Rivkin further argued that the sanctions enforced on Russia after the Crimea annexation in 2014 did not suffice to deter President Putin's expansionist aspirations.

Not all *WSJ* articles relay a negative frame of President Obama. Three of the news articles that discuss the Russian intervention employ a neutral tone toward his administration. These articles report on topics such as the international reactions to the Russian bombing campaign and the negotiations between the United States and Russia to de-escalate the situation in Syria. None of these three articles, however, portray the Obama administration positively. Even the *WP*, which also built a negative frame of President Obama, published two pieces in period IV highlighting positive aspects of the US president's policy. In one of these articles, WSJ journalists Jay Solomon, Carol Lee, and Farnaz Fassihi gathered the opinion of nearly ten world leaders about the prospects of world stability in light of Russia's growing involvement in Syria.[67] The three journalists wrote the article almost as a report, rather than a news story with a particular angle.

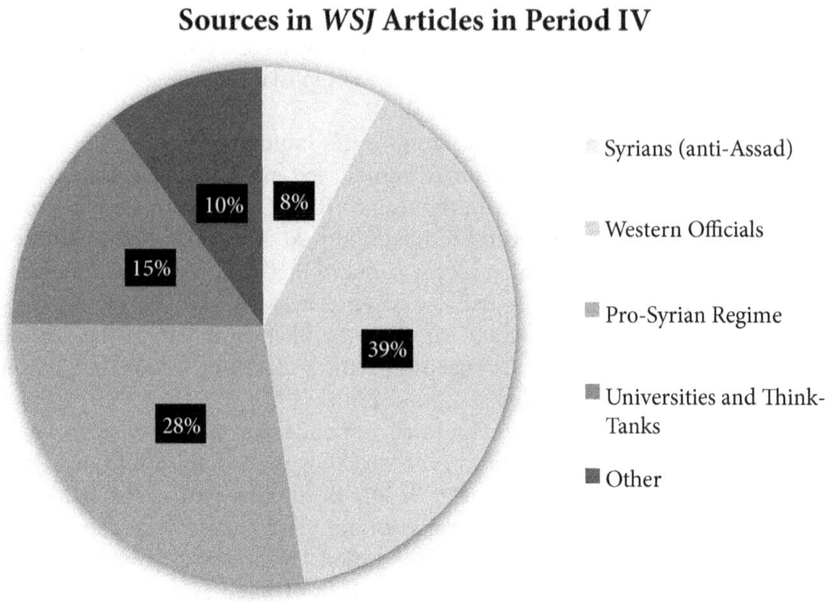

Sources in *WSJ* Articles in Period IV

- Syrians (anti-Assad): 8%
- Western Officials: 10%
- Pro-Syrian Regime: 15%
- Universities and Think-Tanks: 28%
- Other: 39%

Figure 5.3 Sources in *WSJ* articles in period IV.

Several *WSJ* articles in period IV analyze the intervention from the perspective of Russian foreign policy. Most of these articles discuss the reasons that led President Putin to increase Russian involvement in Syria. Another unsigned opinion article, published one day before the beginning of the military campaign, claims that Russia and Iran sought to spread their influence in the Middle East:

> The Putin-Tehran goal in Syria is part of a strategy to build an arc of influence that extends from western Afghanistan through the eastern Mediterranean. It seeks to diminish US influence in the region, pushing on the open door of Mr. Obama's desire to leave. The goal is to isolate US allies in Kurdish Iraq and Israel, while forcing the Sunni Arabs to accommodate the Shiite-Russian alliance or face internal agitation and perhaps external conflict.[68]

Olga Razumovskaya, a *WSJ* journalist based in Moscow at the time, authored a news article that analyzes the narrative of the Russian media about the Syrian conflict. Razumovskaya suggested that the Russian government used its leverage over the media to boost Russian national pride and improve President Putin's approval ratings. She wrote, "Russian state media news coverage showed Mr. Putin as being ready to take decisive action to do in the Middle East what the West could not. There has been almost no criticism voiced of his policy."[69]

Yaroslav Trofimov, by contrast, argued that the Russian president's main goal was to protect Bashar al-Assad and Syria's "Alawi region." Trofimov also claimed that Russia did not distinguish the different rebel groups, deeming all of them terrorist organizations: "Russia, like the Assad regime, does not make much of a distinction between Islamic State, whose ranks include many Chechens and other Russian citizens, more moderate Islamist rebels backed by Saudi Arabia, Turkey, or Qatar, and even more moderate Syrian fighters supported by the United States."[70] The above articles testify that Russia's reasons to intervene in the Syrian conflict were multifaceted and not reducible to one single factor. The analysis of Russian foreign policy is consistent across the three newspapers.

In period IV, the *WSJ* published several articles that discuss European foreign policy and the refugee crisis. The European Union and the United States shared similar views of the Syrian conflict by the time of the Russian intervention, both of them opposing the Assad regime and the Islamic State, on one hand, and pressing for a political settlement between the regime and the Syrian opposition, on the other. However, the refugee crisis caused deep divisions within the European Union, especially concerning the allocation of refugees among the member states. Deborah Ball, a London-based *WSJ* editor for Europe, Middle East, and Africa, signs a news article that discusses these divisions. The article focuses on the opinions of then-Italian Prime Minister Matteo Renzi. Russia should be part of any political negotiation, Renzi argued, and the West should not intervene in Syria if it wished to prevent a "new Libya."[71] Ball pointed out that Renzi disapproved of how Hungarian Prime Minister Viktor Orbán handled the refugee crisis. The article highlights the divisions inside the European Union and the fact that its leaders seemed favorable to a political agreement that included Russia and Bashar al-Assad.

Another article that focuses on European foreign policy reports on Donald Tusk's speech at the UN General Assembly. Tusk, who at the time was the president of the European Council, addressed the refugee crisis and the possible solutions to the Syrian conflict. He maintained a strong anti-Assad stance, arguing that most Syrian refugees arriving in Europe fled Syrian state terrorism, not ISIS. He also mentioned that a political solution could not be "a formula for defining a new division [of Syria] into spheres of influence."[72] These articles reinforce the hypothesis that the *WSJ* attached importance to the geopolitical aspects of the Syrian crisis. In fact, the newspaper's coverage of the geopolitics of the Syrian conflict in period IV is more extensive than that of the humanitarian crisis in the country or the development of the Syrian civil war.

As stated in the introduction of this section, the coverage of period IV in the *WSJ* emphasizes the international reactions to the Russian intervention. Apart from discussing it from the perspective of the United States, *WSJ* journalists shed light on the views of the European Union, Russia, Saudi Arabia, Iran, and Syria. For example, Solomon highlighted in a news piece that Saudi officials were concerned about the consequences of the Russian bombing campaign: "Saudi and other Arab officials warned the Obama administration … that Russia's military intervention in Syria risked fueling a new flood of funds and fighters into the ranks of extremist groups Islamic State and al-Qaeda and could aid their efforts to claim even more territory in the Middle East."[73]

Sam Dagher and Asa Fitch, in turn, discussed the role of Iran, explaining in detail the size and scope of the country's expanding role as an ally of the Syrian regime. The article does not share a particularly anti-Iran frame. Instead, the authors quoted several experts, who provided factual information about Iranian involvement in the conflict, and Iranian diplomats, who explained their reasons for intervening in Syria. Dagher and Fitch's opening paragraph set the tone of the article: "Iran is expanding its already sizable role in Syria's multisided war in the wake of Russia's airstrikes, despite the risk of antagonizing the US and its Persian Gulf allies who want to push aside President Bashar al-Assad."[74]

In conclusion, the *WSJ* relayed frames that are essentially anti-Obama, anti-Assad, and anti-Russia in period IV. Compared with the other two newspapers, the *WSJ*'s coverage is the most international, focusing mostly on the possible geopolitical outcomes of the Russian intervention. However, the number of reports echoing Syrian voices on the ground is lower than in the *NYT* and the *WP*. The critical frame of President Obama is evident mainly in opinion articles signed by columnists who stressed the shortcomings of the US president's policy. *WSJ* authors were not as direct as their *WP* colleagues in proposing policy changes. One author proposed the increment of sanctions on Russia to pressure President Putin to reduce his involvement in the conflict. Another suggested that the United States ought to establish safe zones in Syria.

…

The Russian intervention in the Syrian civil war proved to be one of the conflict's determinant events, as it changed the course of the war in favor of the Assad regime and led to the intensification of debates in the United States. The coverage of the Russian bombing campaign is extensive in the three newspapers analyzed in this book. As we have seen, the *NYT* continued to relay a pro-Obama frame, although its journalists highlighted the contradictions and ambiguities of his policy. The *NYT* also gave prominence to the debates inside the Democratic Party, especially the discussions involving President Obama and former secretaries of state John Kerry and Hillary Clinton. In period II, which covered the Eastern Ghouta chemical attack, the NYT also focused on the internal debates inside the White House and the Democratic Party. The *WP* covered the beginning of the Russian intervention differently, relaying a negative frame of President Obama and suggesting policies to deal with Syria's new scenario. A few *WP* articles, however, portray US foreign policy positively. In period IV, *WP* authors advocated the establishment of a no-fly zone and support for Kurdish groups. The *WSJ* also condemned Obama's Syria policy, describing it as inconsistent with US interests in the Middle East. Although the newspaper seemed worried about Russian expansionism in the Middle East, most *WSJ* authors did not suggest alternative policies.

Chapter 6

THE FALL OF EASTERN ALEPPO (PERIOD V)

The fall of eastern Aleppo in December 2016 decided the outcome of the Syrian civil war. As pro-Assad forces reconquered the area on December 22, ending a four-year-long struggle for the control of Aleppo, the Syrian regime effectively secured a military victory over rebel forces. Before the March 2011 uprising, the province of Aleppo was Syria's economic heart, concentrating the bulk of its industry and agriculture, and its capital constituted the country's largest urban center. In 2011, the province of Aleppo had around 33 percent of Syria's industry, especially in the textile sector, and contributed 29 percent of the country's GDP.[1] Aleppo's business and merchant class constituted one of the pillars that sustained the Assad regime in power.

The city of Aleppo had been divided since July 2012, when rebel groups—mainly the Liwa al-Tawhid coalition—captured the eastern part of the city, starting what would become one of the longest and bloodiest battles of the Syrian conflict. Christopher Phillips described Liwa al-Tawhid as a collection of groups linked to the Free Syrian Army and the Muslim Brotherhood.[2] According to a report of Stanford University's Center for International Security and Cooperation, Liwa al-Tawhid was an "Aleppo-based militant group that was formed by several small opposition brigades to fight the Assad Regime in July 2012."[3] The report further argues that "the group's goal was to replace the Assad Regime with a moderate Islamic state that had a basis in Shariah law, but included civilian rule, elections, and protection for minorities."

Anti-Assad demonstrations had been occurring in the city of Aleppo since the beginning of the revolution, but it was not until May 2012 that the protests became massive and widespread. On May 18, for example, regime forces used live ammunition to repress thousands of Syrians protesting peacefully in different parts of Aleppo. The largest of these protests took place on the Aleppo University campus, which had become the heart of the insurrection in the city. The armed struggle began in July 2012, and by December, the Syrian government had lost crucial positions in the city, initiating the shelling and aerial bombing of residential and historic areas.

In July 2016, after a long stalemate, the fight for the control of Aleppo took a significant turn, when regime forces cut the most important supply line used by rebels to bring essential products into the city. The siege of eastern Aleppo created the ideal conditions for a military assault, which the Syrian regime launched in September 2016. During the offensive, the Syrian army received crucial assistance from the Lebanese Hezbollah, other Iranian-backed Shia militias, and Russian aircraft and military advisers.

During the air offensive over Aleppo, numerous civilian targets, such as hospitals, street markets, and schools, were bombed. Martin Chulov, Kareem Shaheen, and Emma Graham-Harrison, writing for the *Guardian*, wrote,

> Médecins Sans Frontières said east Aleppo's hospitals had been hit by bombs in more than thirty separate attacks since the siege began in July and there was no possibility of sending help or more supplies. Schools, roads, and homes have also been bombed repeatedly as the Syrian leader's allies attempt to drive opposition communities out of the city and, by doing so, change the face of the nearly six-year war.[4]

The Violations Documentation Center, a Syrian civil monitoring group, claimed that Russia bombing campaigns killed around 500 civilians in Aleppo between September 19 and October 18, 2016.[5]

Western governments and international organizations denounced that the siege of Aleppo constituted an unprecedented humanitarian catastrophe. Ban Ki-moon, then the UN secretary-general, accused Russia of using weapons, such as bunker-busting and incendiary bombs, which were banned by international conventions. Leila Nachawati, a Syrian-Spanish media scholar, compared the siege and recapture of Aleppo to the massacres of Srebrenica and Guernica: "Aleppo has fallen, and the impunity that follows the city's capture brings us to Srebrenica and Guernica. Al-Assad has 'liberated' Aleppo in the same way as Milosevic 'liberated' Yugoslavia and Franco 'liberated' Spain: subjecting entire populations to terror and bombs."[6]

As regime forces encircled eastern Aleppo, residents of the besieged area uploaded desperate accounts on social media. Lina Shamy, an activist and architect who lived in Aleppo during the siege, described the situation with powerful words:

> Two days later, another barrel bomb fell, on a building close to our house. A hospital had moved next door. Regime and Russian jets were intentionally bombing hospitals and clinics. We grabbed a bag of clothes and moved to another house. President al-Assad's forces were inching closer, and our new house was in the firing range. We moved again, to a friend's home.[7]

In December 2016, several rebel groups, both civilian and armed, operated in eastern Aleppo. The most important armed groups were Ahrar al-Sham, al-Jabhat al-Shamiya, Jaish al-Mujahideen, Feilaq al-Sham, Fawj al-Awl, and Jabhat Fatah al-Sham (formerly known as Jabhat al-Nusra or al-Nusra Front).[8] According to Jennifer Cafarella and Genevieve Casagrande, two researchers at the conservative Institute for the Study of War,[9] most of these groups embraced Islamist or jihadist ideology. And three of them (al-Jabhat al-Shamiya, Fawj al-Awl, and Jaish al-Mujahideen) received US support. Cafarella and Casagrande made a clear distinction between Islamist and Salafi-Jihadi groups. In their opinion, it was necessary to make alliances with and support groups considered Islamists as they could curb the growth of the more extremist sections of the armed movement. The two groups considered Salafi-Jihadi were Ahrar al-Sham and Jabhat Fatah al-Sham. Several moderate secularist groups, most of them affiliated with the Free Syrian Army, were also active in Aleppo, although they were not as numerous and resourceful as those previously mentioned. Moreover, rebel groups were divided and clashed with each other for hegemony. Among the civilian groups, we can list the Syrian Civil Defense (also known as the White Helmets),[10] a network of local coordination committees, media groups (such as the Aleppo Media Center), and international NGOs.

The siege of Aleppo amplified the tensions inside the UN Security Council. In a meeting held on September 25, 2016, Samantha Power, the US ambassador to the United Nations at the time, accused Russia of bombing mostly civilian areas in Syria; France and the UK followed suit. Vitaly Churkin, then the Russian ambassador to the United Nations, responded by saying that the 2003 invasion of Iraq was the origin of most problems in Syria, as it had created the conditions for the expansion of terrorist groups in the Middle East.[11] Churkin further argued that jihadist groups such as Jabhat Fatah al-Sham, which had recently announced its dissociation from al-Qaeda, were preventing cease-fire agreements. He also accused Fatah al-Sham of using its access to humanitarian aid as a political weapon. In turn, Staffan de Mistura, then the special envoy of the UN secretary-general for Syria, argued that a military solution in Syria was impossible and that the Security Council ought to press for the cessation of hostilities in Aleppo.[12] Because of the significant differences of opinions among its members, the UN Security Council was unable to pass a meaningful resolution to deal with Aleppo's crisis.

Foreign powers had long held the upper hand in Syria, and by the end of 2016, the fate of the Syrian conflict lay mostly in the hands of Russia and Turkey. On December 13, 2016, the two countries reached a cease-fire agreement that foresaw the evacuation of civilians and rebel fighters from eastern Aleppo to the northwestern province of Idlib. On December 22, the evacuation was completed, sealing the recapture of Aleppo by the Assad regime. Russia's influence in the conflict had grown steadily since President Putin authorized a military intervention in September 2015 to shore up the Assad regime.

As for Turkey, it had launched Operation Euphrates Shield in August 2016 in order to dislodge ISIS from the border city of Jarablus and counter the expansion of the Kurdish forces fighting the terrorist organization. During the siege of Aleppo, Turkey refrained from supporting rebel forces in what was seen as an exchange for the Russian green light to the Turkish invasion of Syria. Different analysts corroborated the claim that Turkey sought the "authorization" of Russia before seizing the Syrian city of Jarablus and its surroundings. According the Aron Lund, a fellow at Century International and Middle East analyst at the Swedish Defense Research Agency,

For the Kurdish leadership in Syria, things are clear: a secret deal has been struck among the governments in Ankara, Damascus, and Tehran. Indeed, Turkey seems confident that its intervention [in Jarablus in August 2016] will not be too stridently opposed by Assad's allies. And although Russia has expressed "concern," it is difficult to imagine that Turkey, as a NATO member housing part of the US nuclear arsenal, would order its army into a country patrolled by the Russian Air Force without some sort of agreement on how to handle the situation.[13]

The fact that the United States (and the United Nations) played a reduced role in the negotiations that led to the end of the Aleppo crisis suggested that Western powers had negligible influence on the ground. Phillips described this new geopolitical reality: "While 2016 began with the United States and Russia negotiating to end the conflict, by the year's end Moscow appeared to have outmaneuvered Washington diplomatically and militarily."[14]

Al-Assad's recapture of eastern Aleppo was arguably the most decisive event in the Syrian civil war; it also symbolized the failure of the US approach to the conflict. Nikolaos van Dam, a former Dutch diplomat and Middle East expert, explained why the international community was unable to act during the fall of eastern Aleppo:

[Western and Arab Gulf countries] were powerless to intervene politically or militarily [in Aleppo in December 2016], because they had already excluded any military intervention in Syria several years before, and no longer had any real influence over the Syrian regime (with which they had broken off relations years before), nor over its allies Russia and Iran, to change their policies concerning Syria. Moreover, they apparently had not provided the military opposition groups with enough military support to be able to win the battle for Aleppo.[15]

It is noteworthy that the final act of the battle of Aleppo occurred only a few weeks before Donald Trump's inauguration as US president. As the Obama era approached an end, there was immense speculation about how the Trump administration would handle the Syrian conflict. As previously discussed, President Obama favored a cautious approach to the Syrian uprising and civil war, opting for a nonconfrontational policy toward Russia (although the two countries frequently clashed at the UN Security Council) and prioritizing the fight against ISIS starting from 2014. By 2016, President Obama's Syria policy combined airstrikes against ISIS (as part of an international coalition) and support to militias (especially the Syrian Democratic Forces) that acted as ground forces against the terrorist organization. It was not clear whether Donald Trump would follow the same strategy.

In a report for the *WSJ*, Raja Abdulrahim and Dion Nissenbaum suggested that a change could be in sight:

The apparent defeat of the opposition in Aleppo represents a blow to the Obama administration. The implications for the incoming administration of Donald Trump are unclear, but seem to fit with the president-elect's vision of US involvement in Syria. During his campaign, Mr. Trump implied he would work with both Moscow and the Assad regime against Islamic State extremists, while saying the United States had been unsuccessful in identifying any moderate rebels.[16]

Although Donald Trump's Syria policy was uncertain, it was clear that the future US president and his national security team held a more aggressive attitude toward Iran. General Jim Mattis, who would serve as secretary of defense during the first two years of Donald Trump's presidency, criticized the Obama administration for its "passive" approach toward Tehran. With the benefit of hindsight, it is possible to affirm that Donald Trump's Middle East policy had two fundamental pillars: provide unrestrained support to Israel and increased hostility toward Iran. Against this backdrop, Trump officials devised a Syria policy that many observers deemed incoherent.

For example, Bret McGurk, a diplomat who served in senior national security positions under George W. Bush, Barack Obama, and Donald Trump, wrote in January 2020, "Washington's policy is defined by incoherence: maximalist ends, minimalist means, false assumptions, few allies, all pressure, no diplomacy. The Middle East in turn is stuck on an escalatory ladder."[17] McGurk further argued, "The United States must maintain a significant military force forward and ready in the Middle East, even as its fight against ISIS has stalled and its guiding grand strategy calls for shifting resources out of the region altogether."

In October 2019, James Jeffrey, President Trump's special envoy to Syria, stated that US objectives in Syria were threefold: "to get Iranian forces out of the country, to ensure the lasting defeat of ISIS, and, through a political process, to change the behavior of the Syrian government—without seeking regime change per se."[18] Nonetheless, several foreign policy analysts deemed it impossible to push Iranian forces out of Syria without antagonizing Russia. The following sections show that the *NYT*, the *WP*, and the *WSJ* paid particular attention to analyzing the foreign policy views of President Trump and those who would serve as his advisers. In particular, *WP* and *WSJ* authors wrote extensively about this topic.

On several occasions, President Trump reiterated his willingness to withdraw US troops from Iraq, Syria, and Afghanistan, although delivering on this promise proved complex. In October 2019, after several contradictory statements, President Trump ordered the withdrawal of all US troops stationed in northeastern Syria. This decision spawned criticism from various politicians and political commentators, including Republican Senator Lindsey Graham, who was considered one of Trump's closest allies. A few weeks later, Mark Esper, who had been appointed as secretary of defense in July 2019, declared that the United States would finally maintain a presence in Syria mostly to protect oil fields from ISIS.

Foreign Policy reporter Jack Detsch suggested that the protection of oil fields amounted to an important reason for US engagement in northeastern Syria since the Obama period. Detsch wrote, "The United States has been laying the groundwork, with the US-led coalition fighting the Islamic State in Iraq and Syria building up an SDF force designed to protect petroleum fields in Hasakah and Deir Ezzor provinces, which are controlled by the Kurdish-dominated group."[19] In fact, the topic of how much disengagement can the United States afford in the Middle East is contentious. Several observers argue that the United States is still deeply entangled in the region. For example, in January 2020, in the aftermath of the killing of Iranian General Qasem Soleimani, McGurk wrote, "Trump himself said he intended to end wars and move forces out of the Middle East region altogether. The unforeseen escalatory cycle is evidence of a policy not working as intended."[20] Despite the recent withdrawal of US troops from Iraq and Afghanistan, it is unlikely that the United States will fully disengage from the Middle East in the near future.

President Trump's Syria policy had elements of continuity with his predecessor's in at least two respects. First, both presidents avoided unconditional confrontation with Russia and unrestrained action to oust Bashar al-Assad. Richard Gowan, the research director at the NYU Center on International Cooperation, argued that US officials at the UN (under both Barack Obama and Donald Trump) always prioritized the preservation of good diplomatic relations with Russia.[21] In his opinion, this approach did not change substantially during the first year of Trump's presidency.[22]

Second, both presidents saw the defeat of ISIS as a priority. Regarding their ISIS policy, McGurk highlighted, "The strategy to destroy the ISIS caliphate was developed under Obama and then carried forward, with minor modifications, under Trump; throughout, it focused on enabling local fighters to reclaim their cities from ISIS and then establish the conditions for displaced people to return."[23] One of President Obama's last decisions was to send two hundred additional troops to support Kurdish groups fighting ISIS in Syria. Phillips, arguing along similar lines, wrote that "although [President Trump's] bombastic style might have been distinctive, the end result was little different from Obama's: marginalization in western Syria alongside further entrenchment in the post-ISIS east."[24] In fact, Donald Trump's announcement of his intention to withdraw US troops from Syria was based on the assumption that ISIS was no longer a threat to US interests.

In period V, two topics dominate the coverage of the Syrian conflict in the three newspapers analyzed in this book: US foreign policy, more specifically the differences between presidents Obama and Trump, and the battle of Aleppo. The three newspapers suggested that the Trump presidency would represent a shift in US Middle East policy, although the specifics of such change were not evident. When assessing the Obama years, the *WP* and the *WSJ* continued to relay a critical frame of the Obama administration, whereas the *NYT* offered a more neutral view. As we will see, none of the newspapers focused on suggesting policies, preferring instead to speculate on the possible changes that would come with Donald Trump.

6. The Fall of Eastern Aleppo

Period V comprises the week from December 6 to December 12, 2016. The siege and fall of eastern Aleppo attracted significant media coverage during these seven days. On December 12, Russia and Turkey announced a cease-fire and the beginning of the evacuation of the area, which ended on December 22 after numerous interruptions and setbacks. The total number of articles analyzed in period V is forty-five, of which thirty-seven are news articles and eight are opinion pieces (see Table 6.1). None of the three newspapers published editorials during those seven days. Thirty-eight authors sign or co-sign articles in period V; twenty-two men and sixteen women.

The *NYT* published ten articles, the *WP* published twenty, and the *WSJ*, fifteen. As previously mentioned, the most recurrent topics and subtopics are US foreign policy and the battle of Aleppo (see Figure 6.1). Whereas the *NYT* prioritized the coverage of the battle and siege of Aleppo, the *WP* and the *WSJ* focused on the diplomatic and geopolitical aspects of the conflict.

Table 6.1 Number of articles per newspaper and genre in period V

	News	Opinion	Total
NYT	8	2	10
WP	16	4	20
WSJ	13	2	15
TOTAL	37	8	45

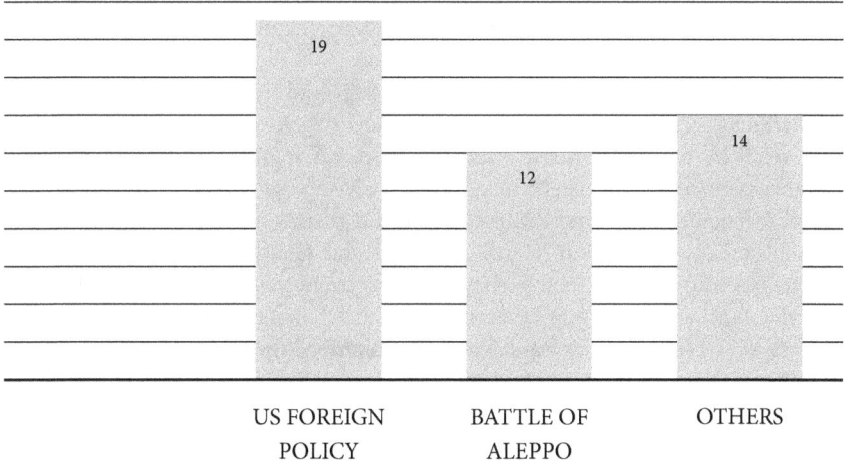

Figure 6.1 Topics in period V.

The NYT *Relays a Neutral Frame of Obama's Syria Policy*

The *NYT* published ten articles in period V: eight news articles and two opinion pieces. The most relevant topics are US foreign policy and the siege of Aleppo. Most *NYT* articles in period V focus on the humanitarian and military aspects of the battle of Aleppo, leaving the geopolitical aspects in the background. The articles that discuss US foreign policy relay a neutral frame of President Obama's Syria policy. Although the *NYT* did not openly support the US president's policy (as it did in periods I, II, and III), in period V, *NYT* journalists refrained from criticizing his policy and using sources that expressed anti-Obama views. Other topics tackled by the newspaper include Russian foreign policy, ISIS, and the refugee crisis.

One opinion piece discusses the options available for the United States to end the Syrian civil war in a way that would benefit its national security interests. In the article, Peter Galbraith, a former ambassador under President Bill Clinton, endorsed two policies; namely that the United States cooperate with Russia on a diplomatic level and, on a military level, support the Syrian-Kurdish forces fighting ISIS. For Galbraith, the country should pursue three overarching objectives: "The United States has an interest in a result that allows as many Syrians as possible to go home, that ensures the total defeat of the Islamic State and other extremist groups, and that safeguards the Syrian Kurds, who have been America's principal ally against the Islamic State."[25]

Galbraith further argued that the best way to achieve these objectives was to establish a "close collaboration with Russia." The former diplomat also stated that a deal with President Putin was feasible, as both countries shared similar goals in Syria, such as defeating ISIS and creating safe conditions for the refugees to return to the country. Concerning the relationship with the Kurds, Galbraith maintained, "The United States must provide long-term guarantees to the Syrian Kurds, who now control a large territory, not all of which is Kurdish." Galbraith seemed overly concerned with the possibility of the Assad regime recapturing Syria's oil resources, which were mostly in Kurdish-controlled areas.

On December 6, 2016, President Obama delivered his last presidential speech on national security. The outgoing US president took the opportunity to assess and reaffirm his antiterrorist strategy before an audience formed mostly of military personnel. The speech received extensive media coverage, including from the three newspapers analyzed herein, although the frames varied depending on the media organization. Gardiner Harris and Charlie Savage, the two *NYT* journalists who covered the speech, wrote an account that is more descriptive than analytical, an approach that favored President Obama's narrative. Using several extracts of the speech, Harris and Savage summarized the key points of the Obama administration's antiterrorist strategy.

For example, President Obama highlighted the fact that no foreign terrorist organization had successfully perpetrated an attack on US soil during his two presidencies. This had been achieved, he continued, even as the United States withdrew nearly 180,000 troops from Iraq and Afghanistan. The US president also argued that his approach to fighting wars was more effective than President George W. Bush's, as it "did not bankrupt the Treasury or cause thousands of deaths."[26] In an allusion to Donald Trump's foreign policy views, President Obama insisted that the United States should not magnify the role of terrorism: "[Terrorists] do not pose an existential threat to our nation and we cannot make the mistake of elevating them as if they do … These terrorists can never directly destroy our way of life but we can do it for them if we lose track of who we are and the values that this nation was founded on." Throughout the report, the two *NYT* journalists contrasted President Obama's opinions with remarks from Donald Trump. In one of these comparisons, they stated, "Trump has proposed banning immigration from Muslim countries, and some Republicans have proposed scrutiny of Muslim communities in the United States. Mr. Obama criticized such proposals."[27]

In Harris and Savage's article, the use of these two frame devices (use of quotations from the speech and comparison of Obama's and Trump's foreign policy views) induces the reader to sympathize with President Obama's policy. The only citation that was not from President Obama came from John McCain, who described the US president's speech as a "feeble attempt to evade the harsh judgment of history."[28] The late Republican senator also criticized President Obama's alleged indifference to the carnage perpetrated by the Syrian regime and ISIS against ordinary Syrians. McCain's statement appears toward the end of the article, which suggests that both journalists avoided exposing *NYT* readers to a distinctly anti-Obama narrative. This article constitutes a remarkable opportunity for researchers to examine the role of sources in frame-building. As we will see, the *WP* and the *WSJ* framed the speech differently, relying for that purpose on different sources, mostly commentators who criticized the outgoing US president.

One *NYT* article in period V briefly mentions the limited role that the United States played in the negotiations that led to the surrender and evacuation of eastern Aleppo. In the article, Anne Barnard and Hwaida Saad wrote, "As a turning point in the war approaches, countries like the United States, which have long demanded that President Bashar al-Assad step down, are reduced to wrangling with Russia … over how to protect or evacuate the civilians."[29] Barnard and Saad did not elaborate on why the United States had lost influence in Syria. According to several observers, however, it was partly due to President Obama's lack of audacity to intervene in the conflict; *WP* and *WSJ* authors reiterated this idea on numerous occasions.

Five *NYT* news articles report on the siege of Aleppo. Most of them employ a similar structure, which combines a depiction of the situation on the ground with a discussion about the international reactions to the Aleppo crisis. To describe the situation on the ground, *NYT* journalists relied mostly on accounts from civilians and rebel fighters trapped inside the besieged area. The international reactions, on the other hand, relied on statements from UN and government officials. The discussion revolved around three factors: the humanitarian crisis, the military developments, and the diplomatic consequences of the fall of Aleppo. It is noteworthy that Barnard authored or co-authored all five articles, which partly explains their similar structure. The sources used in these articles include civilians in Aleppo, rebel fighters, humanitarian organizations (among them the United

Nations, the Red Cross, and the White Helmets), as well as anti- and pro-Assad government officials. Civilians and humanitarian organizations constituted the majority of the sources, which indicates that Barnard and the other *NYT* journalists prioritized the humanitarian crisis over the military and diplomatic aspects of the battle of Aleppo (see Figure 6.2).

For example, in an article published on December 8, Barnard affirmed,

> Pleas for help from eastern Aleppo escalated …,with doctors warning that they could no longer provide more than first aid. Some residents reached via telephone and text message were fleeing from the front lines into the center of the shrinking enclave, while others stayed near the edges, hoping to evacuate but complaining that the combatants would not pause to let them escape.[30]

Barnard had access to civilians, such as doctors, nurses, and local activists, who provided firsthand accounts of the siege and evacuation of Aleppo. These accounts played an essential role in building the anti-Russia and anti-Assad frames, as they constituted vivid evidence of the brutality that surrounded the recapture of eastern Aleppo.

In another article, a rebel fighter is quoted as saying that the area's population faced extermination: "A rebel fighter with the Nour al-Din al-Zenki group[31], reached in a hiding place near the Old City, said that several neighborhoods had fallen and that defeat appeared inevitable. 'Aleppo

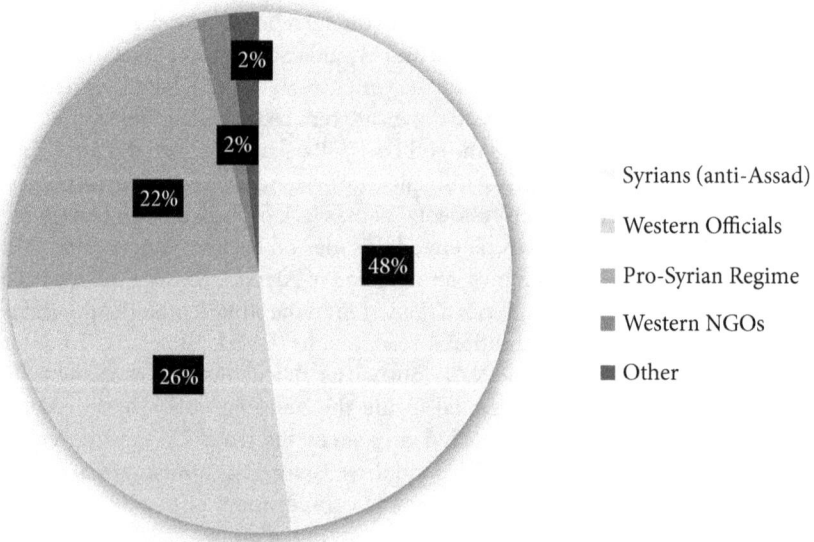

Figure 6.2 Sources in *NYT* articles in period V.

has fallen,' he said. 'If there are no UN initiatives, I expect the regime will exterminate us all.'"[32] Similar accounts appear in other articles, although they usually portray residents and fighters as victims, rather than as active agents in a political struggle. For example, Barnard and Nick Cumming-Bruce quoted Rupert Colville, a spokesman for the United Nations high commissioner for human rights, as saying, "Civilians are caught between warring parties that appear to be operating in flagrant violation of international humanitarian law. All sides are deeply culpable."[33] By saying that civilians were caught between warring parties, the UN spokesperson removed any vestige of agency from the population trapped inside eastern Aleppo.

Notwithstanding the anti-Russia and anti-Assad frames, *NYT* journalists did not abstain from criticizing Syrian rebel groups. For example, in one of her five pieces, Barnard stated, "Years of aerial bombing and artillery bombardment have wrecked many eastern Aleppo neighborhoods, destroying clinics, schools, and homes. Rebels have also indiscriminately shelled government-held neighborhoods in western Aleppo."[34] Barnard did not provide much detail about the shelling of western Aleppo, although in other articles she also referred to the opposition's misconduct during the siege.

In two pieces, *NYT* journalists highlighted that anti-Assad forces in eastern Aleppo were divided. In one of them, Barnard and Saad wrote, "Infighting and mistrust among rebels have hastened their collapse. During the week, al-Qaeda-linked fighters attacked US-backed groups and took their supplies."[35] In the second piece, Barnard and Nick Cumming-Bruce noted that "rebel groups inside east Aleppo [were] fragmented and [did] not always act in concert."[36] As we have seen, several rebel groups were active in Aleppo in December 2016. Although analysts generally classified them as Islamists, moderate secularists, or Salafi-Jihadis, reducing the Syrian opposition to these three subgroups is overly simplistic. Usually, it creates distorted pictures of the situation on the ground. Because of its enormous fragmentation and heterogeneity, understanding the ideologies and financial resources of the anti-Assad movement (both armed and unarmed) requires a much deeper examination.

In brief, the *NYT* coverage of the Syrian conflict in period V relays a neutral frame of the Obama administration's Syria policy. *NYT* authors did not contrast President Obama's speech on national security with the facts on the ground in Syria or with the opinions of different politicians and foreign policy experts. Only one news article briefly mentions the limited role of the United States in the negotiations that led to the evacuation of eastern Aleppo. Instead of carrying out an in-depth analysis of foreign policy during the Obama era, *NYT* journalists compared Obama's and Trump's foreign policy standpoints, which induced the reader to sympathize with the outgoing president. In period V, the *NYT* gave prominence to reporting on the situation in eastern Aleppo, and to do that, *NYT* journalists relied on firsthand accounts from civilians, rebel fighters, and members of humanitarian organizations. These accounts played a key role in building anti-Assad and anti-Russia frames.

The WP *Criticizes Obama's and Trump's Views on Syria*

The *WP* published twenty articles in period V, ten more than the *NYT*. The topics discussed are similar to those in the *NYT*: US foreign policy and the battle of Aleppo. Unlike the *NYT*, however, the *WP* gave more importance to US foreign policy, publishing nine articles with that as their focus. Even in articles about the siege, *WP* journalists paid significant attention to the diplomatic discussion around the events in Aleppo. Of the twenty articles analyzed in this section, sixteen are news pieces and four are opinion columns. In period V, the *WP* coverage is unquestionably critical of the Obama administration, both in news and opinion articles. In news articles, *WP* journalists differed from their *NYT* colleagues in that they relied mainly on sources expressing a critical view of President Obama's Syria policy.

On December 7, journalists Greg Jaffe and David Nakamura published a report about the US president's speech on his national security strategy. Jaffe and Nakamura contrasted President Obama's ideas with counterarguments from critics of the outgoing president, such as Donald Trump and Jim Mattis. On one occasion, the two *WP* journalists stated, "The critique from Trump and Mattis is that the president did not do enough to prevent the Islamic State from taking root in Iraq and Syria and has moved too slowly to destroy it. In Mattis, Trump has chosen a former military commander who … described Obama's strategy to defeat the Islamic State as 'unguided' and 'replete with half measures.'"[37] The notion that President Obama's Syria policy contributed to the growth of ISIS is recurrent throughout the *WP* coverage of the Syrian conflict. In another passage of the text, Jaffe and Nakamura reiterated the idea: "The president's critics contend that Obama did not push hard enough to keep American troops in the country and that the vacuum created by their departure created an opening for the Islamic State."

Two days later, David Ignatius published an opinion piece analyzing President Obama's antiterrorism policy. Ignatius's main argument is that the US president used supposedly "impermissible" tactics: "One unlikely legacy of Obama's presidency is that he made the secret, once-impermissible tactic of targeted killing the preferred tool of American counterterrorism policy."[38] Ignatius was critical of the Joint Special Operations Command (JSOC), which he described as a "supersecret group that manages most military counterterrorism strikes." JSOC was created in 1980 in the aftermath of the Iran hostage crisis to plan and conduct special operations of the US military. The Carter administration's handling of the crisis was deemed as a colossal failure (more than 50 American citizens were held hostage for more than a year in the US embassy in Tehran) and US officials concluded that a special command should be created. Since then, JSOC has played a key role on several special operations of the US military, such as the invasion of Panama in 1989 and the killing of Osama Bin-Laden in 2011, among others. JSOC was in charge of most anti-ISIS operations during both Obama presidencies.

In his article, Ignatius highlighted the fact that President Obama was proud of using drone strikes against alleged terrorists. Ignatius cited "military sources," as saying that JSOC conducted more than twenty thousand drone attacks in Afghanistan, Iraq, and Syria. According to the *WP* columnist, in Iraq and Syria alone, the strikes killed between twenty and twenty-five thousand ISIS operatives. He did not question the importance of adopting counterterrorism policies; he seemed more concerned about their implementation. The *WP* columnist criticized President Obama's "small-footprint tactics, as opposed to big conventional attacks."[39] This article constitutes a direct challenge to the Obama administration in that it questions a crucial aspect of the US president's antiterrorism strategy.

The *WP* published at least three articles in period V that analyze Donald Trump's foreign policy views. Journalists Gregg Jaffe and Gregg Miller sign a news piece that describes the views of the generals who would form Donald Trump's national security team. The journalists argued that these "retired generals" held highly bellicose views on Iran and Islamic terrorism: "President-elect Donald Trump is assembling a national security team dominated by retired generals who share a deep distrust of Iran and have characterized the threat of militant Islam in far direr terms than Obama administration officials and intelligence assessments."[40] Unlike Obama administration officials, Jaffe and Miller continued, Donald Trump's national security team did not consider Russia and China threats on the same level as Iran and "militant Islam." The two *WP* journalists did not explain what the members of Trump's national security team understood by "militant Islam." This type of sweeping generalization, which indicates that several US journalists see the Middle East through Orientalist lenses, can be found often in the *WP* coverage of the Syrian conflict.

Jaffe and Miller also pointed out the contradictions between Donald Trump's impulsive behavior and lack of foreign policy experience and the fact that his advisers had vast combat experience, and therefore maintained a more pragmatic attitude. Their article does not build an unequivocal pro-Obama or pro-Trump frame, although critical narratives of President Obama predominate.

Jackson Diehl, a member of the *WP* editorial board specializing in foreign policy, wrote an opinion piece in which he examined Donald Trump's Islamophobic ideas. Diehl argued that Trump's approach toward Islam and Islamic terrorism differed from George W. Bush's and Barack Obama's. He predicted that Trump's presidency would constitute the "third and darkest phase to neutralize the threat of Islamic extremism." Diehl wrote,

> The outlines of what might well be called the Trump crusade are easily located in the rhetoric of Stephen Bannon, Michael Flynn, Jeff Sessions,[41] and other Trump appointees. They describe a "long history of the Judeo-Christian West struggle against Islam," as Bannon put it, or "a world war against a messianic mass movement of evil people," as Flynn ... has written.[42]

Diehl anticipated that, despite taking a more aggressive stance against Iran, Trump would not change US policy on Syria significantly. On one side, the priority would continue to be defeating ISIS; on the other, Diehl continued, there would be no significant shift in the attitude toward Iran and the Assad regime: "The new administration will look for showy ways to challenge Iran, but it is unlikely to do so in the place where it would matter most: Syria. Trump's civilizational conflict will be experienced not by Shiite militias or Sunni terrorists—who will surely welcome it—but by average citizens across the Muslim world." This forecast proved correct. Whereas on the domestic level the Trump administration passed numerous laws that can be considered Islamophobic, in Syria, the United States did not change the approach toward Iran significantly.

One news article, written by Josh Rogin, a *WP* foreign policy analyst, examines the fact that two Syrian opposition leaders traveled to Washington in December 2016 to try to meet Donald Trump. Rogin took the opportunity to analyze how the two leaders saw the conflict and what they expected to accomplish in the possible meeting with the future US president. Both Syrian political leaders belonged to the National Coalition for Syrian Revolutionary and Opposition Forces; an alliance formed in November 2012 by multiple anti-Assad groups. The National Coalition gained the support of several countries, such as the United States, Turkey, France, and the UK. The *WP* analyst reminded readers that Donald Trump was critical of the support that the United States had provided to segments of the Syrian opposition. According to Rogin, the two leaders did not necessarily oppose a collaboration between the United States and Russia. As they were aware of Donald Trump's strong anti-Iran stance, the two Syrian leaders expected to reach an understanding with the future US president that could benefit the Syrian opposition.

Rogin quoted one of the Syrian oppositionists, Abdul Ilah Fahad, as saying that Russia and Iran could not be treated equally. In Fahad's words, "Working with Russia while isolating Iran would also benefit America's allies in the region, including Israel and the Gulf Arab states."[43] Rogin's article also reinforces the negative frame of President Obama relayed in the *WP* in period V. For example, the foreign policy analyst reported that the Syrian opposition "felt betrayed" by the Obama administration: "Despite years of work to build ties, those representing the opposition are convinced that President Obama overpromised and underdelivered."[44]

Several *WP* articles report on the battle of Aleppo, either as their main or subtopic. Most of these articles combine the analysis of the situation on the ground with the diplomatic discussion around the battle of Aleppo and its geopolitical consequences. In contrast to the *NYT*, which emphasized the situation on the ground, *WP* authors treated these two aspects equally. The majority of the sources quoted in these articles consist of pro-Assad politicians, humanitarian organizations (including the United Nations and the Syrian Observatory for Human Rights), and anti-Assad officials (see Figure 6.3).

Civilians and fighters trapped inside Aleppo account for a minority of the sources quoted in the *WP* in period V. The newspaper relayed unequivocal anti-Russia and anti-Assad frames, highlighting that both regimes were responsible for the bombing and shelling of civilian areas. For example, Louisa Loveluck and Karen DeYoung wrote, "The eastern districts of the city have been under siege since July, with bombardment by Syrian and Russian warplanes killing hundreds of civilians and destroying hospitals that treated the wounded."[45]

6. The Fall of Eastern Aleppo   137

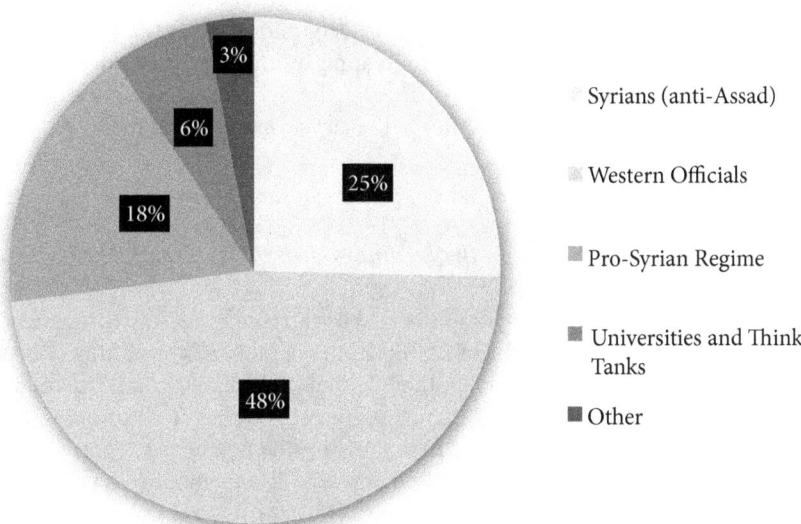

Figure 6.3 Sources in *WP* articles in period V.

When portraying the situation on the ground, *WP* journalists relied more on civilians than rebel fighters. Like in the *NYT*, these civilians were, in most cases, presented as victims, rather than as active subjects in the Syrian uprising and civil war. Loveluck, for instance, quoted two civilians in one news article as saying that they were waiting to die. One of these Aleppo residents' actual words were: "Life in Aleppo has become a slow death, you watch everything and everyone dear to you disappear."[46] Another civilian is quoted as saying, "I am waiting to die or be captured by the Assad regime … Pray for me and always remember us."[47]

Rebel fighters were quoted on three occasions: one belonged to the Islamist group Jaish al-Islam, the second, to the previously mentioned Nour al-Din al-Zenki Movement, and the third, to the Free Syrian Army. The frame vis-à-vis the Syrian opposition is negative, which is consistent with the pattern found in *WP* articles throughout this book. For example, Loveluck and DeYoung quoted Rupert Coville (UN Human Rights spokesperson) as saying that opposition groups had been firing at civilians trying to escape eastern Aleppo: "During the last two weeks, Fatah al-Sham Front and the Abu Amara Battalion[48] are alleged to have abducted and killed an unknown number of civilians who requested the armed groups to leave their neighborhoods, to spare the lives of civilians."[49]

In conclusion, the *WP* coverage of the fall of eastern Aleppo is more complete than in the *NYT* in terms of topics addressed and sourcing practices. The newspaper depicted the Obama administration in negative terms, a trend that remained consistent throughout this research. The critical frame of President Obama is built both in news and opinion articles. The *WP* devoted several articles in period V to analyzing Donald Trump's foreign policy views. In one of these articles, the author predicted that his Syria policy would not differ substantially from President Obama's. When covering the siege of Aleppo, *WP* journalists gave more emphasis to its diplomatic and geopolitical aspects than their *NYT* colleagues, who focused more on the situation on the ground. In period V, *WP* journalists relayed hostile frames of Russia, the Syrian regime, and the Syrian opposition—also a constant feature of the newspaper's coverage of the Syrian conflict.

The WSJ *Focuses on the Incoming Trump Administration*

The *WSJ* published fifteen articles in period V: thirteen of these articles are news and two are opinion pieces. The most frequent topics and subtopics are US foreign policy and the siege of Aleppo. Although the *WSJ* relayed a critical frame of President Obama, implying that the US president had been too soft on ISIS and had not confronted Russia and the Assad regime, the newspaper reported mostly on the incoming Trump administration. The *WSJ* also maintained an anti-Russia and anti-Assad tone.

The newspaper published several articles in period V that analyze the relationship between Russia and Western countries in the face of the Syrian conflict. When covering the fall of eastern Aleppo, *WSJ* journalists used sources that were based in Aleppo, such as activists and rebel fighters, along with members of humanitarian organizations and government officials; however, diplomats and other government officials prevailed over civilians, rebel fighters, and humanitarian workers (see Figure 6.4).

In an article published on December 6, 2016, *WSJ* journalist Carol Lee analyzed President Obama's speech on national security. Lee argued that several of the US president's most relevant foreign policy decisions, such as the withdrawal of troops from Iraq and the more extended use of drones in counterterrorism operations, stemmed from his decision to "scale back America's military presence overseas." The *WSJ* journalist also claimed that President Obama's central message with the speech was that the United States could fight terrorism while "staying true" to its principles. Lee relied mostly on extracts of the speech and comments from Mathew Levitt, a former official under President George W. Bush. The article does not express a recognizable anti- or pro-Obama frame, although most of Obama's statements are contrasted with Levitt's divergent opinions. For example, Lee quoted the former Bush official affirming that terrorist threats had increased during the Obama administration. She also reminded *WSJ* readers that President Obama faced "sharp" criticism for refusing to intervene in the Syrian civil war and that the conflict had become worse since then.

Like her *NYT* and *WP* colleagues, Lee highlighted the fact that the outgoing president was keen to draw a line between his and Donald Trump's views on countering terrorism. In her words, "Mr. Obama, in a national-security speech delivered just weeks before he leaves the White House, repeatedly drew a contrast between his ideas and those of Republican President-elect

Sources in *WSJ* Articles in Period V

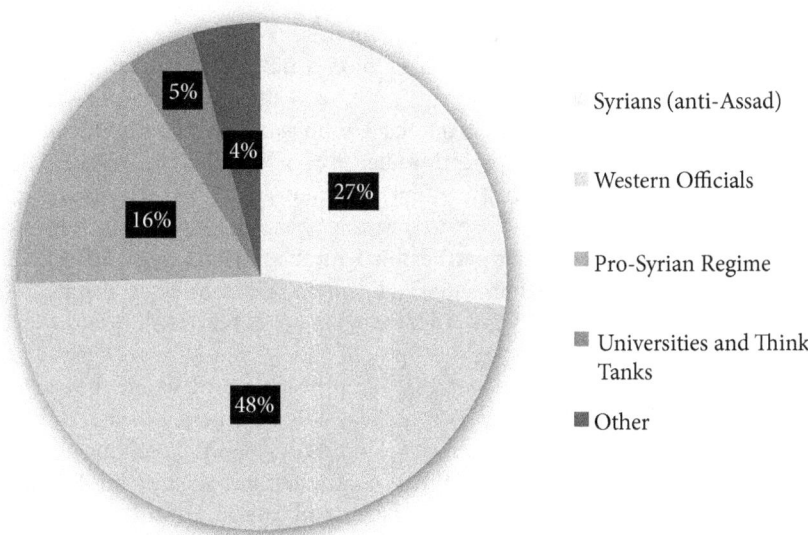

Figure 6.4 Sources in *WSJ* articles in period V.

Donald Trump while making a case for why his successor should adhere to his approach, which was shaped by his early decision to scale back America's military presence overseas."[50]

Journalists Gordon Lubold and Julian Barnes wrote an article in which they compared Barack Obama's and Donald Trump's anti-ISIS policies. The journalists quoted "analysts" as saying that there would be no fundamental differences between the two presidents, although the Trump administration would give more autonomy to the military. According to Lubold and Barnes, "The Obama White House's approach [had] been to use local forces and carefully limit the exposure of American personnel to combat."[51] They also argued that the Trump administration could reduce "White House oversight of operational decisions and [move] some tactical authority back to the Pentagon."

Lubold and Barnes quoted Michael Flynn, Donald Trump's first national security adviser, criticizing the Obama administration for not granting sufficient freedom to the military for it to define the extension of anti-ISIS operations. Flynn continued by saying that "the new administration [would] do a full reassessment of the authorities at the military's disposal to execute the fight against Islamic State." The two *WSJ* journalists also cited military officials (without disclosing their identities) assuring their readiness for an incoming administration that might pursue a harder line against the Islamic State. To contrast these opinions, they quoted members of the Obama administration defending their president's approach. The frame toward President Obama is neutral, a tone that is attained by using both pro- and anti-Obama sources. Additionally, the article suggests a conflict between the Obama administration and the US military; however, the two journalists did not provide much detail about it.

Gerald Seib, by contrast, wrote an opinion article in which he claimed that Donald Trump's Middle East strategy would constitute a significant shift with respect to President Obama's. Seib quoted Trump as saying that the United States would stop "attempting to topple [Middle Eastern] regimes."[52] Trump's Middle East policy, the *WSJ* columnist continued, would consist of four fundamental pillars: firstly, an end to the efforts to oust the Syrian president Bashar al-Assad; secondly, the establishment of a partnership with Russia to defeat the Islamic State; thirdly, a "warmer" relationship with the Egyptian president Abdel Fattah el-Sisi; and finally, increased hostility toward Iran and the possible dissolution of the Iran nuclear deal.

Furthermore, Seib pointed out that Trump's approach would be radically different from President George W. Bush's Middle East policy in that he would be "less willing to intervene in the region militarily." The *WSJ* columnist further argued that Trump's future strategy had contradictions, such as the fact that a closer partnership with Russia would mean empowering Iran: "A partnership with Russia to defeat the Islamic State also means empowering not just Russia's friend there, Syrian President al-Assad, but also Mr. al-Assad's chief regional ally, Iran. Iran has placed a huge bet on its relationship with Mr. al-Assad as the key to its hopes to expand its regional influence."[53] Some of Seib's prognoses, such as that Donald Trump would withdraw from the Iran nuclear deal, proved correct, although others, such as the potential partnership with Russia to defeat ISIS, fell short of the mark.

Carol Lee and Felicia Schwartz wrote an article about Donald Trump's national security team. The *WSJ* journalists noted that the group was highly heterogeneous (it included generals, business people, and conservative politicians), which meant that its members differed on several topics, such as climate change, trade, and the Iran nuclear deal. According to Lee and Schwartz, the key agreement among Trump's future national security team was that the "US approach to global affairs" should undergo a radical shift.[54] They also mentioned the conflicting views of Donald Trump and Rex Tillerson, who would serve as Trump's first secretary of state. Tillerson worked in the oil industry before joining the Trump administration, and some of his remarks on issues such as climate change and the relationship with Iran contrasted with Trump's opinions.

Lee and Schwartz continued the article by highlighting that Tillerson's good relationship with President Putin implied that the United States would undertake a different approach toward Russia: "Mr. Tillerson's relationship with Mr. Putin suggests Mr. Trump plans to press ahead with a warmer relationship between Washington and Moscow. It is unclear what that means for relations with Europe, however, which backs sanctions on Russia over its intervention in Ukraine." The article, which is more descriptive than analytical, relays a neutral tone regarding Donald Trump and his possible foreign policy.

An unsigned opinion piece published on December 14 discusses the role of Russia and the Assad regime in the Syrian civil war. The piece relays an unequivocal anti-Russia and anti-Assad frame, accusing both regimes of deceiving the international community about their commitment to fighting the Islamic State:

> Mr. Putin has long claimed that his forces in Syria are fighting jihadists, especially ISIS. But the reality is that the Bashar al-Assad government and Russians have long focused nearly all of their military attention against the moderate opposition forces. Those are the forces backed by the Saudis and sometimes even by the United States. Mr. al-Assad wants to destroy them first because they pose the most serious long-term threat to the regime.[55]

The author also criticized the Obama administration for avoiding a confrontation with Russia and the Assad regime. In period V, the *WSJ* analyzed Russia's role in the Syrian civil war and its relationship with Western countries in detail, emphasizing these aspects over others, such as the situation on the ground in eastern Aleppo.

Some *WSJ* authors did not subscribe to Donald Trump's views on Russia and Putin. For example, Laurence Norman signs a news article about the frictions between the European Union and Russia over the Aleppo crisis. Norman relied solely on European officials to build his narrative, which lent the article an unmistakable anti-Russia perspective. The article's first paragraph sets the tone: "Senior UK and French diplomats said … that the renewed Islamic State push into the Syrian city of Palmyra demonstrated that Russian forces were focused on propping up President Bashar al-Assad's regime, not tackling terrorism in the country."[56] Despite the anti-Russia frame, Norman mentioned that the European Union was particularly divided over how to deal with Russia: "The European Union has been divided over whether to also target Russian people and entities. A number of countries, including the Czech Republic, Austria, and Italy, have opposed that."

In another article, Norman discussed the perspectives of the Iran nuclear deal under a Trump administration. The journalist focused on how European officials feared US abandonment of the deal. He quoted European diplomats along with members of the incoming Trump administration and the Islamic Republic News Agency (IRNA). Norman suggested that the European Union and the United States could take different stances on how to engage with Iran: "European diplomats have been clear that, if the United States tears up the deal or takes actions that spark a crisis over it, the bloc will not feel obliged to put European sanctions back in place on Iran."[57] The *WSJ* journalist's suggestion proved correct. When the Trump administration effectively pulled out of the Iran nuclear deal in May 2018, the European Union not only criticized the decision but also stepped up efforts to keep the deal in place. In the article, Norman also quoted the UN atomic agency claiming that all parts were complying with the deal, an affirmation that relayed a positive significance to the nuclear agreement. However, it is not possible to identify a clear frame for or against the deal.

Four *WSJ* articles focus on the fall of eastern Aleppo and its geopolitical consequences. The articles report on the Russian offensive over eastern Aleppo, the evacuation agreement, and the humanitarian crisis in the besieged area. They combine the analysis of the situation on the ground with a description of the diplomatic debates among key international actors. As previously discussed, both the *NYT* and the *WP* used a similar style to report on the fall of eastern Aleppo. Like their *WP* colleagues, *WSJ* journalists gave particular importance to unveiling the geopolitical aspects of the events in Aleppo. An analysis of the *WSJ* sourcing practices shows that government officials, both pro- and anti-Assad, constitute the majority of the sources used in these four articles. These sources include officials from countries like Russia, Syria, the United States, and France, and also officials and spokespeople of the United Nations and other humanitarian organizations. These four articles contribute to building an anti-Russia frame in period V.

The Syrian opposition, in turn, is the focus of only one article: a report on the attempts by rebel leaders to meet Donald Trump. At the beginning of the text, *WSJ* journalist Yaroslav Trofimov described Syrian rebels as "Sunni opposition," which suggests that he divided anti-Assad groups predominantly along sectarian lines. In Trofimov's words, "Syria's Sunni opposition does not have many reasons to be optimistic these days as the reinvigorated regime conquers Aleppo amid international indifference. But leaders of the rebel alliance cling to the hope that when Donald Trump tackles the Syrian crisis, his longstanding hostility to Iran will offset his desire to improve relations with Russia."[58] Later in the text, however, the journalist qualified the leaders that reached out to Trump as "moderate."

Throughout the sample of articles analyzed in this book, the *WSJ* has framed the Syrian opposition in ambiguous and simplistic terms—at times as extremist, at times as moderate. In part, this depiction stems from the fact that the Syrian opposition was in fact diverse and heterogeneous. Nevertheless, it is also true that *WSJ* authors did not seem interested in providing in-depth coverage of the anti-Assad movement. The *WP* held an even more hostile view of anti-Assad rebels, portraying them mostly as Islamists or jihadists. In the above article, Trofimov correctly anticipated that Syrian rebels were unlikely to receive support from the Trump administration.

In brief, the *WSJ* coverage of the Syrian conflict in period V focuses mostly on Donald Trump's Middle East and Syria policies. Although the general attitude toward Trump's foreign policy views was neutral, *WSJ* journalists showed concern about his willingness to build closer ties with Russian President Vladimir Putin. The newspaper relayed a negative frame of Russia and the Assad regime, which consistently features in the *WSJ* coverage of the Syrian conflict. Additionally, *WSJ* journalists paid greater attention to the diplomatic debates that surrounded the fall of eastern Aleppo than to its military and humanitarian aspects. In period V, the *WSJ* continued to relay a critical frame of President Obama, although analyzing the Obama administration did not seem to be a priority for *WSJ* authors.

...

The fall of eastern Aleppo and the presidential transition in the United States dominate the coverage of the Syrian conflict in period V. Each of the three newspapers analyzed in this book discussed these two topics but with varying degrees of balance between them. Whereas *NYT* journalists focused on the humanitarian aspects of the battle of Aleppo, the *WP* and the *WSJ* centered their coverage on its diplomatic and geopolitical sides. Critical narratives of President Obama are less frequent in the *NYT* than in the other two newspapers. As we have seen, the *NYT* relayed a neutral frame of Obama, highlighting the contradictions of his Syria policies. The *WP* and the *WSJ*, by contrast, continued to portray the Obama administration negatively. On the other hand, the *WP* and the *WSJ* discussed the incoming Trump administration in more detail than the *NYT*, analyzing his personal views and those of his foreign policy advisers. The three newspapers framed Russia and the Assad regime negatively, and *WSJ* authors openly opposed Trump's intentions to build closer ties with Putin. For *WP* and *WSJ* authors, Obama's and Trump's Syria policies showed elements of continuity and discontinuity. The *NYT*, by contrast, framed the two presidents' policies as being predominantly opposed.

Chapter 7

THE US-UK-FRENCH AIRSTRIKES AGAINST SYRIA (PERIOD VI)

In April 2018, Syria was still a divided country, a patchwork of territories controlled by different groups, hardly resembling the dynamic, multiethnic society that it once was. The Assad regime and its allies were in charge of most of the country, including Aleppo, Homs, and the bulk of Greater Damascus. The Kurdish People's Protection Units (YPG) had become the second-largest force in Syria, controlling a large portion of territory, inhabited mostly by Kurds and Arabs, in northeastern Syria. The YPG is the armed wing of the Democratic Union Party (PYD), which was created in 2003 by members of the Turkey-based Kurdistan Workers' Party (PKK). Among the PYD's founders was Osman Öcalan, the brother of Abdullah Öcalan, the Kurdish leader who has been in a Turkish prison since 1999. The YPG was the backbone of the Syrian Democratic Forces (SDF), a US-supported coalition of groups created in 2015 primarily to fight the Islamic State. Anti-Assad rebel forces, on the other hand, were almost entirely crammed into the province of Idlib, although opposition groups held small pockets of territory in other parts of the country. The Islamic State, which once controlled more than 30 percent of Syria, was reduced to a few brigades squeezed into small areas near the Syrian-Iraqi border.

The focus of the Syrian regime was on regaining the pockets of resistance still under the control of opposition groups. In April 2018, regime forces recaptured Eastern Ghouta after a two-month offensive that claimed thousands of civilian lives. Because of its location in the outskirts of Damascus, the Syrian regime considered the area to be of strategic importance. Eastern Ghouta was then under the control of the Salafist group Jaish al-Islam, although other rebel groups were also active in the besieged enclave. At the beginning of July 2018, a few months after retaking Eastern Ghouta, the regime reconquered the southern city of Dara'a on the Syrian-Jordanian border. The victory in Dara'a had symbolic significance for the Assad regime, as many considered the city the cradle of the Syrian revolution, the place where the first protests erupted in March 2011. Several observers anticipated that it was only a matter of time until regime forces took control of the entire country.

The Assad regime continued to employ all sorts of military tactics to recapture territory, including the use of barrel bombs and chemical weapons. The use of such weapons, which have an extremely low level of precision, meant that the Syrian regime failed to distinguish between civilian and combatant targets, a practice considered a war crime under international conventions. A study conducted by the Global Public Policy Institute, a nonprofit think tank based in Berlin, found that pro-Assad forces used chemical weapons on more than three hundred different occasions between December 2011 and April 2018.[1]

In 2018 alone, it used sarin and chlorine—two gases that cause severe damage to the nerve and respiratory systems—in the Damascene locality of Douma at least three times. These attacks were reported in situ by civilians, citizen journalists, and later confirmed by different organizations, including the Organization for the Prohibition of Chemical Weapons, Forensic Architecture—a multidisciplinary research group based at Goldsmiths, University of London—and Bellingcat—an investigative journalism website based in the Netherlands.[2] The worst of the three attacks, which left a death toll of approximately forty-two people and hundreds of people injured, occurred on April 7, 2018. According to the Violations Documentation Center and to Douma residents, the Syrian Air Force dropped bombs containing the toxic substances on two occasions during that day.

The Douma chemical attack prompted the United States, France, and the UK to launch a series of airstrikes on April 14 against three government locations in Syria: a scientific research center, a chemical weapons facility, and a storage facility. The leaders of the three countries claimed that the airstrikes were carried out in response to the use of sarin and chlorine in Douma. President Trump declared that US security was at stake: "The purpose of our actions tonight is to establish a strong deterrent against the production, spread, and use of chemical weapons. Establishing this deterrent is a vital national security interest of the United States."[3] Theresa May, who was then the British prime minister, framed the attacks similarly, stating that the use of chemical weapons represented a "stain on humanity" that could not be "normalized."

President Trump used the occasion to highlight that his Syria policy was different from President Obama's in that he would not tolerate the crossing of certain "lines" by the Syrian regime. The remark was an obvious reference to the "red line" set by President Obama in 2012 during a press conference in the White House (see Chapter 3). Trump also took the opportunity to criticize Russian President Vladimir Putin, saying that his support for the Syrian regime would entail a "big price to pay." In fact, this occasion was one of the few on which the US president used recriminatory language against his Russian counterpart. The April 2018 airstrikes against Syria constituted the second time that President Trump authorized the use of military force against Syria. In April 2017, in the aftermath of another chemical attack, this time in the village of Khan Sheikhoun, the United States bombed the al-Shayrat airbase near the city of Homs.

Although the three governments justified the joint airstrikes on the grounds that they would act as a deterrent against the use of chemical weapons by the Syrian regime, the attitude of Western powers regarding the use of these kinds of weapons is inconsistent, as Stephen Zunes argued. In a piece written for *Truthout*, a nonprofit news organization, the international relations scholar claimed that the US government turned a blind eye to the use of poisonous gases by the Iraqi regime against Kurdish civilians in March 1988, during the Iran-Iraq War: "The March

1988 massacre in the northern Iraqi city of Halabja, where [Saddam] Hussein's forces murdered up to five thousand Kurdish civilians with chemical weapons, was downplayed by the Reagan administration, with some officials even falsely claiming that Iran was actually responsible. The United States continued sending aid to Iraq even after the regime's use of poison gas was confirmed."[4] Zunes further argued that, apart from being a moral outrage, "the use of any ordnance [not only chemical weapons] on civilian targets is illegal under international law."

The US-UK-French joint airstrikes against Syria triggered an intense debate about their actual impact on the country's civil war. Furthermore, the question of whether or not the attacks represented a departure from President Obama's Syria policy came under the spotlight, receiving a significant amount of media attention. Most analysts agreed that, despite the harsh language used by President Trump against Russia, Iran, and the Syrian regime, the airstrikes would have a negligible impact on the Syrian civil war. For example, *NYT* journalist Peter Baker wrote,

> The strike essentially left in place the status quo on the ground. It did little if anything to weaken Mr. Assad beyond any chemical weapons stores it destroyed, leaving him to continue waging war on his own people through conventional means. It did nothing to exact the "big price" Mr. Trump promised to impose on Russia and Iran for enabling Mr. Assad's chemical attacks.[5]

Michael Crawley, Andrew Restuccia, and Tom McTague, writing for *Politico*, adopted a similar tone:

> The attacks were on a smaller scale than some analysts had predicted, reasoning that Trump needed to send a tougher signal than he did a year ago [when the United States attacked the al-Shayrat airbase in April 2017] given that his last strike had clearly not deterred Assad's continued use of chemical weapons as a tool to put down an armed rebellion that has raged since early 2011.[6]

Various Syrian civil groups also voiced their concerns about the ineptitude of the airstrikes to deter the Syrian regime.

Raja Abdulrahim, writing for the *WSJ*, noted that the Trump administration had no intention to change the course of US foreign policy toward Syria: "Before and during the strikes, the US-led coalition—which is focused solely on battling Islamic State militants—told rebel groups that it backs in Syria that the attack should not be interpreted as a shift to war against the Assad regime."[7] Abdulrahim quoted two members of US-backed groups in Syria, which were part of the anti-ISIS coalition led by the United States, as saying that they had received expressed orders from the US military not to attack Assad regime forces in the aftermath of the 2018 joint airstrikes.

The attack's legality also came under scrutiny. Because the Trump administration did not seek congressional approval before authorizing the use of military force against the Syrian regime, several Democrats regarded the airstrikes as an illegal act of war. In response, Trump officials argued that the Authorization for Use of Military Force, a joint resolution approved in 2001 in the aftermath of the September 11 attacks, provided the legal grounds for the government's actions. However, the Trump administration was not entirely unified about acting against the Assad regime without the imprimatur of the US Congress. Then-Secretary of Defense Jim Mattis pushed for congressional authorization, but President Trump overrode him. Mattis convinced the US president to limit the airstrikes to three targets, though, something that, in his opinion, would prevent the action from triggering a Russian response.

The Trump administration was also reproached, this time by both Democrats and Republicans, for not having a more comprehensive Syria policy. Whereas a few distinguished Republicans advocated a more assertive attitude to counter Russian and Iranian influence in Syria, several Democratic politicians opposed the use of military force against the Syrian regime. Republican Senator Lindsey Graham, for example, complained about US military leaders being reluctant to confront Russia. In his opinion, the United States should not act in Syria just as a "chemical weapons police." Congresswoman Nancy Pelosi, then-House Democratic leader, opposed the airstrikes and demanded a "clear, comprehensive Syria policy."

The debate about the magnitude of US involvement in Syria was directly linked to President Trump's proposal to withdraw US troops from the country, a policy that he had been championing since the 2016 presidential elections. Politicians and experts on both sides of the political spectrum expressed concern over this possibility, arguing that it would harm US interests in the Middle East. Jennifer Cafarella wrote in July 2018,

> A US retreat from eastern Syria, where it currently has some two thousand troops, would create a vacuum that various belligerents would compete to fill. Assad and his backers, Turkey, and jihadist groups such as al-Qaeda and ISIS all hope to gain control of the areas that the US-SDF alliance seized from ISIS. A US withdrawal will only accelerate this conflict.[8]

Senator Graham called the possible move a "stain on the honor of the United States." As mentioned, Democratic politicians also opposed the idea, maintaining that the United States could not withdraw the support that it had been giving to the Kurdish groups fighting ISIS in northeastern Syria.

This chapter analyzes the coverage of the 2018 airstrikes in the *NYT*, the *WP*, and the *WSJ*. The importance of the US-UK-French joint attacks for this book lies in two factors. First, they constituted one of the few occasions on which the United States used military force against the Syrian regime, and as such, they were followed by an intense public debate. Since the emergence of ISIS in 2014, US foreign policy had focused on defeating the terrorist organization. Support for anti-Assad rebel groups was residual during the Obama administration and was virtually eliminated in the Trump years. Second, the attacks presented an opportunity to analyze how the three newspapers reacted to President Trump's erratic Syria policy.

As we have seen in previous chapters, the attitude toward the Obama administration affected how the newspapers covered the Syrian conflict. In April 2018, the three newspapers adopted different discourses regarding the joint airstrikes, and the question that arises is the extent to which these views were affected by their attitude toward the Trump administration.

Period VI comprises nine days, from April 12 to April 20, 2018. The number of articles analyzed is ninety, making period VI the second largest dataset in this book. Of these, sixty-seven are news articles, fourteen are op-eds, four are news analyses, three are editorials, and two are transcripts of statements delivered by US President Donald Trump, British Prime Minister Theresa May, and French President Emmanuel Macron (see Table 7.1). In period VI, seventy-six authors sign or co-sign articles. Of these, fifty-one are men and twenty-five are women. The *NYT* published twenty-seven articles, the *WP*, twenty-eight, and the *WSJ*, thirty-four. In period VI, two topics dominate the coverage of the Syrian conflict: the airstrikes and US foreign policy.

The three newspapers presented different frames of the airstrikes and, consequently, of President Trump's Syria policy. *NYT* authors opposed the attacks on the grounds that the Trump administration did not seek congressional approval. The newspaper was critical of the Trump administration's policy, arguing that the US president lacked a clear strategy toward the conflict. It was not clear, however, what strategy the US government should adopt.

WP authors, by contrast, favored the attacks but maintained that they had been too limited. As this book demonstrates, the *WP* consistently demanded a more interventionist US policy in Syria. *WP* and *NYT* authors presented a critical frame of the Trump administration, although the two newspapers endorsed different policies. *WSJ* authors presented a third view, arguing that the attacks had been justified, and refraining from challenging President Trump's approach to the conflict. Despite their divergent views, the three newspapers agreed that the attacks would not change the course of the Syrian civil war and that Trump's Syria policy did not aim at regime change.

Table 7.1 Number of articles per newspaper and genre in period VI

	News	News Analysis	Opinion	Editorial	Transcripts	Total
NYT	16	4	5	1	2	**28**
WP	23	0	4	1	0	**28**
WSJ	28	0	5	1	0	**34**
Total	67	4	14	3	2	**90**

The NYT Opposes the Airstrikes

In period VI, the *NYT* published sixteen news articles, five opinion pieces, four news analyses, two transcripts of speeches and statements,[9] and one editorial. The number of op-ed and news analysis articles (ten in total) suggests that the *NYT* coverage of the Syrian conflict in period VI is more analytical than usual. The only period in which the newspaper published a higher number of opinion pieces is period IV, which covers the beginning of the Russian campaign in Syria. In periods I, II, III, and V, the *NYT* published fewer opinion pieces than in periods IV and VI.

As previously seen, a remarkable feature of the *NYT* coverage of the Russian intervention in Syria (period IV) is the portrayal of Russia in negative terms. Opinion pieces play a significant role in conveying negative frames, as they provide the broader context in which the reader will situate the news articles published by the newspaper. Therefore, the fact that the *NYT* built a negative frame of the Trump administration in period VI explains the high number of opinion articles. The most discussed topics and subtopics in period VI are the joint airstrikes, US foreign policy, and Russian foreign policy.

Six *NYT* articles assert that the joint airstrikes against Syria were limited and would not change the situation on the ground substantially. Four of these articles are news analyses, one is an opinion piece, and another is a news article. One day after the attacks, for example, Ben Hubbard wrote, "[Syria] will remain mired in its painful status quo: a multilayered conflict with the Syrian people stranded in battles between global and regional powers. The United Nations will keep organizing talks that do not bring peace, and the [UN] Security Council will remain too divided to stop the bloodshed."[10] Hubbard continued by claiming that the attacks "were meticulously planned and executed to avoid altering the overall dynamics of the conflict and keep the United States from getting dragged further in."

Several analysts argued that the attacks' limited scope resulted from President Trump's unwillingness to provoke Russia (and to a certain extent Iran). Michael Wolgelenter, who was then the *NYT*'s news editor in London, maintained that "the United States and its allies tried to walk a fine line with the airstrikes, sending a strong message to President Bashar al-Assad of Syria without provoking a military response from Russia and Iran."[11] Thomas Gibbons-Neff went a step further, claiming that the Assad regime would continue to use chemical weapons against civilians. To substantiate this view, the *NYT* journalist quoted a Pentagon report according to which the airstrikes did not undermine the Assad regime's capability of producing these kinds of weapons. Gibbons-Neff wrote, "[The report] found that the Syrian president is expected to continue researching and developing chemical weapons for potential future use, according to an American intelligence analyst who has seen the document and described it to the *New York Times* on the condition of anonymity."[12]

David Sanger and Ben Hubbard agreed with this view, stating in a news article that it would be relatively easy for the Assad regime to replace the weapons destroyed by the airstrikes. The two journalists quoted Michael Knights, a fellow at the Washington Institute for Near East Policy, as saying that it would be impossible to destroy Bashar al-Assad's chemical weapons capabilities. In Knights' words, "[you] either have to deter the regime from using [chemical weapons] by imposing significant costs, or you have to get rid of the regime. But there is no way you can get rid of the capability."[13] The article does not suggest that the United States should seek regime change, as Knight's words may imply, but it expressed sharp criticism at both the Obama and the Trump administrations' Syria policies. Sanger and Hubbard criticized former Secretary of State John Kerry for stating that the best way to prevent the use of chemical weapons by the Assad regime was through diplomatic channels. This skepticism toward diplomacy indicates that the two journalists favored more decisive US policy in Syria. This notion represents a departure from previous views shared by *NYT* journalists, who regularly opposed US interventionism in the conflict.

The *NYT* relayed an anti-Trump frame in period VI. The newspaper criticized the US president's lack of a clear Syria policy. In a news analysis, Peter Baker argued that President Trump had "competing impulses" in Syria. On the one hand, Baker argued, the US president intended to maintain President Obama's policy to fight the Islamic State and, on the other, he felt compelled to fulfill his promise to withdraw the United States from foreign conflicts. The journalist quoted several experts as saying that the attacks would fail to deter the Syrian regime (see Figure 7.1). One of the experts is Colin Kahl, who served as national security adviser to Joe Biden when he served as US vice president. According to Kahl, "[the] relatively cautious nature of the strike signaled that we were deterred from taking larger action, potentially undercutting the credible US threat of doing more down the line if the regime continues to use chemical weapons."[14]

Emma Ashford, a researcher at the Cato Institute,[15] shared the view that the airstrikes would fail to deter the Syrian regime. However, her argument is different from Kahl's, whose article implies that the United States should "take larger action" in Syria. Ashford, by contrast, advocated a more cautious approach, arguing that the joint airstrikes had been less effective in deterring the Syrian regime than President Obama's 2013 chemical weapons deal with Russia: "In 2013, Mr. Obama chose not to approve military strikes against Syria. Instead, he negotiated the removal of most of Syria's chemical weapons, an imperfect compromise, but one that reduced the risk of chemical weapons attacks on civilians for several years."[16] Moreover, Ashford criticized President Trump, both on a political and personal level. On one side, she argued that his foreign policy was "military-centric," on the other, that the US president was always seeking media attention and was unable to control his impulses.

In an editorial published on April 13, the *NYT* editorial board opposed the airstrikes, arguing, "Under the UN Charter, there are two justifications for using force against another country without its consent: in self-defense and with the UN Security Council's permission. The former does not apply in this case, and the latter would be impossible, given Russia's veto power in the Council."[17] The editorial board also called for the passing of legislation restraining the power of US presidents to attack third countries unilaterally.

Despite adopting an anti-Trump frame, *NYT* authors did not overlook the similarities between Obama's and Trump's approach to the Syrian conflict. Susan Rice, who served as national security adviser during President Obama's second term, wrote an op-ed arguing that both presidents had "proven more alike than not" in their Syria policies.[18] Rice highlighted the fact that both administrations prioritized defeating ISIS over toppling the Syrian president. The former Obama official further claimed that the United States had consistently avoided confrontation with Russia and a broader entanglement in the Syrian civil war, pursuing a political solution instead. She also mentioned that both Obama and Trump "drew a controversial distinction" between conventional and chemical weapons, even though the Assad regime had killed far more civilians with so-called conventional weapons. According to her, the firmer stance against chemical weapons had to do with the fact that the United States had a vested interest in upholding the system of international norms.

In Rice's view, both US presidents shared the belief that chemical weapons violated international law. She concluded the article by suggesting that although the United States should "refrain from deposing Mr. Assad militarily" and "renew its push for a negotiated settlement to the conflict," it should maintain troops in the country to "help secure, rebuild, and establish effective local governance in liberated areas." By highlighting the similarities between Obama and Trump, Rice dissented from most *NYT* authors. As we have seen in the previous chapter, in period V, the *NYT* underscored the differences between both leaders. In terms of policy proposals, however, Rice's piece epitomizes the view of the Syrian conflict relayed by most *NYT* authors in the dataset analyzed herein.

Gene Healey and John Glaser, who are also foreign policy researchers at the Cato Institute, sign an opinion article outlining their views of US foreign policy. Although the piece is not directly about Syria, the fact that it was published in the context of the 2018 airstrikes makes it relevant for this book. Healey and Glaser delivered a sharp critique on the war on terror strategy. More specifically, they discussed the Authorization for Use of Military Force (AUMF), which allows US presidents to employ military force against the perpetrators of the 2001 terrorist attacks and other designated terrorist groups.

The two scholars argued that the war on terror strategy did not fulfill its intended objective of deterring these organizations. According to Healey and Glaser, the strategy produced the opposite outcome, as the number of active terrorist groups in the countries where the United States intervened since 2001 had actually increased: "In the seven countries that the United States either invaded or bombed since September 11 [Afghanistan, Iraq, Pakistan, Syria, Libya, Yemen, and Somalia], the number of individual terrorist attacks rose by an astonishing 1,900 percent from 2001 to 2015. If anything, open-ended war in the Middle East has made us less safe, not more."[19] The authors did not clarify what they meant by "individual terrorist attacks."

Additionally, Healy and Glaser argued, the so-called Corker-Kaine resolution would expand (not restrain as its advocates claimed) presidential powers to start new wars. The Corker-Kaine resolution was presented in April 2018 to the US Congress by Republican Senator Bob Corker and Democratic Senator Tim Kaine with the objective of reframing the original AUMF, which had been enacted into law on September 18, 2001. The resolution expanded the number of organizations and countries against which the US president was authorized to use force without congressional approval. The two Cato researchers also claimed that the new resolution would turn "the constitutional war making process upside down," since it kept the initiative with the president. Healey and Glaser's piece constitutes a clear challenge to President Trump's decision to attack Syria and also to the idea that terrorism is an existential threat to the United States.

In period VI, *NYT* authors analyzed the divisions within the US political establishment in detail. Democrats and Republicans held opposing views of the 2018 airstrikes, as Cooper, Gibbons-Neff, and Hubbard reported: "Early reaction to the strikes from Capitol Hill appeared to break down along party lines, with Republicans expressing support for the president and Democrats questioning whether Mr. Trump has a well-thought-out strategy for what happens after the military action is over."[20] At least two other authors reported on the differences between Republicans and Democrats on the issue. Although the debate largely followed a partisan divide, a few Republican senators criticized President Trump's lack of a Syria policy, as Nicholas Fandos reported. He quoted McCain stating that the US president needed to lay out US goals, "not just with regard to ISIS, but also the … conflict in Syria and malign Russian and Iranian influence in the region."[21]

Helene Cooper, in turn, signs an article that analyzes the differences between Jim Mattis and President Trump. She claimed that Mattis failed to convince the US president to seek congressional approval before authorizing the airstrikes. Cooper further argued that the frictions between the two politicians reflected a more comprehensive debate inside the Republican Party: "Neoconservative members of the Republican foreign policy establishment have started to air concerns that Mr. Mattis is ceding strategic territory to Iran and Russia in Syria."[22] The above articles illustrate that the Syrian conflict continued to be a highly controversial topic in US politics during the Trump presidency. It also suggests that *NYT* authors were eager to show the contradictions and weaknesses of the Trump administration.

Several *NYT* articles analyze the relationship between the United States and Russia. This issue comprises a fundamental part of the coverage of the Syrian conflict. On different occasions since the beginning of the uprising, the two countries were involved in intense debates at the UN Security Council and other international fora. The US mainstream media reported avidly on this controversial relationship. Nevertheless, the issue gained extra prominence during the Trump administration, which was probably a result of the president's stated sympathies toward President Putin.

In one of the articles that discusses this issue, Hubbard quoted Maha Yahya, the director of the Carnegie Middle East Center in Beirut, as saying that the United States should seek an agreement with Russia to solve the Syrian conflict. Yahya argued that such an agreement would require intense diplomatic activity, which the Trump administration was unwilling to undertake: "The only solution, [Yahya] said, is a settlement between Russia and the United States that other powers, like Turkey and Iran, could eventually be brought into. But reaching such an agreement would involve an intensity of diplomatic efforts that Mr. Trump's administration is not interested in."[23]

NYT authors continued to portray Russia negatively. For example, Cory Gardner, a Republican and a member of the US Senate Committee on Foreign Relations, signs an opinion article advocating the inclusion of Russia in the list of countries that support terrorism. Gardner wrote, "The moral case for such a designation is sound. Russia has invaded its neighbors Georgia and Ukraine, it supports the murderous regime of Bashar al-Assad and our enemies in Afghanistan, and it is engaged in active information warfare against Western democracies, including meddling in the 2016 United States elections."[24] Gardner's article constitutes one of the few occasions in the sample analyzed in this book in which a Republican authored an opinion piece for the *NYT*. The piece is highly critical of Russia, functioning as a critique of President Trump's intention to improve US-Russia relations.

Two other articles analyze the state of the relationship between the two countries. Sewell Chan signs a news piece discussing the UN Security Council's rejection of a resolution condemning the US-UK-French airstrikes against Syria. Chan quoted Vasily Nebenzia, the Russian ambassador to the United Nations, as saying that the aggression had been against a sovereign state that was "on the front lines of the fight against terrorism."[25] According to Nebenzia, the United States had shown a remarkable disregard for international law by acting before the Organization for the Prohibition of Chemical Weapons determined whether or not chemical weapons had been used in Douma.

In another article, Peter Baker reported on President Trump's intentions to impose sanctions on Russia for "enabling the Syrian government's use of chemical weapons." Baker argued that the sanctions would come despite President Trump's attempts to get closer to President Putin. The *NYT* journalist underscored that Syria was not the only area of contention between the United States and Russia: "New sanctions … would be the third round enacted by the Trump administration against Russia in the past four weeks. Last month, the administration targeted Russian companies and individuals for intervening in the 2016 election and mounting cyberattacks against Western facilities."[26] Despite "the deterioration in relations between Moscow and the West," Baker went on to argue that it was unlikely that the airstrikes would mean a greater US involvement in the Syrian civil war.

In conclusion, the *NYT* coverage of the 2018 airstrikes against Syria is critical of the Trump administration. The higher number of op-ed and news analysis articles contributes to building this frame. Most *NYT* authors agreed that the airstrikes were limited and would hardly impact the Syrian civil war. The *NYT* editorial board, in turn, opposed the airstrikes on the grounds that they violated the UN Charter. Additionally, an article signed by two foreign policy experts condemns the war on terror strategy, suggesting that the US Congress should limit the powers of presidents to wage war abroad. One article implies that the United States should act boldly to deter the Assad regime from using chemical weapons, although it does not provide specific details about how this should be done. In period VI, *NYT* authors quoted more Republicans than in the other periods analyzed in this book, suggesting an eagerness to explore the fissures within the Republican Party in order to build a negative frame of the Trump administration.

Sources in *NYT* Articles in Period VI

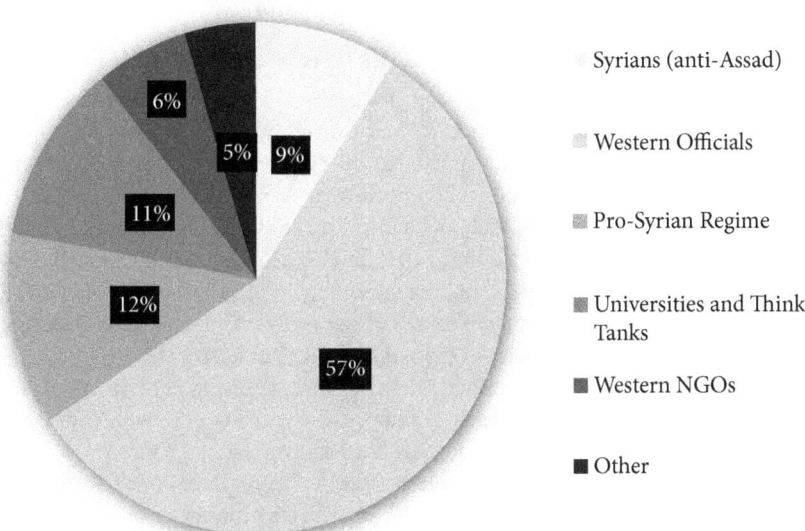

Figure 7.1 Sources in *NYT* articles in period VI.

Lastly, the *NYT* maintained its critical view of Russia, although some authors argued directly (or implied) that a deal between the United States and Russia was the most feasible way to resolve the Syrian conflict.

The WP *Considers the Airstrikes Insufficient*

The *WP* published twenty-eight articles in period VI. Of these, twenty-three are news articles, four are opinion pieces, and one is an editorial. The most discussed topics in the *WP* coverage of the Syrian conflict in period VI are US foreign policy, the airstrikes against Syria, and the relationship between the United States and Russia. Like the *NYT*, the *WP* adopted a critical attitude toward the Trump administration, criticizing the US president for the lack of a well-defined Syria policy and his intention to withdraw US troops from the country.

As in previous periods, *WP* authors advocated that the United States play a more active role in the Syrian conflict. For example, an editorial published one day after the airstrikes states that "the departure of the Assad regime" was the only way to end the use of chemical weapons against civilians.[27] By arguing that "it was wrong for Mr. Trump to call [the] operation a 'Mission Accomplished,'" the editorial board implied that the removal of Bashar al-Assad should be carried out by the United States. This position, however, is not unanimous in the *WP* coverage of the Syrian conflict in period VI. As we will see, other authors claimed that a political arrangement involving the United States, Russia, the Syrian government, and the so-called moderate opposition was the best way to move forward and end the conflict.

Most *WP* journalists maintained that the 2018 airstrikes in Syria were limited and would produce minor impacts on the ground. Liz Sly and Louisa Loveluck, for example, claimed that the attacks "had caused no serious casualties and had probably not destroyed Syria's capacity to develop and deploy banned chemical substances."[28] Sly and Loveluck quoted Amr al-Azm, a professor of history at Shawnee State University in Ohio, as saying that the attacks would not prevent the Assad regime from winning the war. Al-Azm also claimed that the airstrikes were "more about the Western allies making sure their red lines were addressed rather than trying to seriously damage the Assad regime, prevent the further killing of civilians, or reduce the capacity of the Assad regime to keep fighting."

WP journalist Paul Sonne agreed with the view expressed in Sly and Loveluck's article, arguing that it was unclear whether the Syrian regime would stop using chemical weapons. Sonne quoted Robert Ford stating that the United States would have to conduct follow-up attacks against the Assad regime. Ford suggested that the US government considered regime change as a legitimate approach. In Ford's words, "[w]e are getting closer to a regime-change scenario because [Assad is] bombing almost every day. To me, that is drawing us in. I have zero confidence that we could control where that goes then."[29] Sonne's article suggests that the United States should play a larger role in the Syrian civil war, constituting an accurate summary of the *WP*'s view in period VI. Sonne quoted several officials or experts who urged the United States to act (see Figure 7.2). Besides quoting former ambassador Ford, he quoted Kenneth Pollack, a former CIA analyst and resident scholar at the American Enterprise Institute.[30] Pollack said, "As long as you have a strategy that leaves Assad in place and allows him to slaughter his people as he sees fit, he is going to do so. And he is probably going to use chemical warfare agents."[31]

WP authors were particularly critical of President Trump. *WP* columnist Michael Gerson wrote an opinion article that draws attention to President Trump's double standard in Syria: "Trump's position ... has its own share of inconsistencies. It prioritizes the lives of children killed by a nerve agent above the lives of children killed by a barrel bomb. Targeting civilians—through bombing, forced starvation, torture, and the repeated use of chemical weapons—has been an essential element of Syrian President Bashar al-Assad's strategy."[32] Gerson went further, claiming that both Trump and Obama had similar priorities in Syria, namely the defeat of the Islamic State and the opposition to the use of chemical weapons. The foreign policy scholar suggested that the best policy would be arming moderate opposition groups so they would be able to force the Assad regime to a negotiation.

WP columnist Eugene Robinson criticized the Trump administration for not having a clear Syria strategy. Describing President Trump's policy as "international lurching," Robinson argued that his Syria approach was unclear and confusing. For him, Trump is a realist, a president who believed that foreign relations are a

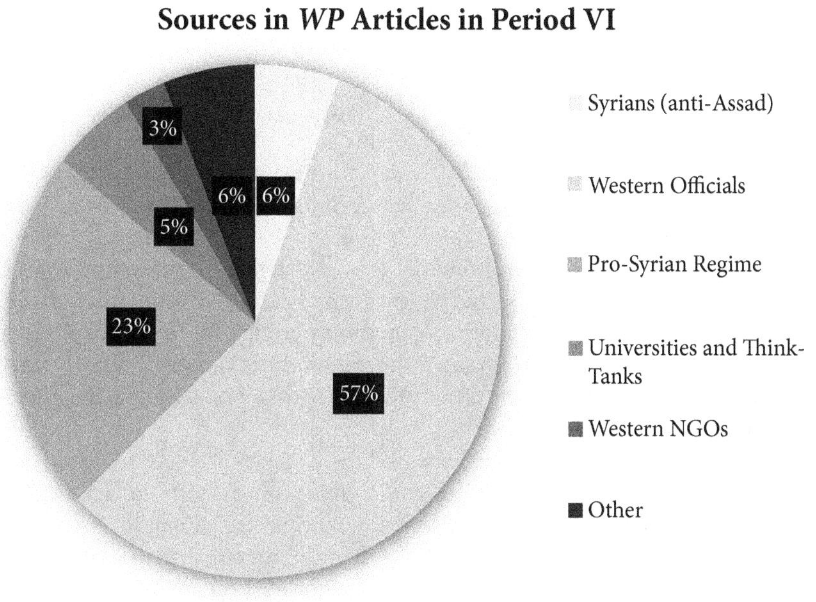

Sources in *WP* Articles in Period VI

- Syrians (anti-Assad): 57%
- Western Officials: 23%
- Pro-Syrian Regime: 5%
- Universities and Think-Tanks: 6%
- Western NGOs: 6%
- Other: 3%

Figure 7.2 Sources in *WP* articles in period VI.

"zero-sum game in which [other countries] must lose so that [the United States] may win." Robinson also maintained that the United States used to embody liberal principles in foreign policy: "If the aim of foreign policy were to keep everybody guessing, Trump would be a smashing success. But that is no proper goal for the leader of the free world. Rhetorically, at least, the United States used to stand for freedom, democracy, and human rights throughout the world."[33] The *WP* columnist continued his argument by accusing President Trump of sympathizing with dictators while ignoring democratic leaders.

In period VI, *WP* authors did not spare President Obama from criticism. Karen DeYoung, for example, argued that the lack of a coherent Syria strategy dated back to the Obama era. According to DeYoung, President Obama failed to support Syrian rebels decisively and enforce the "red line" against the use of chemical weapons. The *WP* journalist continued by stating that US policy in Syria had primarily consisted of controlling the northeastern part of the country with the help of Kurdish militias. DeYoung believed that President Trump intended to change this approach:

> Trump appeared to undercut that goal [of controlling northeastern Syria with the help of Kurdish militias] in recent weeks when he voiced, to the surprise of many within the administration, plans to withdraw US forces as soon as the last militant remnants are defeated. In turn, he has solicited military and financial

contributions from regional partners, especially among the gulf states, to send troops and pay for stability operations.[34]

In a similar line, Greg Jaffe claimed that President Trump's guiding foreign policy principle was "[doing] the opposite of his predecessor."[35] For Jaffe, the April airstrikes had been an attempt by Trump to differentiate himself from Obama and show how weak his predecessor had been in the face of international crises. Jaffe was critical of President Obama, stating that he had continuously hesitated to challenge the Assad regime militarily. Such a statement implies that the United States should play a more active role in the Syrian civil war, through direct intervention or military support to opposition groups. In his article, Jaffe also highlighted the conflicts within the Trump administration, reporting that the US president had "shocked" some of his officials when announcing his intentions to remove US troops from Syria.

Several other *WP* authors underscored the divisions inside President Trump's cabinet. For instance, Josh Rogin, commenting on Trump's indecisiveness to sanction Russia, wrote, "Trump's disagreement with his national security team on Syria spilled into public view this week when the president pulled back on new Syria-related sanctions on Russia, even though US Ambassador to the United Nations Nikki Haley had already announced them."[36] In period VI, at least five *WP* articles analyze the disagreements between President Trump and different members of his cabinet.

Mike DeBonis and Karoun Demirjian widened the scope, examining the divisions within the entire US political establishment. In a news article published two days after the airstrikes, the two journalists offered an outline of the polarization besetting both US mainstream parties. They argued that Congress was "divided on what [the Syria] strategy should be and how much latitude Trump and his successors should be given to intervene in Syria and elsewhere in the Middle East."[37] For DeBonis and Demirjian, the US political elite struggled to decide how much autonomy presidents should have to wage war abroad. Whereas some of the politicians quoted in the article criticized the attacks for being too limited, others expressed concern that they were carried out without congressional approval. DeBonis and Demirjian quoted Democrats and Republicans equally in their article.

As mentioned in the beginning of this section, the *WP* published an editorial on April 14 that approved the attacks and regarded its stated objective, deterring the deployment of chemical weapons, as legitimate. The *WP* editorial board also expressed their approval of US authorities trying "to minimize the risk of a direct military confrontation with Russia or Iran."[38] However, the editorial not only opposes the planned withdrawal from Syria but also states that the "departure of the Assad regime" was the only way to "ensure that Syrians [did] not suffer more atrocities." Moreover, the editorial board argued that the United States should strengthen its military positions in the country in order to counter Russian and Iranian influence in the Middle East: "Moscow and Tehran will not be swayed by moral arguments. The United States must use the leverage it has on the ground, by maintaining and, if necessary, further fortifying its position in the country."

Various *WP* authors warned that the withdrawal of US troops from Syria would constitute an unprecedented mistake. In the previously mentioned opinion piece, Rogin provided a list of possible consequences of leaving the country:

> The dangers of a precipitous US withdrawal from Syria are severe: Iran and Russia would entrench themselves militarily, our partners in Syria would conclude we abandoned them, US credibility would suffer, and regional allies would look elsewhere for leadership. It is highly likely that Syrian leader Bashar al-Assad would continue his mass atrocities, and it is within the realm of possibility that the Islamic State could reemerge.[39]

The *WP* columnist argued that US allies had lost the civil war, and it was time for the United States to de-escalate tensions with Russia. Rogin's article implies that the US government should negotiate a political solution with Russia and the Syrian government. However, for this plan to succeed, US troops needed to remain in the country.

WP authors proposed different solutions to the Syrian conflict. The newspaper discussed these possible solutions more extensively than the *NYT*. Although the editorial published on April 14 calls for the ousting of the Assad regime, some *WP* analysts differed from this view, defending instead an arrangement between the different actors involved in the conflict. For instance, *WP* columnist Kathleen Parker opposed the removal of Bashar al-Assad on the grounds that it was unclear which force would fill the void. "If we were ultimately 'successful' [in removing Assad], would we be initiating yet another long-term occupation in the Middle East?" Parker asked.[40] Although her article does not elaborate on possible solutions to the conflict, it implies that a political agreement between Trump and Putin was the best outcome. In period VI, at least two other authors advocated a political solution in Syria.

Gerson, for instance, argued that the best outcome for the United States would be a "well-armed coalition of moderate rebels forcing the [Syrian] regime to the negotiating table, resulting in a coalition government that includes some regime elements but not Assad."[41] In his opinion, the above scenario was highly unlikely to occur because the United States had lost several years carrying out an erratic, incoherent Syria policy.

On another note, several *WP* articles discuss the growing tensions between the United States and Russia in the aftermath of the airstrikes. The *WP* covered this topic in more detail than the *NYT*. Despite the escalation of accusations and the threat of new US sanctions against Russia, most authors agreed that Russia would not retaliate. Anton Troianovski, the newspaper's Russia correspondent at the time, argued that the joint airstrikes had not damaged Russian positions in Syria: "While Russia slammed the missile attack rhetorically, it signaled that the strike had not crossed the threshold that would bring Russian retaliation. Moscow's response shows that Washington appears to have succeeded in delivering a blow that did not provoke Russia militarily."⁴² Russia's balanced response, Troianovski continued, had to do with the fact that the country was trying to portray itself as a more relevant and reliable player in the Middle East. The *WP* journalist further argued that the airstrikes did not affect Russia's strategy of "[cementing] a long-term foothold in the Middle East."

In conclusion, the *WP* coverage of the Syrian conflict in April 2018 is consistent with the discourses it produced in the previous periods analyzed in this research. The newspaper continued to advocate a more active US involvement in Syria and the Middle East. Several *WP* authors suggested that the 2018 airstrikes had been limited and would not change the situation on the ground. Additionally, the newspaper's coverage is consensual in opposing the withdrawal of US troops from Syria. One author argued that the United States should step up the support given to the moderate Syrian opposition. In another article, it was implied that the country would have to carry out follow-up attacks against the Syrian regime in order to deter the use of chemical weapons against civilians.

In period VI, the *WP* shared a negative frame of both the Trump and the Obama administrations, reproving them for lacking well-defined Syria policies. Two *WP* authors suggested that President Trump's Syria policy was slightly different from his predecessor's. With respect to possible solutions to the Syrian conflict, the newspaper did not relay a single position. Two columnists openly defended a political arrangement between the different actors involved in the conflict. The *WP* editorial board, in turn, argued that the departure of the Assad regime was the best guarantee of stability, although it did not specify how this objective would be achieved.

The WSJ *Adopts an Advisory Tone toward Trump*

The *WSJ* published thirty-four articles in period VI. Twenty-eight of these are news pieces, five are opinion articles, and one is an editorial. Two topics predominate in the *WSJ* coverage of the Syrian conflict in period VI: US foreign policy and the airstrikes against Syria. However, the newspaper discussed other issues, such as the Syrian civil war, ISIS, and the geopolitics of the Middle East. In general, the newspaper adopted a neutral frame of President Trump, avoiding explicit criticism of him, as the other two newspapers had done, but occasionally mentioning the inconsistencies of his Syria policy. *WSJ* authors suggested that the United States should play a more decisive role in Syria, mostly to contain the Syrian and Iranian regimes.

As with the *NYT* and the *WP*, *WSJ* authors claimed that the 2018 airstrikes were limited and would not bring a fundamental change to the Syrian civil war. The newspaper expressed this view both in news and opinion articles. For example, Raja Abdulrahim wrote a news piece about how the attacks had not damaged the Syrian regime's capability to use conventional weapons. Abdulrahim argued that so-called conventional weapons had caused most casualties in the conflict and that the Assad regime would continue to use them against civilians. She wrote,

While chemical-weapons facilities were the target of the military strikes, President Bashar al-Assad's main tool of war has been conventional arms such as rockets, barrel bombs, and mortars. Those have caused the vast majority of more than 400,000 deaths in a seven-year civil war and helped him win back large parts of the country. By contrast, chemical weapons have killed fewer than 2,000 people, according to activist and human rights groups.[43]

The three newspapers analyzed in this book shared the view that the joint airstrikes would have a limited impact on the Syrian regime's military capability.

WSJ authors agreed with the widely held assessment that the Trump administration needed a more coherent strategy for the Syrian conflict. Foreign policy scholars Ryan Crocker and Michael O'Hanlon argued that the airstrikes constituted an unprecedented opportunity for the "West" to develop such a strategy. The two scholars proposed a policy that included more US military engagement in the country and the prolongation of the alliance with Kurdish groups in northeastern Syria. They also stated that the United States should momentarily refrain from pursuing the removal of Bashar al-Assad:

> [T]he West has no way to make [Bashar al-Assad] leave at present. That means the United States and the international community need to redefine the United Nations process in Geneva, which currently seeks to create a new leadership to replace Mr. Assad ... For now, the Geneva talks should focus less on political transition and more on technical issues like distributing relief and reviving agriculture.[44]

Although several *WSJ* articles emphasize the inconsistencies of President Trump's Syria policy, the newspaper did not portray his presidency negatively. Instead, it adopted a cautious tone toward the Trump administration, acting more as an adviser of the president than an opponent or an independent observer. For example, Walter Russel Mead stated that President Trump's Middle East policy could be successful if the president forged the right alliances: "The Trump agenda has a real chance of success in the Middle East—but only if the Trump administration can master the dark arts of alliance management. That may seem unlikely, but if there is one thing we have learned about this president, it is that he can be tactically flexible in pursuit of his goals."[45]

Mead was one of the few commentators that did not echo the idea that the Trump administration lacked a Syria policy. Like *WP* columnist Eugene Robinson, he saw the US president as a realist who was willing to build alliances with any Middle Eastern country opposed to Russia and Iran, "irrespective of its human-rights record." Mead also argued that President Trump's main goal in Syria was to "avoid bailing out without getting sucked in." While other analysts deemed this to be a contradiction, Mead saw it as a pursuit of balance. And "alliance management" comprised the key factor in determining the outcome of this policy.

Michael Gordon and Dion Nissenbaum adopted the same advisory tone toward President Trump. In a news article published on April 14, they quoted a former state department official as saying that the airstrikes could only be effective if the US government conducted follow-up strikes in combination with aggressive diplomacy. Gordon and Nissenbaum seemed to believe that President Trump was willing to authorize a sustained operation against the Syrian regime if it continued to use chemical weapons indiscriminately. They wrote, "Mr. Trump appeared to be trying to do exactly that [carry out a significant follow-up of the airstrikes] by asserting that the US was prepared for a 'sustained' operation, though his defense secretary said the strike was a 'one-time shot.'"[46] Also, the article suggests, the United States should maintain a military presence in the country. The two *WSJ* journalists stated that it was "unclear how the United States [hoped] to encourage a diplomatic settlement for Syria if Mr. Assad, Russia, and Iran still [held] the high cards on the battlefield."

Yaroslav Trofimov analyzed the consequences of US troops withdrawing from Syria, concluding that it would increase the possibility of a conflict between Israel and Iran. In an opinion piece that dissects the growing tensions between both countries, Trofimov asserted that the move would constitute an enormous service to Russia and Iran, as they were better positioned to fill the void left by the United States: "President Donald Trump's stated desire to withdraw US forces from Syria—which, if it happens, would be a major strategic boon to Iran and Russia—is only fueling Israel's sense that it must act against Iran before it is too late."[47]

Trofimov's piece portrays Iran in highly negative terms. To build this perspective, he quoted different foreign policy experts and Israeli officials (see Figure 7.3). One

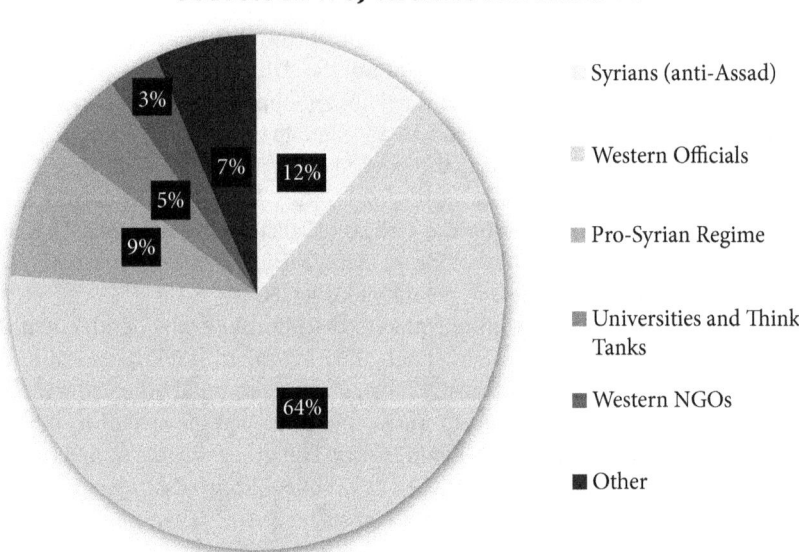

Figure 7.3 Sources in *WSJ* articles in period VI.

of the quoted officials is retired Major General Yaakov Amidror, who stated that Iran had shifted its priority in the region "from preventing a collapse of Syrian President Bashar al-Assad's regime to preparing for a future confrontation with Israel." The fact that the *WSJ* journalist did not use any Iranian sources to contrast this controversial statement gives the piece a pro-Israel bias. Amidror, who served as Israeli Prime Minister Benjamin Netanyahu's national security adviser from 2011 to 2013, also claimed that Israel was "ready to take the risk of a war" to prevent Iran from building its nuclear capability.

WSJ authors examined the divisions inside the Trump administration in at least two articles. In one of them, Gordon Lubold and Dion Nissenbaum argued that the Trump national security team was divided into two factions.[48] The first of these promotes a more assertive foreign policy toward Russia, Iran, and North Korea, as these countries represented threats to the United States. This group, whose members included formers National Security Adviser John Bolton and Secretary of State Mike Pompeo, also favored an attack that undermined the Syrian regime's full military capability, not only its chemical weapons facilities. The second faction, which supported a more cautious foreign policy approach, was led by Jim Mattis. The fact that President Trump opted for a more restrained attack, Lubold and Nissenbaum argued, illustrated that Mattis wielded noticeable influence over the US president.

The *WSJ* also reported on the disagreements within the entire US establishment. As previously discussed, these divisions seemed to follow a partisan line, with Republicans favoring the airstrikes and Democrats criticizing that President Trump did not seek congressional approval before authorizing them. The divisions between both political parties also revolved around the president's legal authority to use military force abroad. In one of the articles about the issue, *WSJ* journalist Chris Gordon argued that "congressional lawmakers reacted swiftly to President Donald Trump's decision to launch missiles against Syria in responses that reflected the partisan divide over foreign policy, military intervention, and Mr. Trump's role as commander-in-chief."[49] In spite of arguing that the debate followed party lines, Gordon recognized that a few Republicans, such as Senator Lindsey Graham, criticized the airstrikes for being too limited.

In period VI, the *WSJ* is the newspaper that most openly asserted what the US Syria policy should be. An editorial published on April 16 proposes a US-imposed no-fly zone in northeastern Syria to protect the Kurdish groups fighting the Islamic State. The enforcement of a safe zone would be combined with diplomatic efforts to deter Russia and economic sanctions against the Syrian regime. The editorial refrains from demanding that Bashar al-Assad step down, as some *WSJ* columnists had previously done, especially in period II, which covers the 2013 Eastern Ghouta chemical attack. In April 2018, however, the newspaper argued that the United States should keep a military presence in the region so that it would find itself in a better position in the event of negotiations with Russia and the Syrian regime.

The *WSJ* editorial board adopted an anti-Iran tone, suggesting that the country nurtured imperial ambitions in the Middle East and that the United States should counter them by supporting regional opponents of the Ayatollah regime. The editorial board wrote, "The better US strategy is to support regional opponents of Iranian imperialism and try to turn Syria into the Ayatollah's Vietnam. Only when Russia and Iran begin to pay a larger price in Syria will they have any incentive to negotiate an end to the war or even contemplate a peace based on dividing the country into ethnic-based enclaves."[50] Although there were no specific examples of who these regional opponents of Iran were, the reference was probably to countries such as Saudi Arabia and Israel.

Interestingly, one of the options mentioned in the editorial consisted of the division of Syria into "ethnic-based enclaves." Although the editorial board does not specify the ethnicities or sects it refers to, the enclaves would probably be formed by Sunnis, Alawites, and Kurds. This idea brings to mind the 1916 Sykes-Picot Agreement, whereby Britain and France divided the Middle East among themselves in the aftermath of the First World War. The difference is that, in 2018, the spoils of the Syrian war would be divided between the United States and Russia. The *WSJ* editorial published on April 16 is also critical of the Obama administration, accusing it of failing to deter the use of chemical weapons and prevent Russia and Iran from advancing their agendas in the Middle East.

In another article, Mark Dubowitz and Richard Goldberg held that the United States should be ready to wage "financial warfare" against Iran for its role in shoring up the Syrian regime. The two authors, who belonged to the conservative think tank Foundation for Defense of Democracies, argued that the Iran Nuclear Deal should be reformulated, as it was insufficient to deter the Iranian regime's nuclear ambitions. Dubowitz and Goldberg also claimed that US Syria policy had been in a state of paralysis since the deal had come into effect. The only way to contain Iran and Syria, the two scholars continued, was to exert durable financial pressure against the two countries:

> A Syria strategy that leaves these Iranian financial spigots open is doomed to fail. Why haven't they been blocked? For fear of jeopardizing the 2015 nuclear accord, the Joint Comprehensive Plan of Action, which relieved sanctions on Iranian banks, regime assets, and economic sectors. This policy paralysis needs to end, and this weekend's [April 14, 2018] military strike, conducted in close coordination with France and Britain, should lead to a trans-Atlantic understanding that allows true financial warfare against the Iran-Syria nexus to commence.[51]

Like other *WSJ* articles in period VI, Dubowitz and Goldberg's piece adopts an advisory tone toward the Trump administration.

In period VI, *WSJ* authors opted to focus on the differences between the Obama and the Trump administrations. For example, Sune Engel Rasmussen and Raja Abdulrahim noted in a news article that US policy in Syria had "shifted away" from supporting anti-Assad rebels: "The singular focus of Friday's strikes on chemical weapons reflected the changing US priorities in Syria under the Trump administration, which has shifted away from even minimal support for rebel groups seeking to oust the Assad regime."⁵² The attitude of focusing on the differences between the two administrations illustrates the frame that the *WSJ* built in period VI concerning US foreign policy. If combined with the fact that the newspaper adopted an advisory tone toward the Trump administration and was critical of President Obama's Syria policy, it can be inferred that most *WSJ* authors sympathized with President Trump, or at least avoided direct criticism toward his administration. The *NYT* and the *WP*, by contrast, adopted a more confrontational stance toward President Trump's Syria policy, although their attitude concerning the Obama years varied.

The *WSJ* offered comprehensive coverage of the Syrian civil war. Several articles analyze the situation on the battlefield, providing first-hand accounts from different actors involved in the conflict. The articles show that the Assad regime continued to regain territory from rebel groups and that its indiscriminate targeting of civilians worsened the humanitarian crisis in Syria. One of the articles about the civil war analyzes the growth of Hayat Tahrir al-Sham, the former al-Qaeda affiliate that had become one of the most powerful groups in Idlib.⁵³ *WSJ* journalist Rasmussen argued that the group was imposing a religious dictatorship based on Sharia law. The article omits the numerous other groups also active in Idlib during that time, which implies that most Syrian rebel groups still active in the country had an Islamist agenda.

Despite the reluctance of *WSJ* authors to criticize President Trump in period VI, some articles underscore the contradictions and limitations of his policy. In period VI, not only did the *WSJ* focus on the differences between Trump's and Obama's Syria policies, it also continued to hold a critical stance on the Obama administration, criticizing it for failing to contain Russia, Iran, and the Syrian regime. Moreover, *WSJ* authors did not call for the immediate removal of Bashar al-Assad, preferring instead to highlight that negotiation with Russia and the Syrian regime would be necessary. However, the tone in relation to Iran continued to be bitterly confrontational, with several authors demanding a more aggressive policy to contain the Ayatollah regime's expansionist strategy in the Middle East. A key aspect of this proposed policy was maintaining a military presence in Syria and establishing a no-fly zone in northeastern Syria.

...

The April 2018 joint airstrikes against the Assad regime did not represent a substantial shift in US foreign policy toward the Syrian conflict. Nevertheless, they sparked an intense debate within the US political establishment and foreign policy circles. The *NYT*, the *WP*, and the *WSJ* participated actively in these discussions, portraying different frames of President Trump's Syria policy. As we have seen, the *NYT* shared a negative frame of the Trump administration. Although the newspaper criticized the US president for lacking a coherent Syria policy, it did not elaborate on what this policy should be. *NYT* authors challenged President Trump's militaristic tone and continued to endorse President Obama's noninterventionist approach, as the newspaper had done in most of the other periods analyzed in this book. In period VI, *NYT* authors used more Republican sources than in the other periods, which is explained by the newspaper's eagerness to give a platform to Republican critics of Trump.

The *WP*, in turn, advocated that the United States pursue a more aggressive Syria policy. *WP* authors criticized the Obama administration for failing to arm moderate rebels and confront the Syrian regime militarily. In period VI, the *WP* did not share a homogenous view about the future of Bashar al-Assad. While the editorial board advocated the removal of the Syrian president, the majority of *WP* authors argued that a political agreement among the different actors seemed a more feasible outcome. The newspaper relayed an anti-Trump stance in period VI, deeming the airstrikes insufficient and opposing Trump's proposal to withdraw US troops from Syria.

Unlike their *NYT* and *WP* colleagues, *WSJ* authors adopted a neutral tone toward the Trump administration. It acted almost as an adviser of the US president, although some *WSJ* authors underscored the contradictions of his policy. The newspaper emphasized the differences between Trump's and Obama's Syria approaches. It also relayed an anti-Iran frame and advocated a more active US involvement in the conflict. One of the policies suggested by *WSJ* authors was a no-fly zone in northeastern Syria. In period VI, the three newspapers reported on the divisions within the Trump administration regarding the April 2018 airstrikes.

CONCLUSION

The Coverage of the Syrian Conflict and the Crisis of US Journalism

More than twelve years after the first protests erupted in Syria in March 2011, the country is still immersed in an information black hole. The Syrian media landscape is currently fragmented into three subsystems controlled by the Syrian government, opposition forces, and Kurdish groups, respectively. Working conditions for independent journalists remain unbearable, with media practitioners facing restrictions and all sorts of intimidations. In government-held areas, the Syrian regime continues to exert tight control over media narratives, as most news outlets are either controlled by the government or owned by close allies of Syrian President Bashar al-Assad. Moreover, the regime makes every effort to inhibit dissonant voices, especially by forbidding independent media organizations from operating freely.

Freedom House classifies Syria as one of the most unfree countries in the world. In a report published in 2023, the organization stated,

> All media [in Syria] must obtain permission to operate from the Interior Ministry. Private media in government-controlled territory are generally owned by figures associated with the regime. Media freedom varies in territory held by other groups, but local outlets are typically under heavy pressure to support the dominant militant faction in their area ... Journalists face physical danger throughout Syria, especially from regime forces and extremist groups.[1]

Syria ranked 175th (of 180 countries) in the 2023 World Press Freedom Index, produced by the NGO Reporters without Borders.[2] The NGO also claimed that "a total of sixty-six journalists have been killed in Syria since 2016 and at least fifty-eight journalists are still classified as imprisoned, held hostage, or missing in connection with the civil war that began with an uprising in 2011."[3] Just like before the uprising, only a few international media groups operate inside the country, a reality that hinders the development of a healthy media landscape.

Journalists, activist groups, and media organizations overcame innumerable obstacles to report on the Syrian conflict. The conditions inside Syria were hazardous, but the external environment was also adverse, as several countries pursued different agendas in the Syrian civil war. The fact that the so-called international community was divided over how to respond to the conflict influenced the coverage of the Syrian uprising and civil war in various ways. It is not an exaggeration to refer to the media coverage of the Syrian conflict as a "war of narratives" in which different views vied for dominance.

For instance, in the United States, the conversation was intense and involved various political players—from elite politicians to government officials, the US military, and civil society groups. Although the deployment of a considerable number of US ground troops was never a tangible option for either the Obama or the Trump administrations, debates revolved mainly around the appropriate degree of US involvement in the conflict and how to counter the influence of countries considered opponents.

As argued throughout this book, the three newspapers analyzed herein took active stands in the discussion about US foreign policy on Syria. Whereas the *NYT* usually aligned with the Obama administration, supporting President Obama's cautious policy toward the Syrian conflict and his attempts to disengage the United States militarily from the Middle East, the *WP* and the *WSJ* promoted narratives that criticized the US president for lacking a clear Syria policy. Regarding the Trump administration, the alignments were slightly different, with the *NYT* and the *WP* spreading anti-Trump frames and the *WSJ* adopting a neutral attitude toward the former US president.

The analysis of the articles that formed the six periods of this book is unambiguous about the foreign policy approaches advanced by each of the three newspapers. The *NYT* spread a multilateralist foreign policy approach, advocating that the United States exercise world hegemony in collaboration with allies and within the framework of international organizations. Conversely, the *WP* and the *WSJ* relayed a realist foreign policy view, arguing that the US government should prioritize its interests in the Middle East by taking a firmer stance against Russia, Iran, and the Syrian regime. The *WP* and the *WSJ* endorsed an interventionist approach in Syria, even if sometimes it meant that the United States would act alone. The specifics of such an intervention, however, were not always made explicit. Some *WP* and *WSJ* authors advocated the enforcement of sanctions against Russia and the Syrian regime as well as creating a no-fly zone to protect civilians and US-backed groups. A minority of authors in these two newspapers argued that US policy should focus on supporting Syrian rebels more energetically.

In fact, the coverage of the Syrian opposition in the three newspapers is superficial and mostly negative (see Table 8.1 for a summary of the frames per newspaper and period). Various news reports misrepresented and trivialized the Syrian opposition, depicting them at times as incapable of defeating the Syrian regime and at other times as dominated by Islamist forces. In Western media, far more coverage was given to Syrian oppositionist groups than the movements that fought the US-led occupations in Iraq and Afghanistan—mainly because the US government opposed the Syrian regime. However, despite receiving greater coverage, Syrian oppositionist groups were still depicted in overly simplistic terms.

At the beginning of the uprising in March 2011 (period I), the three newspapers framed the protests as part of a pro-democracy movement against an authoritarian regime. The *WP* and the *WSJ* adopted a critical frame of President Obama, urging him to actively support the demonstrations. Whereas the *WSJ* advocated that the United States backed Syrian opposition groups, the *WP* proposed a different policy, leaning toward the imposition of sanctions against the Syrian regime. In period I, several *WP* authors highlighted the similarities between the situations in Libya and Syria, which suggested that the option of intervention in the latter was not unreasonable. *NYT* authors, by contrast, opposed this notion, upholding that the United States should not adopt the same approach in Syria as it had done in Libya.

As the Syrian regime stepped up the repression against the protests and the conflict turned into an armed struggle, the number of advocates of intervention increased. Period II, which covers the aftermath of the Eastern Ghouta chemical attack, marked the zenith of this discussion. In August 2013, both the *WP* and the *WSJ* supported the use of military force against President Bashar al-Assad. Authors writing for the *WSJ* went even further, advocating regime change as the outcome that would best fit the interests of the United States. Several *WSJ* articles state that the United States should carry out an air campaign to support so-called moderate opposition groups to overthrow the Syrian president. *WP* authors did not go as far as upholding regime change, although various articles claim that President Obama should act forcefully against the Syrian regime. The *NYT*, conversely, supported President Obama's decision not to launch a unilateral attack against the Syrian government and to seek congressional approval before employing military force.

With the expansion of ISIS in Iraq and Syria in July 2014 (period III), the attitude of the three newspapers shifted. The *NYT*, the *WP*, and the *WSJ* went on to argue that the fight against the terrorist organization should become a priority and that the United States should carry out airstrikes against ISIS. In part, the fact that the US political elite built a solid consensus around this idea explains the shift. The change of attitude also suggests that the war on terror narrative still wields influence on members of the US elite, the editorial boards of the three newspapers, and various journalists and analysts working for the elite press. Journalists tend to assimilate, at least in part, the principles shared by the institutions for which they work. Thus, in light of the emergence and expansion of ISIS in 2014, the discussion about regime change virtually disappeared from the coverage of the Syrian conflict in the three analyzed newspapers.

In period IV, which covers the first days of the Russian intervention in Syria in September/October 2015, the three newspapers maintained their general attitudes toward the Obama administration. However, the tone regarding President Obama's Syria policy changed. The *WP* and the *WSJ* increased their levels of criticism, condemning the US president for being responsible for the Syrian turmoil and demanding an aggressive response against Russia and the Syrian regime. In period IV, neither the *WP* nor the *WSJ* advocated regime change as the best solution for the conflict. Instead, authors from both newspapers insisted that the United States should step up sanctions against Russia and Syria and create safe zones to protect civilians and US-backed groups (especially those fighting ISIS). In turn, most *NYT* authors refrained from openly criticizing President Obama, although a few articles highlight the limitations of his policy.

The coverage of US foreign policy on Syria in periods V and VI, which cover the fall of Aleppo in December 2016 and the US-UK-French joint airstrikes against Syria in April 2018, includes analysis of Donald Trump's views. His ascent to the presidency changed the conversation in various ways. In December 2016, one month before Trump's inauguration as the 45th US president, the news media gave considerable coverage to his foreign policy ideas. The *NYT* focused primarily on the perceived disparities between Obama and Trump, especially regarding their views on Russia, Iran, and terrorism. One of the framing devices used by *NYT* authors was quoting President Obama and other administration officials without contrasting their statements with opposing views. By omitting criticism of President Obama, the *NYT* induced the reader to sympathize with his policies. The *WP* and the *WSJ*, by contrast, chose to highlight the elements of continuity and disruption between Obama and Trump.

In April 2018 (period VI), the *NYT* criticized the Trump administration for carrying out the airstrikes against Syria in violation of the UN Charter. *NYT* authors also claimed that President Trump lacked a clear Syria policy. The *WP* and the *WSJ*, on the other hand, endorsed the airstrikes but argued that they had been limited and, therefore, would not change the situation on the ground substantially.[4] Both newspapers continued to spread an interventionist frame, demanding a more aggressive US policy in Syria and opposing the withdrawal of troops from the country, which was one of President Trump's stated goals in April 2018. Whereas the *WP* criticized President Trump for his ambiguous Syria strategy, the *WSJ* adopted an advisory tone toward the US president.

Overall, despite their different framings of the policies pursued by the US government throughout the Syrian conflict, the general focus of the three newspapers was similar: more than half of the articles analyzed in this book have US foreign policy as a topic or subtopic, which indicates that this issue dominates the coverage of international events in the US elite press. The fact that US foreign policy occupies such a central position endorses the notion that mainstream newspapers and the political elite cultivate an organic relationship that materializes predominantly through the sourcing practices of journalists.

Sources constitute the backbone of news articles and, therefore, are the most visible framing device in this type of text. The overwhelming majority of the sources that appear in this research's dataset are somehow connected to either the two mainstream US political parties or a few elite universities and Think tanks (see Figure 8.1). For instance, *NYT* authors mostly quoted Democratic politicians and members of the Obama administration. *WSJ* authors, on the other hand, relied primarily on Republican politicians to substantiate their articles about US foreign policy on Syria. The sourcing practices of *WP* authors were more balanced, with politicians from both parties equally appearing in the articles analyzed in this research. Statements from sources that do not belong to US elite circles hardly appear in the coverage of the Syrian conflict in the *NYT*, the *WP*, and the *WSJ*.

For Michael Schudson, journalists tend to quote public officials and policymakers because they are in a privileged position to predict the outcome of events:

> In covering foreign policy, for instance, journalists want experts who know or are close to the key diplomatic players, who can authoritatively explain the policy choices at hand, and who are willing to make predictions about how events will unfold. They lean toward former public officials, retired military leaders, and think tank policy adepts who frame issues in a narrow, technical way rather than scholars who have done primary research on the country or conflict at hand or leading religious spokespersons who would address issues in moral rather than strategic terms.[5]

Table 8.1 Summary of frames per newspaper and period

	NYT	WP	WSJ
Period I (Beginning of the Uprising)	• Pro-Syrian protests • Pro-Obama • Pro-Libya intervention • Anti-intervention in Syria	• Pro-Syrian protests • Critical of Obama • Libya and Syria similar • Pro-sanctions against Syria	• Pro—Syrian protests • Critical of Obama • Pro-support for Syrian opposition • The *WSJ* expressed doubts about the fall of Assad
Period II (Eastern Ghouta Chemical Attack)	• Pro-Obama • Anti-intervention against Syrian regime	• Critical of Obama • Pro-intervention against Syrian regime	• Critical of Obama • Pro-intervention against Syrian regime • Pro-regime change in Syria
Period III (Emergence of ISIS)	• Pro-Obama • Pro-intervention against ISIS • Pro-alliances with local groups to fight ISIS • Syrian opposition mostly Islamist	• Critical of Obama • Pro-intervention against ISIS • Anti-alliances with local groups to fight ISIS • Syrian opposition mostly Islamist	• Critical of Obama • Pro-intervention against ISIS • Pro-alliances with local groups to fight ISIS • Syrian opposition mostly Islamist
Period IV (Russian Intervention)	• Pro-Obama • The *NYT* highlighted the inconsistencies of Obama's policy • Pro-support for Kurdish militias	• Critical of Obama • Obama responsible for chaos in Syria • Pro-no-fly zones in Syria and sanctions against Syria and Russia • Pro-support for Kurdish militias	• Critical of Obama • Obama responsible for the growth of ISIS • Pro-creation of safe zones in Syria and stepping up of sanctions against Russia

(*Continued*)

	NYT	WP	WSJ
Period V (Battle of Aleppo)	• Neutral frame of Obama • The *NYT* prioritized humanitarian crisis over geopolitical consequences of the battle of Aleppo • Pro-support for Syrian-Kurdish groups • Highlighted the contrasts between Obama and Trump	• Critical of Obama • Obama too soft on ISIS, Russia, and the Syrian regime • Trump's policy will not differ from Obama's • The *WP* highlighted the elements of continuity and discontinuity between Obama and Trump • Anti-Syrian opposition	• Critical of Obama • Obama too soft on ISIS, Russia, and the Syrian regime • The *WSJ* focused mostly on Trump's policy • Neutral frame of Trump • The *WSJ* expressed concern over Trump's ties with Russia • The *WSJ* highlighted the elements of continuity and discontinuity between Obama and Trump
Period VI (US-UK-French Airstrikes)	• Anti-airstrikes against Syria • Anti-Trump • The *NYT* highlighted the disagreements within the Republican Party • Anti-Assad and Russia • The *NYT* refrained from suggesting policies	• Pro-airstrikes against Syria • Airstrikes were limited • Anti-Trump and critical of Obama • Pro-political settlement in Syria	• Pro-airstrikes against Syria • Neutral frame of Trump • The *WSJ* occasionally pointed out the inconsistencies of Trump's policy • Pro-no-fly zone in northern Syria to protect Kurds

By selecting the sources from which they take statements and the order in which these statements appear in news articles, journalists disclose valuable information about their framing practices. Todd Gitlin argued that framing involves the selection of what is newsworthy and what is not: "Media are mobile spotlights, not passive mirrors of the society; selectivity is the instrument of their action. A news story adopts a certain frame and rejects or downplays material that is discrepant. A story is a choice, a way of seeing an event that also amounts to an established system of power and knowledge."[6]

The recurrence of topics and reasoning devices over a period of time constitutes another central aspect of frame-building. By repeating ideas and presenting information in a certain way, newspapers make them more salient to the public. The three newspapers analyzed herein consistently highlighted specific aspects of the foreign policy pursued by the US government toward the Syrian conflict.

This book argues that elite dissent exerted a profound impact on how the *NYT*, the *WP*, and the *WSJ* framed the Syrian conflict. If elite dissent is growing, we need to revise the theoretical frameworks that see the news media as unequivocal propaganda tools of the elites. News framing analysts ought to focus on how increasing elite dissent shapes mainstream media narratives. The propaganda model represents a singular contribution to the scholarship on media power, as it is arguably the first theoretical framework to integrate in the analytical process the political economy of the media, the relationship between political institutions and news organizations, and how these elements affect news content production.

However, with the end of the Cold War, the model became in many ways obsolete. Growing divisions within elite circles replaced the broad foreign policy consensus around anticommunism. Additionally, the second filter identified by Herman and Chomsky in *Manufacturing Consent*, namely, the notion that advertising is the primary income source of the mass media, lost validity. According to the Pew Research Center, the primary source of income of the largest US newspapers in 2020 was their digital circulation, especially revenue generated by paywalls.[7]

In the last two decades, the media have developed a symbiotic relationship with Internet giants because most news organizations now rely primarily on social media to reach audiences. Advertising dried up, migrating almost entirely to companies such as Facebook and Google. Margaret Sullivan explained this structural transformation:

> An even more profound change was coming from two dominant technology platforms, Google and Facebook, who have been able to attract the vast portion of digital advertising. By some estimates, the "duopoly" was sucking up 60 percent of all digital advertising revenue in the United States by the middle of the last decade. From the point of view of traditional publishers, this seemed almost diabolical because the platforms benefited from "content"—the news stories, videos, photo galleries, etc.—that the old-school companies supplied, but siphoned off most of the revenue.[8]

The cascading activation model, by contrast, incorporates elite dissent into the examination of news frames. Nevertheless, its narrow definition of power, on the one hand, and the fact that it underestimates the role played by the political economy of the media in the shaping of news content, on the other, amount to essential flaws of the model proposed by Robert Entman. Media scholar Des Freedman contributed to the debate about media power by introducing the notion that the combination of elite dissent and the emergence of protest movements create opportunities for new forms of media to develop and for alternative discourses to reach larger audiences.[9] The case of Syria confirms this view: At the beginning of the uprising, a powerful movement of citizen journalists took advantage of the Internet and other digital technologies to radically transform a media landscape characterized by a unilateral, top-down information flow.

Higher levels of attachment to elite narratives are a result of the US press becoming increasingly concentrated in the hands of fewer media conglomerates. Although the data is not fully accessible, different media analysts agree that the *NYT*, the *WP*, and the *WSJ* have increased their market share quotas, both in revenue and readership. A more concentrated news media landscape, with fewer outlets with the resources to compete effectively in the marketplace, explains the intensification of frame competition currently seen among mainstream newspapers. However, this transformation also leads to a narrower variety of opinions available to the public. As Freedman argued, "media ownership patterns, while unable to reveal the full dynamics of how the media function, are one of the crucial elements in the reproduction of media power."[10]

Matthew Hindman and James Webster have pointed out that the Internet and the "attention economy" increased the levels of market concentration in the news media industry.[11] Although the expansion of the digital world enabled the emergence of a large number of alternative media outlets, users tend to migrate to the wealthier websites, which have the resources to produce larger quantities of quality content. As a result of this trend, local journalism is disappearing. Sullivan, for instance, argued, "Some of the most trusted sources of news—local sources, particularly local newspapers—are slipping away, never to return. The cost to democracy is great. It takes a toll on civic engagement—even on citizens' ability to have a common sense of reality and facts, the very basis of self-governance."[12] Only in the United States, more than 1,300 communities have lost any form of news coverage, a phenomenon that is increasing what several analysts have dubbed "news deserts."[13] Between 2007 and 2014, more than half of the jobs in journalism were lost due to the closure of hundreds of US newspapers.[14]

Additionally, online readers have greater exposure (through social media, search engines, and all sorts of algorithms) to the outlets with which they share a greater ideological affinity. In this scenario, numerous news organizations feel compelled to emphasize their political leanings in order to maintain and increase their share of readers and subscribers. It is outside the scope of this book to examine the journalistic business models that prevail in the United States. However, private media corporations predominate in the country, and public subsidies to news organizations are virtually inexistent. Victor Pickard argued that the lack of support for a public media system has far-reaching consequences. In his opinion, a strong public media "can provide a baseline for reliable information and act as a safety net when the market fails to support adequate levels of news production."[15]

The excessive indexing of mainstream newspapers to elite views also has broader implications for the role of journalism within a democratic society. The close affiliation between the political elite and mainstream newspapers threatens the right of citizens to a fair, diverse, and unbiased coverage of the events that surround them and somehow affect their lives. Because journalistic narratives will always be partial representations of the world, the news media ought to facilitate citizens' access to a diversity of topics, issues, and perspectives. And this is a far cry from making elite debates the primary focus in the coverage of world events.

For journalism to function as a public good, it is essential that the press gives voice to a wide range of sources and opinions, such as those of scholars who are not aligned with the mainstream, advocacy groups, unions, independent research centers, and the ordinary people who are directly affected by the issues at hand. The production of alternative content (not solely informed by members of the

Sources in *NYT, WP,* and *WSJ* Articles in Period I to VI

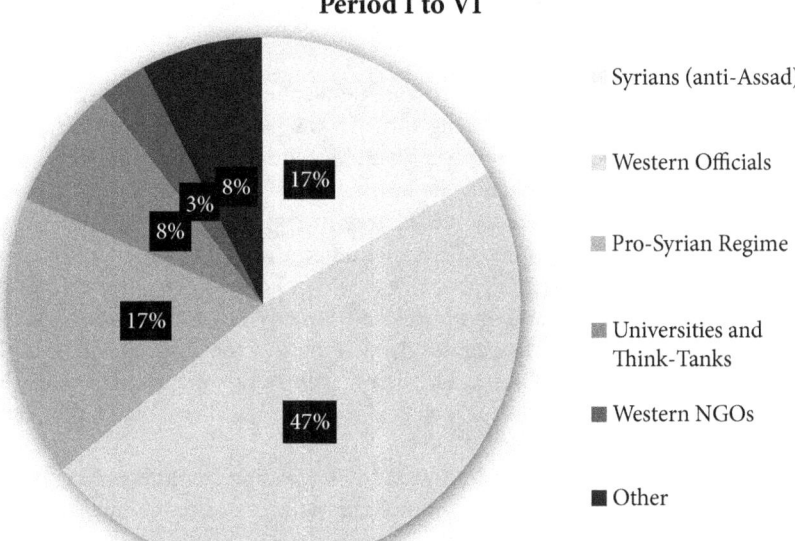

Figure 8.1 Sources in *NYT, WP,* and *WSJ* articles in periods I to VI.

political establishment) and the fostering of a healthy public debate amount to crucial aspects of media pluralism.

Public good journalism implies fairness and diversity, but above all, it should mean that journalists adopt a critical attitude toward political and economic powers. If newspapers become more dependent on elite groups, both financially and as sources of information, journalists will not enjoy the freedom to scrutinize the activities of decision-makers. Without this independence, the press will fail to adequately inform and educate the citizenry.

Pickard argued that it is crucial to create noncommercial forms of journalism in order to achieve media pluralism: "Removing commercial values (an emphasis on sensational, conflict-driven, trivial news that attracts attention to advertising) and adding public values (an emphasis on high-quality information, diverse voices and views, and reporting that confronts concentrated power and social problems) could foster a journalism that is universally accessible but attentive to diverse cultures and contexts."[16]

This book demonstrates that the coverage of the Syrian conflict in the *NYT*, the *WP*, and the *WSJ* falls short of achieving these journalistic desiderata. Above all, the three newspapers reproduced the narratives of specific segments of the US political elite, and by focusing on these narratives, they neglected important aspects of the conflict. Frame competition must not be mistaken for media pluralism. For example, Syrians authored fewer than 2 percent of the articles analyzed in this research and they constitute a minority of the sources that appear in these articles. When quoted, Syrians are usually depicted as victims, rather than as agents in the conflict.

This fact illustrates that US mainstream newspapers failed to give voice to those most affected by the Syrian uprising and civil war, and who were potentially in a more advantaged position to devise possible solutions to the conflict. A public discussion about Syria should include the millions of displaced people, the families of those missing or murdered under torture in regime prisons, and the activists and intellectuals who have lived in and studied the region for several decades. US mainstream newspapers explained the Syrian conflict primarily through the prism of the US political and military establishments, not of those who have been part of the decades-long struggle for democracy and social justice in Syria. This failure indicates that old Orientalist tropes, such as the one according to which Middle Eastern societies are incapable of representing themselves, still pervade Western media organizations.

In *Covering Islam*, Edward Said used the expression "antithetical knowledge" to refer to ideas formulated by those opposed to the mainstream. In Said's words,

> By antithetical knowledge I mean the kind of knowledge produced by people who quite consciously consider themselves to be writing in opposition to the prevailing orthodoxy. As we shall see, they do so for varying reasons and in different situations, but all of these people have a pronounced sense that how and for what reason they study Islam are questions that require deliberation and explicitness.[17]

This type of knowledge, however, is virtually absent from the coverage of the Syrian conflict in the *NYT*, the *WP*, and the *WSJ* during the six analyzed periods. Instead of critical knowledge, what often appears in the articles that formed this book's dataset may be described as neocolonial perceptions such as democracy-building, US national interest, terrorism, and regional stability.

In line with Said's argument, Muhammad Idrees Ahmad claimed that avoiding the representation of Syrian voices constitutes a symptom of the crisis of Western journalism:

> When Western media, which [have] some commitment to accuracy and objectivity, [move] on, or when [they fail] to amplify local voices with direct knowledge of the situation, [they leave] an information vacuum. In the case of Syria, that is filled by Russian and Iranian media, whose coverage is of an entirely different nature. The aim of these outlets, which are less concerned with facts than with upholding state-sanctioned narratives, is obfuscation.[18]

Ahmad further argued that "events in Syria [were] only registered when they intersected with Western interests." This book confirms this view and goes one step further, by establishing that different media organizations align with specific segments of the elites.

News framing analysis has become an influential paradigm among scholars willing to undertake news content analysis. Its strength lies in the heterogeneous conceptualization of news frames and its urge for researchers to look at the entirety of the news cycle. This research suggests that news framing analysts should go beyond a narrow textual analysis, limited to assessing the positive and negative attitudes that news texts adopt regarding a specific issue and undertake instead a careful examination of the conditions in which these texts emerge and how media discourses relate to institutional narratives. The analysis of the coverage of the Syrian conflict in the *NYT*, the *WP*, and the *WSJ* unveils some of the structural flaws of US journalism and draws attention to the fact that policymakers, media practitioners, and communication scholars ought to devise alternatives to a model that has become excessively driven by elite interests.

APPENDIX: THE SCIENCE OF NEWS FRAMES

This appendix discusses the questions that inspired this project and the methodology employed in the analysis of the dataset. As stated in the introduction, the broader objective of this book is the examination of the coverage of the Syrian conflict in the *NYT*, the *WP*, and the *WSJ*. More specifically, the book focuses on how the three newspapers framed the Syrian uprising and civil war in six different events of the conflict. This study integrates a large body of research about the relationship between media, conflict, and foreign policy in the United States.

I argue that it is necessary to analyze power relations in order to understand the interaction between political systems, media organizations, and the public. As Kevin Carragee and Wim Roefs argued, "Determining which frames dominate particular news texts would provide the systematic assessment of content demanded by … critics. Frames, as imprints of power, are central to the production of hegemonic meanings."[1] The notion that frames are "imprints of power" permeates this project and underpins the methodological choices I made when collecting and analyzing this book's dataset. The main theoretical framework used in this research is the news-framing paradigm, as it allows for an integrative and holistic consideration of the news cycle.

Philosopher of science Thomas Kuhn claimed that paradigms provide road maps to the activity of researchers: "Our most recent examples show that paradigms provide scientists not only with a map but also with some of the directions essential for map-making. In learning a paradigm the scientist acquires theory, methods, and standards together, usually in an inextricable mixture."[2] Choosing which paradigm to employ in a research enterprise involves a myriad of factors that relate to the researcher's ontological and epistemological preferences as well as the questions that motivate the project in the first place.

As previously mentioned, the present study employs the news framing paradigm because it enables a more comprehensive view of the discursive practices of media organizations. Robert Entman explained how the news framing paradigm provides the means for a more consistent content analysis:

> The major task of determining textual meaning should be to identify and describe frames; content analysis informed by a theory of framing would avoid treating all negative or positive terms or utterances as equally salient and influential. Often, coders simply tote up all messages they judge as positive and negative and draw conclusions about the dominant meanings. They neglect to measure the salience of elements in the text, and fail to gauge the relationships of the most salient clusters of messages—the frames—to the audience's schemata.[3]

According to Entman, the identification of frames should not be reduced to summing up positive and negative descriptors of a topic. He suggested that it is more important to determine how salient certain ideas are in a text and how they combine with other notions to form dominant frames. Baldwin van Gorp added that "the linkage between the explicit elements of the news text and the central framing idea, which is part of a larger cultural level, requires some interpretation by the person who is doing the analysis."[4] For van Gorp, frames are embedded in cultural systems that influence journalistic practices and the assimilation of news texts by the public. Thus, the news framing paradigm constantly urges us to transcend the limits of the text and avoid a simple text-centered linguistic analysis. Gregory Philo accepted this idea, arguing, "If the analysis remains 'within the text' it is not possible to explain the social relationships which underpin the presentation of the descriptions and accounts which appear."[5]

Philo was referring to the limitations of critical discourse analysis (CDA) as an analytical approach for researchers undertaking news content analysis. According to Dianna Mullet, the aim of CDA is the "discovery of latent or hidden beliefs that appear in language disguised as analogies, metaphors, or other conceptual expressions."[6] CDA aims to unpack how language reproduces dominant ideologies and unequal power relations. By focusing primarily on the linguistic components of texts, CDA leaves out essential extra-textual elements, such as the identity of sources, the identification of absent narratives, and other contextual aspects of the production process. Philo further argued,

> The key point is that to distinguish between types of rhetoric necessitates an analysis of political structures, purposes, and strategies. It requires an account of the social and political system and conflicting interest within it, beyond what can be seen from an immediate text. Without this we cannot comment on the difference between rhetoric and reality in terms of the intentions of the speaker, the validity of representations, and the relation between accounts that are featured and alternative versions of truth.[7]

The perception of the news production process as a totality that is underpinned by social relations constitutes one of the distinctive features of the news framing paradigm. This notion enables media scholars to interpret news texts in novel ways. As Paul D'Angelo argued, "[s]cholars gravitate to news framing analysis precisely because its integrative approach allows them to adapt and hone various theoretical frameworks in order to do empirical research that bears ultimately on a core assumption of the discipline: that mediated messages, by virtue of their organizational basis and technological dissemination, are impactful and consequential."[8]

The methodology used in this research combines news framing analysis with the theories of media power discussed in this book's introduction and first chapter. In brief, these theories assume that mass media organizations operate within specific networks of power relations, and, therefore, recognizing these relations is a precondition for the analysis of discourses and frames. Des Freedman defined media power as a "set of relationships that help to organize the deployment of the symbolic resources that play a vital role in social reproduction and that, in conjunction with other institutions and processes, help to structure our knowledge about, our ability to participate in, and our capacity to change the world."[9]

In this light, researchers undertaking news content analysis ought to consider the broader social environment in which journalistic practices materialize. D'Angelo has shown his support for this idea by stating that "news framing denotes how journalists, their sources, and audiences work within conditions that shape the messages they construct as well as the ways they understand and interpret these messages."[10]

Certain aspects of news texts—such as the amount of context given, the recurrence of topics, the organization of the information, and the sourcing practices of journalists—shape journalistic messages in different ways and play a determinant role in the construction of news frames. According to Entman, "The text contains frames, which are manifested by the presence or absence of certain keywords, stock phrases, stereotyped images, sources of information, and sentences that provide thematically reinforcing clusters of facts or judgments."[11] For time and resource constraints, this study does not examine the impact of the frames of the Syrian conflict on the public, limiting its scope to comparing the frames relayed by the three newspapers to the narratives of the US political establishment.

I opted for this research design (a comparative approach) because the Syrian conflict has been surrounded from the beginning by an unusual amount of elite debate, and the frames relayed in the three newspapers are unquestionably connected to these different elite narratives. Furthermore, the conversations I had with some of the journalists who covered the conflict provided insufficient data for me to draw robust conclusions about how and why newspapers align with one part of the elites or another. Most journalists I spoke to refrained from discussing the links between mainstream media and elite discourses. As previously discussed, the idea that journalists can cover events objectively, if they apply specific techniques and follow fixed routines, is still widely hegemonic among media practitioners working for mainstream newspapers. For this reason, an ethnographic study that relied on a large sample of in-depth interviews or newsroom observations was discarded.

This study contributes to the framing scholarship in different ways. For instance, it constitutes one of the first attempts to analyze the frames of the Syrian conflict in mainstream newspapers, and as such, it sheds light on the coverage of one of the most complex and tragic conflicts of this century. The unusual volume of elite debate surrounding the Syrian uprising and civil war represents a unique opportunity to analyze how the news media behave in the face of elite dissent.

The issues inherent in the study of a long conflict, such as the Syrian civil war, pose enormous challenges to media scholars undertaking news framing analysis. First, the overwhelming amount of news reports (in all genres and formats) makes the selection of a representative dataset an intricate process, especially for researchers engaging in qualitative content analysis. The data collection began with the selection of six events that represented turning points in the Syrian conflict. Thus, although I based this selection on objective factors, such as a military shift in the conflict or a battle that resulted in a large number of casualties, my subjectivity played an undeniable part in this process.

Second, the fact that the Syrian civil war is in many ways an ongoing conflict prevented me from taking full advantage of hindsight, which can be of great assistance in sociological research. Although scholarly works on the causes and nature of the Syrian conflict abound, several questions about US attitudes to this unprecedented event remain unanswered. This research has the potential to fill some of the existing gaps in our understanding of how the US media covered the Syrian uprising and civil war.

Identifying News Frames

The scholarship is inconclusive regarding which methodology is the most effective for the identification of news frames. Entman described framing analysis as a "fractured paradigm" that requires further refinement. In 1993, he claimed that "nowhere is there a general statement of framing theory that shows exactly how frames become embedded within and make themselves manifest in a text, or how framing influences thinking."[12] Although much progress has been achieved since the publication of Entman's "Framing: Toward Clarification of a Fractured Paradigm," and new approaches for identifying frames have been devised, the issue is still subjected to fruitful debate in academic circles.

In a more recent article, Claes de Vreese argued that researchers still employ highly diverse methods when undertaking framing analysis: "Previous research on frames in the news shares little conceptual ground and most studies draw on tentative working definitions or operational definitions of frames designed for the purpose of the specific study. Therefore there is little consensus as how to identify frames in the news."[13]

Daniela Dimitrova argued that comparative studies are the most appropriate to identify news frames: "A comparative design takes the essence of framing—putting a topic, issue, event, or person into a particular context in order to shape how someone else thinks about and acts toward it—and moves the level of explanatory context up a rung."[14] Emma Björnehed and Josefina Erikson agree with Dimitrova, being of the opinion that frame analysis is only possible in the context of a permanent comparison between media and institutional discourses.[15]

The emergence of a media landscape dominated by digital platforms added new layers to the analysis of news frames. Knüpfer and Entman argued that "platforms such as Facebook, YouTube, Reddit, or Twitter, along with the corporate interests and company policies that govern them, will hold increasing sway over who gets heard by whom and under what conditions they may exchange points of view."[16]

One of the most stimulating discussions among scholars is on the question of whether or not a consensual approach to identifying frames is necessary. For example, D'Angelo argued against the view that the lack of a unified methodological approach constitutes an obstacle for news framing research. According to him, "[t]he three paradigms endemic to communication, called cognitive, constructionist, and critical, enable the news framing research program to function."[17] For D'Angelo, the different research traditions are arbitrarily (yet efficiently) used by frame researchers, making news framing analysis a multiparadigmatic research program.

This idea challenges the Kuhnian notion that a broad epistemological consensus is a precondition for a normal and functioning scientific environment. In the case of framing, even if a wide consensus is lacking, the paradigm has become a popular analytical framework in content analysis and political communication. I argue that the framing paradigm has undergone what philosopher of science Jürgen Renn labeled a "re-centering process." Renn explained this process as follows:

> The transition from an old to a new system of knowledge is typically attended by a shift of the intellectual center of gravity. We may call this process "re-centering." What was initially peripheral, whether as a domain of application, as an argument, or as auxiliary concepts of constructions, may now come to the center and emerge as part of the constitution and core of a new knowledge system.[18]

Renn further argued that the transition from an old to a new paradigm is neither the result of an abrupt disruption, as Kuhn believed, nor the result of a cumulative and gradual process. The transformation of a system of knowledge is caused rather by the reorganization of existing paradigms into new ones.[19]

According to D'Angelo, four main types of frames—journalist, audience, issues, and news (content) frames—constitute the news framing process.[20] It has been argued that frame-building is mostly determined by culture and politics, being the result of conscious and unconscious operations that take place during the production, distribution, and reception of news content. Journalist frames amount to the views and thoughts that journalists develop about the persons, events, or issues on which they report. Although journalist frames play a decisive role in news framing, they must not be mistaken for the broader notion of news frames, which refer to "written, spoken, graphical, and visual message modalities that journalists use to contextualize an event, issue, and/or person within one or more stories."[21]

Audience frames, in turn, refer to how news receivers process the information they obtain from the media and how this information affects their perceptions and behaviors. Audience frames may also be studied as part of what the scholarship has labeled "reception studies." The third type of frame (issue frames) designates the opinions of governments, advocacy groups, and other organizations and individuals that have a stake in the issue at hand. Issue frames appear in news texts mostly through sourcing and quoting. Sourcing practices, therefore, are a powerful indicator of news frames.

The fourth type of frames in D'Angelo's typology (news frames) functions as a common denominator of journalist and issue frames, as they synthesize the views of journalists and those of the sources they use in a news text. Furthermore, the framing literature tends to classify frames as either generic or issue-specific. Whereas issue-specific frames are exclusive to a particular person, issue, or event, generic frames encompass a broader scope and can appear alongside different topics. This research, however, adopts the notion of hybrid frames, which will be discussed in further detail later in this appendix.

Joseph Cappella and Kathleen Jamieson claimed that a frame must meet four criteria to be classified as such: "First, a news frame must have identifiable conceptual and linguistic characteristics. Second, it should be commonly observed in journalistic practice. Third, it must be possible to distinguish the frame reliably from other frames. Fourth, a frame must have representational validity (i.e. be recognized by others) and not be merely a figment of a researcher's imagination."[22]

Research in political communication and framing analysis has advanced enormously in the last twenty years, especially since the introduction of automated means of content analysis and increased accessibility to sizable online archives. D'Angelo argued that frame scholars should "look for patterns of framing in a corpus of stories."[23] Thus, the identification of frames is only possible if researchers check for recurrent topics, ideas, causal relations, sourcing practices, and policy recommendations. The more extensive the sample and the more consistent the patterns, the more precise the contours of the frames will be. After all, as Entman explained, "The *sine qua non* of successful framing is magnitude—magnifying those elements of the depicted reality that favor one side's position, making them salient, while at the same time shrinking those elements that might be used to construct a counterframe."[24]

The analysis of one single story on a particular topic will not suffice for making conclusive claims about how the topic is being framed. Since the same medium may employ opposing narratives about an issue, the frequency of similar frames in a period of time plays a crucial role. In order to identify news frames, researchers need to deconstruct news texts and analyze how the information is organized and presented to the receiver. Not only content matters, but also the format in which this content is displayed. Teun van Dijk argued that a news text is above all a "reconstruction of available discourses."[25] Adam Berinsky and Donald Kinder, in turn, claimed that frames are also good stories: "Framing information in ways that conform to the structure of a good story appears to change understanding, and understanding … appears to shape opinion."[26] The two scholars added that "the macrostructure of a text—the overall organization of the component pieces of that text—plays an especially important role in memory and comprehension."[27]

It should be evident by now that frame analysis does not boil down to simple textual analysis. It aims instead to examine the totality of the relations that circumscribe a media text. Nevertheless, framing also holds a linguistic dimension, entailing different techniques that are used in the writing process. Journalism and media scholar Baldwin van Gorp coined the phrase "frame package" to refer to these techniques. In his words, "[e]ach reconstructed frame is presented by a frame package; that is, by an integrated structure of framing devices and a logical chain of reasoning devices that demonstrates how the frame functions to represent a certain issue."[28]

According to this definition, a combination of framing and reasoning devices accounts for the activity of frame building. Some of the frame devices enumerated by van Gorp are metaphors, historical examples, catchphrases, depictions, lexical choices, actions and settings, and visual images. The use of frame devices combined with the establishment of relations of causality creates the frames that will be shared with news receivers. In van Gorp's view, "[t]he reasoning devices refer to the defining functions of frames … and they form a route of causal reasoning which may be evoked when an issue is associated with a particular frame."[29]

When analyzing the coverage of the Students for a Democratic Society—one of the most relevant student activist organizations in the United States during the 1960s—in mainstream media, Gitlin found a number of framing devices, such as trivialization, emphasis on internal dissent, marginalization, undercounting, and disparagement of the movement's effectiveness.[30] As this book argues, similar devices appear in the coverage of the Syrian conflict in the US mainstream press. Frame identification requires a combination of technical procedures, such as linguistic and textual analyses, with a political and sociological evaluation of the context in which these frames emerge.

Selecting and Analyzing the Dataset

The six events used in the compilation of this book's dataset had considerable geopolitical implications and, for that reason, attracted substantial media attention. The fact that the coverage of the Syrian uprising and civil war alternated between periods of saturation and silence constituted an additional challenge in the data collection. Since my primary interest lay in comparing the frames of the three newspapers, I selected events which put Syria in the spotlight, and when the number of media reports was higher. For each of the selected events, several articles were compiled using the *NYT* search engine and, in the case of the *WP* and the *WSJ*, ProQuest databases. The keyword "Syria" was used to filter the articles. Once a first batch of articles was assembled, an initial triage was undertaken to ensure that all texts related to the Syrian conflict. A few articles were subsequently discarded, and the remainder were organized according to period and newspaper. The six periods are:

I. The beginning of the Syrian uprising: March 15 to March 30, 2011
II. The Eastern Ghouta chemical attack: August 20 to August 26, 2013
III. The expansion of ISIS in Iraq and Syria: July 6 to July 31, 2014
IV. The beginning of the Russian intervention in Syria: September 28 to October 4, 2015
V. The fall of eastern Aleppo: December 6 to December 12, 2016
VI. The US-UK-French joint attacks against Syria: April 12 to April 20, 2018

The total dataset amounts to 414 articles (see Tables A.1 and A.2 for a more detailed breakdown of the articles). The total number of articles of the *NYT*, the *WP*, and the *WSJ* are 112, 141, and 161, respectively. Each article was summarized and assigned a topic, a subtopic, and a genre (news, opinion, editorial, news analysis, interview, background, and speech transcripts). This meta-classification, which took place before the actual coding of the articles, provided a first glimpse of the most common frames (see Table A.3 for a list of the ten most recurrent topics and subtopics in the dataset). The summaries proved to be an essential part of the data analysis, as they gave me an efficient way to revisit each article at any point during the research, making the identification of recurrent topics and frames easier.

The assignation of topics and subtopics revealed that frames may not, as various scholars argue, be simply classified either as generic frames, which are generalizable to any issue, or issue-specific frames, which are specific to a given affair because these categories often overlap. Thus, I prefer to work with the notion of hybrid frames. According to Michael Brüggemann and D'Angelo, "Conceiving of frames as hybrids of issue-specific frames and generic frames represents a promising way to defragment news framing analysis. It provides a way to see issue framing and generic framing as part of a holistic process that ultimately becomes represented analytically in terms of a topic—or domain-specific typology with hybrid frames located at the center."[31] Even frames that are considered to be generic frames, such as humanitarian crisis and conflict framings, acquire unique characteristics when applied in the coverage of specific events, issues, or players. Therefore, the notion of hybrid frames was used in this research, and the coding process reflected this decision.

Table A.1 Number of Articles per Newspaper and Period

	Period I	Period II	Period III	Period IV	Period V	Period VI	Total
NYT	15	20	12	27	10	28	**112**
WP	24	25	11	33	20	28	**141**
WSJ	16	40	21	35	15	34	**161**
Total	**55**	**85**	**44**	**95**	**45**	**90**	**414**

Table A.2 Number of Articles per Newspaper and Genre

	News	Opinion	Editorial	News Analysis	Interview	Background	Transcript	Total
NYT	72	23	4	8	0	2	3	**112**
WP	93	34	11	1	1	0	1	**141**
WSJ	128	31	1	1	0	0	0	**161**
Total	**293**	**88**	**16**	**10**	**1**	**2**	**4**	**414**

Table A.3 Most Recurrent Topics and Subtopics

Topics	Topics	Subtopics	Subtopics
1. Foreign Policy (US)	6. Foreign Policy (Europe)	1. Foreign Policy (US)	6. Syrian Regime
2. Civil War	7. ISIS	2. Foreign Policy (Russia)	7. Syrian Government Repression
3. Chemical Attacks (Ghouta)	8. Protests in Syria	3. Civil War	8. Protests in Syria
4. Foreign Policy (Russia)	9. War on Terror	4. War on Terror	9. International Reactions
5. US Airstrikes in Syria	10. Syrian Government Repression	5. Chemical Attacks (Ghouta)	10. Russian Intervention

During the data analysis, I paid particular attention to references to the US administration (in periods I to V to the Obama administration and in period VI to the Trump administration), US foreign policy, and the foreign policies of countries such as Russia, France, Iran, Turkey, Saudi Arabia, and Qatar. Since the framings of the Syrian regime and ISIS were overwhelmingly negative in the three newspapers, my analysis of these topics did not go into much detail. Particular focus was also given to policy propositions, especially those related to possible retaliation against the Syrian regime and ISIS, support (or lack thereof) to the Syrian opposition, and the deployment of US ground troops to Syria. The preceding chapters demonstrate that these issues constituted the most controversial aspects of the US foreign policy debate during the Syrian conflict.

The journalists' sourcing practices were also subjected to scrutiny, as they revealed relevant information about the newspapers' editorial lines and the journalists' framing choices. For each article, I created a list of the sources quoted. Most sources consisted of US politicians and academics working at a few prestigious universities and think tanks. An accessory objective of this research is to compare the frames relayed in op-ed and news articles. Although most news organizations have separate teams for these two journalistic genres, it is impossible to isolate their production process entirely. This book argues that, in most cases, the three newspapers relayed similar frames in these two types of articles, although, as is typical of the genre, the op-ed pieces express the opinions of their authors more directly.

The articles analyzed in this book were stored and coded in the qualitative data analysis software NVivo. Pat Bazeley and Kristi Jackson defined code as "an abstract representation of an object or phenomenon, or, more prosaically, a way of identifying themes in a text."[32] The two scholars, who are experts in qualitative data analysis, added that "coding in qualitative research, in its simplest sense, is a way of 'tagging' text with codes, of indexing it, in order to facilitate later retrieval."[33]

The analysis of the dataset began without previously established codes, as they overly reflect the subjectivity of the researcher. Most codes emerged during the analysis of the texts of period I, although they needed to be continuously refined throughout the data analysis. The three most recurrent codes are "US Foreign Policy," "Critique on US Foreign Policy," and "Divisions in the US Political Establishment" (see Table 9.4 for a full list of the most recurrent codes). As the data analysis progressed, these general codes were narrowed down to more specific subcodes, as each period required its own set of particular codes. Codes were used to index small fragments of the articles, not the entire text.

Once the coding of the entire dataset was completed, I undertook a close examination of the most recurrent codes in order to identify hegemonic frames. Since the articles had been previously classified by period, newspaper, and journalistic genre, it was possible to retrieve one or more codes and create clusters of codes and subcodes. The frequency of codes was subjected to scrutiny, but most importantly, their contents and how they related to other codes in the texts to form reasoning devices and, ultimately, frames. However, frames and codes are not synonyms. A frame is a cluster of codes and reasoning devices organized in a certain way in one or more texts.

The next step of the data analysis involved determining which frames were dominant in each newspaper and period. As van Gorp claimed, "[o]nce a repertoire

Table A.4 Most Recurrent Codes and Subcodes

Actors	Narratives	Policies	Syrian Conflict
Arab League	Arab Spring	Divisions in Europe	Chemical Attacks
Assad-Syrian Regime	Orientalism	Geopolitics	Civil War
Free Syrian Army	Historical	Regional Disputes	Consequences of the Syrian Conflict
Hezbollah	Analysis	Russian Foreign Policy	
International Community	Regime Narrative	US Foreign Policy	Ethnic Divisions in Syria
Iran	Russia, Syria Against the West	—Critique on US Foreign Policy	Government Repression
Iraq		—Divisions in the US Establishment	Humanitarian Crisis
ISIS	War on Terror		Origins of the Conflict
Islamists		—Geostrategic Importance of Syria	Protests in Syria
Israel			
Kurds			
Rebels			
Refugees			
Regional Actors			
Saudi Arabia			
Syrian Opposition			
Turkey			
UK			
UN			
US			

of frames is defined, two questions need to be answered. First, is the list of frames complete? Second, are these frames the most dominant ones?"[34] This stage of the analysis was informed by the notion that the recurrence and repetition of ideas, topics, and reasoning devices amount to a critical aspect of frame-building. On several occasions, however, the newspapers relayed conflicting frames about a specific issue. After all, it is not uncommon that op-ed authors writing for the same newspaper express different opinions on a particular issue. When conflicting frames were found in the same newspaper, I classified them as either hegemonic or outlier frames.

The analysis of the dataset demonstrates that the three newspapers followed consistent patterns throughout the six periods, which shows that the sample used in this book accurately represents the coverage of the Syrian conflict in the *NYT*, the *WP*, and the *WSJ*. These patterns relate to factors such as the topics discussed, the use of sources, and foreign policy proposals.

NOTES

Introduction

1. Bassam Haddad, "Why Syria Is Unlikely to Be Next ... for Now," *Carnegie Endowment for International Peace*, March 9, 2011.
2. Nadim Houry quoted in Cajsa Wikstrom, "Syria: 'A Kingdom of Silence,'" *Al Jazeera*, February 9, 2011.
3. Cristina Roca, "How the Syrian War Changed How War Crimes Are Documented," *New Humanitarian*, June 1, 2017; Olympe Lemut, "Shooting the War in Syria," *Newlines*, June 25, 2021.
4. Christopher Phillips, *The Battle for Syria*, 8.
5. Edward Said, *Covering Islam*, 150–1.
6. Ibid.
7. Todd Gitlin, *The Whole World Is Watching*, 6.
8. Ibid., 7.
9. Robert Entman, "Toward Clarification of a Fractured Paradigm," 52.
10. Kareem Shaheen, "'Save Us': Aleppo Civilians Plead for Help as Airstrikes Resume," *Guardian* (UK edition), December 14, 2016.
11. Ben Hubbard, "Assad's Lesson from Aleppo: Force Works, with Few Consequences," *New York Times*, December 16, 2016.
12. Ibid.
13. The Tahrir Institute for Middle East Policy focuses on democratic transitions in the Middle East, claiming to prioritize the views of local experts and advocates.
14. RT, "Liberation of E. Aleppo from Militants Complete—Russian Military," *RT*, December 16, 2016.
15. I use the terms "Salafism" and "Islamic fundamentalism" indistinctively in the book.
16. Freedom House, "Freedom of the Press 2017," 9.
17. Muhammad Idrees Ahmad, "RT and Syria: The Triumph of Narrative over Facts," *News Line*, March 2017.
18. Enab Baladi, "Thousands Still Besieged in Aleppo ... Activists Fear for Their Fate," *Enab Baladi*, December 21, 2016.
19. Michael Schudson, *The Sociology of News*, 75.
20. Bill Kovach and Tom Rosenstiel, *The Elements of Journalism*, 101.
21. Edward Herman and Noam Chomsky, *Manufacturing Consent*, loc. 1131–3 of 14175, Kindle.
22. Ibid., loc. 1134–7 of 14175, Kindle.
23. Edward Said, *Orientalism*, 30.
24. Ibid.
25. Edward Herman and Noam Chomsky, *Manufacturing Consent*, loc. 278–80 of 14175, Kindle.
26. Stuart Hall, "Encoding and Decoding in the Television Discourse," 13.
27. Robert Entman and Nikki Usher, "Framing in a Fractured Democracy," 300.

28 Robert Entman, *Projections of Power*, 9.
29 Des Freedman, *The Contradictions of Media Power*, 140.
30 Sara Fischer, "Trump Bump: NYT and WaPo Digital Subscriptions Tripled since 2016," *Axios*, November 24, 2020; Amy Watson, "Wall Street Journal: Circulation 2018–2020," *Statista*, December 18, 2020.
31 Viktor Pickard, *Democracy without Journalism?*, 75.
32 Ibid., 11–12.
33 Michael Schudson, *The Sociology of News*, 72.
34 Daniel Hallin and Paolo Mancini, *Comparing Media Systems*, 9.
35 Ibid., 11.
36 Victor Navasky, foreword to *Journalism after September 11*, eds. Barbie Zelizer and Stuart Allan, xv.
37 Sara Fischer, "Trump Bump: NYT and WaPo Digital Subscriptions Tripled since 2016," *Axios*, November 24, 2020.
38 Steve Barkin and Mark Levy, "All the News That's Fit to Correct," 220.
39 Amy Mitchell et al., "Political Polarization & Media Habits," *Pew Research Center*, October 21, 2014.
40 WashPostPR, "The Washington Post Announces Expanded International Coverage," *Washington Post PR* (blog), *Washington Post*, February 13, 2018.
41 Michael Levin, "Seven Years Later: What Exactly Did Rupert Murdoch Do to the Wall Street Journal?," *HuffPost*, July 31, 2015.
42 Editorial Board, "The Iraqi Debacle," *Wall Street Journal*, June 15, 2014.
43 Lucia Graves, "The Wall Street Journal's Trump Problem," *Guardian* (UK edition), September 10, 2017.
44 Daniel Shane, "The Wall Street Journal Kills Off Its International Print Editions," *CNN*, September 29, 2017.
45 Sean Aday, "The US Media, Foreign Policy, and Public Support for War," in *The Oxford Handbook of Political Communication*, eds. Kate Kenski and Kathleen Jamieson, 315.
46 Ibid.

Chapter 1

1 Peter Baker, "'Mission Accomplished!' But What Is the Mission in Syria?," *New York Times*, April 14, 2018.
2 BBC News, "Syria Airstrikes: US Still 'Locked and Loaded' for New Chemical Attacks," *BBC News*, April 15, 2018.
3 Kari Paul, "Obama Says Presidents Should Avoid Social Media in Apparent Trump Jab," *Guardian* (UK edition), September 18, 2019.
4 Ben Rhodes, *The World as It Is*, loc. 1508 of 7562, Kindle.
5 Walter Russel Mead, *Special Providence*, 15.
6 W. Lance Bennett, "The News about Foreign Policy," in *Taken by Storm*, eds. W. Lance Bennett and David Paletz, 19.
7 Sean Aday, "The US Media, Foreign Policy, and Public Support for War," in *The Oxford Handbook of Political Communication*, eds. Kate Kenski and Kathleen Jamieson, 316.
8 Victor Pickard, *Democracy without Journalism*, 35.

9   Dina Matar, "First Framing and News," in *Reporting the Middle East*, ed. Zahera Harb, 41.
10 Walter Russel Mead, *Special Providence*, 49.
11 Jürgen Habermas, "Political Communication in Media Society," 411–12.
12 Walter Lippmann and Charles Merz, "A Test of the News," *New Republic*, August 4, 1920, 3.
13 Howard Friel and Richard Falk, *The Record of the Paper*, 95.
14 Ibid.
15 Edward Herman and Noam Chomsky, *Manufacturing Consent*, loc. 105–7 of 14175, Kindle.
16 Ibid., loc. 1790–2 of 14175, Kindle.
17 The US government funded different paramilitary, right-wing groups in Nicaragua that opposed the leftist Sandinista government that came to power in 1979. The most important of these groups was the so-called Contra, which received millions of dollars from the Reagan administration. The International Court of Justice ruled that the links between US state institutions, such as the CIA, and the Contra violated international law.
18 W. Lance Bennett, "Toward a Theory of Press-State Relations in the United States," 103.
19 W. Lance Bennett, "Press-Government Relations in a Changing Media Environment," in *The Oxford Handbook of Political Communication*, eds. Kate Kenski and Kathleen Jamieson, 251.
20 Edward Herman and Noam Chomsky, *Manufacturing Consent*, loc. 2117–20 of 14175, Kindle.
21 Daniel Hallin, *Uncensored War*, 61.
22 Ibid., 12.
23 Ibid., 213.
24 Edward Herman and Noam Chomsky, *Manufacturing Consent*, loc. 1045–7 of 14175, Kindle.
25 Edward Herman and Noam Chomsky, "The Propaganda Model after 20 Years," interview by Andrew Mullen, November 2009.
26 Ibid.
27 Jon Western and Joshua Goldstein, "Humanitarian Intervention Comes of Age," *Foreign Affairs*, November/December 2011.
28 Eytan Gilboa et al., "Moving Media and Conflict Studies beyond the CNN Effect," 655.
29 Piers Robinson, *The CNN Effect*, 25.
30 Ibid., 37.
31 Chris York, "'Whitewashing War Crimes': How UK Academics Promote Pro-Assad Conspiracy Theories about Syria," *HuffPost*, August 22, 2018; Chris York and Ewan Somerville, "Professor Piers Robinson Leaves Sheffield Uni Post after Accusations of Promoting Conspiracy Theories," *HuffPost*, April 17, 2019.
32 The 2013 Eastern Ghouta chemical attack and the 2018 Douma chemical attack are discussed in more detail in Chapters 4 and 8.
33 Piers Robinson, "War and Media since 9/11," 559.
34 Piers Robinson, "9/11 Unmasked by David Ray Griffin and Elizabeth Woodworth: A Review," *OffGuardian* (blog), September 10, 2018.
35 George Kennan, "Somalia, Through a Glass Darkly," *New York Times*, September 30, 1993.
36 Ibid.

37 Steven Livingstone, "Clarifying the CNN Effect," 3.
38 Sean Aday, "The US Media, Foreign Policy, and Public Support for War," in *The Oxford Handbook of Political Communication*, eds. Kate Kenski and Kathleen Jamieson," 316.
39 Peter Jakobsen, "Focus on the CNN Effect Misses the Point," 134.
40 Lyse Doucet, "Syria & the CNN Effect," 144.
41 Samer Abboud, *Syria*, 44–5.
42 Donatella Della Ratta, *Shooting a Revolution*, 124–5.
43 Committee to Protect Journalists, "Ten Most Censored Countries," *Committee to Protect Journalists*, May 2, 2012.
44 The Middle East Institute is a Washington-based institution founded in 1946 and dedicated to the study of the Middle East.
45 Antoun Issa, "Syria's New Media Landscape."
46 Kholoud Helmi, "Revolutionary Women: Makers of the New Media in Syria," interview by SOAS Syria Society, *Syrian Corner*, February 8, 2018.
47 Ibid.
48 Omar al-Ghazzi, "'Forced to Report': Affective Proximity and the Perils of Local Reporting on Syria," 2.
49 Ibid., 9.
50 Lyse Doucet, "Syria & the CNN Effect," 142.
51 Donatella Della Ratta, *Shooting a Revolution*, 138–9.
52 Perry Anderson, *American Foreign Policy and Its Thinkers*, 183.
53 Robert Entman, *Projections of Power*, 5.
54 Stephen Ambrose and Douglas Brinkley, *Rise to Globalism*, 474.
55 Ian Lustick, *Trapped in the War on Terror*, 71.
56 George W. Bush, introduction to the National Security Strategy 2002, September 17, 2002.
57 Adam Isacson and Nicole Ball, "US Military and Police Assistance to Poorly Performing States," in *Short of the Goal: US Policy and Poorly Performing States*, eds. Nancy Birdsall, Milan Vaishnav, and Robert Ayres, 415.
58 Gilbert Achcar, *The Clash of Barbarisms*, 28.
59 Pippa Norris, Montague Kern, and Marion Just, "Framing Terrorism," in *Framing Terrorism*, eds. Pippa Norris, Montague Kern, and Marion Just, 15.
60 Robert McChesney, "September 11 and the Structural Limitations of US Journalism," in *Journalism after September 11*, eds. Barbie Zelizer and Stuart Allan, 93.
61 Robert Entman, *Projections of Power*, 115.
62 Ibid., 113.
63 Michael Schudson, "What's Unusual about Covering Politics as Usual," in *Journalism after September 11*, eds. Barbie Zelizer and Stuart Allan, 41.
64 Operation Desert Fox was a bombing campaign against Iraqi targets conducted by the United States and the UK in December 1998.
65 John Richardson, *Analyzing Newspapers*, 187–8.
66 Robert Entman, *Projections of Power*, 122.
67 Des Freedman, *The Contradictions of Media Power*, 119–20.

Chapter 2

1 Samer Abboud, *Syria*, 63.
2 Gilbert Achcar, *The People Want*, 24.
3 Omar Dahi and Yasser Munif, "Revolts in Syria," 327.

4   Ibid., 327–8.
5   Michael Bröning, "The Sturdy House That Assad Built," *Foreign Affairs*, March 7, 2011.
6   Hillary Clinton quoted in Glenn Kessler, "Hillary Clinton's Uncredible Statement on Syria," *Washington Post*, April 4, 2011.
7   Bashar al-Assad, "Interview with Syrian President Bashar al-Assad," *Wall Street Journal*, January 31, 2011.
8   Christopher Phillips, *The Battle for Syria*, 154.
9   Frederic C. Hof, "How Close Did Israel Come to Peace with Syria," interview by Faysal Itani, *New Lines Magazine*, May 5, 2022.
10 Ibid.
11 Mark Landler, "Unrest in Syria and Jordan Poses New Threat to US Policy," *New York Times*, March 26, 2011.
12 New York Times, "In Syria Demonstrations Are Few and Brief," *New York Times*, March 16, 2011.
13 Michael Slackman, "Syria Tries to Ease Deep Political Crisis," *New York Times*, March 27, 2011.
14 Mark Landler, "Unrest in Syria and Jordan Poses New Threat to US Policy," *New York Times*, March 26, 2011.
15 Robert Gates quoted in Mark Landler and Thom Shanker, "Gates and Clinton Unite to Defend Libya Intervention, and Say It May Last a While," *New York Times*, March 27, 2011.
16 Barack Obama quoted in Helene Cooper, "Obama Cites Limits of US Role in Libya," *New York Times*, March 28, 2011.
17 Helene Cooper, "Obama Cites Limits of US Role in Libya," *New York Times*, March 28, 2011.
18 Mark Landler, "Unrest in Syria and Jordan Poses New Threat to US Policy," *New York Times*, March 26, 2011.
19 Ibid.
20 Thomas Friedman, "Hoping for Arab Mandelas," *New York Times*, March 26, 2011; Thomas Friedman, "Tribes with Flags," *New York Times*, March 22, 2011.
21 Thomas Friedman, "Looking for Luck in Libya," *New York Times*, March 29, 2011.
22 Fukuyama's actual words in the introduction of his well-known book are: "While earlier forms of government were characterized by grave defects and irrationalities that led to their eventual collapse, liberal democracy was arguably free from such fundamental internal contradictions." See Francis Fukuyama, *The End of History and the Last Man*, xi.
23 Thomas Friedman, "Looking for Luck in Libya," *New York Times*, March 29, 2011.
24 Ronald Bruce St. John, "The Changing Libyan Economy: Causes and Consequences."
25 See Gilbert Achcar, *The People Want*; Adam Hanieh, *Lineages of Revolt*.
26 Francis Fukuyama, *The End of History and the Last Man*, xiv–xv.
27 Edward Said, *Orientalism*, 30.
28 Ibid., 132.
29 Thomas Friedman, "Hoping for Arab Mandelas," *New York Times*, March 26, 2011.
30 Janine Zacharia, "Israel, Long Critical of Assad, May Prefer He Stay after All," *Washington Post*, March 30, 2011; Leila Fadel, "Amid Protests, Syrian President Accepts Cabinet's Resignation," *Washington Post*, March 29, 2011; Edward Cody, "Arab League Condemns Broad Bombing Campaign in Libya," *Washington Post*, March 20, 2011.

31. Washington Post, "Syrian Forces Fire into Air as Protesters Call for Assad's Exit," *Washington Post*, March 29, 2011.
32. Elliot Abrams, "Ridding Syria of a Despot," *Washington Post*, March 26, 2011.
33. Editorial Board, "Opposing Syria's Crackdown," *Washington Post*, March 24, 2011.
34. Editorial Board, "Can Syria's Dictator Reform?," *Washington Post*, March 29, 2011.
35. Ibid.
36. Zalmay Khalilzad, "A Regional Strategy for Democracy in the Middle East," *Washington Post*, March 15, 2011.
37. David Ignatius, "Obama's Fuzzy Narrative in the Mideast," *Washington Post*, March 25, 2011.
38. David Ignatius, "Obama Speech Offers Clarity on Libya Policy," *Washington Post*, March 28, 2011.
39. Jim Hoagland, "Obama Recalibrates American Power," *Washington Post*, March 29, 2011.
40. Editorial Board, "The UN's Human 'Rights' Council," *Washington Post*, March 26, 2011.
41. Elliot Abrams, "Ridding Syria of a Despot," *Washington Post*, March 26, 2011.
42. Thomas Friedman, "Looking for Luck in Libya," *New York Times*, March 29, 2011.
43. Elliot Abrams, "Ridding Syria of a Despot," *Washington Post*, March 26, 2011.
44. Robert Gates quoted in David Ignatius, "Gates Underlines the Dangers in the Middle East," *Washington Post*, March 22, 2011.
45. The Golan Heights were part of Syria before Israel captured and occupied them during the 1967 Six-Day War.
46. Janine Zacharia, "Israel, Long Critical of Assad, May Prefer He Stay after All," *Washington Post*, March 30, 2011.
47. Zalmay Khalilzad, "Freedom's Call," *Washington Post*, March 16, 2011.
48. Ahed al-Hendi, "Syrians Cry 'Freedom!' Too," *Wall Street Journal*, March 26, 2011.
49. Jay Solomon, "US Won't Back New Intervention," *Wall Street Journal*, March 27, 2011.
50. Naftali Bendavid, "Republicans Show Divisions over the US Intervention," *Wall Street Journal*, March 29, 2011.
51. Wall Street Journal, "The Syrian Revolt," *Wall Street Journal*, March 26, 2011.
52. Jay Solomon, "US Won't Back New Intervention," *Wall Street Journal*, March 27, 2011.
53. Wall Street Journal, "The Shaky House of Assad," *Wall Street Journal*, March 22, 2011.
54. Wall Street Journal, "The Syrian Revolt," *Wall Street Journal*, March 26, 2011.
55. Farnaz Fassihi and Jay Solomon, "Syrian Regime Rocked by Protests," *Wall Street Journal*, March 26, 2011.
56. Barack Obama quoted in Farnaz Fassihi, "Syrian Cabinet Steps Down," *Wall Street Journal*, March 29, 2011.
57. Jay Solomon, "US Won't Back New Intervention," *Wall Street Journal*, March 27, 2011.

Chapter 3

1. Navi Pillay quoted in David Jolly, "Death Toll in Syrian Civil War Near 93,000, UN Says," *New York Times*, June 13, 2013.
2. The Carter Center was founded in 1982 by former US President Jimmy Carter and his wife Rosalynn Carter.

3   The Carter Center, "Syria Countrywide Conflict Report," 24.
4   *Shahada* is the Islamic belief in the oneness of god.
5   Yassin al-Haj Saleh, *The Impossible Revolution*, 159.
6   Amnesty International, "Human Slaughterhouse: Mass Hangings and Extermination at Saydnaya Prison, Syria," *Amnesty International USA*, February 3, 2017.
7   Médecins Sans Frontières (MSF), "Thousands Suffering Neurotoxic Symptoms Treated in Hospitals Supported by MSF," *MSF International*, August 24, 2013.
8   United Nations, "'Clear and Convincing' Evidence of Chemical Weapons Use in Syria, UN Team Reports," *UN News*, September 13, 2013.
9   Christopher Phillips, *The Battle for Syria*, 169.
10 Muhammad Idrees Ahmad, "Obama's Legacy Is Tarnished as Putin Fills the Vacuum in Syria," *The National*, October 10, 2015.
11 Ben Hubbard and Hwaida Saad, "Images of Death in Syria, but No Proof of Chemical Attacks," *New York Times*, August 21, 2013.
12 Editorial Board, "The Corpses in Syria," *New York Times*, August 23, 2013.
13 Robert Entman, *Projections of Power*, 5.
14 Ben Hubbard, Mark Mazzetti, and Mark Landler, "Blasts in the Night, a Smell, and a Flood of Syrian Victims," *New York Times*, August 26, 2013.
15 Mark Landler, Mark Mazzetti, and Alissa Rubin, "Obama Officials Weigh Response to Syrian Assault," *New York Times*, August 22, 2013.
16 John Kerry, "Text of Kerry's Statement on Chemical Weapons in Syria," *New York Times*, August 26, 2013.
17 Ben Hubbard, "Signs of Chemical Attacks Detailed by Aid Group," *New York Times*, August 24, 2013.
18 Mark Landler and Michael Gordon, "Air War in Kosovo Seen as Precedent in Possible Response to Syria Chemical Attack," *New York Times*, August 23, 2013.
19 Thom Shanker, "General Says Syrian Rebels Aren't Ready to Take Power," *New York Times*, August 21, 2013.
20 Martin Dempsey quoted in Ibid.
21 Editorial Board, "The Corpses in Syria," *New York Times*, August 23, 2013.
22 Edward Luttwak, "In Syria, America Loses if Either Side Wins," *New York Times*, August 24, 2013.
23 Ibid.
24 Ben Rhodes, *The World as It Is*, chapter 18.
25 Editorial Board, "The Corpses in Syria," *New York Times*, August 23, 2013.
26 Scott Shane and Ben Hubbard, "Confident Syria Used Chemicals," *New York Times*, August 25, 2013.
27 According to Stephen Walt, an international relations scholar and *Foreign Policy* columnist, the Washington Institute for Near East Policy is "an influential organization in the Israel lobby." See Stephen Walt, "Robert Satloff Doth Protest Too Much," *Foreign Policy*, April 9, 2010.
28 The Council describes itself as an independent, nonpartisan, nonprofit organization that takes no institutional policy positions.
29 France held a highly interventionist stance in the aftermath of the Eastern Ghouta attack.
30 The Center for Public Justice advertises itself as an American-Christian think tank which undertakes to bring a Christian worldview to bear on policy issues.
31 Editorial Board, "Syrian Attack Should Prompt US Investigation into Chemical Weapons," *Washington Post*, August 21, 2013.

32 Jennifer Rubin, "The Gruesome Repudiation of 'Leading from Behind,'" *Right Turn* (blog), *Washington Post*, August 25, 2013.
33 Editorial Board, "Syria Response Can't Rely Solely on Military Might," *Washington Post*, August 26, 2013.
34 Liz Sly, "UN Inspectors Visit Site of Alleged Chemical Attack in Syria after Coming under Sniper Fire," *Washington Post*, August 26, 2013.
35 Eugene Robinson, "Assad Must Be Punished," *Washington Post*, August 26, 2013.
36 Will Englund, "Russia Says Western Attack on Syria Would Be 'Catastrophic,'" *Washington Post*, August 26, 2013.
37 Martin Dempsey quoted in Loveday Morris and Karen DeYoung, "Syrian Activists Accuse Government of Deadly Chemical Attack near Damascus," *Washington Post*, August 22, 2013.
38 Loveday Morris and Karen DeYoung, "Syrian Activists Accuse Government of Deadly Chemical Attack near Damascus," *Washington Post*, August 22, 2013.
39 Adam Berinsky and Donald Kinder, "Making Sense of Issues through Media Frames," 641.
40 Karen DeYoung and Anne Gearan, "After Syria Chemical Allegations, Obama Considering Limited Military Strike," *Washington Post*, August 26, 2013.
41 Karen DeYoung and Colum Lynch, "In Syria Chemical Attack Allegations, US and Allies Push for Immediate Probe," *Washington Post*, August 22, 2013.
42 Anne Gearan, Loveday Morris, and Colum Lynch, "UN to Inspect Site of Alleged Chemical Weapons Attack in Syria," *Washington Post*, August 25, 2013.
43 Mahmoud Irdaisat quoted in Liz Sly, "UN Inspectors Visit Site of Alleged Chemical Attack in Syria after Coming under Sniper Fire," *Washington Post*, August 26, 2013.
44 Eliot Cohen, "Syrian Will Require More than Cruise Missiles," *Washington Post*, August 25, 2013.
45 Michael Gerson, "Syrian War Leaves No Easy Choices," *Washington Post*, August 26, 2013.
46 Taylor Luck, "As Syrian Rebels' Losses Mount, Teenagers Begin Filling Ranks," *Washington Post*, August 24, 2013.
47 Michael Gerson, "Syrian War Leaves No Easy Choices," *Washington Post*, August 26, 2013.
48 Walter Russell Mead, "The Failed Grand Strategy in the Middle East," *Wall Street Journal*, August 24, 2013.
49 Ibid.
50 Jay Solomon and Julian Barnes, "In Mideast, US Policy Models Bog Down," *Wall Street Journal*, August 21, 2013.
51 Pete du Pont, "Obama's Foreign Failure," *Wall Street Journal*, August 27, 2013.
52 Wall Street Journal, "Double-Secret Probation for Bashar," *Wall Street Journal*, August 25, 2013.
53 Wall Street Journal, "Syria Side Effect," *Wall Street Journal*, August 26, 2013.
54 Andrew Roberts, "Syria's Gas Attacks on Civilization," *Wall Street Journal*, August 25, 2013.
55 According to its website, "[t]he Fund for Investigative Journalism provides grants and other support to independent journalists and news organizations to produce high-quality, unbiased, nonpartisan investigative stories that have an impact."
56 Gary Fields, "Law Makers Call for US Response in Syria," *Wall Street Journal*, August 25, 2013.

57 Sam Dagher, Maria Abi-Habib, and Ellen Knickmeyer, "Arab League Cautious as US Gears for Strike," *Wall Street Journal*, August 27, 2013.
58 Serge Halimi, "The Challenge Is Bigger than Trump," *Le Monde Diplomatique* (English Edition), February 2020.
59 Bret Stephens, "Target Assad," *Wall Street Journal*, August 27, 2013.
60 Wall Street Journal, "Loose Lips on Syria," *Wall Street Journal*, August 27, 2013.
61 Wall Street Journal, "The Problem Is Assad," *Wall Street Journal*, August 27, 2013.
62 Ellen Knickmeyer and Nour Malas, "Arab Allies Withhold Public Support for US Strike on Syria," *Wall Street Journal*, August 27, 2013.
63 Adam Entous, Julian Barnes, and Inti Landauro, "US Weighs Plan to Punish Assad," *Wall Street Journal*, August 23, 2013.
64 Farnaz Fassihi, "Syrian Strike Could Dash Hope for Iran Talks," *Wall Street Journal*, August 27, 2013.
65 Joshua Mitnick, "Israel Worries Rise over a Syrian Attack," *Wall Street Journal*, August 27, 2013.
66 Adam Entous, Nour Malas, and Margaret Coker, "A Veteran Saudi Power Player Works to Build Support to Topple Assad," *Wall Street Journal*, August 25, 2013.
67 Jay Solomon, "In Turkey, Syrian Rebels Hope US Strikes Could Swing War," *Wall Street Journal*, August 26, 2013.

Chapter 4

1 Michael Weiss and Hassan Hassan, *ISIS*, 130.
2 Ibid., 137.
3 Christopher Phillips, *The Battle for Syria*, 207.
4 Stephen Zunes, "The US and ISIS," *Progressive Magazine*, August 26, 2014.
5 Josh Rogin, "Pentagon Wanted to Arm the Syrian Opposition," *Foreign Policy*, February 7, 2013.
6 Hillary Clinton, "Hillary Clinton: 'Failure' to Help Syrian Rebels Led to the Rise of ISIS," interview by Jeffrey Goldberg, *The Atlantic*, August 10, 2014.
7 Hillary Clinton, "Hillary Clinton: 'Failure' to Help Syrian Rebels Led to the Rise of ISIS," interview by Jeffrey Goldberg, *The Atlantic*, August 10, 2014.
8 Ben Rhodes, *The World as It Is*, loc. 4881 of 7562, Kindle.
9 Thomas Friedman, "Obama on the World," *New York Times*, August 8, 2014.
10 Gilbert Achcar, *Morbid Symptoms*, 24.
11 Peter Moore, "One Year Later, Americans Back Military Action in Syria," *YouGov*, August 29, 2014.
12 John McCain and Lindsey Graham, "Stop Dithering, Confront ISIS," *New York Times*, August 29, 2014.
13 Aaron Zelin, "Al-Qaeda Disaffiliates with the Islamic State of Iraq and al-Sham," Washington Institute for Near East Policy, February 3, 2014.
14 Wilson Center, "Timeline: The Rise, Spread, and Fall of the Islamic State," Wilson Center, October 28, 2019.
15 Combined Joint Task Force—Operation Inherent Resolve. "About CJTF-OIR." Operation Inherent Resolve, accessed May 27, 2020.
16 Matthieu Aikins, "The Promise of Aleppo's Radicals," *New York Times*, July 7, 2014.

17 Clemens Wergin, "Is Obama's Foreign Policy Too European?," *New York Times*, July 8, 2014.
18 Michael Cohen, "Obama's Understated Foreign Policy Gains," *New York Times*, July 9, 2014.
19 David Sanger, *Confront and Conceal*, loc. 161 of 7721, Kindle.
20 Michael O'Hanlon and Edward Joseph, quoted in Jake Flanagin, "Iraq—or Sunnistan, Shiitestan and Kurdistan," *Op-Talk* (blog), *New York Times*, July 7, 2014.
21 Leslie Gelb and Joseph Biden, quoted in Jake Flanagin, "Iraq—or Sunnistan, Shiitestan and Kurdistan," *Op-Talk* (blog), *New York Times*, July 7, 2014.
22 Michael O'Hanlon and Edward Joseph, quoted in Jake Flanagin, "Iraq—or Sunnistan, Shiitestan and Kurdistan," *Op-Talk* (blog), *New York Times*, July 7, 2014.
23 Hwaida Saad, "Militants Said to Kill Scores at Syrian Base," *New York Times*, July 25, 2014.
24 Somini Sengupta, "Bid to Deliver Aid to Syria May Set Stage for a UN Clash," *New York Times*, July 13, 2014.
25 Rick Gladstone, "UN Council, in Unanimous Vote, Backs Aid Delivery to Syrians in Rebel Areas," *New York Times*, July 14, 2014.
26 Somini Sengupta, "Defying Syria, United Nations Sends in Trucks Carrying Aid," *New York Times*, July 24, 2014.
27 Ban Ki-moon quoted in Ibid.
28 Hwaida Saad and Alan Cowell, "Assad Begins a Third Term in Syria, Vowing to Look after Its People," *New York Times*, July 16, 2014.
29 Marc Thiessen, "Obama's Legacy of Failure," *Washington Post*, July 7, 2014.
30 John Kerry quoted in Dana Milbank, "Another Swing and a Miss for Obama's Foreign Policy," *Washington Post*, July 14, 2014.
31 John Kerry brokered an agreement between the two leading candidates in the 2014 Afghan elections, Ashraf Ghani and Abdullah Abdullah. According to the deal, both politicians would share power and form a national unity government.
32 Editorial Board, "US Should Aid Those Who Fight Terror, Not Abet Human Rights Abuses," *Washington Post*, July 7, 2014.
33 The Wilson Center is a public-private partnership funded with both public funds and private donations. The media watch group FAIR described the center as a "centrist" think tank. See Michael Dolny, "FAIR STUDY: Think Tank Spectrum 2012," FAIR, July 1, 2013.
34 Jane Harman, "The United States Must Advance a Mideast Policy Based on Collaboration," *Washington Post*, July 10, 2014.
35 Fareed Zakaria, "Obama Caves to Conventional Wisdom in Syria," *Washington Post*, July 10, 2014.
36 In 1982, former Syrian President Hafez al-Assad crushed a rebellion against his government in the Syrian city of Hama, killing more than 20,000 people. Several observers described the rebellion as a Sunni uprising led by the Syrian Muslim Brotherhood.
37 Fareed Zakaria, "Obama Caves to Conventional Wisdom in Syria," *Washington Post*, July 10, 2014.
38 Eugene Robinson, "The Downside of Giving Weapons to Rebels in Ukraine or Syria," *Washington Post*, July 21, 2014.
39 Ray Takeyh, "How to Break the Iran Nuclear Stalemate," *Washington Post*, July 18, 2014.
40 Editorial Board, "The West Must Prepare for a Wounded Putin to Become Even More Aggressive," *Washington Post*, July 30, 2014.

41 The Carnegie Middle East Center is considered one of the top think tanks in the Middle East and North Africa.
42 Yezid Sayigh quoted in Liz Sly and Ahmed Ramadan, "Assad, Inaugurated to Third Term, Tells the World: I Told You So," *Washington Post*, July 16, 2014.
43 Bashar al-Assad quoted in Liz Sly and Ahmed Ramadan, "Assad, Inaugurated to Third Term, Tells the World: I Told You So," *Washington Post*, July 16, 2014.
44 Bret Stephens, "The Post-Pax Americana World," *Wall Street Journal*, July 7, 2014.
45 Adam Entous and Julian Barnes, "Pentagon Envisions 'Small' Training Program for Syria Opposition," *Wall Street Journal*, July 16, 2014.
46 Jonathan Foreman, "Building the US-Kurdistan Special Relationship," *Wall Street Journal*, July 10, 2014.
47 Jay Solomon, "Failed Mideast Peace Effort Sidelines US in Current Strife," *Wall Street Journal*, July 9, 2014.
48 Jay Solomon and Carol Lee, "Obama Contends with Arc of Instability Unseen since '70s," *Wall Street Journal*, July 13, 2014.
49 Jason Riley, "Hillary's Foreign Policy Gambit," *Wall Street Journal*, July 7, 2014.
50 Laurence Norman, "EU Adds New Targets for Syria Sanctions," *Wall Street Journal*, July 22, 2014.
51 Stephen Fidler, "Europe Narrows Divide over Russian Sanctions," *Wall Street Journal*, July 25, 2014.
52 Andrew Grossman, "Syria Is Breeding Western Terrorists, US Warns," *Wall Street Journal*, July 8, 2014.
53 Stacy Meichtry, "France Steps Up Effort to Stop Syria-Bound Fighters," *Wall Street Journal*, July 9, 2014.
54 Siobhan Gorman, "US Faces Growing Threats, 9/11 Commission Cautions," *Wall Street Journal*, July 22, 2014.
55 Maria Abi-Habib, "Islamist Militants Gain in Syria," *Wall Street Journal*, July 24, 2014.
56 Margaret Coker, "The New Jihad," *Wall Street Journal*, July 11, 2014.

Chapter 5

1 Charles Lister, "Why Assad Is Losing," *Brookings Institution*, May 5, 2015.
2 William Spindler, "2015: The Year of Europe's Refugee Crisis," *UNHCR UK*, December 8, 2015.
3 Somini Sengupta, "Refugee Crisis in Europe Prompts Western Engagement in Syria," *New York Times*, September 30, 2015.
4 Russian Defense Ministry quoted in John Daly, "The Real Cost of Russia's Syrian Campaign," *United Press International*, March 6, 2017.
5 Christopher Phillips, *The Battle for Syria*, 217.
6 Ibid., 218.
7 President Obama, "Remarks by President Obama to the United Nations General Assembly," *The White House*, September 28, 2015.
8 Gilbert Achcar, *Morbid Symptoms*, 60.
9 Ibid., 54.
10 Barack Obama, "The Obama Doctrine," interview by Jeffrey Goldberg, *The Atlantic*, April 2016.
11 Perry Anderson, *American Foreign Policy and Its Thinkers*, 232.

12 Robert Blackwill and Philip Gordon, "Containing Russia, Again," *Foreign Affairs*, January 18, 2018.
13 Ibid.
14 Anna Borshchevskaya, "In Syria, Putin Risks Repeating the Soviet Union's Afghanistan Mistake," *Washington Institute for Near East Policy*, September 15, 2015; Thomas Friedman, "Syria, Obama and Putin," *New York Times*, September 30, 2015; Andrew Roth, "Putin's Endgame in Syria?," *Washington Post*, September 29, 2015.
15 Editorial Board, "Russia's Dangerous Escalation in Syria," *New York Times*, October 2, 2015.
16 Editorial Board, "Putin and Obama Have Profound Differences on Syria," *New York Times*, September 28, 2015.
17 Ibid.
18 Michael Gordon and Gardiner Harris, "Obama and Putin Play Diplomatic Poker over Syria," *New York Times*, September 28, 2015.
19 Khoodair Khusheif quoted in Anne Barnard, "Syrian Rebels Say Russia Is Targeting Them Rather than ISIS," *New York Times*, September 30, 2015.
20 Anne Barnard and Andrew Kramer, "Russia Carries Out Airstrikes in Syria for Second Day," *New York Times*, October 1, 2015.
21 Editorial Board, "Russia's Dangerous Escalation in Syria," *New York Times*, October 2, 2015.
22 Peter Baker, "John Kerry Rushes In Where Obama Will Not Tread," *New York Times*, September 29, 2015.
23 Ibid.
24 Peter Baker, "Syria Exposes Split between Obama and Clinton," *New York Times*, October 3, 2015.
25 Ross Douthat, "Is Putin Winning?," *New York Times*, October 3, 2015.
26 Thomas Friedman, "Syria, Obama and Putin," *New York Times*, September 30, 2015.
27 Ibid.
28 Anne Barnard and Neil MacFarquhar, "Vladimir Putin Plunges into a Caldron in Syria: Saving al-Assad," *New York Times*, October 1, 2015.
29 Somini Sengupta, "Russian Foreign Minister Defends Airstrikes in Syria," *New York Times,* October 1, 2015.
30 Steven Myers, "In Putin's Syria Intervention, Fear of a Weak Government Hand," *New York Times*, October 4, 2015.
31 Somini Sengupta, "Refugee Crisis in Europe Prompts Western Engagement in Syria," *New York Times*, September 30, 2015.
32 Sinan Ulgen, "Turkey Can't Be Europe's Gatekeeper," *New York Times*, October 1, 2015.
33 Peter Baker and Neil MacFarquhar, "Obama Sees Russia Failing in Syria Effort," *New York Times*, October 2, 2015.
34 Northeastern Syria is known to Syrian Kurds as "Rojava."
35 Carne Ross, "The Kurd's Democratic Experiment," *New York Times*, September 30, 2015.
36 Editorial Board, "Both Mr. Putin and Mr. Obama Are Wrong on Syria," *Washington Post*, September 28, 2015.
37 Fareed Zakaria, "In Syria, Whose Side Is the United States On?," *Washington Post*, October 1, 2015.
38 The Center for a New American Security claims to be an independent, bipartisan organization that produces research to "shape and elevate" the US national security debate.

39 Phillip Carter, "Why Foreign Troops Can't Fight Our Fights," *Washington Post*, October 2, 2015.
40 Karen DeYoung, Juliet Eilperin, and Greg Miller, "US Will Not Directly Confront Russia in Syria, Obama Says," *Washington Post*, October 2, 2015.
41 Missy Ryan, "Russian, Syrian Partnership Poses a New Challenge for US in Iraq," *Washington Post*, September 28, 2015.
42 Editorial Board, "How We Got to the Syria Mess," *Washington Post*, October 2, 2015.
43 Charles Krauthammer, "Obama's Syria Debacle," *Washington Post*, October 1, 2015.
44 Fareed Zakaria, "The Self-Destruction of American Power," *Foreign Affairs*, July/August 2019.
45 David Petraeus quoted in Walter Pincus, "Petraeus on Putin: His Provocations Are Designed to Protect His Interests," *Washington Post*, September 28, 2015.
46 Hillary Clinton quoted in Karen DeYoung, Juliet Eilperin, and Greg Miller, "US Will Not Directly Confront Russia in Syria, Obama Says," *Washington Post*, October 2, 2015.
47 David Ignatius, "The US Cannot Pass Syria On to Putin," *Washington Post*, September 29, 2015.
48 Juliet Eilperin, "At UN, Obama Touts Diplomacy over Military Force as Conflicts Mount,'" *Washington Post*, September 27, 2015.
49 Juliet Eilperin, "Obama's Multilateralist Vision for the World Collides with Great-Power Reality," *Washington Post*, September 29, 2015.
50 According to the media watch group FAIR, the Brookings Institutions and the Council on Foreign Relations are the first and the third most cited "centrist" think tanks, respectively. See Michael Dolny, "FAIR STUDY: Think Tank Spectrum 2012," *FAIR*, July 1, 2013.
51 Anne Applebaum, "Putin's Power Plays," *Washington Post*, September 27, 2015.
52 Adam Taylor, "Russia's Airstrikes in Syria Mark a Huge Departure for Moscow," *Washington Post*, September 30, 2015.
53 David Ignatius, "Russia and the 'Facts on the Ground' in Syria," *Washington Post*, October 1, 2015.
54 Andrew Roth, "Putin's Endgame in Syria?," *Washington Post*, September 29, 2015.
55 Andrew Roth and Thomas Gibbons-Neff, "Russia's Military Is Unlikely to Turn the Tide in Syria's War," *Washington Post*, October 3, 2015.
56 Petraeus quoted in Walter Pincus, "Petraeus on Putin: His Provocations Are Designed to Protect His Interests," *Washington Post*, September 28, 2015.
57 UN Syria Commission of Inquiry, "Rampant Human Rights Violations and War Crimes as War-Torn Idlib Faces the Pandemic," *United Nations Human Rights Office of the High Commission*, July 7, 2020; Human Rights Watch, "Syria/Russia: Strategy Targeted Civilian Infrastructure," *Human Rights Watch*, October 15, 2020.
58 Gerald Seib, "Syria War Tests Obama's Security Doctrine," *Wall Street Journal*, September 28, 2015.
59 Bret Stephens, "An Unteachable President," *Wall Street Journal*, September 28, 2015.
60 Wall Street Journal, "What US Retreat Looks Like," *Wall Street Journal*, October 1, 2015.
61 The Human Rights Foundation claims to be a nonpartisan, nonprofit organization that promotes and protects human rights globally, focusing on "closed" societies.
62 Garry Kasparov, "Putin Takes a Victory Lap While Obama Watches," *Wall Street Journal*, September 29, 2015.

63 Nader Hashemi and Danny Postel, "The Sectarianization Thesis," in *Sectarianization*, eds. Nader Hashemi and Danny Postel, 3.
64 Wall Street Journal, "Obama's 'Dangerous Currents,'" *Wall Street Journal*, September 28, 2015.
65 Carol Lee, "Obama Criticizes Russia over Syria Airstrikes," *Wall Street Journal*, October 2, 2015.
66 Paula Dobriansky and David Rivkin, "Congress Can Respond to Putin with More Sanctions," *Wall Street Journal*, October 4, 2015.
67 Jay Solomon, Carol Lee, and Farnaz Fassihi, "Arabs Spurn Military Push by Moscow Inside Syria," *Wall Street Journal*, September 30, 2015.
68 Wall Street Journal, "Obama's 'Dangerous Currents,'" *Wall Street Journal*, September 29, 2015.
69 Olga Razumovskaya, "Putin's Domestic Media Blitz Focuses on Islamic State Threat in Russia," *Wall Street Journal*, October 2, 2015.
70 Yaroslav Trofimov, "Russia Entry Adds New Fuel to Syria War," *Wall Street Journal*, October 1, 2015.
71 Matteo Renzi quoted in Deborah Ball, "Italy Prime Minister Renzi Calls for Russia to Be Part of Solution to Syria Crisis," *Wall Street Journal*, September 29, 2015.
72 Donald Tusk quoted in Laurence Norman, "EU's Tusk Says Europe Will Cope with Refugee Crisis," *Wall Street Journal*, September 29, 2015.
73 Jay Solomon, "Russia's Move in Syria Risks Aiding Militants, Saudis Warn," *Wall Street Journal*, October 1, 2015.
74 Sam Dagher and Asa Fitch, "Iran Expands Role in Syria in Conjunction with Russia's Airstrikes," *Wall Street Journal*, October 2, 2015.

Chapter 6

1 SANA Syrian Arab News Agency, "Do You Know That Aleppo Is the Economic, Commercial and Industrial Capital of Syria?," *SANA*, November 23, 2021.
2 Christopher Phillips, *The Battle for Syria*, 128.
3 Mapping Militant Organizations, "Liwa al-Tawhid," Stanford University, July 2016.
4 Martin Chulov, Kareem Shaheen, and Emma Graham-Harrison, "East Aleppo's Last Hospital Destroyed by Airstrikes," *Guardian* (UK edition), November 19, 2016.
5 Human Rights Watch, "Russia/Syria: War Crimes in Month of Bombing Aleppo," *Human Rights Watch*, December 1, 2016.
6 Leila Nachawati, "Alepo, Como Srebrenica y Gernika," *Otras Miradas* (blog), *Público*, December 16, 2016; my translation.
7 Lina Shamy, "I Went to Aleppo to Study. I Left in a Convoy of Refugees," *New York Times*, January 20, 2017.
8 Jennifer Cafarella and Genevieve Casagrande, "Syrian Armed Opposition Forces in Aleppo," 5–6.
9 The Institute for the Study of War claims to be a nonpartisan, nonprofit public policy research organization, though it receives financial support from large private corporations, such as Microsoft, IronNet Cybersecurity, and Capital Bank.
10 The Syrian Civil Defense is a grassroots group formed in 2014 to respond to aerial bombardments in rebel-controlled areas.

11. RT, "'As If She Was Mother Teresa Herself': Russia's Churkin Snubs US Power's Speech at UNSC," *RT*, December 14, 2016.
12. Staffan de Mistura quoted in United Nations, "Amid Bloodshed in Aleppo, Special Envoy for Syria Briefs Security Council, Calling on Russian Federation, United States to Save Ceasefire at 'Eleventh Hour,'" *United Nations*, September 25, 2016.
13. Aron Lund, "After Murky Diplomacy, Turkey Intervenes in Syria," *Carnegie Middle East Center*, August 24, 2016.
14. Christopher Phillips, *The Battle for Syria*, 233.
15. Nikolaos van Dam, *Destroying a Nation*, 134–5.
16. Raja Abdulrahim and Dion Nissenbaum, "Evacuations Set to Begin as Assad Reclaims Aleppo," *Wall Street Journal*, December 13, 2016.
17. Brett McGurk, "The Cost of an Incoherent Foreign Policy," *Foreign Affairs*, January 22, 2020.
18. James Jefrey quoted in Kathy Gilsinan, "Trump Is Killing a Fatally Flawed Syria Policy," *The Atlantic*, October 8, 2019.
19. Jack Detsch, "US Troops Really Are in Syria to Protect the Oil—for the Kurds," *Foreign Policy*, August 5, 2020.
20. Brett McGurk, "The Cost of an Incoherent Foreign Policy," *Foreign Affairs*, January 22, 2020.
21. Richard Gowan, "End Times Diplomacy at the UN," 18.
22. Gowan's journal article was published in the summer of 2017.
23. Bret McGurk, "Hard Truths in Syria," *Foreign Affairs*, May/June 2019.
24. Christopher Phillips, *The Battle for Syria*, 233.
25. Peter Galbraith, "How the War Ends in Syria," *New York Times*, December 6, 2016.
26. Barack Obama quoted in Gardiner Harris and Charlie Savage, "Obama, in Major National Security Speech, Defends Counterterrorism Legacy," *New York Times*, December 6, 2016.
27. Gardiner Harris and Charlie Savage, "Obama, in Major National Security Speech, Defends Counterterrorism Legacy," *New York Times*, December 6, 2016.
28. John McCain quoted in Ibid.
29. Anne Barnard and Hwaida Saad, "'We Are Dead Either Way': Agonizing Choices for Syrians in Aleppo," *New York Times*, December 10, 2016.
30. Anne Barnard, "Russia Says Aleppo Combat Has Ceased; Residents Disagree," *New York Times*, December 8, 2016.
31. According to Hosam al-Jablawi, a Syrian citizen journalist, the Nour al-Din al-Zenki movement was a moderate armed group founded in the countryside of Aleppo in 2011 that was part of the Free Syrian Army. In 2017, after the Assad regime recaptured Aleppo, the group joined the Islamist coalition Hay'at Tahrir al-Sham. Nour al-Din al-Zenki leaders justified the merging by arguing that both the international community and moderate groups inside Syrian had stopped supporting them. For more information, see al-Jablawi, Hosam, "Nour al-Din al-Zenki Movement: How a Once Moderate Group Joined Fateh al-Sham," *Atlantic Council*, February 17, 2017.
32. Anne Barnard, "In Rebel-Held Aleppo, Residents Report Increasing Desperation," *New York Times*, December 7, 2016.
33. Anne Barnard and Nick Cumming-Bruce, "Chaos and Desperation as Thousands Flee Aleppo amid Government Advance," *New York Times*, December 9, 2016.
34. Anne Barnard, "In Rebel-Held Aleppo, Residents Report Increasing Desperation," *New York Times*, December 7, 2016.

35. Anne Barnard and Hwaida Saad, "'We Are Dead Either Way': Agonizing Choices for Syrians in Aleppo," *New York Times*, December 10, 2016.
36. Anne Barnard and Nick Cumming-Bruce, "Chaos and Desperation as Thousands Flee Aleppo amid Government Advance," *New York Times*, December 9, 2016.
37. Greg Jaffe and David Nakamura, "Obama Defends His Wartime Strategy and Laments Trump's Likely Change of Course," *Washington Post*, December 6, 2016.
38. David Ignatius, "Obama's Tenure Ends with a Turf War over Killing Terrorists," *Washington Post*, December 8, 2016.
39. Ibid.
40. Greg Jaffe and Greg Miller, "Trump's Generals, Hardened by War, See Militant Islam, Iran as Dire Dangers," *Washington Post*, December 9, 2016.
41. Stephen Bannon served as the White House's chief strategist during President Trump's first seven months in office. Bannon is a well-known voice of the far-right in the United States. Michael Flynn was Trump's national security adviser for twenty-two days. He is a retired general who was involved in counterterrorism operations in the Iraq and Afghanistan Wars. Jeff Sessions is a Republican politician who served as US attorney general during 2017 and 2018.
42. Jackson Diehl, "Trump's Coming War against Islam," *Washington Post*, December 11, 2016.
43. Abdul Ilah Fahad quoted in Josh Rogin, "In Washington, Syrian Opposition Offers to Work with Trump and Russia," *Washington Post*, December 11, 2016.
44. Josh Rogin, "In Washington, Syrian Opposition Offers to Work with Trump and Russia," *Washington Post*, December 11, 2016.
45. Louisa Loveluck and Karen DeYoung, "Syrian Army Retakes Aleppo's Old City as Rebels Discuss Exit," *Washington Post*, December 7, 2016.
46. Ahmed al-Shaer quoted in Louisa Loveluck, "Syrian Forces Push Aleppo Rebels to Brink as City Nears 'Total Collapse,'" *Washington Post*, December 12, 2016.
47. Ameen al-Halabi quoted in Louisa Loveluck, "Syrian Forces Push Aleppo Rebels to Brink as City Nears 'Total Collapse,'" *Washington Post*, December 12, 2016.
48. Like Fatah al-Sham, the Abu Amara Batallion was also regarded as a terrorist group by Western analysts.
49. Rupert Coville quoted in Louisa Loveluck and Karen DeYoung, "Hundreds of Men Vanish as They Flee Aleppo, UN Official Says," *Washington Post*, December 9, 2016.
50. Carol Lee, "Obama Defends His Antiterror Strategy in Argument Aimed at His Successor," *Wall Street Journal*, December 6, 2016.
51. Gordon Lubold and Julian Barnes, "Pentagon Prepares Tougher Options on Fighting Militants to Show Trump Team," *Wall Street Journal*, December 9, 2016.
52. Gerald Seib, "Listen Closely: Donald Trump Proposes Big Mideast Strategy Shift," *Wall Street Journal*, December 12, 2016.
53. Ibid.
54. Carol Lee and Felicia Schwartz, "Trump's Team Differs on Foreign Policy Issues," *Wall Street Journal*, December 13, 2016.
55. Wall Street Journal, "Russia's Syria Doublespeak," *Wall Street Journal*, December 12, 2016.
56. Laurence Norman, "European Diplomats Attack Russia's Syria Position after Islamic State Retakes Palmyra," *Wall Street Journal*, December 12, 2016.
57. Laurence Norman, "Europe Hopeful Trump Will Stick with Iran Nuclear Deal," *Wall Street Journal*, December 13, 2016.
58. Yaroslav Trofimov, "Syrian Rebels Pin Hopes on Trump," *Wall Street Journal*, December 8, 2016.

Chapter 7

1. Tobias Schneider and Theresa Lütkefend, "Nowhere to Hide: The Logic of Chemical Weapons Use in Syria," Global Public Policy Institute, February 17, 2019.
2. Malachy Browne et al., "One Building, One Bomb: How Assad Gassed His Own People," *New York Times*, June 25, 2018.
3. Donald Trump, "President Trump on Syria Strikes," *New York Times*, April 13, 2018.
4. Stephen Zunes, "History Shows Hypocrisy of US Outrage over Chemical Weapons in Syria," *Truthout*, April 24, 2018.
5. Peter Baker, "'Mission Accomplished!' But What Is the Mission in Syria?," *New York Times*, April 14, 2018.
6. Michael Crowley, Andrew Restuccia, and Tom McTague, "US, Britain and France Launch Airstrikes on Syria," *Politico*, April 14, 2018.
7. Raja Abdulrahim, "Strikes Spare Assad's Conventional Arsenal," *Wall Street Journal*, April 14, 2018.
8. Jennifer Cafarella, "Don't Get Out of Syria," *Foreign Affairs*, July 11, 2018.
9. The first transcript is President Trump's speech following the airstrikes and the second, the statements of British Prime Minister Theresa May and French President Emmanuel Macron.
10. Ben Hubbard, "After US Strikes, Syria Return to War as Usual," *New York Times*, April 15, 2018.
11. Michael Wolgelenter, "Seven Takeaways from the Airstrikes on Syria," *New York Times*, April 14, 2018.
12. Thomas Gibbons-Neff, "Missile Strikes Are Unlikely to Stop Syria's Chemical Attacks, Pentagon Says," *New York Times*, April 19, 2018.
13. Michael Knights quoted in David Sanger and Ben Hubbard, "A Hard Lesson in Syria: Assad Can Still Gas His Own People," *New York Times*, April 14, 2018.
14. Colin Kahl quoted in Peter Baker, "'Mission Accomplished!' But What Is the Mission in Syria?," *New York Times*, April 14, 2018.
15. The media watch group FAIR describes the Cato Institute as a center-right think tank. For more information see Michael Dolny, "FAIR STUDY: Think Tank Spectrum 2012," FAIR, July 1, 2013.
16. Emma Ashford, "Trump's Syria Strikes Show What's Wrong with US Foreign Policy," *New York Times*, April 13, 2018.
17. Editorial Board, "A Coordinated Attack on Syria," *New York Times*, April 13, 2018.
18. Susan Rice, "Trump's Problem in Syria? It Was Obama's Too," *New York Times*, April 17, 2018.
19. Gene Healey and John Glaser, "Repeal, Don't Replace, Trump's War Powers," *New York Times*, April 17, 2018.
20. Helene Cooper, Thomas Gibbons-Neff, and Ben Hubbard, "US, Britain and France Strike Syria over Suspected Chemical Weapons Attack," *New York Times*, April 13, 2018.
21. John McCain quoted in Nicholas Fandos, "Divided on Strikes, Democrats and Republicans Press for Clearer Syria Strategy," *New York Times*, April 14, 2018.
22. Helene Cooper, "Mattis Wanted Congressional Approval before Striking Syria. He Was Overruled," *New York Times*, April 17, 2018.
23. Maha Yahya quoted in Ben Hubbard, "After US Strikes, Syria Return to War as Usual," *New York Times*, April 15, 2018.
24. Cory Gardner, "Is Russia Sponsoring Terrorism?," *New York Times*, April 18, 2018.

25 Vasily Nebenzia quoted in Sewell Chan, "UN Security Council Rejects Russian Resolution Condemning Syrian Airstrikes," *New York Times*, April 13, 2018.
26 Peter Baker, "Trump to Impose New Sanctions on Russia over Support for Syria," *New York Times*, April 14, 2018.
27 Editorial Board, "Trump Was Right to Strike Syria. But the Mission Is Far from Accomplished," *Washington Post*, April 14, 2018.
28 Liz Sly and Louisa Loveluck, "Assad Is Defiant as US-Led Strikes in Syria Show No Sign of Threatening His Hold on Power," *Washington Post*, April 14, 2018.
29 Paul Sonne, "Trump's Strikes on Syria Risk Retaliation, Escalation in a War He Wants to Avoid," *Washington Post*, April 15, 2018.
30 According to *Encyclopedia Britannica*, the American Enterprise Institute is a private nonprofit American institution of research founded in 1943 by American industrialist Lewis H. Brown. The *Encyclopedia* also states that it supports limited government, private enterprise, and democratic capitalism. The institute is also described as a right-wing think tank. For more information, see Peter Bondarenko, "American Enterprise Institute," in *Encyclopedia Britannica*, accessed October 10, 2021.
31 Paul Sonne, "Trump's Strikes on Syria Risk Retaliation, Escalation in a War He Wants to Avoid," *Washington Post*, April 15, 2018.
32 Michael Gerson, "The Real Mission in Syria Was Never Attempted," *Washington Post*, April 17, 2018.
33 Eugene Robinson, "Trump Is Smashingly Successful—at Sowing Utter Confusion," *Washington Post*, April 20, 2018.
34 Karen DeYoung, "Lawmakers Worry about Securing US Goals in Syria as Trump Looks for the Exit," *Washington Post*, April 19, 2018.
35 Greg Jaffe, "Trump Tries to Appear Strong in Syria Even as He Plans to Withdraw," *Washington Post*, April 14, 2018.
36 Josh Rogin, "Inside Michael Flynn's Plan to Persuade Trump to Stay in Syria," *Washington Post*, April 20, 2018.
37 Mike DeBonis and Karoun Demirjian, "Lawmakers Agree There Should Be a 'Strategy' on Syria—But What That Should Be Is an Open Question," *Washington Post*, April 14, 2018.
38 Editorial Board, "Trump Was Right to Strike Syria. But the Mission Is Far from Accomplished," *Washington Post*, April 14, 2018.
39 Josh Rogin, "Inside Michael Flynn's Plan to Persuade Trump to Stay in Syria," *Washington Post*, April 20, 2018.
40 Kathleen Parker, "The Dogs of War Are Howling," *Washington Post*, April 14, 2018.
41 Michael Gerson, "The Real Mission in Syria Was Never Attempted," *Washington Post*, April 17, 2018.
42 Anton Troianovski, "Russia Responds to Airstrikes in Syria with Harsh Words but No Fire," *Washington Post*, April 14, 2018.
43 Raja Abdulrahim, "Strikes Spare Assad's Conventional Arsenal," *Wall Street Journal*, April 14, 2018.
44 Ryan Crocker and Michael O'Hanlon, "After the Syria Attack, a Strategy," *Wall Street Journal*, April 15, 2018.
45 Walter Russel Mead, "Trump's Realist Syria Strategy," *Wall Street Journal*, April 16, 2018.
46 Michael Gordon and Dion Nissenbaum, "US Upholds Its Red Line in Syria, While Steering Clear of Russia's," *Wall Street Journal*, April 14, 2018.

47. Yaroslav Trofimov, "Iran's Moves in Syria Raise Risk of Conflict with Israel," *Wall Street Journal*, April 19, 2018.
48. Gordon Lubold and Dion Nissenbaum, "Trump Bowed to Pentagon Restraint on Syria Strikes," *Wall Street Journal*, April 16, 2018.
49. Chis Gordon, "Partisan Divide Defines Congressional Reaction to Syria Strikes," *Wall Street Journal*, April 14, 2018.
50. Editorial Board, "A Trump Strategy for Syria," *Wall Street Journal*, April 16, 2018.
51. Mark Dubowitz and Richard Goldberg, "Use Iran Sanctions to Stop Assad," *Wall Street Journal*, April 18, 2018.
52. Sune Engel Rasmussen and Raja Abdulrahim, "A Day after US Airstrikes in Syria, Assad Launches New Onslaught against Rebels," *Wall Street Journal*, April 15, 2018.
53. Sune Engel Rasmussen, "As Islamic State Fades in Syria, Another Militant Group Takes Root," *Wall Street Journal*, April 18, 2018.

Conclusion

1. Freedom House, "Syria: Freedom in the World 2023."
2. Reporters without Borders, "Syria: 2023 World Press Freedom Index," Reporters without Borders, 2023.
3. Reporters without Borders, "Syria: Third Journalist Killed in 2022 and Another Injured in Turkish Airstrikes," Reporters without Borders, November 23, 2022.
4. *NYT* authors also argued that the airstrikes would not change the situation on the ground.
5. Michael Schudson, *The Sociology of News*, 45–6.
6. Todd Gitlin, *The Whole World Is Watching*, 49–52.
7. Pew Research Center, "Newspapers Fact Sheet," Pew Research Center, June 29, 2021.
8. Margaret Sullivan, *Ghosting the News*, 30.
9. Des Freedman, *The Contradictions of Media Power*, 139.
10. Ibid., 58–9.
11. Matthew Hindman, *The Internet Trap*; James Webster, *The Marketplace of Attention*.
12. Margaret Sullivan, *Ghosting the News*, 13.
13. Penelope Abernathy, "The Expanding News Desert."
14. Matthew Hindman, *The Internet Trap*, 132.
15. Victor Pickard, *Democracy without Journalism?*, 137.
16. Ibid., 167.
17. Edward Said, *Covering Islam*, 157.
18. Muhammad Idrees Ahmad, "Syrians Die in Western Media Darkness," *New York Review*, July 20, 2021.

Appendix

1. Kevin Carragee and Wim Roefs, "The Neglect of Power in Recent Framing Research," 222.
2. Thomas Kuhn, "The Nature and Necessity of Scientific Revolutions," in *Philosophy of Science*, eds. Martin Curd, J.A. Cover, and Christopher Pincock, 92.
3. Robert Entman, "Framing: Toward Clarification of a Fractured Paradigm," 57.

4   Baldwin van Gorp, "Strategies to Take Subjectivity Out of Framing Analysis," in *Doing News Framing Analysis*, eds. Paul D'Angelo and Jim Kuypers, 90.
5   Gregory Philo, "Can Discourse Analysis Successfully Explain the Content of Media and Journalistic Practice?," 187.
6   Dianna Mullet, "A General Critical Discourse Analysis Framework for Educational Research," 120.
7   Gregory Philo, "Can Discourse Analysis Successfully Explain the Content of Media and Journalistic Practice?," 187.
8   Paul D'Angelo, prologue to *Doing News Framing Analysis II*, ed. Paul D'Angelo, xvii.
9   Des Freedman, *The Contradictions of Media Power*, 30.
10 Paul D'Angelo, prologue to *Doing News Framing Analysis II*, ed. Paul D'Angelo, xxiv.
11 Robert Entman, "Framing: Toward Clarification of a Fractured Paradigm," 52.
12 Ibid., 51.
13 Claes de Vreese, "News Framing: Theory and Typology," 53.
14 Daniela Dimitrova, "Comparative News Framing Analysis," in *Doing New Framing Analysis II*, ed. Paul D'Angelo, 274.
15 Emma Björnehed and Josefina Erikson, "Making the Most of the Frame," 111.
16 Curd Knüpfer and Robert Entman, "Framing Conflicts in Digital and Transnational Media Environments," 485.
17 Paul D'Angelo, "News Framing as a Multiparadigmatic Research Program: A Response to Entman," 851.
18 Jürgen Renn, *The Evolution of Knowledge*, 85.
19 Ibid., 84–5.
20 Paul D'Angelo, prologue to *Doing News Framing Analysis II*, ed. Paul D'Angelo, xxvi.
21 Ibid., xxx.
22 Joseph Cappella and Kathleen Jamieson quoted in Claes de Vreese, "News Framing: Theory and Typology," 54.
23 Paul D'Angelo, prologue to *Doing News Framing Analysis II*, ed. Paul D'Angelo, xxv.
24 Robert Entman, *Projections of Power*, 31.
25 Teun van Dijk, *Discourse Analysis*, 28 quoted in Paul D'Angelo, prologue to *Doing News Framing Analysis II*, ed. Paul D'Angelo, xxiv.
26 Adam Berinsky and Donald Kinder, "Making Sense of Issues through Media Frames," 654.
27 Ibid., 643.
28 Baldwin van Gorp, "Strategies to Take Subjectivity Out of Framing Analysis," in *Doing News Framing Analysis*, eds. Paul D'Angelo and Jim Kuypers, 91.
29 Ibid.
30 Todd Gitlin, *The Whole World Is Watching*, 27–8.
31 Michael Brüggemann and Paul D'Angelo, "Defragmenting News Framing Research," in *Doing New Framing Analysis II*, ed. Paul D'Angelo, 107.
32 Pat Bazeley and Kristi Jackson, *Qualitative Data Analysis with NVivo*, 70.
33 Ibid.
34 Baldwin van Gorp, "Strategies to Take Subjectivity Out of Framing Analysis," in *Doing News Framing Analysis*, eds. Paul D'Angelo and Jim Kuypers, 97.

BIBLIOGRAPHY

Abboud, Samer N. *Syria*. Second edition. Cambridge, UK: Polity Press, 2016.
Abdulrahim, Raja. "Many in Aleppo See Choices Reduced to Displacement, Submission or Death." *Wall Street Journal*, December 9, 2016. https://www.wsj.com/articles/many-in-aleppo-see-choices-reduced-to-displacement-submission-or-death-1481315844.
Abdulrahim, Raja. "Strikes Spare Assad's Conventional Arsenal." *Wall Street Journal*, April 14, 2018. https://www.wsj.com/articles/after-strikes-assad-seeks-to-show-normalcy-1523727307.
Abdulrahim, Raja. "Syria Expands Control to Most of Aleppo." *Wall Street Journal*, December 12, 2016. https://www.wsj.com/articles/syria-rebels-near-defeat-in-aleppo-1481544160.
Abdulrahim, Raja, and Dion Nissenbaum. "Evacuations Set to Begin as Assad Reclaims Aleppo." *Wall Street Journal*, December 13, 2016. https://www.wsj.com/articles/aleppo-civilians-have-nowhere-safe-to-run-red-cross-says-1481628920.
Abdulrahim, Raja, and Maria Abi-Habib. "Nearing Defeat, Rebels Seek Talks on Fate of Aleppo." *Wall Street Journal*, December 7, 2016. https://www.wsj.com/articles/syria-rebels-call-for-aleppo-cease-fire-1481123217.
Abernathy, Penelope Muse. "The Expanding News Desert—The Loss of Local News." Center for Innovation and Sustainability in Local Media, University of North Carolina at Chapel Hill, 2018. https://www.usnewsdeserts.com/reports/expanding-news-desert/.
Abi-Habib, Maria. "Islamist Militants Gain in Syria." *Wall Street Journal*, July 24, 2014. https://online.wsj.com/articles/islamic-state-militants-confront-syria-forces-in-rare-confrontation-1406239224.
Abrams, Elliott. "Ridding Syria of a Despot." *Washington Post*, March 25, 2011. https://www.washingtonpost.com/opinions/ridding-syria-of-a-despot/2011/03/25/AFSRRVYB_story.html.
Abu Amer, Adnan. "How Do Palestinians See the Syrian War?." *Al Jazeera*, October 20, 2018. https://www.aljazeera.com/opinions/2018/10/20/how-do-palestinians-see-the-syrian-war.
Achcar, Gilbert. *The Clash of Barbarisms: The Making of the New World Disorder*. Updated and expanded edition. London: Routledge, 2016.
Achcar, Gilbert. *Morbid Symptoms: Relapse in the Arab Uprising*. Stanford, CA: Stanford University Press, 2016.
Achcar, Gilbert. *The People Want: A Radical Exploration of the Arab Uprising*. London: Saqi Books, 2013.
Aday, Sean. "The US Media, Foreign Policy, and Public Support for War." In *The Oxford Handbook of Political Communication*, edited by Kate Kenski and Kathleen Hall Jamieson, 315–32, 2017. https://doi.org/10.1093/oxfordhb/9780199793471.013.025_update_001.
Ahmad, Muhammad Idrees. "Obama's Legacy Is Tarnished as Putin Fills the Vacuum in Syria." *The National*, October 10, 2015. https://www.thenationalnews.com/opinion/obama-s-legacy-is-tarnished-as-putin-fills-the-vacuum-in-syria-1.33078.

Ahmad, Muhammad Idrees. "RT and Syria: The Triumph of Narrative over Facts." *News Line*. March 2017. https://newslinemagazine.com/magazine/rt-syria-triumph-narrative-facts/.

Ahmad, Muhammad Idrees. "Syrians Die in Western Media Darkness." *New York Review*, July 20, 2021. https://www.nybooks.com/daily/2021/07/20/syrians-die-in-western-media-darkness/.

Aikins, Matthieu. "The Promise of Aleppo's Radicals." *New York Times*, July 7, 2014. https://www.nytimes.com/2014/07/08/opinion/the-promise-of-aleppos-radicals.html.

Alaaldin, Ranj. "Imperfect Allies and Non-State Actors: Lessons from the 1991 No-Fly Zone in Iraq." *Brookings*, May 28, 2021. https://www.brookings.edu/blog/order-from-chaos/2021/05/28/imperfect-allies-and-non-state-actors-lessons-from-the-1991-no-fly-zone-in-iraq/.

al-Assad, Bashar. "Interview with Syrian President Bashar Al-Assad." *Wall Street Journal*, January 31, 2011. https://www.wsj.com/articles/SB10001424052748703833204576114712441122894.

al-Ghazzi, Omar. "'Forced to Report': Affective Proximity and the Perils of Local Reporting on Syria." *Journalism*, January 5, 2021, 1–15. https://doi.org/10.1177/1464884920984874.

al-Haj Saleh, Yassin. *The Impossible Revolution: Making Sense of the Syrian Tragedy*. London: Hurst & Company, 2017.

al-Hendi, Ahed. "Syrians Cry 'Freedom!' Too." *Wall Street Journal*, March 26, 2011. https://www.wsj.com/articles/SB10001424052748704425804576220803275650930.

Allison, Roy. "Russia and Syria: Explaining Alignment with a Regime in Crisis." *International Affairs* 89, no. 4 (July 2013): 795–823. https://doi.org/10.1111/1468-2346.12046.

Ambrose, Stephen E., and Douglas G. Brinkley. *Rise to Globalism: American Foreign Policy since 1938*. 9th revised edition. New York: Penguin, 2012.

Amnesty International. "Human Slaughterhouse: Mass Hangings and Extermination at Saydnaya Prison, Syria." *Amnesty International USA*, February 3, 2017. https://www.amnestyusa.org/reports/human-slaughterhouse-mass-hangings-and-extermination-at-saydnaya-prison-syria/.

Anderson, Perry. *American Foreign Policy and Its Thinkers*. Brooklyn, NY: Verso Books, 2014.

Applebaum, Anne. "Putin's Power Plays." *Washington Post*, September 27, 2015. https://www.washingtonpost.com/opinions/what-putin-will-do-to-stay-in-power/2015/09/27/12a964b0-63b7-11e5-8e9e-dce8a2a2a679_story.html.

Ashford, Emma. "Trump's Syria Strikes Show What's Wrong with US Foreign Policy." *New York Times*, April 13, 2018. https://www.nytimes.com/2018/04/13/opinion/trump-us-foreign-policy.html.

Associated Press. "Bashar al-Assad Wins Re-Election in Syria as Uprising against Him Rages On." *Guardian* (UK edition), June 4, 2014. http://www.theguardian.com/world/2014/jun/04/bashar-al-assad-winds-reelection-in-landslide-victory.

Associated Press. "Obama's Middle East Envoy Steps Up Diplomatic Push in Syria." *Guardian* (UK edition), July 26, 2009. https://www.theguardian.com/world/2009/jul/26/george-mitchell-syria-peace-talks.

Baker, Peter. "John Kerry Rushes in Where Obama Will Not Tread." *New York Times*, September 29, 2015. https://www.nytimes.com/2015/09/30/world/middleeast/john-kerry-rushes-in-where-obama-will-not-tread.html.

Baker, Peter. "'Mission Accomplished!' But What Is the Mission in Syria?" *New York Times*, April 14, 2018. https://www.nytimes.com/2018/04/14/us/politics/trump-syria-policy.html.

Baker, Peter. "Syria Exposes Split between Obama and Clinton." *New York Times*, October 3, 2015. https://www.nytimes.com/2015/10/04/world/syria-exposes-split-between-obama-and-clinton.html.

Baker, Peter, and Neil MacFarquhar. "Obama Sees Russia Failing in Syria Effort." *New York Times*, October 2, 2015. https://www.nytimes.com/2015/10/03/world/middleeast/syria-russia-airstrikes.html.

Baker, Peter, and Rick Gladstone. "President Trump Talked Tough. But His Strike on Syria Was Restrained." *New York Times*, April 13, 2018. https://www.nytimes.com/2018/04/13/world/middleeast/trump-syria-attack.html.

Barkin, Steve M., and Mark R. Levy. "All the News That's Fit to Correct: Corrections in the Times and the Post." *Journalism & Mass Communication Quarterly* 60, no. 2 (June 1983): 218–25. https://doi.org/10.1177/107769908306000202.

Barnard, Anne. "Aleppo Close to Falling under Complete Control of Syrian Government." *New York Times*, December 12, 2016. https://www.nytimes.com/2016/12/12/world/aleppo-syrian-government.html.

Barnard, Anne. "In Rebel-Held Aleppo, Residents Report Increasing Desperation." *New York Times*, December 7, 2016. https://www.nytimes.com/2016/12/07/world/middleeast/syria-aleppo.html.

Barnard, Anne. "Russia Says Aleppo Combat Has Ceased; Residents Disagree." *New York Times*, December 8, 2016. https://www.nytimes.com/2016/12/08/world/middleeast/syria-aleppo-rebels-russia-lavrov-assad.html.

Barnard, Anne. "Syrian Rebels Say Russia Is Targeting Them Rather than ISIS." *New York Times*, September 30, 2015. https://www.nytimes.com/2015/10/01/world/middleeast/syrian-rebels-say-russia-targets-them-rather-than-isis.html.

Barnard, Anne, and Andrew E. Kramer. "Russia Carries Out Airstrikes in Syria for 2nd Day." *New York Times*, October 1, 2015. https://www.nytimes.com/2015/10/02/world/middleeast/russia-syria-airstrikes-isis.html.

Barnard, Anne, and Hwaida Saad. "Accounts of Syrian Prisons Describe a Volatile Mix of Chaos and Control." *New York Times*, August 24, 2013. https://www.nytimes.com/2013/08/25/world/middleeast/accounts-of-syrian-prisons-describe-a-volatile-mix-of-chaos-and-control.html.

Barnard, Anne, and Hwaida Saad. "'We Are Dead Either Way': Agonizing Choices for Syrians in Aleppo." *New York Times*, December 10, 2016. https://www.nytimes.com/2016/12/10/world/middleeast/we-are-dead-either-way-agonizing-choices-for-syrians-in-aleppo.html.

Barnard, Anne, and Neil MacFarquhar. "Vladimir Putin Plunges into a Caldron in Syria: Saving Assad." *New York Times*, October 1, 2015. https://www.nytimes.com/2015/10/02/world/middleeast/vladimir-putin-plunges-into-a-cauldron-saving-assad.html.

Barnard, Anne, and Nick Cumming-Bruce. "Chaos and Desperation as Thousands Flee Aleppo amid Government Advance." *New York Times*, December 9, 2016. https://www.nytimes.com/2016/12/09/world/middleeast/syria-aleppo-united-nations.html.

Bazeley, Pat, and Jackson Kristi. *Qualitative Data Analysis with NVivo*. Second edition. Thousand Oaks, CA: SAGE Publications Ltd, 2013.

BBC News. "Remembering the Kurdish Uprising of 1991." *BBC News*, April 7, 2016. https://www.bbc.co.uk/news/in-pictures-35967389.

BBC News. "Syria Air Strikes: Theresa May Says Action 'Moral and Legal.'" *BBC News*, April 17, 2018. https://www.bbc.com/news/uk-politics-43775728.

BBC News. "Syria Air Strikes: US Still 'Locked and Loaded' for New Chemical Attacks." *BBC News*, April 15, 2018. https://www.bbc.co.uk/news/world-middle-east-43771840.

BBC News. "Syria War: What We Know about Douma 'Chemical Attack.'" *BBC News*, July 10, 2018. https://www.bbc.com/news/world-middle-east-43697084.

Bendavid, Naftali. "Republicans Show Divisions over the US Intervention." *Wall Street Journal*, March 30, 2011. https://www.wsj.com/articles/SB10001424052748703461504576231090786495316.

Bennett, W. Lance. "The News about Foreign Policy." In *Taken by Storm: Media, Public Opinion and US Foreign Policy in the Gulf War*, edited by W. Lance Bennett and David L. Paletz, 12–40. Chicago: University of Chicago Press, 1994.

Bennett, W. Lance. "Press–Government Relations in a Changing Media Environment." In *The Oxford Handbook of Political Communication*, edited by Kate Kenski and Kathleen Hall Jamieson, 249–62, 2017. https://doi.org/10.1093/oxfordhb/9780199793471.013.40.

Bennett, W. Lance. "Toward a Theory of Press-State Relations in the United States." *Journal of Communication* 40, no. 2 (June 1, 1990): 103–27. https://doi.org/10.1111/j.1460-2466.1990.tb02265.x.

Berinsky, Adam J., and Donald R. Kinder. "Making Sense of Issues through Media Frames: Understanding the Kosovo Crisis." *Journal of Politics* 68, no. 3 (August 1, 2006): 640–56. https://doi.org/10.1111/j.1468-2508.2006.00451.x.

Björnehed, Emma, and Josefina Erikson. "Making the Most of the Frame: Developing the Analytical Potential of Frame Analysis." *Policy Studies* 39, no. 2 (February 12, 2018): 109–26. https://doi.org/10.1080/01442872.2018.1434874.

Blackwill, Robert D., and Philip H. Gordon. "Containing Russia, Again." *Foreign Affairs*, January 18, 2018. https://www.foreignaffairs.com/articles/russian-federation/2018-01-18/containing-russia-again.

Bondarenko, Peter. "American Enterprise Institute." *Encyclopedia Britannica*, accessed October 10, 2021. https://www.britannica.com/topic/American-Enterprise-Institute.

Borger, Julian. "'Syria Is Bleeding': Aleppo Facing War's Worst Humanitarian Crisis, UN Says." *Guardian* (UK edition), September 29, 2016. http://www.theguardian.com/world/2016/sep/29/aleppo-syria-war-humanitarian-crisis-un.

Borger, Julian. "Syrian Chemical Attack Used Sarin and Was Worst in 25 Years, Says UN." *Guardian* (UK edition), September 17, 2013. https://www.theguardian.com/world/2013/sep/16/syrian-chemical-attack-sarin-says-un.

Borger, Julian, and Kareem Shaheen. "Russia Accused of War Crimes in Syria at UN Security Council Session." *Guardian* (UK edition), September 26, 2016. http://www.theguardian.com/world/2016/sep/25/russia-accused-war-crimes-syria-un-security-council-aleppo.

Borshchevskaya, Anna. "In Syria, Putin Risks Repeating the Soviet Union's Afghanistan Mistake." The Washington Institute for Near East Policy, September 15, 2015. https://www.washingtoninstitute.org/policy-analysis/syria-putin-risks-repeating-soviet-unions-afghanistan-mistake.

Bourdieu, Pierre. *Distinction: A Social Critique of the Judgement of Taste*. London: Routledge & Kegan Paul, 1984.

Bröning, Michael. "The Sturdy House That Assad Built," *Foreign Affairs*, March 7, 2011. https://www.foreignaffairs.com/articles/syria/2011-03-07/sturdy-house-assad-built.

Brown, Katy, and Aurelien Mondon. "Populism, the Media, and the Mainstreaming of the Far-Right: *The Guardian*'s Coverage of Populism as a Case Study." *Politics* 41, no. 3 (September 30, 2020): 279–95. https://doi.org/10.1177/0263395720955036.

Browne, Malachy, Christoph Koettl, Singhvi Anjali, Natalie Reneau, Barbara Marcolini, Yousur Al Hlou, and Drew Jordan. "One Building, One Bomb: How Assad Gassed His Own People." *New York Times*, June 25, 2018. https://www.nytimes.com/interactive/2018/06/25/world/middleeast/syria-chemical-attack-douma.html.

Brüggemann, Michael, and Paul D'Angelo. "Defragmenting News Framing Research: Reconciling Generic and Issue-Specific Frames." In *Doing News Framing Analysis II: Empirical and Theoretical Perspectives*, edited by Paul D'Angelo, 90–111. New York, NY: Routledge, 2018.

Bumiller, Elisabeth, and David D. Kirkpatrick. "Obama Warns Libya, but Attacks Go On." *New York Times*, March 18, 2011. https://www.nytimes.com/2011/03/19/world/africa/19libya.html.

Busby, Ethan, D. J. Flynn, and James N. Druckman. "Studying Framing Effects on Political Preferences: Existing Research and Lingering Questions." In *Doing News Framing Analysis II: Empirical and Theoretical Perspectives*, edited by Paul D'Angelo, 27–50. New York; London: Routledge, 2018.

Bush, George W. Introduction to "The National Security Strategy 2002" by the White House. September 17, 2002. https://georgewbush-whitehouse.archives.gov/nsc/nss/2002/.

Cafarella, Jennifer. "Don't Get Out of Syria." *Foreign Affairs*, July 11, 2018. https://www.foreignaffairs.com/articles/syria/2018-07-11/dont-get-out-syria.

Cafarella, Jennifer, and Genevieve Casagrande. "Syrian Armed Opposition Forces in Aleppo." *Backgrounder*. Institute for the Study of War, February 13, 2016. http://www.understandingwar.org/sites/default/files/Syrian%20Armed%20Opposition%20Forces%20in%20Aleppo_0.pdf.

Calamur, Krishnadev. "Assad Is Still Using Chemical Weapons in Syria." *The Atlantic*, February 6, 2018. https://www.theatlantic.com/international/archive/2018/02/syria-chemical-weapons/552428/.

Calamur, Krishnadev. "How Will This Attack on Syria Be Any Different?" *The Atlantic*, April 14, 2018. https://www.theatlantic.com/international/archive/2018/04/us-syria-strike/557552/.

Carragee, Kevin M., and Wim Roefs. "The Neglect of Power in Recent Framing Research." *Journal of Communication* 54, no. 2 (2004): 214–33. https://doi.org/10.1111/j.1460-2466.2004.tb02625.x.

The Carter Center. "Syria Countrywide Conflict Report." *The Syria Conflict Mapping Project*, August 20, 2013. https://www.cartercenter.org/resources/pdfs/peace/conflict_resolution/syria-conflict/NationwideReport-aug-20-2013.pdf.

Carter, Phillip. "Why Foreign Troops Can't Fight Our Fights." *Washington Post*, October 2, 2015. https://www.washingtonpost.com/opinions/why-foreign-troops-cant-fight-our-fights/2015/10/02/7f569ba2-66d5-11e5-9ef3-fde182507eac_story.html.

Castells, Manuel. *Networks of Outrage and Hope: Social Movements in the Internet Age*. Cambridge, UK; Malden, MA: Polity Press, 2012.

Chivers, C. J. "American Tells of Odyssey as Prisoner of Syrian Rebels." *New York Times*, August 22, 2013. https://www.nytimes.com/2013/08/23/world/middleeast/american-tells-of-odyssey-as-prisoner-of-syrian-rebels.html.

Chulov, Martin. "The Rise and Fall of the ISIS 'Caliphate.'" *Guardian* (UK edition), March 24, 2019. http://www.theguardian.com/world/2019/mar/23/the-rise-and-fall-of-the-isis-caliphate.

Chulov, Martin, Kareem Shaheen, and Emma Graham-Harrison. "East Aleppo's Last Hospital Destroyed by Airstrikes." *Guardian* (UK edition), November 19, 2016. http://www.theguardian.com/world/2016/nov/19/aleppo-hospitals-knocked-out-airstrikes.

Clinton, Hillary. "Hillary Clinton: 'Failure' to Help Syrian Rebels Led to the Rise of ISIS." Interview by Jeffrey Goldberg. *The Atlantic*, August 10, 2014. https://www.theatlantic.com/international/archive/2014/08/hillary-clinton-failure-to-help-syrian-rebels-led-to-the-rise-of-isis/375832/.

CNN Wire Staff. "Obama Warns Syria Not to Cross 'Red Line.'" *CNN*, August 21, 2012. https://www.cnn.com/2012/08/20/world/meast/syria-unrest/index.html.

Cody, Edward. "Arab League Condemns Broad Bombing Campaign in Libya." *Washington Post*, March 20, 2011. https://www.washingtonpost.com/world/arab-league-condemns-broad-bombing-campaign-in-libya/2011/03/20/AB1pSg1_story.html.

Cohen, Eliot A. "Syria Will Require More than Cruise Missiles." *Washington Post*, August 25, 2013. https://www.washingtonpost.com/opinions/syria-will-require-more-than-cruise-missiles/2013/08/25/8c8877b8-0daf-11e3-85b6-d27422650fd5_story.html.

Cohen, Michael A. "Obama's Understated Foreign Policy Gains." *New York Times*, July 9, 2014. https://www.nytimes.com/2014/07/10/opinion/obamas-understated-foreign-policy-gains.html.

Coker, Margaret. "The New Jihad." *Wall Street Journal*, July 11, 2014. https://online.wsj.com/articles/why-the-new-jihadists-in-iraq-and-syria-see-al-qaeda-as-too-passive-1405096590.

Coleman, Renita, Maxwell McCombs, Donald Shaw, and David Weaver. "Agenda Setting." In *The Handbook of Journalism Studies*, edited by Karin Wahl-Jorgensen and Thomas Hanitzsch, 147–60. New York: Routledge, 2008.

Combined Joint Task Force - Operation Inherent Resolve. "About CJTF-OIR." *Operation Inherent Resolve*, accessed May 27, 2020. https://www.inherentresolve.mil/About-CJTF-OIR/.

Committee to Protect Journalists. "Ten Most Censored Countries." *Committee to Protect Journalists*, May 2, 2012. https://cpj.org/reports/2012/05/10-most-censored-countries-2/.

Communication Theory. "Limited Effects Theory." Last modified February 10, 2019. https://www.communicationtheory.org/limited-effects-theory/.

Cooper, Helene. "Mattis Wanted Congressional Approval before Striking Syria. He Was Overruled." *New York Times*, April 17, 2018. https://www.nytimes.com/2018/04/17/us/politics/jim-mattis-trump-syria-attack.html.

Cooper, Helene. "Obama Cites Limits of US Role in Libya." *New York Times*, March 28, 2011. https://www.nytimes.com/2011/03/29/world/africa/29prexy.html.

Cooper, Helene, and Eric Schmitt. "US to Deploy Hundreds of Troops to Guard Oil Fields in Syria, Pentagon Officials Say." *New York Times*, October 25, 2019. https://www.nytimes.com/2019/10/25/world/middleeast/esper-troops-syria.html.

Cooper, Helene, and Michael R. Gordon. "Russia Buildup Seen as Fanning Flames in Syria." *New York Times*, September 29, 2015. https://www.nytimes.com/2015/09/30/world/russia-buildup-seen-as-fanning-flames-in-syria.html.

Cooper, Helene, Thomas Gibbons-Neff, and Ben Hubbard. "US, Britain and France Strike Syria over Suspected Chemical Weapons Attack." *New York Times*, April 13, 2018. https://www.nytimes.com/2018/04/13/world/middleeast/trump-strikes-syria-attack.html.

Crocker, Ryan, and Michael O'Hanlon. "After the Syria Strike, a Strategy." *Wall Street Journal*, April 15, 2018. https://www.wsj.com/articles/after-the-syria-strike-a-strategy-1523817912.

Crowley, Michael, Andrew Restuccia, and Tom McTague. "US, Britain and France Launch Airstrikes on Syria." *Politico*, April 14, 2018. https://www.politico.eu/article/donald-trump-strikes-syria-chemical-weapons-russia-france-united-kingdom/.

Dadouch, Sarah. "In the Cradle of the Syrian Revolution, Renewed Violence Shows Reconciliation Is Still Elusive." *Washington Post*, September 19, 2021. https://www.washingtonpost.com/world/middle_east/syria-civil-war-daraa/2021/09/18/fa637108-1593-11ec-a5e5-ceecb895922f_story.html.

Dahi, Omar S., and Yasser Munif. "Revolts in Syria: Tracking the Convergence between Authoritarianism and Neoliberalism." *Journal of Asian and African Studies* 47, no. 4 (2012): 323–32. https://doi.org/10.1177/0021909611431682.

Daly, John C. K. "The Real Cost of Russia's Syrian Campaign." *United Press International*, March 6, 2017. https://www.upi.com/Top_News/Voices/2017/03/06/The-real-cost-of-Russias-Syrian-campaign/7981488823565/.

D'Angelo, Paul. "News Framing as a Multiparadigmatic Research Program: A Response to Entman." *Journal of Communication* 52, no. 4 (December 1, 2002): 870–88. https://doi.org/10.1111/j.1460-2466.2002.tb02578.x.

D'Angelo, Paul. Prologue to *Doing News Framing Analysis II: Empirical and Theoretical Perspectives*, edited by Paul D'Angelo. New York; London: Routledge, 2018, xxiii–xl.

Dagher, Sam, and Asa Fitch. "Iran Expands Role in Syria in Conjunction with Russia's Airstrikes." *Wall Street Journal*, October 2, 2015. https://www.wsj.com/articles/iran-expands-role-in-syria-in-conjunction-with-russias-airstrikes-1443811030.

Dagher, Sam, Maria Abi-Habib, and Ellen Knickmeyer. "Arab League Cautious as US Gears for Strike." *Wall Street Journal*, August 27, 2013. https://online.wsj.com/article/SB10001424127887323906804579038462208619236.html.

DeBonis, Mike, and Karoun Demirjian. "Lawmakers Agree There Should Be a 'Strategy' on Syria—But What That Should Be Is an Open Question." *Washington Post*, April 14, 2018. https://www.washingtonpost.com/powerpost/in-congress-both-critics-and-supporters-of-syria-strike-call-for-clearer-strategy/2018/04/14/76969ca2-3f94-11e8-974f-aacd97698cef_story.html.

Della Rata, Donatella. *Shooting a Revolution: Visual Media and Warfare in Syria*. Digital Barricades. London: Pluto Press, 2018. https://www.vlebooks.com/Vleweb/Product/Index/2033340?page=0.

Detsch, Jack. "US Troops Really Are in Syria to Protect the Oil—for the Kurds." *Foreign Policy*, August 5, 2020. https://foreignpolicy.com/2020/08/05/kurds-oil-syria-us-troops-trump/.

de Vreese, Claes H. "News Framing: Theory and Typology." *Information Design Journal & Document Design* 13, no. 1 (January 2005): 51–62.

DeYoung, Karen. "Lawmakers Worry about Securing US Goals in Syria as Trump Looks for the Exit." *Washington Post*, April 19, 2018. https://www.washingtonpost.com/world/national-security/lawmakers-worry-about-securing-us-goals-in-syria-as-trump-looks-for-the-exit/2018/04/18/96dfc52a-4335-11e8-ad8f-27a8c409298b_story.html.

DeYoung, Karen. "Obama, Advisers Weigh Response to Syrian Attack as Military Assets Are Repositioned." *Washington Post*, August 24, 2013. https://www.washingtonpost.com/world/national-security/obama-advisers-weigh-response-to-syrian-attack-military-action-is-among-options/2013/08/24/c1cc5508-0cc3-11e3-9941-6711ed662e71_story.html.

DeYoung, Karen, and Anne Gearan. "After Syria Chemical Allegations, Obama Considering Limited Military Strike." *Washington Post*, August 26, 2013. https://www.washingtonpost.com/world/national-security/2013/08/26/599450c2-0e70-11e3-8cdd-bcdc09410972_story.html.

DeYoung, Karen, and Colum Lynch. "In Syria Chemical Attack Allegations, US and Allies Push for Immediate Probe." *Washington Post*, August 22, 2013. https://www.washingtonpost.com/world/national-security/in-syria-chemical-attack-allegations-us-and-allies-push-for-immediate-probe/2013/08/22/00f76f2a-0b6f-11e3-8974-f97ab3b3c677_story.html.

DeYoung, Karen, Juliet Eilperin, and Greg Miller. "US Will Not Directly Confront Russia in Syria, Obama Says." *Washington Post*, October 2, 2015. https://www.washingtonpost.com/world/national-security/2015/10/02/44c1f7fc-6932-11e5-9223-70cb36460919_story.html.

Diehl, Jackson. "Trump's Coming War against Islam." *Washington Post*, December 11, 2016. https://www.washingtonpost.com/opinions/global-opinions/trumps-coming-war-against-islam/2016/12/11/edf3241c-bd60-11e6-91ee-1adddfe36cbe_story.html.

Dimitrova, Daniela V. "Comparative News Framing Analysis: Explaining and Measuring Patterns of Frames in Political News." In *Doing News Framing Analysis II: Empirical and Theoretical Perspectives*, edited by Paul D'Angelo, 274–91. New York; London: Routledge, 2018.

Dolny, Michael. "FAIR STUDY: Think Tank Spectrum 2012." *FAIR*, July 1, 2013. https://fair.org/extra/fair%E2%80%88study-think-tank-spectrum-2012/.

Doucet, Lyse. "Syria & the CNN Effect: What Role Does the Media Play in Policy-Making?" *Daedalus* 147, no. 1 (January 2018): 141–57. https://doi.org/10.1162/DAED_a_00480.

Douthat, Ross. "Is Putin Winning?" *New York Times*, October 3, 2015. https://www.nytimes.com/2015/10/04/opinion/sunday/ross-douthat-is-putin-winning.html.

Dubowitz, Mark, and Richard Goldberg. "Use Iran Sanctions to Stop Assad." *Wall Street Journal*, April 18, 2018. https://www.wsj.com/articles/use-iran-sanctions-to-stop-assad-1524087596.

du Pont, Pete. "Obama's Foreign Failure." *Wall Street Journal*, August 27, 2013. https://online.wsj.com/article/SB10001424127887324591204579037880644807254.html.

Editorial Board. "Both Mr. Putin and Mr. Obama Are Wrong on Syria." *Washington Post*, September 28, 2015. https://www.washingtonpost.com/opinions/a-siren-song-at-the-un/2015/09/28/814ee01e-6616-11e5-8325-a42b5a459b1e_story.html.

Editorial Board. "Can Syria's Dictator Reform?" *Washington Post*, March 29, 2011. https://www.washingtonpost.com/opinions/can-syrias-dictator-reform/2011/03/29/AFdznHyB_story.html.

Editorial Board. "A Coordinated Attack on Syria." *New York Times*, April 13, 2018. https://www.nytimes.com/2018/04/13/opinion/donald-trump-syria-military.html.

Editorial Board. "The Corpses in Syria." *New York Times*, August 23, 2013. https://www.nytimes.com/2013/08/23/opinion/the-corpses-in-syria.html.

Editorial Board. "How We Got to the Syria Mess." *Washington Post*, October 2, 2015. https://www.washingtonpost.com/opinions/origins-of-a-disaster/2015/10/02/69b058c2-6907-11e5-9ef3-fde182507eac_story.html.

Editorial Board. "The Iraq Debacle." *Wall Street Journal*, June 15, 2014. https://online.wsj.com/articles/the-iraq-debacle-1402615473.

Editorial Board. "Opposing Syria's Crackdown." *Washington Post*, March 23, 2011. https://www.washingtonpost.com/opinions/opposing-syrias-crackdown/2011/03/23/ABdqbvKB_story.html.

Editorial Board. "Putin and Obama Have Profound Differences on Syria." *New York Times*, September 28, 2015. https://www.nytimes.com/2015/09/29/opinion/putin-and-obama-have-profound-differences-on-syria.html.

Editorial Board. "Russia's Dangerous Escalation in Syria." *New York Times*, October 2, 2015. https://www.nytimes.com/2015/10/02/opinion/russias-dangerous-escalation-in-syria.html.

Editorial Board. "Syria Response Can't Rely Solely on Military Action." *Washington Post*, August 26, 2013. https://www.washingtonpost.com/opinions/syria-response-cant-rely-solely-on-military-action/2013/08/26/cafe7f5a-0e64-11e3-bdf6-e4fc677d94a1_story.html.

Editorial Board. "Syrian Attack Should Prompt US Investigation into Chemical Weapons." *Washington Post*, August 21, 2013. https://www.washingtonpost.com/opinions/syrian-attack-should-prompt-us-investigation-into-chemical-weapons/2013/08/21/92d263f4-0a7b-11e3-8974-f97ab3b3c677_story.html.

Editorial Board. "A Trump Strategy for Syria." *Wall Street Journal*, April 16, 2018. https://www.wsj.com/articles/trumps-next-syria-challenge-1523819596.

Editorial Board. "Trump Was Right to Strike Syria. But the Mission Is Far from Accomplished." *Washington Post*, April 14, 2018. https://www.washingtonpost.com/opinions/global-opinions/trump-was-right-to-strike-syria-but-the-mission-is-far-from-accomplished/2018/04/14/e1e34bc2-3fee-11e8-974f-aacd97698cef_story.html.

Editorial Board. "The United Nations' Human 'Rights' Council." *Washington Post*, March 26, 2011. https://www.washingtonpost.com/opinions/the-united-nations-human-rights-council/2011/03/25/AFSRyPeB_story.html.

Editorial Board. "US Should Aid Those Who Fight Terror, Not Abet Human Rights Abuses." *Washington Post*, July 7, 2014. https://www.washingtonpost.com/opinions/us-should-aid-those-who-fight-terror-not-abet-human-rights-abuses/2014/07/07/a07a0794-05f4-11e4-a0dd-f2b22a257353_story.html.

Editorial Board. "The West Must Prepare for a Wounded Putin to Become Even More Aggressive." *Washington Post*, July 30, 2014. https://www.washingtonpost.com/opinions/the-west-must-prepare-for-a-wounded-putin-to-become-even-more-aggressive/2014/07/30/d80efcd8-1804-11e4-85b6-c1451e622637_story.html.

Eilperin, Juliet. "At UN, Obama Touts Diplomacy over Military Force as Conflicts Mount." *Washington Post*, September 27, 2015. https://www.washingtonpost.com/politics/obama-goes-to-un-to-preach-cooperation-even-as-conflict-mounts/2015/09/27/12e21176-651e-11e5-9ef3-fde182507eac_story.html.

Eilperin, Juliet. "Obama's Multilateralist Vision for the World Collides with Great-Power Reality." *Washington Post*, September 29, 2015. https://www.washingtonpost.com/politics/obamas-multilateralist-vision-for-the-world-collides-with-great-power-reality/2015/09/29/aa482b7c-66e5-11e5-9ef3-fde182507eac_story.html.

Ellison, Sarah. *War at the Wall Street Journal: Inside the Struggle to Control an American Business Empire*. Boston: Houghton Mifflin Harcourt, 2010.

Enab, Baladi. "Thousands Still Besieged in Aleppo … Activists Fear for Their Fate." *Enab Baladi*, December 21, 2016. https://english.enabbaladi.net/archives/2016/12/thousands-still-besieged-aleppo-activists-fear-fate/.

Englund, Will. "Russia Says Western Attack on Syria Would Be 'Catastrophic.'" *Washington Post*, August 26, 2013. https://www.washingtonpost.com/world/middle_east/russia-says-western-attack-on-syria-would-be-catastrophic/2013/08/26/4a7ea122-0e5d-11e3-a2b3-5e107edf9897_story.html.

Entman, Robert M. "Framing Media Power." In *Doing News Framing Analysis*, edited by Paul D'Angelo and Jim A. Kuypers, 331–55. New York; London: Routledge, 2010.

Entman, Robert M. "Framing: Toward Clarification of a Fractured Paradigm." *Journal of Communication* 43, no. 4 (1993): 51–8.
Entman, Robert M. *Projections of Power: Framing News, Public Opinion, and US Foreign Policy*. Chicago: University of Chicago Press, 2003.
Entman, Robert M., and Nikki Usher. "Framing in a Fractured Democracy: Impacts of Digital Technology on Ideology, Power and Cascading Network Activation." *Journal of Communication* 68, no. 2 (April 1, 2018): 298–308. https://doi.org/10.1093/joc/jqx019.
Entous, Adam, and Julian E. Barnes. "Pentagon Envisions 'Small' Training Program for Syria Opposition." *Wall Street Journal*, July 16, 2014. https://online.wsj.com/articles/pentagon-envisions-small-training-program-for-syria-opposition-1405520641.
Entous, Adam, and Sam Dagher. "US Talks Tough on Syria, Ramps Up Attack Planning." *Wall Street Journal*, August 25, 2013. https://online.wsj.com/article/SB10001424127887323407104579034633663263254.html.
Entous, Adam, Julian E. Barnes, and Inti Landauro. "US Weighs Plans to Punish Assad." *Wall Street Journal*, August 23, 2013. https://online.wsj.com/article/SB10001424127887323665504579029122081493110.html.
Entous, Adam, Nour Malas, and Margaret Coker. "A Veteran Saudi Power Player Works to Build Support to Topple Assad." *Wall Street Journal*, August 25, 2013. https://online.wsj.com/article/SB10001424127887323423804579024452583045962.html.
Fadel, Leila. "Amid Protests, Syrian President Accepts Cabinet's Resignation." *Washington Post*, March 29, 2011. https://www.washingtonpost.com/world/syrian-president-accepts-cabinets-resignations/2011/03/29/AFVTAjuB_story.html.
Fandos, Nicholas. "Divided on Strikes, Democrats and Republicans Press for Clearer Syria Strategy." *New York Times*, April 14, 2018. https://www.nytimes.com/2018/04/14/us/politics/congress-syria-trump.html.
Fassihi, Farnaz. "Syria Frees Prisoners as Unrest Continues." *Wall Street Journal*, March 26, 2011. https://www.wsj.com/articles/SB10001424052748704517404576224533067681492.
Fassihi, Farnaz. "Syria Strike Could Dash Hopes for Iran Talks." *Wall Street Journal*, August 27, 2013. https://online.wsj.com/article/SB10001424127887324906304579037233239608824.html.
Fassihi, Farnaz. "Syria Warns Protesters to Stop." *Wall Street Journal*, March 28, 2011. https://www.wsj.com/articles/SB10001424052748704396904576226293686597156.
Fassihi, Farnaz. "Syrian Cabinet Steps Down." *Wall Street Journal*, March 29, 2011. https://www.wsj.com/articles/SB10001424052748704559904576230233227123572.
Fassihi, Farnaz. "Syrian Leader Shuns Reform." *Wall Street Journal*, March 31, 2011. https://www.wsj.com/articles/SB10001424052748703806304576232423584690828.
Fassihi, Farnaz, and Jay Solomon. "Syria Regime Rocked by Protests." *Wall Street Journal*, March 26, 2011. https://www.wsj.com/articles/SB10001424052748704517404576223350109783770.
Feldman, Sarah. "Halfway into 2019, News Subscriptions Continue to Grow." *Statista*, August 2, 2019. https://www.statista.com/chart/18893/digital-news-subscribers/.
Fidler, Stephen. "Europe Narrows Divide over Russian Sanctions." *Wall Street Journal*, July 25, 2014. https://online.wsj.com/articles/eu-narrows-divide-over-russian-sanctions-1406240060.
Fields, Gary. "Lawmakers Call for US Response on Syria." *Wall Street Journal*, August 25, 2013. https://online.wsj.com/article/SB10001424127887323906804579034723096767510.html.

Fischer, Sara. "Trump Bump: NYT and WaPo Digital Subscriptions Tripled since 2016." *Axios*, November 24, 2020. https://www.axios.com/washington-post-new-york-times-subscriptions-8e888fd7-5484-44c7-ad43-39564e06c84f.html.

Flanagin, Jake. "Iraq—or Sunnistan, Shiitestan and Kurdistan." *Op-Talk* (blog). *New York Times*, July 7, 2014. https://op-talk.blogs.nytimes.com/2014/07/07/iraq-or-sunnistan-shiitestan-and-kurdistan/.

Foreman, Jonathan. "Building the US - Kurdistan Special Relationship." *Wall Street Journal*, July 10, 2014. https://online.wsj.com/articles/the-u-s-should-guarantee-kurdish-independence-1405020652.

Franck, Georg. "The Economy of Attention." *Journal of Sociology* 55, no. 1 (March 1, 2019): 8–19. https://doi.org/10.1177/1440783318811778.

Freedman, Des. *The Contradictions of Media Power*. London; New York: Bloomsbury Academic, 2014.

Freedman, Robert O. "George W. Bush, Barack Obama, and the Arab-Israeli Conflict from 2001 to 2011." In *Israel and the United States: Six Decades of US-Israeli Relations*, edited by Robert O. Freedman, 37–78. Boulder, CO: Routledge, 2012.

Freedom House. *Freedom of the Press 2017*. Press Freedom's Dark Horizon. April 2016. https://freedomhouse.org/sites/default/files/FOTP_2017_booklet_FINAL_April28.pdf.

Freedom House. "Syria: Freedom in the World 2023," 2023. https://freedomhouse.org/country/syria/freedom-world/2023.

Friedman, Thomas L. "Hoping for Arab Mandelas." *New York Times*, March 26, 2011. https://www.nytimes.com/2011/03/27/opinion/27friedman.html.

Friedman, Thomas L. "Looking for Luck in Libya." *New York Times*, March 29, 2011. https://www.nytimes.com/2011/03/30/opinion/30friedman.html.

Friedman, Thomas L. "Obama on the World." *New York Times*, August 8, 2014. https://www.nytimes.com/2014/08/09/opinion/president-obama-thomas-l-friedman-iraq-and-world-affairs.html.

Friedman, Thomas L. "Syria, Obama and Putin." *New York Times*, September 30, 2015. https://www.nytimes.com/2015/09/30/opinion/thomas-friedman-syria-obama-and-putin.html.

Friedman, Thomas L. "Tribes with Flags." *New York Times*, March 22, 2011. https://www.nytimes.com/2011/03/23/opinion/23friedman.html.

Friel, Howard, and Richard A. Falk. *The Record of the Paper: How the New York Times Misreports US Foreign Policy*. London; New York: Verso Books, 2004.

Fukuyama, Francis. *The End of History and the Last Man*. New York: Free Press, 1992.

Galbraith, Peter W. "How the War Ends in Syria." *New York Times*, December 6, 2016. https://www.nytimes.com/2016/12/06/opinion/how-the-war-ends-in-syria.html.

Gearan, Anne, Loveday Morris, and Colum Lynch. "UN to Inspect Site of Alleged Chemical Weapons Attack in Syria." *Washington Post*, August 25, 2013. https://www.washingtonpost.com/world/national-security/un-to-inspect-alleged-chemical-weapons-attack-in-syria-lawmakers-call-for-us-military-response/2013/08/25/e171162e-0d94-11e3-bdf6-e4fc677d94a1_story.html.

Gerson, Michael. "The Real Mission in Syria Was Never Attempted." *Washington Post*, April 17, 2018. https://www.washingtonpost.com/opinions/the-real-mission-in-syria-was-never-attempted/2018/04/16/9f6cbb00-4199-11e8-8569-26fda6b404c7_story.html.

Gerson, Michael. "Syrian War Leaves No Easy Choices." *Washington Post*, August 26, 2013. https://www.washingtonpost.com/opinions/michael-gerson-a-complex-path-to-ending-syrias-war/2013/08/26/c7173532-0e7b-11e3-bdf6-e4fc677d94a1_story.html.

Gibbons-Neff, Thomas. "Missile Strikes Are Unlikely to Stop Syria's Chemical Attacks, Pentagon Says." *New York Times*, April 19, 2018. https://www.nytimes.com/2018/04/19/world/middleeast/syria-strikes.html.

Gilbert, Ben. "Rebel Infighting Kills Thousands of Syrians." *Al Jazeera America*, February 28, 2014. http://america.aljazeera.com/articles/2014/2/28/infighting-killsthousandsofsyrianrebels.html.

Gilboa, Eytan, Maria Gabrielsen Jumbert, Jason Miklian, and Piers Robinson. "Moving Media and Conflict Studies beyond the CNN Effect." *Review of International Studies* 42, no. 4 (October 2016): 654–72. https://doi.org/10.1017/S026021051600005X.

Gilsinan, Kathy. "Trump Is Killing a Fatally Flawed Syria Policy." *The Atlantic*, October 8, 2019. https://www.theatlantic.com/politics/archive/2019/10/trumps-confusing-syria-policy/599629/.

Gitlin, Todd. "The Pro-War Post." *American Prospect*, March 18, 2003. http://prospect.org/article/pro-war-post.

Gitlin, Todd. *The Whole World Is Watching: Mass Media in the Making and Unmaking of the New Left*. Berkeley, CA Los Angeles; London: University of California Press, 2003.

Gladstone, Rick. "UN Council, in Unanimous Vote, Backs Aid Delivery to Syrians in Rebel Areas." *New York Times*, July 14, 2014. https://www.nytimes.com/2014/07/15/world/middleeast/un-security-council-authorizes-strengthened-syria-aid.html.

Goffman, Erving. *Frame Analysis: An Essay on the Organization of Experience*. Cambridge, MA: Harvard University Press, 1974.

Gordon, Chris. "Partisan Divide Defines Congressional Reaction to Syria Strikes." *Wall Street Journal*, April 14, 2018. https://www.wsj.com/articles/partisan-divide-defines-congressional-reaction-to-syria-strikes-1523745696.

Gordon, Michael R., and Dion Nissenbaum. "US Upholds Its Red Line in Syria, While Steering Clear of Russia's." *Wall Street Journal*, April 14, 2018. https://www.wsj.com/articles/u-s-upholds-its-red-line-in-syria-while-steering-clear-of-russias-1523680020.

Gordon, Michael R., and Gardiner Harris. "Obama and Putin Play Diplomatic Poker over Syria." *New York Times*, September 28, 2015. https://www.nytimes.com/2015/09/29/world/middleeast/obama-and-putin-clash-at-un-over-syria-crisis.html.

Gordon, Michael R., and Mark Landler. "Kerry Cites Clear Evidence of Chemical Weapon Use in Syria." *New York Times*, August 26, 2013. https://www.nytimes.com/2013/08/27/world/middleeast/syria-assad.html.

Gorman, Siobhan. "US Faces Growing Threats, 9/11 Commission Cautions." *Wall Street Journal*, July 22, 2014. https://online.wsj.com/articles/u-s-faces-growing-threats-9-11-commission-cautions-1406002558.

Gowan, Richard. "End Times Diplomacy at the UN." *Journal of International Affairs* 70, no. 2 (2017): 17–28. https://www.jstor.org/stable/90012617.

Graves, Lucia. "The Wall Street Journal's Trump Problem." *Guardian* (UK edition), September 10, 2017. https://www.theguardian.com/media/2017/sep/10/the-wall-street-journals-trump-problem.

Grix, Jonathan. *The Foundations of Research*. Second edition. Palgrave Study Skills. Basingstoke; New York: Palgrave Macmillan, 2010.

Grossman, Andrew. "Syria Is Breeding Western Terrorists, US Warns." *Wall Street Journal*, July 8, 2014. https://online.wsj.com/articles/holder-calls-on-u-s-allies-to-disrupt-grooming-of-islamic-terrorists-1404826340.

Habermas, Jürgen. "Political Communication in Media Society: Does Democracy Still Enjoy an Epistemic Dimension? The Impact of Normative Theory on Empirical

Research." *Communication Theory* 16, no. 4 (November 2006): 411–26. https://doi.org/10.1111/j.1468-2885.2006.00280.x.

Haddad, Bassam. "Why Syria Is Unlikely to Be Next … for Now." *Carnegie Endowment for International Peace*, March 9, 2011. https://carnegieendowment.org/sada/42936.

Halimi, Serge. "The Challenge Is Bigger than Trump." *Le Monde Diplomatique (English Edition)*, February 2020. https://mondediplo.com/2020/02/01us.

Hall, Stuart. "Encoding and Decoding in the Television Discourse." *Discussion Paper*. Centre for Cultural Studies, University of Birmingham, 1973.

Hallin, Daniel C. *The Uncensored War: The Media and Vietnam*. New York; London: Oxford University Press, 1986.

Hallin, Daniel C., and Paolo Mancini. *Comparing Media Systems: Three Models of Media and Politics*. Cambridge, United Kingdom: Cambridge University Press, 2004. http://ebookcentral.proquest.com/lib/soas-ebooks/detail.action?docID=266614.

Hanieh, Adam. *Lineages of Revolt: Issues of Contemporary Capitalism in the Middle East*. Chicago, IL: Haymarket Books, 2013.

Harman, Jane. "The United States Must Advance a Mideast Policy Based on Collaboration." *Washington Post*, July 10, 2014. https://www.washingtonpost.com/opinions/the-united-states-must-advance-a-mideast-policy-based-on-collaboration/2014/07/10/ccd7eeaa-0761-11e4-a0dd-f2b22a257353_story.html.

Harris, Gardiner, and Charlie Savage. "Obama, in Major National Security Speech, Defends Counterterrorism Legacy." *New York Times*, December 6, 2016. https://www.nytimes.com/2016/12/06/us/politics/obama-in-major-national-security-speech-to-defend-counterterrorism-legacy.html.

Hashemi, Nader, and Danny Postel. "The Sectarianization Thesis." In *Sectarianization: Mapping the New Politics of the Middle East*, edited by Nader Hashemi and Danny Postel, 1–22. New York: Oxford University Press, 2017.

Healy, Gene, and John Glaser. "Repeal, Don't Replace, Trump's War Powers." *New York Times*, April 17, 2018. https://www.nytimes.com/2018/04/17/opinion/repeal-replace-trump-war-powers.html.

Helmi, Kholoud. "Revolutionary Women: Makers of the New Media in Syria." Interview by SOAS Syria Society. *Medium*, February 13, 2018. https://medium.com/stories-soas/revolutionary-women-makers-of-the-new-media-in-syria-c55bf3315234.

Herman, Edward S., and Noam Chomsky. *Manufacturing Consent: The Political Economy of the Mass Media*. London: The Bodley Head Random House, 2008. Kindle.

Herman, Edward S., and Noam Chomsky. "The Propaganda Model after 20 Years: Interview with Edward S. Herman and Noam Chomsky." Interview by Andrew Mullen. *Westminster Papers in Communication and Culture* 6, no. 2 (October 1, 2009): 12–22. https://doi.org/10.16997/wpcc.121.

Hindman, Matthew. *The Internet Trap: How the Digital Economy Builds Monopolies and Undermines Democracy*. Princeton, NJ: Princeton University Press, 2018.

Hinnebusch, Raymond, Marwan J. Kabalan, Bassma Kodmani, and David Lesch. "Syrian Foreign Policy and the United States: From Bush to Obama." *Syria Studies* 2, no. 1 (2010): 1–58.

Hoagland, Jim. "Obama Recalibrates American Power." *Washington Post*, March 29, 2011. https://www.washingtonpost.com/opinions/obama_recalibrates_american_power/2011/03/29/AFIqwDvB_story.html.

Hof, Frederic C. "How Close Did Israel Come to Peace with Syria." Interview by Faysal Itani. *New Lines Magazine*. May 5, 2022. https://newlinesmag.com/review/how-close-did-israel-come-to-peace-with-syria/.

Hollar, Julie. "Here's the Evidence Corporate Media Say Is Missing of WaPo Bias against Sanders." *FAIR*, August 15, 2019. https://fair.org/home/heres-the-evidence-corporate-media-say-is-missing-of-wapo-bias-against-sanders/.

Horkheimer, Max, and Theodor W. Adorno. "The Culture Industry: Enlightenment as Mass Deception." In *Dialectic of Enlightenment: Philosophical Fragments*, edited by Gunzelin Schmid Noeri. Translated by Edmund Jephcott, 94–136. Stanford, CA: Stanford University Press, 2002. http://ebookcentral.proquest.com/lib/soas-ebooks/detail.action?docID=5406369.

Hubbard, Ben. "After US Strikes, Syria Returns to War as Usual." *New York Times*, April 15, 2018. https://www.nytimes.com/2018/04/15/world/middleeast/syria-us-airstrike.html.

Hubbard, Ben. "Assad's Lesson from Aleppo: Force Works, with Few Consequences." *New York Times*, December 16, 2016. https://www.nytimes.com/2016/12/16/world/middleeast/syria-aleppo-assad-autocrats-obama.html.

Hubbard, Ben. "Signs of Chemical Attack Detailed by Aid Group." *New York Times*, August 24, 2013. https://www.nytimes.com/2013/08/25/world/middleeast/syria-updates.html.

Hubbard, Ben, and Hwaida Saad. "Images of Death in Syria, but No Proof of Chemical Attack." *New York Times*, August 21, 2013. https://www.nytimes.com/2013/08/22/world/middleeast/syria.html.

Hubbard, Ben, Mark Mazzetti, and Mark Landler. "Blasts in the Night, a Smell, and a Flood of Syrian Victims." *New York Times*, August 26, 2013. https://www.nytimes.com/2013/08/27/world/middleeast/blasts-in-the-night-a-smell-and-a-flood-of-syrian-victims.html.

Human Rights Watch. "Russia/Syria: War Crimes in Month of Bombing Aleppo." *Human Rights Watch*, December 1, 2016. https://www.hrw.org/news/2016/12/01/russia/syria-war-crimes-month-bombing-aleppo.

Human Rights Watch. "Syria/Russia: Strategy Targeted Civilian Infrastructure." *Human Rights Watch*, October 15, 2020. https://www.hrw.org/news/2020/10/15/syria/russia-strategy-targeted-civilian-infrastructure.

Ignatius, David. "Gates Underlines the Dangers in the Middle East." *Washington Post*, March 22, 2011. https://www.washingtonpost.com/opinions/gates_underlines_the_dangers_in_the_middle_east/2011/03/22/ABYhTMDB_story.html.

Ignatius, David. "Obama Speech Offers Clarity on Libya Policy." *Washington Post*, March 28, 2011. https://www.washingtonpost.com/opinions/obama-speech-offers-clarity-on-libya-policy/2011/03/28/AF8Ud8qB_story.html.

Ignatius, David. "Obama's Fuzzy Narrative in the Mideast." *Washington Post*, March 25, 2011. https://www.washingtonpost.com/opinions/obamas-fuzzy-narrative-in-the-mideast/2011/03/24/AFt0DRYB_story.html.

Ignatius, David. "Obama's Tenure Ends with a Turf War over Killing Terrorists." *Washington Post*, December 8, 2016. https://www.washingtonpost.com/opinions/obamas-tenure-ends-with-a-turf-war-over-killing-terrorists/2016/12/08/b3c371d8-bd84-11e6-91ee-1adddfe36cbe_story.html.

Ignatius, David. "Russia and the 'Facts on the Ground' in Syria." *Washington Post*, October 1, 2015. https://www.washingtonpost.com/opinions/russias-facts-on-the-ground-in-syria/2015/10/01/45fe3bb2-687e-11e5-8325-a42b5a459b1e_story.html.

Ignatius, David. "The US Cannot Pass Syria On to Putin." *Washington Post*, September 29, 2015. https://www.washingtonpost.com/opinions/the-us-cannot-pass-syria-on-to-putin/2015/09/29/f7273434-66df-11e5-9ef3-fde182507eac_story.html.

Isacson, Adam, and Nicole Ball. "US Military and Police Assistance to Poorly Performing States." In *Short of the Goal: US Policy and Poorly Performing States*, edited by Nancy Birdsall, Milan Vaishnav, and Robert L. Ayres, 412–60. Washington, DC: Centre for Global Development, 2006.

Issa, Antoun. "Syria's New Media Landscape." Policy Paper. Middle East Institute, December 2016. https://www.mei.edu/sites/default/files/publications/PP9_Issa_Syrianmedia_web_0.pdf.

Jaffe, Greg. "Trump Tries to Appear Strong in Syria Even as He Plans to Withdraw." *Washington Post*, April 14, 2018. https://www.washingtonpost.com/world/national-security/trump-tries-to-appear-strong-in-syria-even-as-he-plans-to-withdraw/2018/04/14/4bb75fe6-400f-11e8-8d53-eba0ed2371cc_story.html.

Jaffe, Greg, and David Nakamura. "Obama Defends His Wartime Strategy and Laments Trump's Likely Change of Course." *Washington Post*, December 6, 2016. https://www.washingtonpost.com/politics/obama-to-defend-his-terror-strategy-as-trump-names-prepares-to-alter-it/2016/12/05/a585f9de-bb1c-11e6-91ee-1adddfe36cbe_story.html.

Jaffe, Greg, and Greg Miller. "Trump's Generals, Hardened by War, See Militant Islam, Iran as Dire Dangers." *Washington Post*, December 9, 2016. https://www.washingtonpost.com/world/national-security/trumps-generals-hardened-by-war-see-militant-islam-iran-as-dire-dangers/2016/12/09/17f849a0-bd8d-11e6-94ac-3d324840106c_story.html.

Jaffe, Greg, John Hudson, and Philip Rucker. "Trump, a Reluctant Hawk, Has Battled His Top Aides on Russia and Lost." *Washington Post*, April 16, 2018. https://www.washingtonpost.com/world/national-security/trump-a-reluctant-hawk-has-battled-his-top-aides-on-russia-and-lost/2018/04/15/a91e850a-3f1b-11e8-974f-aacd97698cef_story.html.

Jakobsen, Peter Viggo. "Focus on the CNN Effect Misses the Point: The Real Media Impact on Conflict Management Is Invisible and Indirect." *Journal of Peace Research* 37, no. 2 (March 1, 2000): 131–43. https://doi.org/10.1177/0022343300037002001.

Jamieson, Kathleen Hall, and Kate Kenski. "Political Communication: Then, Now, and Beyond." In *The Oxford Handbook of Political Communication*, edited by Kate Kenski and Kathleen Hall Jamieson, 10, 2017. https://doi.org/10.1093/oxfordhb/9780199793471.013.77.

John, Tara. "Everything You Need to Know about the New al-Nusra Front." *Time*, July 29, 2016. https://time.com/4428696/nusra-front-syria-terror-al-qaeda/.

Johnson, Adam. "Washington Post Ran 16 Negative Stories on Bernie Sanders in 16 Hours." *FAIR*, March 8, 2016. https://fair.org/home/washington-post-ran-16-negative-stories-on-bernie-sanders-in-16-hours/.

Jolly, David. "Death Toll in Syrian Civil War Near 93,000, UN Says." *New York Times*, June 13, 2013. https://www.nytimes.com/2013/06/14/world/middleeast/un-syria-death-toll.html.

Kasparov, Garry. "Putin Takes a Victory Lap While Obama Watches." *Wall Street Journal*, September 29, 2015. https://www.wsj.com/articles/putin-takes-a-victory-lap-while-obama-watches-1443568463.

Kennan, George F. "Somalia, Through a Glass Darkly." *New York Times*, September 30, 1993. https://www.nytimes.com/1993/09/30/opinion/somalia-through-a-glass-darkly.html.

Kerry, John. "Text of Kerry's Statement on Chemical Weapons in Syria." *New York Times*, August 26, 2013. https://www.nytimes.com/2013/08/27/world/middleeast/text-of-kerrys-statement-on-chemical-weapons-in-syria.html.

Kessler, Glenn. "Hillary Clinton's Uncredible Statement on Syria." *Washington Post*, April 4, 2011. https://www.washingtonpost.com/blogs/fact-checker/post/hillary-clintons-uncredible-statement-on-syria/2011/04/01/AFWPEYaC_blog.html.

Khalilzad, Zalmay. "A Regional Strategy for Democracy in the Middle East." *Washington Post*, March 15, 2011. https://www.washingtonpost.com/opinions/a-regional-strategy-for-democracy-in-the-middle-east/2011/03/14/ABR8d1Z_story.html.

Knickmeyer, Ellen, and Nour Malas. "Arab Allies Withhold Public Support for US Strike on Syria." *Wall Street Journal*, August 27, 2013. https://online.wsj.com/article/SB100014241278873244906304579038910953494966.html.

Knüpfer, Curd B., and Robert M. Entman. "Framing Conflicts in Digital and Transnational Media Environments." *Media, War & Conflict* 11, no. 4 (December 1, 2018): 476–88. https://doi.org/10.1177/1750635218796381.

Kovach, Bill, and Tom Rosenstiel. *The Elements of Journalism: What Newspeople Should Know and the Public Should Expect*. New York: Crown Publishing Group, 2001.

Krauthammer, Charles. "Obama's Syria Debacle." *Washington Post*, October 1, 2015. https://www.washingtonpost.com/opinions/obamas-world-falls-apart/2015/10/01/50c2a7d6-686f-11e5-8325-a42b5a459b1e_story.html.

Kuhn, Thomas S. "The Nature and Necessity of Scientific Revolutions." In *Philosophy of Science: The Central Issues*, edited by Martin Curd, J. A. Cover, and Chris Pincock, Second edition, 79–93. New York: W.W. Norton, 2013.

Landler, Mark. "Unrest in Syria and Jordan Poses New Test for US Policy." *New York Times*, March 26, 2011. https://www.nytimes.com/2011/03/27/world/middleeast/27diplomacy.html.

Landler, Mark, Mark Mazzetti, and Alissa J. Rubin. "Obama Officials Weigh Response to Syria Assault." *New York Times*, August 22, 2013. https://www.nytimes.com/2013/08/23/world/middleeast/syria.html.

Landler, Mark, and Michael R. Gordon. "Air War in Kosovo Seen as Precedent in Possible Response to Syria Chemical Attack." *New York Times*, August 23, 2013. https://www.nytimes.com/2013/08/24/world/air-war-in-kosovo-seen-as-precedent-in-possible-response-to-syria-chemical-attack.html.

Landler, Mark, and Thom Shanker. "Gates and Clinton Unite to Defend Libya Intervention, and Say It May Last Awhile." *New York Times*, March 27, 2011. https://www.nytimes.com/2011/03/28/world/africa/28policy.html.

Lee, Carol E. "Obama Defends His Antiterror Strategy in Arguments Aimed at His Successor." *Wall Street Journal*, December 6, 2016. https://www.wsj.com/articles/obama-defends-his-antiterror-strategy-in-arguments-aimed-at-his-successor-1481072025.

Lee, Carol E., and Corey Boles. "White House Aims to Make Case to War-Weary Public." *Wall Street Journal*, August 27, 2013. https://online.wsj.com/article/SB10001424127887324906304579039340954396628.html.

Lee, Carol E., Farnaz Fassihi, and Jay Solomon. "Obama Vows 'Long-term Campaign' against Islamic State." *Wall Street Journal*, September 28, 2015. ProQuest. https://search.proquest.com/docview/1717268542?accountid=14565.

Lee, Carol E., and Felicia Schwartz. "Trump's Team Differs on Foreign Policy Issues." *Wall Street Journal*, December 13, 2016. https://www.wsj.com/articles/trumps-team-differs-on-foreign-policy-issues-1481673683.

Lemut, Olympe. "Shooting the War in Syria." *Newlines*, June 25, 2021. https://newlinesmag.com/photo-essays/shooting-the-war-in-syria/.

Levin, Michael. "Seven Years Later: What Exactly Did Rupert Murdoch Do to The Wall Street Journal?" *HuffPost*, July 31, 2015. https://www.huffpost.com/entry/seven-years-later-what-ex_b_7912298.
Lin, Ed. "Carlos Slim Sells $40 Million More in New York Times Stock." *Barron's*, April 20, 2018. https://www.barrons.com/articles/carlos-slim-sells-40-million-more-in-new-york-times-stock-1524244371.
Lippmann, Walter. *Public Opinion*. New York: Harcourt, Brace and Company, 1922.
Lippmann, Walter, and Charles Merz. "A Test of the News: An Examination of the News Reports in the New York Times on Aspects of the Russian Revolution of Special Importance to Americans March 1917–March 1920." *New Republic*, August 4, 1920. http://archive.org/details/LippmannMerzATestoftheNews.
Lister, Charles. "Why Assad Is Losing." Brookings Institution, May 5, 2015. https://www.brookings.edu/opinions/why-assad-is-losing/.
Livingston, Steven. *Clarifying the CNN Effect: An Examination of Media Effects According to Type of Military Intervention*. Cambridge, MA: Harvard University Press, 1997.
Loveluck, Louisa. "Syrian Forces Push Aleppo Rebels to Brink as City Nears 'Total Collapse.'" *Washington Post*, December 12, 2016. https://www.washingtonpost.com/world/middle_east/syrian-forces-push-aleppo-rebels-to-brink-as-city-nears-total-collapse/2016/12/12/0e7e7e82-c079-11e6-afd9-f038f753dc29_story.html.
Loveluck, Louisa, and Karen DeYoung. "Hundreds of Men Vanish as They Flee Aleppo, UN Official Says." *Washington Post*, December 9, 2016. https://www.washingtonpost.com/world/hundreds-of-men-vanish-as-they-flee-aleppo-un-official-says/2016/12/09/e269938e-bdff-11e6-91ee-1adddfe36cbe_story.html.
Loveluck, Louisa, and Karen DeYoung. "Syrian Army Retakes Aleppo's Old City as Rebels Discuss Exit." *Washington Post*, December 7, 2016. https://www.washingtonpost.com/world/syrian-army-retakes-aleppos-old-city-as-rebels-discuss-exit/2016/12/07/6ad0bd42-bc52-11e6-91ee-1adddfe36cbe_story.html.
Lubold, Gordon, and Dion Nissenbaum. "Trump Bowed to Pentagon Restraint on Syria Strikes." *Wall Street Journal*, April 16, 2018. https://www.wsj.com/articles/trump-bowed-to-pentagon-restraint-on-syria-strikes-1523837509.
Lubold, Gordon, and Julian E. Barnes. "Pentagon Prepares Tougher Options on Fighting Militants to Show Trump Team." *Wall Street Journal*, December 9, 2016. https://www.wsj.com/articles/pentagon-prepares-tougher-options-on-fighting-militants-to-show-trump-team-1481330246.
Luck, Taylor. "As Syrian Rebels' Losses Mount, Teenagers Begin Filling Ranks." *Washington Post*, August 24, 2013. https://www.washingtonpost.com/world/middle_east/as-syrian-rebels-losses-mount-teenagers-begin-filling-ranks/2013/08/24/2bdbdfea-0a8f-11e3-9941-6711ed662e71_story.html.
Lund, Aron. "After Murky Diplomacy, Turkey Intervenes in Syria." *Carnegie Middle East Center*, August 24, 2016. https://carnegie-mec.org/diwan/64398?lang=en.
Lustick, Ian S. *Trapped in the War on Terror*. Philadelphia: University of Pennsylvania Press, 2006.
Luttwak, Edward N. "In Syria, America Loses If Either Side Wins." *New York Times*, August 24, 2013. https://www.nytimes.com/2013/08/25/opinion/sunday/in-syria-america-loses-if-either-side-wins.html.
Mapping Militant Organizations. "Liwa al-Tawhid." *Stanford University*. July 2016. https://cisac.fsi.stanford.edu/mappingmilitants/profiles/liwa-al-tawhid.

Marcetic, Branko. "MSNBC Is the Most Influential Network among Liberals – And It's Ignoring Bernie Sanders." *In These Times*, November 13, 2019. http://inthesitimes.com/features/msnbc-bernie-sanders-coverage-democratic-primary-media-analysis.html.

Marx, Karl, and Friedrich Engels. "The German Ideology." In *Collected Works of Karl Marx and Frederick Engels, Vol. 5: Marx and Engels, 1845–1847*. London: Lawrence & Wishart Ltd, 1976.

Matar, Dina. "First Framing and News: Lessons from Reporting Jordan in Crises." In *Reporting the Middle East: The Practice of News in the Twenty-First Century*, edited by Zahera Harb, 33–49. London; New York: I.B. Tauris, 2017.

Mazzetti, Mark, Adam Goldman, and Michael S. Schmidt. "Behind the Sudden Death of a $1 Billion Secret C.I.A. War in Syria." *New York Times*, August 2, 2017. https://www.nytimes.com/2017/08/02/world/middleeast/cia-syria-rebel-arm-train-trump.html.

Mazzetti, Mark, Michael R. Gordon, and Mark Landler. "US Is Said to Plan to Send Weapons to Syrian Rebels." *New York Times*, June 13, 2013. https://www.nytimes.com/2013/06/14/world/middleeast/syria-chemical-weapons.html.

McCain, John, and Lindsey Graham. "Stop Dithering, Confront ISIS." *New York Times*, August 29, 2014. https://www.nytimes.com/2014/08/30/opinion/john-mccain-and-lindsey-graham-confront-isis.html.

McChesney, Robert W. "September 11 and the Structural Limitations of US Journalism." In *Journalism After September 11*, edited by Barbie Zelizer and Stuart Allan. Second edition, 91–100. London; New York: Routledge, 2011.

McGurk, Brett. "The Cost of an Incoherent Foreign Policy." *Foreign Affairs*, January 22, 2020. https://www.foreignaffairs.com/articles/iran/2020-01-22/cost-incoherent-foreign-policy.

McGurk, Brett. "Hard Truths in Syria: America Can't Do More with Less, and It Shouldn't Try." *Foreign Affairs*, May/June 2019. https://www.foreignaffairs.com/articles/syria/2019-04-16/hard-truths-syria.

Mead, Walter Russell. "The Failed Grand Strategy in the Middle East." *Wall Street Journal*, August 24, 2013. https://online.wsj.com/article/SB10001424127887324619504579028923699568400.html.

Mead, Walter Russell. *Special Providence: American Foreign Policy and How It Changed the World*. New York: Knopf, 2012. Kindle.

Mead, Walter Russell. "Trump's Realist Syria Strategy." *Wall Street Journal*, April 16, 2018. https://www.wsj.com/articles/trumps-realist-syria-strategy-1523915612.

Meichtry, Stacy. "France Steps Up Efforts to Stop Syria-Bound Fighters." *Wall Street Journal*, July 9, 2014. https://online.wsj.com/articles/france-plans-travel-ban-for-syria-bound-fighters-1404913652.

Milbank, Dana. "Another Swing and a Miss for Obama's Foreign Policy." *Washington Post*, July 14, 2014. https://www.washingtonpost.com/opinions/dana-milbank-another-swing-and-a-miss-for-obamas-foreign-policy/2014/07/14/e5176cba-0b9f-11e4-b8e5-d0de80767fc2_story.html.

Mitchell, Amy, Jeffrey Gottfried, Jocelyn Kiley, and Katerina Eva Matsa. "Political Polarization & Media Habits." Pew Research Center, October 21, 2014. https://www.journalism.org/2014/10/21/political-polarization-media-habits/.

Mitchell, Amy, Jeffrey Gottfried, Michael Barthel, and Elisa Shearer. "The Modern News Consumer." *Pew Research Center*, July 7, 2016. https://www.journalism.org/2016/07/07/the-modern-news-consumer/.

Mitnick, Joshua. "Israel Worries Rise over a Syrian Attack." *Wall Street Journal*, August 27, 2013. https://online.wsj.com/article/SB10001424127887323906804579039084159645284.html.

Mohammed, Arshad, and Khaled Yacoub Oweis. "US Imposes Sanctions on Syria's Assad." *Reuters*, May 18, 2011. https://www.reuters.com/article/us-syria-idUSLDE73N02P20110518.

Moore, Peter. "One Year Later, Americans Back Military Action in Syria." *YouGov*, August 29, 2014. https://yougov.co.uk/topics/politics/articles-reports/2014/08/29/one-year-later-americans-back-military-action-syri?sectors,political=.

Morris, Loveday, and Karen DeYoung. "Syrian Activists Accuse Government of Deadly Chemical Attack Near Damascus." *Washington Post*, August 22, 2013. https://www.washingtonpost.com/world/syrian-activists-accuse-government-of-deadly-chemical-attack-near-damascus/2013/08/21/aea157e6-0a50-11e3-89fe-abb4a5067014_story.html.

MSF. "Syria: Thousands Suffering Neurotoxic Symptoms Treated in Hospitals Supported by MSF." *Médecins Sans Frontières (MSF) International*, August 24, 2013. https://www.msf.org/syria-thousands-suffering-neurotoxic-symptoms-treated-hospitals-supported-msf.

Mullet, Dianna R. "A General Critical Discourse Analysis Framework for Educational Research." *Journal of Advanced Academics* 29, no. 2 (May 1, 2018): 116–42. https://doi.org/10.1177/1932202X18758260.

Myers, Steven Lee. "In Putin's Syria Intervention, Fear of a Weak Government Hand." *New York Times*, October 4, 2015. https://www.nytimes.com/2015/10/04/world/europe/in-putins-syria-intervention-fear-of-a-weak-government-hand.html.

Nachawati, Leila. "Alepo, Como Srebrenica y Gernika." *Otras Miradas* (blog). *Público*, December 16, 2016. https://blogs.publico.es/otrasmiradas/7412/alepo-como-srebrenica-y-gernika/.

Navasky, Victor. Foreword to *Journalism after September 11*, edited by Barbie Zelizer and Stuart Allan. Second edition, xiii–xviii. London; New York: Routledge, 2011.

New York Times. "In Syria, Demonstrations Are Few and Brief." *New York Times*, March 16, 2011. https://www.nytimes.com/2011/03/17/world/middleeast/17syria.html.

Nissenbaum, Dion. "Pentagon's Plans for Syria Strikes Rely on Missiles." *Wall Street Journal*, August 27, 2013. https://online.wsj.com/article/SB10001424127887324906304579039330444836914.html.

Norman, Laurence. "EU Adds New Targets for Syria Sanctions." *Wall Street Journal*, July 22, 2014. https://online.wsj.com/articles/eu-adds-new-syria-sanctions-targets-1406033066.

Norman, Laurence. "Europe Hopeful Trump Will Stick with Iran Nuclear Deal." *Wall Street Journal*, December 13, 2016. https://www.wsj.com/articles/europe-hopeful-trump-will-stick-with-iran-nuclear-deal-1481661689.

Norman, Laurence. "European Diplomats Attack Russia's Syria Position after Islamic State Retakes Palmyra." *Wall Street Journal*, December 12, 2016. https://www.wsj.com/articles/european-diplomats-attack-russias-syria-position-after-islamic-state-retakes-palmyra-1481555304.

Norman, Laurence. "EU's Tusk Says Europe Will Cope with Refugee Crisis." *Wall Street Journal*, September 29, 2015, ProQuest. https://search.proquest.com/docview/1717316637?accountid=14565.

Norris, Pippa, Montague Kern, and Marion R. Just. "Framing Terrorism." In *Framing Terrorism: The News Media, the Government, and the Public*, 3–23. New York: Routledge, 2003.

Obama, Barack. "The Obama Doctrine." Interview by Jeffrey Goldberg. *The Atlantic*, April 2016. https://www.theatlantic.com/magazine/archive/2016/04/the-obama-doctrine/471525/.

Obama, Barack. "Remarks by President Obama to the United Nations General Assembly." *The White House*, September 28, 2015. https://obamawhitehouse.archives.gov/the-press-office/2015/09/28/remarks-president-Obama-united-nations-general-assembly.

Oweis, Khaled Yacoub. "Syria Blocks Facebook in Internet Crackdown." *Reuters*, November 23, 2007. https://www.reuters.com/article/us-syria-facebook-idUSOWE37285020071123.

Parker, Kathleen. "The Dogs of War Are Howling." *Washington Post*, April 14, 2018. https://www.washingtonpost.com/opinions/the-dogs-of-war-are-howling/2018/04/13/2148f12a-3f56-11e8-8d53-eba0ed2371cc_story.html.

Paterson, Chris. "International News on the Internet: Why More Is Less." *Ethical Space: The International Journal of Communication Ethics* 4, no. 1/2 (2007): 57–66.

Paul, Kari. "Obama Says Presidents Should Avoid Social Media in Apparent Trump Jab." *Guardian* (UK edition), September 18, 2019. http://www.theguardian.com/us-news/2019/sep/18/obama-trump-social-media-tv-twitter.

Pew Research Center. "Newspapers Fact Sheet." *Pew Research Center*, June 29, 2021. https://www.journalism.org/fact-sheet/newspapers/.

Pew Research Center. "Trends and Facts on Newspapers." *Pew Research Center*, June 29, 2021. https://www.journalism.org/fact-sheet/newspapers/.

Phillips, Christopher. *The Battle for Syria: International Rivalry in the New Middle East*. New Haven London: Yale University Press, 2016.

Philo, Gregory. "Can Discourse Analysis Successfully Explain the Content of Media and Journalistic Practice?" *Journalism Studies* 8, no. 2 (April 1, 2007): 175–96. https://doi.org/10.1080/14616700601148804.

Pickard, Victor. *Democracy without Journalism?: Confronting the Misinformation Society*. New York: Oxford University Press, 2019.

Pincus, Walter. "Petraeus on Putin: His Provocations Are Designed to Protect His Interests." *Washington Post*, September 28, 2015. https://www.washingtonpost.com/world/national-security/petraeus-on-putin-his-provocations-are-designed-to-protect-his-interests/2015/09/28/0dc59ade-654e-11e5-9ef3-fde182507eac_story.html.

Postelnicu, Monica. "Two-Step Flow Model of Communication." *Encyclopedia Britannica*, accessed April 16, 2020. https://www.britannica.com/topic/two-step-flow-model-of-communication.

Rasmussen, Sune Engel. "As Islamic State Fades in Syria, Another Militant Group Takes Root." *Wall Street Journal*, April 18, 2018. https://www.wsj.com/articles/as-islamic-state-fades-in-syria-another-militant-group-takes-root-1524064045.

Rasmussen, Sune Engel, and Raja Abdulrahim. "A Day after US Airstrikes in Syria, Assad Launches New Onslaught against Rebels." *Wall Street Journal*, April 15, 2018. https://www.wsj.com/articles/a-day-after-u-s-airstrikes-in-syria-assad-launches-new-onslaught-against-rebels-1523799881.

Razumovskaya, Olga. "Putin's Domestic Media Blitz Focuses on Islamic State Threat in Russia." *Wall Street Journal*, October 2, 2015. https://www.wsj.com/articles/putins-domestic-media-blitz-focuses-on-islamic-state-threat-in-russia-1443805304.

Rehmann, Jan. "Ideology as Alienated Socialization." In *The Oxford Handbook of Karl Marx*, edited by Matt Vidal, Tony Smith, Tomás Rotta, and Paul Prew, 2019. https://doi.org/10.1093/oxfordhb/9780190695545.013.18.

Renn, Jürgen. *The Evolution of Knowledge: Rethinking Science for the Anthropocene.* Princeton: Princeton University Press, 2020.
Reporters without Borders. "Syria: 2023 World Press Freedom Index." *Reporters without Borders*, 2023. https://rsf.org/en/syria.
Reporters without Borders. "Syria: Third Journalist Killed in 2022 and Another Injured in Turkish Airstrikes." *Reporters without Borders*, November 23, 2022. https://rsf.org/en/syria-third-journalist-killed-2022-and-another-injured-turkish-airstrikes.
Rhodes, Ben. *The World as It Is: Inside the Obama White House.* Vintage Digital, 2018. Kindle.
Rice, Susan E. "Trump's Problem in Syria? It Was Obama's Too." *New York Times*, April 17, 2018. https://www.nytimes.com/2018/04/17/opinion/syria-airstrikes-trump-next.html.
Richardson, John. *Analysing Newspapers: An Approach from Critical Discourse Analysis.* Basingstoke, England; New York: Palgrave, 2007.
Riley, Jason L. "Hillary's Foreign Policy Gambit." *Wall Street Journal*, July 7, 2014. https://online.wsj.com/articles/political-diary-hillarys-foreign-policy-gambit-1404758578.
Roberts, Andrew. "Syria's Gas Attack on Civilization." *Wall Street Journal*, August 25, 2013. https://online.wsj.com/article/SB10001424127887323665504579031010578108096.html.
Robinson, Eugene. "Assad Must Be Punished." *Washington Post*, August 26, 2013. https://www.washingtonpost.com/opinions/eugene-robinson-assad-must-be-punished/2013/08/26/3aaceb94-0e8c-11e3-bdf6-e4fc677d94a1_story.html.
Robinson, Eugene. "The Downside of Giving Weapons to Rebels in Ukraine or Syria." *Washington Post*, July 21, 2014. https://www.washingtonpost.com/opinions/eugene-robinson-the-downside-of-giving-weapons-to-rebels-in-ukraine-or-syria/2014/07/21/d67b5090-110d-11e4-98ee-daea85133bc9_story.html.
Robinson, Eugene. "Trump Is Smashingly Successful—at Sowing Utter Confusion." *Washington Post*, April 20, 2018. https://www.washingtonpost.com/opinions/trump-is-smashingly-successful–at-sowing-utter-confusion/2018/04/19/0ca9a4b6-440c-11e8-ad8f-27a8c409298b_story.html.
Robinson, Piers. "9/11 Unmasked by David Ray Griffin and Elizabeth Woodworth: A Review." *OffGuardian* (blog), September 10, 2018. https://off-guardian.org/2018/09/10/9-11-unmasked-by-david-ray-griffin-and-elizabeth-woodworth-a-review/.
Robinson, Piers. *The CNN Effect: The Myth of News, Foreign Policy and Intervention.* London; New York: Routledge, 2002.
Robinson, Piers. "War and Media since 9/11." *European Journal of Communication* 34 (October 1, 2019): 557–63. https://doi.org/10.1177/0267323119875251.
Roca, Cristina. "How the Syrian War Changed How War Crimes Are Documented." *New Humanitarian*, June 1, 2017. https://deeply.thenewhumanitarian.org/syria/articles/2017/06/01/long-read-how-the-syrian-war-changed-how-war-crimes-are-documented.
Rogin, Josh. "In Washington, Syrian Opposition Offers to Work with Trump and Russia." *Washington Post*, December 11, 2016. https://www.washingtonpost.com/opinions/global-opinions/in-washington-syrian-opposition-makes-the-case-for-a-syria-reset/2016/12/11/5ae1b196-be52-11e6-ac85-094a21c44abc_story.html.
Rogin, Josh. "Inside Michael Flynn's Plan to Persuade Trump to Stay in Syria." *Washington Post*, April 20, 2018. https://www.washingtonpost.com/opinions/bring-back-michael-flynns-plan-for-syria/2018/04/19/7b155302-4414-11e8-ad8f-27a8c409298b_story.html.

Rogin, Josh. "Pentagon Wanted to Arm the Syrian Opposition." *Foreign Policy*, February 7, 2013. https://foreignpolicy.com/2013/02/07/pentagon-wanted-to-arm-the-syrian-opposition/.

Ross, Carne. "The Kurds' Democratic Experiment." *New York Times*, September 30, 2015. https://www.nytimes.com/2015/09/30/opinion/the-kurds-democratic-experiment.html.

Roth, Andrew. "Russia's Endgame in Syria? Maybe There Isn't One." *Washington Post*, September 29, 2015. https://www.washingtonpost.com/world/europe/russias-endgame-in-syria-maybe-there-isnt-one/2015/09/29/23e8cc66-63d0-11e5-8475-781cc9851652_story.html.

Roth, Andrew, and Thomas Gibbons-Neff. "Russia's Military Is Unlikely to Turn the Tide in Syria's War." *Washington Post*, October 3, 2015. https://www.washingtonpost.com/world/europe/russias-military-is-unlikely-to-turn-the-tide-in-syrias-war/2015/10/03/1b9fff04-686a-11e5-bdb6-6861f4521205_story.html.

Rubin, Alissa J. "Two Senators Say US Should Arm Syrian Rebels." *New York Times*, February 19, 2012. https://www.nytimes.com/2012/02/20/world/middleeast/mccain-and-graham-suggest-helping-syrian-rebels.html.

Rubin, Barry, ed. *The Muslim Brotherhood: The Organization and Policies of a Global Islamist Movement*. 2010th edition. New York, NY: Palgrave Macmillan, 2010.

Rubin, Jennifer. "The Gruesome Repudiation of 'Leading from Behind.'" *Right Turn* (blog). *Washington Post*, August 25, 2013. https://www.washingtonpost.com/blogs/right-turn/wp/2013/08/25/the-gruesome-repudiation-of-leading-from-behind/.

Rucker, Philip, Carol D. Leonnig, Anton Troianovski, and Greg Jaffe. "Trump Puts the Brakes on New Russian Sanctions, Reversing Haley's Announcement." *Washington Post*, April 16, 2018. https://www.washingtonpost.com/politics/trump-puts-the-brake-on-new-russian-sanctions-reversing-haleys-announcement/2018/04/16/ac3ad4f8-417f-11e8-8569-26fda6b404c7_story.html.

Rucker, Philip, Missy Ryan, Josh Dawsey, and Anne Gearan. "'Big Price to Pay': Inside Trump's Decision to Bomb Syria." *Washington Post*, April 15, 2018. https://www.washingtonpost.com/politics/big-price-to-pay-inside-trumps-decision-to-bomb-syria/2018/04/14/752bdd9a-3ff9-11e8-8d53-eba0ed2371cc_story.html.

RT. "'As If She Was Mother Teresa Herself': Russia's Churkin Snubs US Power's Speech at UNSC." *RT*, December 14, 2016. https://www.rt.com/news/370302-churkin-power-mother-theresa/.

RT. "Liberation of E. Aleppo from Militants Complete - Russian Military." *RT*, December 16, 2016. https://www.rt.com/news/370510-aleppo-women-children-evacuated/.

Ryan, Missy. "Russian, Syrian Partnership Poses a New Challenge for US in Iraq." *Washington Post*, September 28, 2015. https://www.washingtonpost.com/world/national-security/russian-syrian-partnership-poses-a-new-challenge-for-us-in-iraq/2015/09/28/b1190982-65ee-11e5-9223-70cb36460919_story.html.

Saad, Hwaida. "Militants Said to Kill Scores at a Syrian Base." *New York Times*, July 25, 2014. https://www.nytimes.com/2014/07/26/world/europe/isis-militants-said-to-have-killed-syrian-soldiers-outside-raqqa-province.html.

Saad, Hwaida, and Alan Cowell. "Assad Begins a Third Term in Syria, Vowing to Look After Its People." *New York Times*, July 16, 2014. https://www.nytimes.com/2014/07/17/world/middleeast/assad-sworn-in-for-third-term-as-syrian-president.html.

Sadat, Mir H., and Daniel B. Jones. "US Foreign Policy Toward Syria: Balancing Ideology and National Interests." *Middle East Policy Council* XVI, no. 2 (2009): 93–105. http://

www.mepc.org/journal/us-foreign-policy-toward-syria-balancing-ideology-and-national-interests.

Said, Edward W. *Covering Islam: How the Media and the Experts Determine How We See the Rest of the World*. London: Vintage, 1997.

Said, Edward W. *Orientalism*. First Vintage books edition. New York: Vintage Books, 1979.

SANA Syrian Arab News Agency. "Do You Know That Aleppo Is the Economic, Commercial and Industrial Capital of Syria?" *SANA*, November 23, 2021. https://sana.sy/en/?p=255479.

Sanger, David E. *Confront and Conceal: Obama's Secret Wars and Surprising Use of American Power*. New York: Crown Publishers, 2012.

Sanger, David E., and Ben Hubbard. "A Hard Lesson in Syria: Assad Can Still Gas His Own People." *New York Times*, April 14, 2018. https://www.nytimes.com/2018/04/14/us/politics/syria-chemical-weapons-analysis.html.

Savage, Luke. "The Corporate Media's War against Bernie Sanders Is Very Real." *Jacobin*. November 20, 2019. https://jacobinmag.com/2019/11/corporate-media-bernie-sanders-bias-msnbc-warren-biden.

Scheufele, Dietram A., and David Tewksbury. "Framing, Agenda Setting, and Priming: The Evolution of Three Media Effects Models." *Journal of Communication* 57, no. 1 (March 1, 2007): 9–20. https://doi.org/10.1111/j.0021-9916.2007.00326.x.

Schneider, Tobias, and Theresa Lütkefend. "Nowhere to Hide: The Logic of Chemical Weapons Use in Syria." *Global Public Policy Institute*, February 17, 2019. https://www.gppi.net/2019/02/17/the-logic-of-chemical-weapons-use-in-syria.

Schudson, Michael. *The Sociology of News*. Second edition. New York: W. W. Norton & Company, 2011.

Schudson, Michael. "What's Unusual about Covering Politics as Usual." In *Journalism After September 11*, edited by Barbie Zelizer and Stuart Allan. Second edition, 36–47. London; New York: Routledge, 2011.

Schwartz, Felicia. "John Kerry Says US Has 'Grave Concerns' about Russian Airstrikes in Syria." *Wall Street Journal*, September 30, 2015. https://www.wsj.com/articles/john-kerry-says-u-s-has-grave-concerns-about-russian-airstrikes-in-syria-1443645710.

Scott, John. *A Dictionary of Sociology* (Oxford Quick Reference). Fourth edition. Oxford, United Kingdom: OUP Oxford, 2014. Kindle.

Seib, Gerald F. "Listen Closely: Donald Trump Proposes Big Mideast Strategy Shift." *Wall Street Journal*, December 12, 2016. https://www.wsj.com/articles/listen-closely-donald-trump-proposes-big-mideast-strategy-shift-1481561492.

Seib, Gerald F. "Syria War Tests Obama's Security Doctrine." *Wall Street Journal*, September 28, 2015. https://www.wsj.com/articles/syria-war-tests-obamas-security-doctrine-1443454473.

Sengupta, Somini. "Bid to Deliver Aid to Syria May Set Stage for a UN Clash." *New York Times*, July 13, 2014. https://www.nytimes.com/2014/07/14/world/middleeast/bid-to-deliver-aid-to-syria-may-set-stage-for-a-un-clash.html.

Sengupta, Somini. "Defying Syria, United Nations Sends in Trucks Carrying Aid." *New York Times*, July 24, 2014. https://www.nytimes.com/2014/07/25/world/middleeast/defying-syria-united-nations-sends-in-trucks-carrying-aid.html.

Sengupta, Somini. "Refugee Crisis in Europe Prompts Western Engagement in Syria." *New York Times*, September 30, 2015. https://www.nytimes.com/2015/10/01/world/middleeast/europe-refugee-crisis-syria-civil-war.html.

Sengupta, Somini. "Russian Foreign Minister Defends Airstrikes in Syria." *New York Times*, October 1, 2015. https://www.nytimes.com/2015/10/02/world/europe/russia-airstrikes-syria-assad.html.

Şerban, Silviu. "On the Origins of the Gatekeeping Theory and Its Application to Journalism." *Annals of Spiru Haret University, Journalism Studies* 16, no. 2 (2015): 12–24.

Shaheen, Kareem. "'Save Us': Aleppo Civilians Plead for Help as Airstrikes Resume." *Guardian* (UK edition), December 14, 2016. http://www.theguardian.com/world/2016/dec/14/aleppo-civilians-plea-as-airstrikes-resume-syria.

Shamy, Lina. "I Went to Aleppo to Study. I Left in a Convoy of Refugees." *New York Times*, January 20, 2017. https://www.nytimes.com/2017/01/20/opinion/sunday/i-went-to-aleppo-to-study-i-left-in-a-convoy-of-refugees.html.

Shane, Daniel. "The Wall Street Journal Kills Off Its International Print Editions." *CNN*, September 29, 2017. https://money.cnn.com/2017/09/29/media/wall-street-journal-shelves-international-editions/index.html.

Shane, Scott, and Ben Hubbard. "Confident Syria Used Chemicals, US Mulls Action." *New York Times*, August 25, 2013. https://www.nytimes.com/2013/08/26/world/middleeast/syria-says-un-will-get-access-to-site-of-possible-chemical-attack.html.

Shanker, Thom. "General Says Syrian Rebels Aren't Ready to Take Power." *New York Times*, August 21, 2013. https://www.nytimes.com/2013/08/22/world/middleeast/general-says-syrian-rebels-arent-ready-to-take-power.html.

Shaw, Emily. "Frame Analysis." *Encyclopaedia Britannica*, accessed April 14, 2020. https://www.britannica.com/topic/frame-analysis.

Shear, Michael D. "Obama and Advisers to Discuss Syria." *New York Times*, August 24, 2013. https://www.nytimes.com/2013/08/25/world/middleeast/obama-and-advisers-to-discuss-syria.html.

Shoemaker, Pamela J., Tim P. Vos, and Stephen D. Reese. "Journalists as Gatekeepers." In *The Handbook of Journalism Studies*, edited by Karin Wahl-Jorgensen and Thomas Hanitzsch, 73–87. New York: Routledge, 2008.

Slackman, Michael. "Syria Tries to Ease Deep Political Crisis." *New York Times*, March 27, 2011. https://www.nytimes.com/2011/03/28/world/middleeast/28syria.html.

Sly, Liz. "UN Inspectors Visit Site of Alleged Chemical Attack in Syria after Coming under Sniper Fire." *Washington Post*, August 26, 2013. https://www.washingtonpost.com/world/middle_east/un-team-headed-to-site-of-alleged-chemical-attack-comes-under-sniper-fire-turns-back/2013/08/26/5ea074c8-0e3f-11e3-8cdd-bcdc09410972_story.html.

Sly, Liz, and Ahmed Ramadan. "Assad, Inaugurated to 3rd Term, Tells the World: I Told You So." *Washington Post*, July 16, 2014. https://www.washingtonpost.com/world/middle_east/assad-inaugurated-to-3rd-term-says-events-in-region-prove-him-right-about-terrorism/2014/07/16/d7e74dec-eea3-487b-a012-6b8a8a21b1ed_story.html.

Sly, Liz, and Louisa Loveluck. "Assad Is Defiant as US-Led Strikes in Syria Show No Sign of Threatening His Hold on Power." *Washington Post*, April 14, 2018. https://www.washingtonpost.com/world/damascus-defiant-as-trump-orders-strikes-after-syria-chemical-attack/2018/04/14/5ec055a6-3f5c-11e8-955b-7d2e19b79966_story.html.

Solomon, Jay. "Failed Mideast Peace Effort Sidelines US in Current Strife." *Wall Street Journal*, July 9, 2014. https://online.wsj.com/articles/failed-mideast-peace-effort-sidelines-u-s-in-current-strife-1404946094.

Solomon, Jay. "In Turkey, Syrian Rebels Hope US Strikes Could Swing War." *Wall Street Journal*, August 26, 2013. https://online.wsj.com/article/SB10001424127887324906304579037294042386428.html.

Solomon, Jay. "Russia's Move in Syria Risks Aiding Militants, Saudis Warn." *Wall Street Journal*, October 1, 2015. https://www.wsj.com/articles/russias-move-in-syria-risks-aiding-militants-saudis-warn-1443751806.

Solomon, Jay. "US Won't Back New Intervention." *Wall Street Journal*, March 27, 2011. https://www.wsj.com/articles/SB10001424052748703576204576227131356932482.

Solomon, Jay, and Carol E. Lee. "Obama Contends with Arc of Instability Unseen since '70s." *Wall Street Journal*, July 13, 2014. https://online.wsj.com/articles/obama-contends-with-arc-of-instability-unseen-since-70s-1405297479.

Solomon, Jay, and Julian E. Barnes. "In Mideast, US Policy Models Bog Down." *Wall Street Journal*, August 21, 2013. https://online.wsj.com/article/SB10001424127887323980604579027233023070834.html.

Sonne, Paul. "Trump's Strikes on Syria Risk Retaliation, Escalation in a War He Wants to Avoid." *Washington Post*, April 15, 2018. https://www.washingtonpost.com/world/national-security/trumps-strikes-on-syria-risk-retaliation-escalation-in-a-war-he-wants-to-avoid/2018/04/13/5f1059fc-3f7a-11e8-912d-16c9e9b37800_story.html.

Spindler, William. "2015: The Year of Europe's Refugee Crisis." *UNHCR UK*, December 8, 2015. https://www.unhcr.org/news/stories/2015/12/56ec1ebde/2015-year-europes-refugee-crisis.html.

St. John, Ronald Bruce. "The Changing Libyan Economy: Causes and Consequences." *The Middle East Journal* 62 (December 1, 2008): 75–91. https://doi.org/10.3751/62.1.14.

Stephens, Bret. "An Unteachable President." *Wall Street Journal*, September 28, 2015. https://www.wsj.com/articles/an-unteachable-president-1443485444.

Stephens, Bret. "Target Assad." *Wall Street Journal*, August 27, 2013. https://online.wsj.com/article/SB10001424127887323407104579036740023927518.html.

Stephens, Bret. "The Post-Pax Americana World." *Wall Street Journal*, July 7, 2014. https://online.wsj.com/articles/bret-stephens-the-post-pax-americana-world-1404776255.

Sullivan, Kate. "Trump's Syria Withdrawal a 'Stain on the Honor of the United States.'" *CNN*, December 20, 2018. https://www.cnn.com/2018/12/19/politics/lindsey-graham-trump-syria-withdrawal-stain-honor/index.html.

Sullivan, Margaret. *Ghosting the News: Local Journalism and the Crisis of American Democracy*. Columbia Global Reports, 2020.

Takeyh, Ray. "How to Break the Iran Nuclear Stalemate." *Washington Post*, July 18, 2014. https://www.washingtonpost.com/opinions/how-to-break-the-iran-nuclear-stalemate/2014/07/18/ba898726-0e7e-11e4-b8e5-d0de80767fc2_story.html.

Tau, Byron. "Some in Congress Fear White House Will Claim Expanded War Powers after Syria Attack." *Wall Street Journal*, April 18, 2018. https://www.wsj.com/articles/some-in-congress-fear-white-house-will-claim-expanded-war-powers-after-syria-attack-1524083519.

Taylor, Adam. "Russia's Airstrikes in Syria Mark a Huge Departure for Moscow." *Washington Post*, September 30, 2015. https://www.washingtonpost.com/news/worldviews/wp/2015/09/30/russias-airstrikes-in-syria-mark-a-huge-departure-for-moscow/.

Thiessen, Marc A. "Obama's Legacy of Failure." *Washington Post*, July 7, 2014. https://www.washingtonpost.com/opinions/marc-thiessen-obamas-legacy-of-failure/2014/07/07/9148acf8-05e0-11e4-a0dd-f2b22a257353_story.html.

Trofimov, Yaroslav. "Iran's Moves in Syria Raise Risk of Conflict with Israel." *Wall Street Journal*, April 19, 2018. https://www.wsj.com/articles/irans-moves-in-syria-raise-risk-of-conflict-with-israel-1524130202.

Trofimov, Yaroslav. "Russia Entry Adds New Fuel to Syria War." *Wall Street Journal*, October 1, 2015. https://www.wsj.com/articles/russian-entry-adds-new-fuel-to-syria-war-1443719595.

Trofimov, Yaroslav. "Syrian Rebels Pin Hopes on Trump." *Wall Street Journal*, December 8, 2016. https://www.wsj.com/articles/syrian-rebels-pin-hopes-on-trump-1481193000.

Troianovski, Anton. "Russia Responds to Airstrikes in Syria with Harsh Words but No Fire." *Washington Post*, April 14, 2018. https://www.washingtonpost.com/world/russia-responds-to-airstrike-with-harsh-words-but-no-fire/2018/04/14/a02ce438-3f97-11e8-955b-7d2e19b79966_story.html.

Trump, Donald. "President Trump on Syria Strikes: Full Transcript and Video." *New York Times*, April 14, 2018. https://www.nytimes.com/2018/04/13/world/middleeast/trump-syria-airstrikes-full-transcript.html.

Tuchman, Gaye. *Making News: A Study in the Construction of Reality*. New York: Free Press, 1980.

Ulgen, Sinan. "Turkey Can't Be Europe's Gatekeeper." *New York Times*, October 1, 2015. https://www.nytimes.com/2015/10/02/opinion/turkey-cant-be-europes-gatekeeper.html.

UN Syria Commission of Inquiry. "Rampant Human Rights Violations and War Crimes as War-Torn Idlib Faces the Pandemic." *United Nations Human Rights Office of the High Commission*, July 7, 2020. https://www.ohchr.org/EN/NewsEvents/Pages/DisplayNews.aspx?NewsID=26044.

United Nations. "Amid Bloodshed in Aleppo, Special Envoy for Syria Briefs Security Council, Calling on Russian Federation, United States to Save Ceasefire at 'Eleventh Hour.'" United Nations, September 25, 2016. https://www.un.org/press/en/2016/sc12533.doc.htm.

United Nations. "'Clear and Convincing' Evidence of Chemical Weapons Use in Syria, UN Team Reports." *UN News*, September 16, 2013. https://news.un.org/en/story/2013/09/449052-clear-and-convincing-evidence-chemical-weapons-use-syria-un-team-reports.

van Dam, Nikolaos. *Destroying a Nation: The Civil War in Syria*. London; New York: I.B.Tauris, 2017.

van Dijk, Teun A. "Discourse Analysis: Its Development and Application to the Structure of News." *Journal of Communication* 33, no. 2 (June 1, 1983): 20–43. https://doi.org/10.1111/j.1460-2466.1983.tb02386.x.

van Gorp, Baldwin. "Strategies to Take Subjectivity Out of Framing Analysis." In *Doing News Framing Analysis*, edited by Paul D'Angelo, 84–109. New York; London: Routledge, 2010.

Wall, Melissa, and Sahar el-Zahed. "Syrian Citizen Journalism." *Digital Journalism* 3, no. 5 (July 25, 2014): 720–36. https://doi.org/10.1080/21670811.2014.931722.

Wall Street Journal. "Double-Secret Probation for Bashar." *Wall Street Journal*, August 25, 2013. https://online.wsj.com/article/SB10001424127887323665504579028983339691094.html.

Wall Street Journal. "Loose Lips on Syria." *Wall Street Journal*, August 27, 2013. https://online.wsj.com/article/SB10001424127887324591204579039011328308776.html.

Wall Street Journal. "Obama's 'Dangerous Currents.'" *Wall Street Journal*, September 28, 2015. https://www.wsj.com/articles/obamas-dangerous-currents-1443485180.

Wall Street Journal. "The Problem Is Assad." *Wall Street Journal*, August 27, 2013. https://online.wsj.com/article/SB10001424127887323407104579036944187177968.html.

Wall Street Journal. "Russia's Syria Doublespeak." *Wall Street Journal*, December 12, 2016. https://www.wsj.com/articles/russias-syria-doublespeak-1481589744.

Wall Street Journal. "The Shaky House of Assad." *Wall Street Journal*, March 22, 2011. https://www.wsj.com/articles/SB10001424052748703858404576214911264291244.

Wall Street Journal. "Syria Side Effects." *Wall Street Journal*, August 26, 2013. https://online.wsj.com/article/SB10001424127887324591204579035360893940826.html.

Wall Street Journal. "The Syrian Revolt." *Wall Street Journal*, March 26, 2011. https://www.wsj.com/articles/SB10001424052748704517404576222991907156366.

Wall Street Journal. "Thousands in Syria Take to Streets as State Tries to Quell More Unrest." *Wall Street Journal*, March 25, 2011. https://www.wsj.com/articles/SB10001424052748704425804576220424099510348.

Wall Street Journal. "What US Retreat Looks Like." *Wall Street Journal*, October 1, 2015. https://www.wsj.com/articles/what-u-s-retreat-looks-like-1443742339.

Walt, Stephen M. "Robert Satloff Doth Protest Too Much." *Foreign Policy*, April 9, 2010. https://foreignpolicy.com/2010/04/09/robert-satloff-doth-protest-too-much/.

Washington Post. "Syrian Forces Fire into Air as Protesters Call for Assad's Exit." *Washington Post*, March 29, 2011, ProQuest. https://www.proquest.com/docview/858905325?accountid=189667.

WashPostPR. "The Washington Post Announces Expanded International Coverage." *Washington Post PR* (blog). *Washington Post*, February 13, 2018. https://www.washingtonpost.com/pr/wp/2018/02/13/the-washington-post-announces-expanded-international-coverage/.

Watson, Amy. "Wall Street Journal: Circulation 2018–2020." *Statista*, December 18, 2020. https://www.statista.com/statistics/193788/average-paid-circulation-of-the-wall-street-journal/.

Webster, James G. *The Marketplace of Attention: How Audiences Take Shape in a Digital Age*. Cambridge, Massachussetts; London, England: The MIT Press, 2014. Kindle.

Weisman, Jonathan. "House Votes to Authorize Aid to Syrian Rebels in ISIS Fight." *New York Times*, September 17, 2014. https://www.nytimes.com/2014/09/18/us/politics/house-vote-isis.html.

Weiss, Michael, and Hassan Hassan. *ISIS: Inside the Army of Terror*. Second edition. New York: Regan Arts, 2016.

Wergin, Clemens. "Is Obama's Foreign Policy Too European?" *New York Times*, July 8, 2014. https://www.nytimes.com/2014/07/09/opinion/clemens-wergin-is-obamas-foreign-policy-too-european.html.

Western, Jon, and Joshua S. Goldstein. "Humanitarian Intervention Comes of Age," *Foreign Affairs*, November 26, 2013. https://www.foreignaffairs.com/articles/2011-11-01/humanitarian-intervention-comes-age.

Wikstrom, Cajsa. "Syria: 'A Kingdom of Silence.'" *Al Jazeera*, February 9, 2011. https://www.aljazeera.com/features/2011/2/9/syria-a-kingdom-of-silence.

Wilson Center. "Timeline: The Rise, Spread, and Fall of the Islamic State." *Wilson Center*, October 28, 2019. https://www.wilsoncenter.org/article/timeline-the-rise-spread-and-fall-the-islamic-state.

Winseck, Dwayne. "The Political Economies of Media and the Transformation of the Global Media Industries." In *The Political Economies of Media: The Transformation of the Global Media Industries*, edited by Dwayne Winseck and Dal Young Jin, 3–48. London; New York: Bloomsbury Academic, 2011.

Wolgelenter, Michael. "Seven Takeaways from the Airstrikes on Syria." *New York Times*, April 14, 2018. https://www.nytimes.com/2018/04/14/world/middleeast/syria-russia-united-states-airstrikes.html.

York, Chris. "'Whitewashing War Crimes': How UK Academics Promote Pro-Assad Conspiracy Theories about Syria." *HuffPost*, August 22, 2018. https://www.huffingtonpost.co.uk/entry/uk-academics-pro-assad-conspiracy-theories-about-syria_uk_5aa51ea7e4b01b9b0a3c4b10.

York, Chris, and Ewan Somerville. "Sheffield Uni Professor Leaves Post after Accusations of Promoting Conspiracy Theories." *HuffPost*, April 17, 2019. https://www.huffingtonpost.co.uk/entry/piers-robinson_uk_5cb5d5b5e4b082aab08c953f.

Zacharia, Janine. "Israel, Long Critical of Assad, May Prefer He Stay after All." *Washington Post*, March 30, 2011. https://www.washingtonpost.com/world/israel-long-critical-of-assad-may-prefer-he-stay-after-all/2011/03/29/AFIq5JxB_story.html.

Zakaria, Fareed. "In Syria, Whose Side Is the United States On?" *Washington Post*, October 1, 2015. https://www.washingtonpost.com/opinions/in-syria-whose-side-is-the-united-states-on/2015/10/01/27163ec4-6875-11e5-9ef3-fde182507eac_story.html.

Zakaria, Fareed. "Obama Caves to Conventional Wisdom on Syria." *Washington Post*, July 10, 2014. https://www.washingtonpost.com/opinions/fareed-zakaria-obama-caves-to-conventional-wisdom-on-syria/2014/07/10/6a60ad74-085c-11e4-a0dd-f2b22a257353_story.html.

Zakaria, Fareed. "The Self-Destruction of American Power." *Foreign Affairs*, July/August 2019. https://www.foreignaffairs.com/articles/2019-06-11/self-destruction-american-power.

Zelin, Aaron Y. "Al-Qaeda Disaffiliates with the Islamic State of Iraq and al-Sham." Washington Institute for Near East Policy, February 3, 2014. https://www.washingtoninstitute.org/policy-analysis/al-qaeda-disaffiliates-islamic-state-iraq-and-al-sham.

Zunes, Stephen. "History Shows Hypocrisy of US Outrage over Chemical Weapons in Syria." *Truthout*, April 24, 2018. https://truthout.org/articles/history-shows-hypocrisy-of-us-outrage-over-chemical-weapons-in-syria/.

Zunes, Stephen. "The US and ISIS." *Progressive Magazine*, August 26, 2014. https://progressive.org/latest/u.s.-isis/.

INDEX

A
Abdulrahim, Raja 126, 147, 160, 164
Achcar, Gilbert 31, 35–6, 80, 113
Aday, Sean 12, 16–17, 23
Ahmad, Muhammad Idrees 5, 58, 176
Airstrikes Against Syria 145–9, 156, 160, 165
Ahrar al-Sham 84, 92, 101, 124–5
al-Assad, Bashar 45, 74, 88–9
al-Baghdadi, Abu Bakr 78, 82, 99
al-Haj Saleh, Yassin 55
al-Nusra Front 55, 78, 82, 92, 101, 107, 109, 124
al-Qaeda 30, 55, 78–9, 82, 84, 99, 109, 165
Aleppo
    Siege of 3–4, 131–3
    Battle of 123–6, 136–7, 141–3
Arab Spring 1, 35, 39, 42–4, 48, 50
Assad Regime *see* Syrian Regime
Authorization for Use of Military Force (AUMF) 152–3

B
Baker, Peter 15, 107–8, 111, 147, 151, 154
Bennett, W. Lance 16
Biden, Joe 86, 95, 151
Bush, George W. 11, 30–3, 37, 80, 85
Bush, George W. H. 21

C
Cafarella, Jennifer 124, 148
Carnegie Middle East Center 93, 153
Carter, Jimmy 21, 90
Cascading Activation Model, *see also* Entman, Robert 8–9, 16, 28–9, 33, 173
Cato Institute 151, 152
Chemical Weapons 56–8, 65–6, 71–4, 145–64
Chomsky, Noam 6–8, 18–21, 173

Chulov, Martin 124
CIA – 52, 58, 79, 101, 104, 108, 113–14, 116, 156
Clinton, Bill 21, 61, 96
Clinton, Hillary 36, 40, 52, 58, 79–81, 85, 95–7, 104, 106, 108, 114–15, 122, 130
CNN Effect Hypothesis 16, 21–4, 27–8
Cold War 7, 19–23, 28–32, 104, 173
Combined Joint Task Force-Operation Inherent Resolve 79
Cooper, Helene 40–1, 153
Council on Foreign Relations 86, 92, 115
Critical Discourse Analysis 179

D
Dagher, Sam 71, 122
D'Angelo, Paul 179–80, 182–3
Dara'a 145
Dataset of the Book 185, 187
De Mistura, Staffan 125
Democratic Party 11, 108, 111–12, 122
Douma 15, 146, 154
Douthat, Ross 108

E
Eastern Ghouta
    Chemical Attack 55–9, 74
    Recapture of 145
Elite Dissent in the US 22, 27, 33, 49, 58, 61, 79–81, 96–7, 104, 119, 153, 158, 163, 165, 172–3, 180
Enab Baladi 5, 26
End of History 21, 42
Entman, Robert 3, 8–9, 27–9, 31–2, 173, 178–81, 183
European Foreign Policy 97, 100, 102, 110–11, 120–1, 141

F
Facebook 1, 7, 24–5, 38, 173, 181
Fassihi, Farnaz 51–2, 73, 119

Ford, Robert 37, 115, 156
Frames, *see also* Framing, News Frames 2–3, 31, 51–2, 61, 66, 178–80, 181–184
Framing, *see also* Frames, News Frames – 3–5, 7–9, 28–9, 172–3, 177
France 22, 57, 66, 71, 97–8, 125, 136, 146, 164
Free Syrian Army (FSA) 27, 68, 78–9, 84, 99, 101, 123, 125, 137, 187
Freedman, Des 9, 33, 173–4, 180
Friedman, Thomas 42–3, 48, 80, 108–9, 113
Fukuyama, Francis, *see* End of History

G
Gaddafi, Muammar 42, 47, 52, 105
Geopolitics 1–2, 22, 27, 116, 126, 184
Gitlin, Todd 2–3, 18, 172, 184
Global War on Terror, *see* War on terror
Graham, Lindsey 67, 81, 124, 127, 148, 163

H
Habermas, Jürgen 17
Hallin, Daniel 10, 20
Hezbollah 37, 44, 48–9, 51, 68, 80, 101–2, 124, 187
Hubbard, Ben 4, 60–1, 63, 150–1, 153
Humanitarian Aid 66, 87–90, 115, 125
Humanitarian Crisis 3–4, 29, 121, 131–2, 142, 165, 172, 185, 187
Humanitarian Intervention 21–4, 40, 44, 46–7
Humanitarian Organizations 64, 131–3, 136, 138, 142
Hussein, Saddam 18, 22, 30–2, 57, 71–2, 147

I
Ignatius, David 46, 115–16, 134
Indexing Hypothesis 19
International Humanitarian Law 55, 133
International Law 18, 147, 152, 154
IRGC 102
Iran 120, 122, 162–4
Iran Nuclear Deal 85, 115, 140–1, 164
Iraq War 21, 29–33, 42, 48, 85, 95, 113
    Coverage of – 18, 21, 31–2

IS, *see* Islamic State
ISIS, *see* Islamic State
Islamic Front 78, 84, 89
Islamic State 98–9
    Rise and Expansion of – 78–82, 86, 169
Islamist Groups, *see* Sectarianism
Israel 48–9, 73

J
Jabhat Fatah al-Sham *see also* al-Nusra Front 124–5
Jaysh al-Fatah (Army of Conquest) 101, 107, 111
Jaysh al-Islam 137, 145
Joint Special Operations Command (JSOC) 134–5
Journalism
    Citizen 25–7, 173
    Professional 18

K
Kennan, George 23
Kerry, John 103–4, 106–8, 122, 151
Ki-moon, Ban 87–8, 124
Krauthammer, Charles 114
Kuhn, Thomas 178, 182
Kurds
    Iraqi 22, 24, 57, 78, 81, 86, 95, 100
    Syrian 104, 111, 114–15, 117, 126, 130, 145–8, 157, 164, 167

L
Lavrov, Sergei 103, 107, 109–110
Libya 38–44, 48–9, 52, 103, 169–70
Lippmann, Walter 17–18

M
Macron, Emmanuel 149
Manufacturing Consent, *see* Propaganda Model
Mattis, Jim 127, 134, 148, 153, 163
May, Theresa 146, 149
McCain, John 64, 66–7, 79–81, 85, 95–6, 100, 104, 114, 131, 153
Mead, Walter Russel 16–17, 69–70, 161
Médecins Sans Frontières 57, 124
Media
    and foreign policy 12, 15–33
    Western 35, 168, 176

Media Power 8, 173–4, 179–80
Muslim Brotherhood 37, 69, 123, 198
Multilateralism 47, 115, 168

N
NATO 57, 61–2
NATO Intervention in Libya 38, 47, 105
Neoconservatism 12, 44, 50, 70, 114, 153
9/11, *see* September 11
New York Times
    framing of Russia 133, 145
    framing of US foreign policy 42, 62, 86, 107, 111, 130–1, 150–2, 165–6, 168
    political orientation 11, 108
News Content Analysis 177, 179–80
News Framing, *see* Frames, Framing
No-Fly Zone 22, 40, 51, 57, 65, 68, 92, 104, 113–15, 118, 122, 163, 165–6, 168, 171–2

O
Obama, Barack, *see* US Foreign Policy, Obama Administration
Obama Administration
    criticism of in the *NYT* 84–5, 106, 150–1
    criticism of in the *WP* 65–6, 68, 90, 111–13, 115, 133, 157–8
    criticism of in the *WSJ* 70–1, 94–6, 117–19, 138–9, 141
    divisions within 74, 112
    defense of 43, 48, 61, 85, 106, 115
Obama's "red line" speech 57, 63, 74, 90, 108, 113, 146, 156–7
Obama's Foreign Policy Views 103, 117, 138
Obama's Syria Policy 36, 40–2, 51–2, 57–8, 79–80, 128
Objectivity 6–9, 31, 176
Organization for the Prohibition of Chemical Weapons 146, 154
Orientalism, *see also* Said, Edward 8, 43, 62, 71, 92, 109, 118–19, 135, 176, 187

P
Paradigm 7, 21, 177–179, 181–2
the Pentagon 61–2, 92, 94–5, 104, 107, 113–14, 139, 150

Petraeus, David 79, 108, 114–16
Pew Research Center 11, 173
Phillips, Christopher 1, 57, 78, 102, 123, 126, 128
Pickard, Victor 17, 174–5
PKK 145
Political Communication 16, 182–3
Propaganda Model 6–8, 18–21, 28–9
Public Good Journalism 10, 175
Putin, Vladimir 102–103, 109–10
PYD 145

R
Realism 46, 57, 70, 156, 161, 168
Refugee Crisis 101–3, 105–6, 110–11, 118, 121, 130
Republican Party 12, 49–50, 97, 153–5
Rhodes, Ben 15, 63, 80
Robinson, Piers 22–3, 65, 92
Rojava 200
Russia 3, 57, 93, 103–4, 115–17, 120, 125–6, 141
    Press Freedom in 5
Russian Intervention 101–5, 107, 109, 122, 169–70

S
Said, Edward, *see also* Orientalism 2, 7–8, 43, 176
Sanctions
    on Syria 92–3
    on Russia 97–8
Sanger, David 86, 150–1
Saudi Arabia 46, 57, 69, 77, 92, 117, 121, 164, 186
Schudson, Michael 6, 10, 31, 171
Sectarianism 41–2, 48, 55, 63, 78–82, 84, 89, 109, 118–19, 124–5, 133, 135, 142
Seib, Gerald 117, 140
Sengupta, Somini 88, 102, 109–10
September 11 7, 12, 23, 29–32, 80, 98, 148, 152
Sly, Liz 65, 93, 156
Sources
    in the *NYT* 40–1, 63–4, 107, 110, 131
    in the *WP* 44, 64, 66–7, 136–7
    in the *WSJ* 50, 73, 95–6, 138, 141–2

Sourcing Practices 17, 19, 53, 64, 131, 170–1, 174–6, 186
Soviet Union 21, 96, 116
Syria
   US-UK-French airstrikes against 15
   protests in 1–2
Syrian Conflict, *see also* Syrian Uprising and Civil War
   Coverage of 24–7, 58–9, 149, 165, 168, 170, 172–3, 175–6, 180, 184
   Beginning of 35–9, 53, 168–9
Syrian Democratic Forces (SDF) 104, 126, 128, 145, 148
Syrian Government, *see* Syrian Regime
Syrian Media Landscape 25, 167, 173
Syrian Observatory for Human Rights 55, 87, 136
Syrian Opposition 4, 26–7, 36, 57, 61, 77, 80, 89, 92, 101, 109, 133, 136, 142, 145, 147, 168
Syrian Rebels, *see* Syrian Opposition
Syrian Regime, *see also* al-Assad, Bashar 36–8, 53, 55–6, 77, 101, 141, 145–6, 169
Syrian Uprising and Civil War, *see also* Syrian Conflict 55–9, 74, 100, 116

T
Tillerson, Rex 140
Trump, Donald *see* Trump Administration, Trump's Foreign Policy Views, US Foreign Policy
Trump Administration 147–8
   criticism of in the *NYT* 145, 150–1
   criticism of in the *WP* 156–7, 159
   criticism of in the *WSJ* 165
   divisions within 158, 163
Trump's Foreign Policy Views 127, 135–6, 146, 170
Trump's Syria Policy 127–8, 140, 148, 150, 161
Turkey 3, 102, 110–11, 125–6

U
United Nations 106
UN Human Rights Council 45, 47, 77
UN Security Council 37, 40, 45, 65, 72, 87–9, 105, 125–6, 150, 153
US-Russia Relations 102–4, 106, 119, 140, 153–5, 159–60

US Foreign Policy 28–31, 37, 41, 46–7, 58, 63, 69–71, 80–1, 86, 94, 100, 108, 111, 114–15, 130, 135–6, 138, 150, 163–5
US Influence in the Middle East 114, 117–19, 126, 128, 131
US Journalism 8–9, 167, 173–4, 176–177
US Media *see also* US Press, US Journalism 31
US National Security 29–31, 44, 51, 104, 127, 130–1, 135, 138, 140, 146, 163
US Newspapers, *see also* US Media, US Press 10–12
US Political Establishment 96–7, 104, 108, 153, 158, 163
US Press, *see also* US Media, US Newspapers 7, 10, 58, 173

V
Vietnam War 3, 20
Violations Documentation Center 124, 146

W
Wall Street Journal
   framing of Russia 141
   framing of Trump 12
   framing of US foreign policy 50–1, 69, 71–2, 95, 99–100, 122, 138, 161–2, 166, 168
   political orientation 11–12
War on Terror 5, 7, 12, 29–32, 90–1, 94, 119, 130, 152, 154, 169
Washington Institute for Near East Policy 93, 151
Washington Post,
   framing of US foreign policy 44–5, 47, 64–6, 89–91, 93–4, 112–14, 135, 155–9, 166, 168
   political orientation 11
White Helmets 125, 132

Y
YPG 145

Z
Zakaria, Fareed 91–2, 113–14
Zunes, Stephen 79, 146–7

www.ingramcontent.com/pod-product-compliance
Lightning Source LLC
Chambersburg PA
CBHW071825300426
44116CB00009B/1449